COCKBURN AND THE BRITISH NAVY IN TRANSITION

ADMIRAL SIR GEORGE COCKBURN
1772–1853

EXETER MARITIME STUDIES
Series Editors: Michael Duffy and David J. Starkey

British Privateering Enterprise in the Eighteenth Century
by David J. Starkey (1990)

Parameters of British Naval Power, 1650–1850
edited by Michael Duffy (1992)

The Rise of the Devon Seaside Resorts, 1750–1900
by John Travis (1993)

Man and the Maritime Environment
edited by Stephen Fisher (1994)

Manila Ransomed: The British Assault on Manila in the Seven Years War
by Nicholas Tracy (1995)

Trawling: The Rise and Fall of the British Trawl Fishery
by Robb Robinson (1996)

*Pirates and Privateers: New Perspectives on the War on Trade in the
Eighteenth and Nineteenth Centuries*
edited by David J. Starkey, E. S. van Eyck van Heslinga and
J. A. de Moor (1997)

Recreation and the Sea
edited by Stephen Fisher (1997)

COCKBURN AND THE BRITISH NAVY IN TRANSITION

ADMIRAL SIR GEORGE COCKBURN
1772–1853

ROGER MORRISS

UNIVERSITY
of
EXETER
PRESS

First published in 1997 by
University of Exeter Press
Reed Hall, Streatham Drive
Exeter, Devon EX4 4QR
UK

British Library Cataloguing in Publication Data
A catalogue record of this book is available
from the British Library

ISBN 0 85989 526 2

Typeset in 11.5 on 13 pt Garamond 3
by Exe Valley Dataset, Exeter

Printed and bound in Great Britain
by Short Run Press Ltd, Exeter

FOR OLIVE

CONTENTS

ILLUSTRATIONS

Figures

Jacket Illustration:
Napoleon on board the *Bellerophon* at Plymouth in July 1815, before she sailed for Torbay where the former emperor was transferred to the *Northumberland* for the voyage to St Helena. He made public appearances occasionally at the entry port on the upper deck for boatloads of sightseers who crowded around the ships in Torbay. Oil painted by J.J. Chalon, dated 1817. (National Maritime Museum)

Maps

PREFACE

Between the American War of Independence and the Crimean War, Britain and her navy underwent remarkable change. From an economy based predominately on the products of an agrarian sector, Britain became the industrialized 'workshop of the world'. From the loss of her American colonies, Britain emerged the dominant power in Europe and embarked on a period of international maritime primacy. Her sailing navy, from being one among several great forces in Europe, grew to its greatest ever size, undertook war on an unprecedented scale, and subsequently embarked on a period of naval ascendency that has since been termed 'pax britannica'. The British navy itself, reflecting change elsewhere in the British economy, reached the limits of pre-industrial technology and began a process of transition into iron, steam and shell.

These changes, fundamental and far-reaching, affected attitudes to the navy, both external and internal. Indeed, they were accompanied by political change that reshaped naval adminstration and demanded adjustments in standards and commitment both of naval officers and of seamen. For the historian, the task of tracing these changes and their interweaving strands poses problems of relativity and scale. This challenge is here approached through the medium of biography. Change through time on this level is here reduced to registration on a single individual whose service in the navy stretched from the years of peace following the American War of Independence to the years of growing fear of invasion from France in the age of steam. This means of examining the British navy in transition has permitted focus on a variety of interrelated but disparate themes: in particular the professional conduct of the officer corps, the management of seamen, and the politics of administration. While each could of course have been examined separately, one aspect of the navy had relevance for another, and the past had a legacy of experience that can only be appreciated fully by studying the life of an individual in all its aspects.

These themes are thus encapsulated within a narrative from the beginning of the French Revolutionary War to the fall of the Peel ministry in 1846, and set round the career of perhaps the most able administrative officer of his generation. Here, within the context of world affairs, relations with the new United States of America, with Spain and her colonies, and with France in the post-war world are major preoccupations. Cockburn's role in Wellesley's management of Spain between 1810 and 1812 is perhaps worth only a footnote in a greater history. Yet few would dispute his personal impact on the course of world events, both in the Chesapeake in 1814 and in taking Napoleon to St Helena and becoming his first custodian in 1815–16.

Though essentially a biography, this book is thus intended to reveal far more than what happened to its main subject. Only recently has the British navy escaped from the tradition of heroic history that followed the French Revolutionary and Napoleonic wars. There are now new ways of looking at administrative, social and military history and it is hoped this book has benefited from developments in each of these disciplines. There has been a tendency to regard naval history as something separate from life on shore—a field open only to those initiated in its culture. It is the intention of this book to assist in its reintegration within the main stream of historical understanding and to open the subject, so full of potential, to students unversed in naval affairs.

The gestation of this book has itself been a long process. It is largely a work of evenings and weekends, benefiting from few grants of salaried time. It did nevertheless benefit from seventeen years employment at the National Maritime Museum where I was fortunate to enjoy a role that permitted me familiarity with the manuscript collections. Their contents have informed the writing of this book, both in the information and the inspiration they provided.

At the same time, in their professional roles, many colleagues at the National Maritime Museum contributed to research in ways that are too often taken for granted. I must mention in particular the assistance of Roger Quarm, Mary Shephard, Jim Nurse, Chrissie MacLeod and Michael Webb, David Proctor, David Lyon, Barbara Tomlinson, Margaret Andrews, Shamim Patwa and Colin Starkey who all, whether getting out books or facilitating access to pictures, in their interest encouraged and assisted me far more than their professional roles demanded.

Similar roles were played elsewhere by the staff of the Historical Manuscripts Commission, National Register of Archives (Scotland),

National Army Museum, British Library, Public Record Office, National Library of Scotland, Scottish Record Office, City of Sheffield Libraries, Richmond-upon-Thames Reference Library, Essex Record Office, Library of Congress, William L. Clements Library and the Institute of Historical Research. I am grateful to all these institutions for allowing me to quote from historical documents in their possession, and to Her Majesty The Queen for her gracious permission to make use of material from the Royal Archives.

At a more personal level I shall always be grateful to John Dann who, with extraordinary kindness, ensured I had early access to all the Cockburn letters in the Clements Library; Andrew Lambert, with whom I shared references in his early days of research at the National Maritime Museum and who has so fully encouraged the whole Cockburn project since; Michael Duffy, Alan Pearsall, Gillian Hughes, Chris Woolgar, Mary Bullard, Roland Thorne, and the late James Pack. As the only one who saw and commented on my early drafts, I am especially grateful to Mrs E.M. Simpson who did so much of my typing. For reading and suggesting improvements at a late stage, I am particularly grateful to Ken Breen, David K. Brown and Ian Christie.

For permission to reproduce the illustrations, I am pleased to acknowledge with thanks the Trustees of the National Maritime Museum and the Library of Congress. My sincere thanks also go to the administrators of University of London's Isabel Thornley Bequest, a grant from which has much facilitated publication. This final process had been achieved with more kindness than I thought possible in this current age of ruthless economies by the University of Exeter Press. Here, though invidious to single out individuals, I must express my deepest gratitude to Rosemary Rooke, who so ably rendered an often indecipherable typescript into legible print. From beginning to end, many others have suffered and supported this book; the most notable— Judith, Madeleine, Naomi and Anna—have my deepest thanks.

R.M.
Leckhampton
1997

GLOSSARY

Buntades   Emphatic declarations, unswervingly adhered to.

Crimping   The process whereby the debts of seamen were met by agents or crimps from advances on wages by ships' masters requiring crew members, to whom the seamen were then engaged.

Poleacre   A vessel with three masts, usually found in the Mediterranean, and generally carrying square sails upon the mainmast and lateen sails upon the fore and mizen masts.

Razees   The word of French derivation given to a 74- or 64-gun two-deck ship in the Royal Navy which had been cut down forward and aft, so that the lower deck became the upper deck. A ship so altered usually had the capability of carrying a heavier weight of guns than frigates built with only one gun deck, and these guns were carried higher out of the water.

Specie   Coin or other units of precious metal.

Introduction

George Cockburn emerged from the Napoleonic War as Britain's most able admiral, known for his role in both the burning of Washington and the internment of Napoleon.[1] Brought into the Admiralty in 1818, he was to remain there until 1830, returning in 1841 as first naval lord under Peel until 1846. Within a decade, however, his popular reputation was tarnished by association with the government's repressive policies towards radical movements and political disorder, while within the navy he was regarded by Whigs as an opponent of their ideals, especially hated by those he confronted in his bureaucratic capacity. Though trusted by Tories, within a decade of his death in 1853 he was denounced as an administrative tyrant, and thereafter cited as a living example of reactionary conservatism.

At the end of the twentieth century we are still heir to the politics and opinions that brought Cockburn fame and infamy. On the one hand, he was a war hero, on the other he was the opponent of change. The attitudes which formed these opinions have affected how the history of the early nineteenth century has been viewed, and to strip them off is to reveal in a fresh light not only Cockburn himself, but also those events and circumstances with which he had to deal. Before examining Cockburn, it is therefore necessary to look at the tangle of past prejudices which have hitherto affected our view of him.

According to the dominant, Tory strand of the historiography, he was, in the words of his only biographer, 'the man who burned the White House'.[2] Yet this description derives indirectly from Cockburn himself, for recent knowledge of Cockburn stems largely from the *Dictionary of National Biography* in which John Knox Laughton relied for his information on O'Byrne's *Naval Biographical Dictionary*, published in 1849 and dependent, for official approval, on the board upon which Cockburn was the leading naval member. Cockburn wrote his own longhand record of his services during the war,[3] but on points of contention he was publicly reticent. While this might have been diplomatic, it also allowed opinion to reign unchecked. He fully understood the power of the pen in making and breaking reputations, but, except in his official capacity, preferred to keep out of duels with words, especially as differences of opinion clearly coincided with differences of political party.

For the dissident, Whig view of his wartime achievements was virulent even in his own lifetime and occasioned a series of disputes. Thus, for example, on the question of his role in the attack on Washington in 1814, the editor of *The Naval Biography of Great Britain* caused immediate sensation in 1827 by claiming that Cockburn 'took upon himself the responsibility of further proceedings' when the army faltered in its advance, and that 'having determined to make an attack [he] issued an order . . .'. The assumptions behind the claim were immediately attacked by the Whig Colonel De Lacy Evans who served as deputy quartermaster general in the army over which, he maintained, Cockburn had as much authority as 'the youngest midshipman of the fleet'—an assertion the latter did not contest.[4] A second dispute, more dangerous because it was contested, broke out in 1833–7, after the Whig government had posted Cockburn to the North American station. Verbal war was waged on his behalf by James Scott, a subordinate in the American war of 1812. Scott refused to accept allegations of violations of human rights in the supposed routine burning of civilian housing in 1813–14, made in *The Life of a Sailor* in 1833 by Frederick Chamier. He was only a midshipman in 1814, but the dispute in the *United Service Journal* so aroused Scott that he challenged Chamier to a 'hostile meeting'. This was fortunately declined for, though Cockburn congratulated Scott on having done 'equal honour' to his 'heart and head', he deemed 'the precocious' Chamier 'so unimportant' that as late as 1837 he had looked at neither the book nor the correspondence in the journal![5]

In the naval world of the nineteenth century, when loyalty, honour and employment were closely connected, the maintenance of 'truth' mattered. In standing forth against an 'unscrupulous and unworthy slanderer', Scott had the support of numerous other officers who had served under Cockburn and who undoubtedly appreciated that further employment, as well as their sense of integrity, might depend on their expressed opinion. However political circumstances affected whose 'truth' survived. Whig and Tory arguments of the 1820s and 1830s were buttressed by a succession of republications in the 1840s, reinforcing, by hints and slights, the views of both parties. Under the Whig government in 1837 Chamier was invited to revise William James's *Naval History of Great Britain, from the Declaration of War by France in 1793 to the Accession of George IV*, originally compiled with the approval of the Tory Admiralty immediately after the Napoleonic War and published in two editions in 1822–24 and 1826. As was to be expected under a Whig administration, Chamier was asked to extend the work to cover the Battle of Navarino of 1827, which figured the radical Whig admiral, Sir Edward Codrington, and which had taken place under the auspices of William IV when Lord High Admiral, whose innovations were favoured by Whigs but whom Cockburn had forced into resignation in 1828. To counteract Chamier's revision, the Tory view of events was maintained by republication of Captain Edward Brenton's *Naval History of Great Britain*, first published in 1823–25.[6]

The political nature of these past histories of wartime events demands that any re-examination of Cockburn's wartime life and times must delve beneath the surface of contending views. Unfortunately this is even more necessary for the second half of Cockburn's career, which is similarly bedevilled by his own reticence about publicly defending his reputation. For his administrative career there is a sad paucity of information, except that buried deeply in the public records. Some of Cockburn's own letterbooks and journals remain in the United States Library of Congress. But on contentious issues, especially those of recent interest, he left little to vindicate his views and indeed consciously adopted an attitude of indifference to opinions expressed about him in the public press. In 1852 he recalled that 'I never did and now never do pay any attention to the attacks of *The Times* or other newspapers with regard to the management of passing occurrences by those in charge of the department to which they refer.'[7]

His affected indifference applied also to the opinions of enemies in the navy, who often also sat in the House of Commons. These included high-ranking Whig officers like Codrington and Sir Charles Napier, both of whom had fought in the American War of 1812 with him, and Sir George Seymour who served with him in 1841–4 on the Board of Admiralty. Their views of him and his administration have fed popular legend, and indeed, for this era of his life, have achieved wider circulation than any which favoured his administrations. This is largely due to the currency given to the depreciating portrayal of him by Sir John Briggs, whose reminiscences *Naval Administrations 1827–1892* were published by his wife in 1897, shortly after his death. At that time German naval expansion and United States sabre-rattling seemed to recreate the Continental and transatlantic threats of the early nineteenth century. Just as in the 1840s, technological change threatened to render Britain's navy outdated. Briggs was strongly affiliated to the Whig tradition: his father had acted as private secretary to the Whig First Lord Sir James Graham in 1830. He accordingly undertook his reminiscences with the object of proving to Lord Salisbury's government 'the necessity of an adequate navy' to protect the interests of the British Empire, but of one that was at the forefront of technological thinking. He thus looked back to the Tory administrations of the 1820s and 1840s with the intention of showing how wrong conservative administrators were to drag their feet in introducing the latest technology.

Briggs had served as a clerk in the Admiralty office from 1827 and acted as reader to the Board between 1841 and 1865. He cast Cockburn in the role of the archetypal reactionary:

> In his naval capacity he was the most uncompromising representative of things as they were. He seemed to live in the past, and was impressed with the conviction that everything that had been done was right; that what was being done was questionable, and every step in advance was fraught with danger.

His conservatism was said to apply in almost every naval field: in ship design and size, gunnery, tactics, recruitment and discipline.

> The result of the American War [of 1812] taught him no fresh lesson. The superiority of the American vessels in tonnage, broadside, weight of metal and complement made no adequate impression upon him. He considered it was only necessary for a captain to run his ship alongside of his enemy, pour in a broadside, board and take her.

Briggs acknowledged his own inability to understand 'how anyone possessing such a powerful intellect . . . could allow political feeling and personal prejudices to so completely blind his naturally sound judgement'. Nevertheless he indulged in what was tantamount to political polemic. According to him, Cockburn refused to acknowledge the changes that had taken place, were taking place, and must inevitably take place. Every opinion he expressed, every measure he devised, and every step he took were retrograde in their tendencies.[8]

Briggs was unconscious of his own adherence to the idea of progress, like many who followed after him. His opinion of Cockburn was particularly attractive to technological historians who, with hindsight, saw in him the reason why steam was introduced more slowly into the navy than into the merchant service, and why for so long the quarter-deck remained socially superior to the engine room. For, as Briggs maintained, on one occasion he 'went so far as to declare that since the introduction of steam vessels he had never seen a clean deck or a captain who, when he waited upon him, did not look like a sweep'.[9] To technological historians Cockburn became representative of many naval officers in nineteenth-century administration, and of those boards upon which he served in particular.

To review Cockburn's reputation as an administrator is thus to revise the historical view of what Tory boards in the first half of the nineteenth century achieved. Revision of this achievement has long been overdue. Until recently, distaste for administrative history and the difficulties of writing it—combined with a popular preference for hostilities—left naval history in the years between the end of the Napoleonic War and beginning of the Crimean War relatively unknown. This is now changing. Since this work on Cockburn began, new studies have appeared of the development of the sailing battle-fleet, and of ship design, propulsion and armament in the first half of the nineteenth century.[10] Cockburn's importance in maintaining the old while the new was proved is tacitly acknowledged. For he became first naval lord in 1841 at a critical time of transition: when the number of sailing ships in the British navy and in commission was in decline (though still regarded as the main fighting units of the fleet), when the number of steamships was rising, and when propeller propulsion, with all the experimentation necessary to its introduction, challenged the paddle. However, his precise role in the development of the navy is still only touched upon, and largely surmised.[11]

His political role in the navy between 1818 and 1846 is even less known. At a time when population and urban growth was critically altering the balance in British politics, Cockburn formed one of that group attached to Lords Liverpool and Wellington who thought the constitution was threatened. He considered the nature of the naval service, on the part of seamen as well as officers, was dependent on the traditional balance in the constitution. His fear of arbitrary change, especially that undertaken for political gain, also led him to oppose the Duke of Clarence's attempts as Lord High Admiral to follow the advice of others rather than his council. His grasp of the constitutional issues and readiness to confront those who proposed reductions in the control exercised by the Board of Admiralty repeatedly placed him in the front-line of departmental politics. In these struggles, within the Admiralty as well as with other departments, there is no doubt he deferred to the decisions of his political superiors. But, at the same time, he defended those provisions which maintained the maximum employment and training of naval officers and seamen. In consequence, it can be argued that Cockburn had more influence on the evolution of terms of service for personnel than any other naval officer in the first half of the nineteenth century.

There were several reasons for this great influence. The first was the absence of other naval officers of Tory persuasion who had equal experience and ability. A second was the trust he engendered among backbench members of the House of Commons where he became a familiar and respected figure. As a service officer, and in spite of his own party inclination, he was even trusted by the Whig government of 1830 who appointed him commander-in-chief on the North American station, both to get him out of a useful parliamentary seat and to remind the Americans of their vulnerability. Another reason was the power of his personality. From necessity, he had developed early in his life an aura of authority. Briggs wrote that he had 'an indomitable will, considered he could carry everything by mere brute force, and imagined that when he gave an imperative order that which he had commanded must be done'. In his early years his sense of moral rectitude made him appear self-righteous. Later, with his haughty manner and sarcastic tone, he seemed deliberately to be arousing fear and awe in those he encountered. Among government officials in the 1820s he was regarded as 'an ungovernable man, . . . his head turned by the dominion he holds at the Admiralty'.[12] By his last years in office, having reached his 70th year in 1842, he had softened. But by then, burdened with work, frustrated by hostile Board colleagues, few really knew him well.

This man remains an enigma. His own abilities militated against many friendships. Throughout his life he retained a faculty for grasping issues quickly and energetically determining a course of action. Slower brains and dishonourable men frustrated him. In official relations he had few equals and fewer confidantes. He expressed close affection for Nelson, but signed himself the 'dear friend' of nobody until 1810 when writing to Lord Wellesley's secretary, Colonel Shawe.[13] Shawe's place was taken after 1812 by John Wilson Croker, Secretary of the Admiralty, with whom social as well as political bonds developed.[14] By then the Cockburn family had already drawn close to that of the Tory politician Robert Peel— George's younger brother, William, married Peel's sister Elizabeth in 1805, while another brother, Alexander, was one of Peel's closest friends.

Cockburn's personal life, however, remains almost entirely unknown, for most of his private papers seem to have been destroyed.[15] His first known attempt to appear in public with a lady was in May 1802 when Lady Hamilton could offer him only one ticket for the Installation Ball. Otherwise we know only that he married his cousin Mary Cockburn in November 1809 and had two children, one of whom died in 1817. After 1820, when not residing at the Admiralty, he lived a cloistered domestic life at High Beech, near Waltham Abbey, Essex, until he died in 1853, with his wife soon after him.[16] The small family seems to have been a tight, inward-looking community, for Mary Cockburn had weak health and Cockburn strictly separated public from private affairs. Their daughter Augusta only married Captain John Cochrane Hoseason—who assisted Cockburn at the Admiralty—in 1856 after her parents' death, when she was almost 43. She noted to Croker on her father's death that few had had 'the power and the opportunity of appreciating him' as he had done, and that her father 'left behind him a truly Christian example which we cannot but regret should not have been more widely known'.[17]

That his public face was not his private one was acknowledged even by his critic, Briggs, who perceived the haughty and dictatorial bearing was 'totally at variance with his natural disposition'. He was 'very kind, humane, and the friend of all naval officers in trouble and difficulty, and at the Admiralty Board invariably took the lenient view of every case submitted for decision'. He 'was a man of the world, a man of fashion and a courtier, and when he chose could exhibit tact and persuasion.'[18]

These social graces derived from genteel, upper middle-class society of the late eighteenth century. On his mother's side he came from that realm which valued learning, 'engaging, insinuating, shining manners, a distinguished politeness, an almost irresistible address and a superior gracefulness'.[19] She was the daughter of the Reverend Francis Ayscough, Dean of Bristol, who tutored both George III and the Duke of York when boys, and the niece of George, Lord Lyttelton (friend of George III when Prince of Wales). She was a beauty, painted by Sir Joshua Reynolds—a neighbour at Petersham, Surrey—surrounded by her first three boys, of whom she had five between 1770 and 1780: James, George, William, Alexander, and Francis.[20] Their father, Sir James, came from rich, landholding merchant parentage of Ayton and Eyemouth in Berwickshire, Scotland. A dynamic, enterprising figure, he had entered business with, and married the daughter of, Henry Douglas, a wealthy Scots–West India merchant. His first wife bore him three daughters before dying in 1766. Consistently seeking the highest financial rewards, during the Seven Years War he became a commissary, then Commissary General, for the supply of the allied army under Prince Ferdinand, Duke of Brunswick, in Munster, Germany.[21] On his return to England he entered the Court of Directors of the East India Company, purchased plantations in Dominica, and entered Parliament.[22] The wealth he generated permitted him in 1766 to regain for his family the hereditary office of 'principal usher of the white rod in Scotland' and in 1769 to repurchase family estates, all lost to another branch of the family in 1756.[23] With this dignity as well as wealth, he married again in 1769. George was born in 1772.

However the wealth into which he was born was not to last. Sir James's readiness to take high risks contained elements of danger. In 1772, during a crisis in the affairs of the East India Company, he was discredited as a director for withholding information from the proprietors while he bought and sold stock to the value of £10,000 on the Amsterdam market.[24] West Indian and Scottish opportunities provided other outlets for his enterprise. In 1776 he and his partner, Henry Douglas, obtained a contract for supplying 100,000 gallons of Grenada rum to the British army in North America, and the following year had to explain in the House of Commons the 'immense expense' of shipping this cargo.[25]

By this time the two of them were also acting as agents for the Receiver General of the Scottish land tax, for whom they held vast sums of money in their own accounts. Some of this money Sir James advanced as part of a loan to the Nawab of Arcot; one of his partners was drowned, the project fell into confusion, and Sir James found himself hopelessly in debt to creditors who included the Receiver General of the land tax. In 1779 he was forced to accept a secret service pension, negotiated by Lord North. In 1781 he was declared bankrupt. By 1782 he was 'in the extremest distress' and George III changed the secret service pension to a private one on account of the 'former connexions' of Lady Cockburn's father with himself and the royal family.[26] In 1784, without money or influence, Sir James was discarded by the interests controlling his parliamentary contituency. In 1785 his family was forced to move from their house in Petersham, near Richmond in Surrey, a fashionable village on the outskirts of London. But by 1786 he was so deeply in debt he was forced to escape his creditors by obtaining diplomatic immunity as secretary to the Prussian minister in London.[27]

That year, aged 14, George went to sea. His eldest and youngest brothers, James and Francis, entered the army; his two other younger brothers, William and Alexander, entered the Church and diplomatic service. Of his three half-sisters, the two eldest failed to marry, perhaps a consequence of insufficient dowry. George's own education was economical: he attended schools in Marylebone, London, and at Margate, then prepared for the sea at Roy's navigational school in Old Burlington Street, London.[28] His first patron was a neighbour at Petersham, Sir Joshua Rowley, who between 1771 and 1776 served with Sir James on the parish council.[29] In March 1781 his son, Captain Bartholomew Rowley, entered George's name on the books of the frigate *Resource*, then in the West Indies. From there, his name was transferred to the books of the yacht *William and Mary* until May 1786 when Cockburn actually went to sea in the 18-gun *Termagant* as servant to her captain, Rowley Bulteel.[30]

These early years at sea tested the hardihood Cockburn would need to persevere through 22 years of warfare and 17 years at the Admiralty. His first two years were spent in the North Sea and English Channel supporting the revenue service. That winter 18 men deserted in 36 days at Hull where the *Termagant* put in for recaulking after frost, snow and gales off the mouths of the rivers Tyne and Humber.[31] In 1788 Lord Hood obtained for him a berth in the sloop *Ariel* commissioned to survey islands in the Indian Ocean. Servant to her commander, Robert Moorsom, Cockburn studied navigation and chart-making throughout the voyage under her master, Mr Blair. The cruise was not without incident. Sounding around one island in the Great Andaman group one member of the pinnace's crew received an arrow through the arm. That summer sickness forced the sloop back to the coast of India to deposit 40 of her crew in the East India Company hospital at Madras and in October Moorsom was invalided home.

Cockburn went with him,[32] and they reached England by a Company ship in time for Cockburn to enter for his lieutenant's examination in June 1791. He passed after less than five years at sea and still short of his nineteenth birthday even though he should have served six years, been twenty years of age, and served as a midshipman and master's mate.[33] But postings to two more ships, the *Hebe* and *Romney*, each through Hood's influence, permitted him to fulfil these requirments over the next year. At Gibraltar in July 1792, three months after his twentieth birthday, he received an admiral's commission to act as third lieutenant, a rank confirmed in January 1793 by an Admiralty commission into the *Orestes*.

Cockburn was fortunate in obtaining the patronage of Hood who from 1786 was first naval lord at the Board of Admiralty. But his qualification for lieutenant, and the enthusiasm he revealed in the detail of his journals, testify to his commitment to the navy.[34] There, these interests counted for more than the financial assets of parents. Nevertheless, it seems likely that financial difficulties contributed to the personality that developed in these early years—it can be argued that Cockburn had reason to develop privacy about his family circumstances. Of those who entered the navy after 1793, less than four per cent were from merchant stock; certainly even fewer from the families of failed entrepreneurs.[35] Those who knew him early on found him neither well dressed nor charming. Betsy Wynne recorded in 1796 'a fine, sprightly, fashionable man', 'a very pleasant young man', although initially 'quite different'.[36] His financial circumstances were certainly known in the navy in 1797, when his bank account was being shared by other members of the Cockburn family.[37] Only in about 1800, after being deliberately placed at sea to accumulate prizes, did his circumstances and those of his parents appear to improve.

Until that time, with only one break in England during the French Revolutionary War, Cockburn led a life of professional dedication. He worked under Nelson and knew about, but did not imitate, his personal indiscretions: the dalliance with the opera singer Adelaide Correglia at Leghorn, and liaison with Emma Hamilton in Naples and Palermo. Personal indulgence of this nature he later described as weakness. He himself pursued a reputation for honour: 'a system of rules constructed by people of fashion' to facilitate their intercourse with one another, which in the navy demanded avoidance of involvement in the dishonourable misdeeds of others.[38] For this, as Cockburn discovered, was closely connected to the discipline necessary to maintain the respect and loyalty of seamen.

During the Revolutionary War Cockburn learned the lessons essential to a naval captain: not just the methods of managing seamen but the qualities necessary to the successful co-operation of ships at sea. Very quickly he established a reputation for work demanding intelligence: 'service of head' as Nelson termed it. It led directly to employment during the Napoleonic War on duties demanding diplomacy. As these wars lengthened and his experience grew, operations involving negotiations and collaboration between the armed forces became his particular strength. His employment in the Chesapeake in 1813–14, close to the United States capital, gave full use to this experience in combined operations. Other duties were almost wholly political: his employment by Lord Wellesley in 1811–12, for example, to mediate between the Spanish government at Cadiz and Spain's colonies; and his despatch to St Helena with Napoleon. His appointment to the Board of Admiralty in 1818 was of a piece with these duties.

After employment under the Whigs on the North American station in the 1830s and service as first naval lord at the Admiralty under Peel, Cockburn accumulated half a century of almost continuous service. Compared to the part-time employment of officers of the eighteenth century,[39] this length of service in high office was unprecedented. As a political administrator, Cockburn was also qualitatively different from Admiralty commissioners of the eighteenth century. For increasingly he became a public servant. In the early nineteenth century that need to earn a living, that sense of honour with which he served his peers, that paternalism with which he cared for seamen, all merged with a new ethos of public service emanating from Whitehall as office-holders became known as 'civil servants'.

Bridging the gap between the late Georgian and early Victorian navies, Cockburn represented in his views a blending of past and present ideas about naval service. He possessed wisdom accumulated from long naval experience. For example, his own attitudes to flogging, shore leave and desertion were related to his own methods of managing his crews in the 1790s and 1830s. Nothing emphasizes more the central importance he placed on the relationship between officers and seamen; and the peripheral relevance to the navy of reformers' campaigns for mitigation of the conditions seamen suffered. His own practical experience also led him to attach importance to the cultural homogeneity of the officer class, and the value of connections and patronage in the recommendation of potential officers. Possessed of such knowledge, he nevertheless appreciated the necessity for engaging with those in the political arena who thought differently, whether in the House of Commons, at the Board of Admiralty, in other departments of government, or in the Cabinet. His role was always to negotiate or impose what was best for the efficiency of the navy. Through Cockburn, more than any other officer in the first half of the nineteenth century, the needs of the navy were reconciled with public demands concerning the nature of that service.

In plumbing the nature of the naval service, this biography makes no apology for examining the times as well as the life of its subject. For, though naval history in the period of the wars against France and the United States, 1793–1815, is relatively well known, that knowledge still owes a great debt to the historiography of the 'heroic' age immediately succeeding the wars, and to the individualism of the nineteenth century. Then, naval officers were projected as the individuals solely responsible for military events, a natural extension of the manner in which officers themselves necessarily advertised their achievements. For honours, awards, appointments and promotion depended on the projection of claims by the claimants themselves. Yet we now know full well that the great events of that period rested on logistical and administrative achievements far removed from the scene of conflict. An appreciation of Cockburn's part in the war of 1812 against the United States accordingly demands an understanding of the logistical problems of his commanders-in-chief, and of the grand strategy within which Cockburn operated.

Similarly, the problems of the post-war Admiralty need some exploration for Cockburn's part to be properly understood. Not only has the navy in this period attracted few historians, these few have rarely touched upon the greater process of governmental change in the early nineteenth century, of which the Admiralty's problems were but an element. The navy was forcefully affected by the pressures and progress of political and administrative reform; indeed, it was a primary target for Whig reformers. That Cockburn was invariably forced to defend the interests of the navy against proponents of change inevitably cast him in a conservative role. It was the same in the field of technological innovation. Propositions for 'improvements' were constantly coming before the Board of Admiralty, and most had to be rejected without trial. Yet this did not mean Cockburn was not for some changes or responsible for innovations himself. Only an examination of the navy as he managed it permits an informed reassessment of his administrative reputation.

In abandoning heroic individualism to place a relatively unknown naval officer in his administrative context, this biography returns to the day-to-day experience of work in the navy and at the Admiralty over a career lasting sixty years. In covering three decades of operations, followed by thirty years of administration, much has inevitably had to be omitted. Nevertheless the relationship of past experience to current demands, expressed in the political tensions of the period, may reveal the process of transition. If that is revealed, as much as the career of Cockburn, this biography will have achieved its purpose.

CHAPTER 1

The Georgian Navy in the French Revolutionary War, 1793–1801

For Cockburn, as for other naval officers, the declaration of war against Britain by the National Convention of France on 1 February 1793 dramatically altered his life. A reciprocal response set the process of mobilization in motion.[1] Cockburn, a lieutenant of 21 in the *Orestes*, was employed transferring seamen pressed in London from tenders arriving at Gravesend down to the Nore at the mouth of the River Thames, where part of the British fleet lay. On 28 April, after the second delivery of men to the Nore, Cockburn received notice of his appointment to the *Britannia*, equipping at Portsmouth. The impact of the letter completely altered the entries in his log. For the only time in his life, he slipped from objective observations of ship-board operations into accounts of his own movements, a dislocation which persisted until he reached the Mediterranean where he was to spend most of the Revolutionary War. These personal accounts, the first insights we possess into Cockburn's character, illuminate his early interest in those about him.[2]

On 28 April 1793 he 'proceeded to London' to take up his commission from the Admiralty. Being Sunday, he could not receive it and had to return next day. While his things were getting ready—orders for uniform, bed linen and extra clothing—he went to visit his parents at Hurley, returning to London on 3 May.

> At 6 set off for Portsmouth, in company a pert [sic] mate of [an] Indiaman, a boatswain, a merchant's rider, a woman with a child that squalled the whole way, and an old woman whose rotten teeth scented the whole coach. With this group we proceeded with progressive motion till we were overturned about 4 miles before our arrival at Guildford. However there being no harm done (except a lady on the outside having very much bruised her base parts), we having got the coach up right

again, proceeded to Portsmouth where we arrived about 11. But I found myself so unwell that I was unable to go on board. I therefore took up my abode at the Star & Garter & sent for a doctor.

He was 'employed physicking and getting better' and receiving visits from old messmates for two days, after which he waited upon Admiral Hotham (who was to fly his flag in *Britannia*), his flag captain, Holloway, and Lord Hood. Hood was to command the fleet preparing for the Mediterranean, though retaining his seat at the Board of Admiralty, and that afternoon hoisted his flag on board *Victory* to cheers from surrounding ships. Cockburn went on board *Britannia* next day, characteristically listing the wardroom mess as Lieutenants Littlejohn, Peard, Boys, Pater, Serocold, Redmill, Elphinstone, Middleton, Cockburn, the ship's master Jeffreys, Captain Beresford of the 69th Regiment of marines, Subalterns Lyons and Shandy, the chaplain Larwood, purser McIlhaith, and the surgeon Stowe.

After separate manoeuvres, Hotham and Hood's squadrons combined off the Lizard to exercise on their course towards Gibraltar. On a signal for lieutenants on 11 June, Cockburn took a boat to the *Victory* where Hood 'promised to take me on board'. With the fleet in Gibraltar Bay, a party of 26 seamen went to fetch water from Algeciras.

I went with command of the party. Found Algeciras to be a small irregular built town without any fortification and only about 10 guns mounted on a cliff which commands the roads and landing. The soldiers appeared to be in very bad discipline, mounting guard without their coats and some without hats etc etc. The place is governed by a mayor who styles himself Governor who is subject to and receives all orders from the Governor of St Rock. Their churches are very magnificent and they have a very good hospital for the reception of the poor people exclusive of the kings. They shewed us a vast deal of superficial civility such as the Governor coming himself to know if he could be of any assistance to us by lending me men or anything else, and all the gentlemen took their hats off when passing us, but none of them shewed us any English politeness such as asking us to dinner etc etc. I saw some very pretty women but the generality of them was otherwise. They gave us very bad victuals at the Inn, at least to our palates, for everything drowned in bad oil.

Cockburn's observations tell us more about him, perhaps, than about Algeciras. For his perceptions proceeded down a hierarchy from the state of military readiness and discipline, through forms of government, administration and diplomacy, to the appeal of women and food. Cockburn already put politics before his own appetite.

The Mediterranean theatre

As the British fleet edged its way north towards Toulon, Cockburn's attention shifted to the war in which he was involved. In characteristic fashion, he recorded that his own fleet consisted of nineteen sail of the line, a 50-gun ship, a storeship, hospital ship, two fire-ships and several frigates.[3] But a report from Toulon in mid-May had recorded eight of the line and nine other vessels ready for sea, with another twelve of the line and five frigates that could weigh by the end of June.[4] Logistical dominance over the French fleet depended on the assistance of allies, in particular the Spanish. But their aid appeared little more than temporary expedience.

Off Cape Palos on 5 July, a Spanish line of battleships was chased and spoken with. Three days later, at six that evening, several strange sail were sighted; an hour later they became 'a strange fleet of 25 sail'; ten minutes later a fleet of 35 sail. Evening drawing in, two frigates were sent to reconnoitre and the fleet hove to. On *Britannia* that night, several guns were heard and several 'false fires' seen from the strange fleet to windward. As light dawned the signal was relayed to form line of battle. In the distance, however, frigates were seen to make, and receive back, the private signal, confidential to allies. The fleet proved to be Spanish: 25 ships of the line, six frigates and a captured French frigate. Slowly the latter, with a Spanish frigate alongside, advanced into the British line and sent boats on board the *Victory*. Three-quarters of an hour later, the line of battle was cancelled and the British again made sail.

For Cockburn, as for many observers that day, this was the first view of two battle-fleets at sea together. Yet he perceived something wrong. The fleets were those of allies, supposedly meant to co-operate. But neither showed a flicker of amity. Did their respective admirals still feel their mutual hostility of ten years before? 'I cannot help remarking', Cockburn noted down, 'I think the two fleets, though now to act together, passed one another as if they had not got the better of their old grudge, not being within five miles of each other when nearest and not paying the least compliment to or taking the least notice of each other'.[5]

Off Toulon, following another signal for lieutenants, Hood was true to his word: Cockburn was appointed tenth lieutenant of the *Victory*. British involvement in the defence of Toulon seemed to assure the allies of long-term superiority in the Mediterranean. Cockburn in the *Victory* closely witnessed the comings and going of commissioners from the

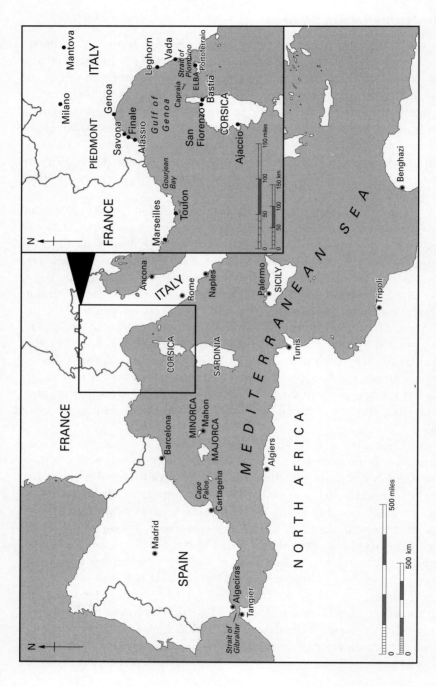

Map 1. The Western Mediterranean

royalist town.[6] But he also noticed the approach of republican forces, the precipitate disembarkation of British troops combined with the sudden occupation by allied warships of the outer harbour.[7] Like Nelson, he too must have marvelled that the strongest place in Europe and twenty-two sail of the line should be given up without a shot being fired.[8] However the investment of the harbour by overwhelming republican forces and the accuracy of their bombardment of allied ships and batteries made the withdrawal of the latter a matter of time.[9] Although ten French ships of the line and several frigates were burnt in the withdrawal, the naval force left to the republicans remained sufficient to pose a threat.

This became evident in 1794. By then Cockburn had risen in two months to first lieutenant in the *Victory* before being appointed, like those who preceded him, to command a sloop, from which in January he was temporarily appointed to command the 36-gun *Inconstant*, and then in February posted captain into the 32-gun *Meleager*. Mainly employed to suppress French trade, she was part of the squadron under Hotham blockading Toulon in June when seven French ships of the line and five frigates escaped. They were lost in the night, but five days later Cockburn was employed to acquaint Hood that they had been seen 'running along shore for Villa Franco' where they were to anchor in defensive positions in 'Gourjean Bay', to be placed under blockade for the rest of the year.[10]

Active co-operation with the Spanish was maintained during 1794. Following the fall of Calvi and extinction of republican resistance on Corsica, Hood exercised his fleet with the Spanish. For a week in August Cockburn acted largely as a messenger between Hood and the Spanish commander. However, in critical encounters with the French fleet in 1795, the allies had to act separately, the British without the confidence of being able decisively to destroy the enemy. Two French ships of the line were taken in mid-March in a general chase, and one destroyed in July.[11] On both occasions the French fleet of 15 of the line was sufficiently strong to have crippled the British force of 13, but in calling off the British chases, Hotham was criticised for being too cautious. British vessels suffered loss and damage that proportionately weakened the fleet and this was critical to the balance of forces. For, in contrast to the French, the facilities for repairing and maintaining the British force in the Mediterranean were limited. Unlike the French, the British fleet was unable to repair serious hull damage, while mast damage was equally likely to disable a ship for a considerable period.

The main problem was the lack of a shore base possessing a dock.

Despite the alliance with Spain, neither the Spanish dockyard at Cartagena nor their refitting yard at Port Mahon, Minorca, was made available to the British fleet. Until 1796 some refitting was possible at Naples or Leghorn, while careening of smaller vessels was possible at the fleet bases of San Fiorenzo and Ajaccio, Corsica. Refitting was also possible at Gibraltar. Yet this yard was distant and often difficult to reach from the north-east, especially in winter against the prevailing winds.[12] It was also without a dock, obliging ships requiring serious hull repairs to return to England. The return of such vessels, especially of ships of the line, left Hood, then Hotham, scarcely sufficient line vessels to match those available to the French.[13]

The wear and tear of sea service was itself sufficient to disable ships already in need of refitting or repair. This was demonstrated to Cockburn in August 1794. On the night of the 22nd a heavy swell sprang the *Meleager*'s mainmast twelve feet below the cap and disabled her for six weeks. Repair in this case demanded only a replacement mast and use of the sheer hulk in San Fiorenzo Bay. Yet masts, in common with other stores, were regularly in short supply. For the *Meleager* a new mainmast was ready in three weeks but was found to be faulty. Three more weeks consequently passed before the *Meleager* was again fit for sea.[14]

Throughout this period, Cockburn was the senior British naval officer at San Fiorenzo. As such, business affecting the *Meleager* took second place to the needs of ships entering harbour and of the land forces on shore. Cockburn co-ordinated demands from ships for cables, cordage and every other type of equipment. In addition, he oversaw the care and accounting for stores, arranged transports for troops and ordnance, and provide a communication centre for ships and squadrons operating nearby.

Not least among the needs of the latter was that for men. Sickness and the provision of prize crews took their toll on ships already undermanned. In June 1794 the *Meleager* was forced back to Corsica with a 'malignant fever' among her crew. Off Bastia two men died where they lay while 47 were committed to hospital. Of these, most remained on shore two weeks.[15] Fresh meat, in the form of live oxen, and chests of lemons were regularly supplied to all ships. But the careful preservation of men never adequately made up the pre-existing deficiency, even with the recruitment of Neapolitans and occasional French refugees.

'Constant rain and excessive bad weather' during the autumn of 1795 only served to emphasise the British lack of a repair base, sufficient supplies of stores, equipment and men. Recycled though they were, the

British ships watching Toulon only grew more worn while the French inside preserved their strength. The French on shore, moreover, gradually extended their control eastwards along the shores of the Gulf of Genoa. After three months' consolidation, on 23 November, the French, 'half naked, determined to conquer or die', drove the Austrian army before them 'eighteen miles without stopping'.[16]

From the sea, British attempts to support the Austrians had only slight effect. In the new year, craft supplying the French army constantly crept along shore from one headland fort to the next. In April and May 1796 Cockburn in *Meleager* took part in successive cutting-out expeditions, seizing cargoes of rice, corn, muskets and ammunition. Two vessels taken on 31 May carried brandy, bread and Austrian prisoners, while another three carried 24-pounder field guns, 13-inch mortars, gun carriages, shells, wheel barrows and entrenching tools—all intended for the siege of Mantua.[17] The French having defeated the allied armies in north Italy four times in four days in April, every Italian state was intimidated.

Spain had also succumbed to French influence. In the Gulf of Genoa the tenor of relations was revealed following the capture of the vessel laden with Austrian prisoners on 31 May 1796. Two days later a boat carrying the crew and a Genoese master came out to the *Meleager*. Cockburn interviewed the master who showed him papers which indicated the vessel had been chartered by the Spanish consul at Savona to carry the prisoners to Barcelona. The Austrian troops, 152 in number, all grenadier guards of the first quality, the oldest only 34 years of age, had been marched under guard to the vessel, given thirty sous each when on board, and told that they were going to join their comrades in Spain. The soldiers, according to Nelson, had no inclination to go to Spain but were sold by the French to the Spanish for a Swiss mercenary regiment employed in Spain.[18]

The Franco-Spanish alliance materialized in a treaty signed on 19 August 1796, but the first Franco-Spanish force to sail left Cadiz on 4 August. After delivering the 'Marquis of Huntly' and other 'gentlemen' to Barcelona for an overland stage of their journey to England, Cockburn carried this news back to Jervis, Hotham's successor as commander-in-chief. The French drive into Italy carried them to Leghorn where Cockburn watched them open fire from the mole on the last of a British convoy of 39 vessels which he conducted to San Fiorenzo Bay. The British occupation of the islands of Elba and Capraja removed stepping stones for a French attack on Corsica. But the Spanish realignment made a Corsican base untenable, a fact made palpable by the sighting off Cape Corse, on 15 October, of a Spanish fleet of '37' vessels.[19] Cockburn, blockading privateers in Leghorn roads, was warned of its possible intention of conducting Corsican partisans in French pay to attack the island. By then, however, the British government had ordered the evacuation of all the islands and British withdrawal from the western Mediterranean.

Trade Suppression

'Political courage in an officer abroad is as highly necessary as military courage.'[20] It was a truth Cockburn learned quickly in the Gulf of Genoa between 1793 and 1796. His work consisted of seizing merchant trading vessels belonging to the French or their allies, and the cargoes of either carried in neutral vessels. All 'goods for the purpose of war', even if not belonging to the enemy but bound to an enemy port, were liable to seizure, while evidence of sales of these goods at such a port was sufficient to justify seizure of the carrying vessel.

This work was a constant concern, pursued even during the course of other duties. In the Gulf it was complicated by three factors: the spread of French influence and land power along the coast, so that neutral or allied ports fell under enemy control; the consequent change in status of ships and cargoes from neutral or allied to enemy; and the difficulties of distinguishing the nationality and status of ships, especially where their owners and masters were consummate in changing their identity.

Cockburn's training began in January 1794 in a squadron under Captain Robert Man, working along the Gulf coast chasing every strange sail that came in sight. On the whole these vessels proved by their conduct whether they had something to hide. French vessels, or vessels trading into French-held ports, crept along the coast passing to and from enemy-occupied territory, taking shelter under the guns of headland forts. Frequently pursuits were fruitless because 'chases' gauged their distances carefully, their timing more often accurate than that of the British ships. Twice on 3 and 4 February 1794 after hectic pursuits, Cockburn in the *Inconstant* was forced to withdraw as forts opened fire.[21] By 1795 these vessels appeared to carry two main, probably complementary, cargoes: grain into the ports of southern France, especially Marseilles; and arms and equipment from those ports to supply the French army in the territories of Piedmont and Genoa.

In contrast, vessels caught readily were invariably those that carried papers attesting the nationality of their owners and their place of residence, the sources of their cargoes, and their destinations as places friendly to Britain. These vessels of allied or neutral status were usually trading long distances, across the Mediterranean and often far beyond. For a few of these, information sources on shore were able to indicate which ones to look out for: a vessel to be allowed free passage in July 1795, for example, carrying 'several well-intentioned Frenchmen' destined for France where it was expected their presence would be 'of considerable use to the common cause'; and a Greek polacre in July 1796 carrying 'emigrants' in the service of the French government, to be seized if at all possible.[22]

But for the vast majority of vessels purporting to be allied or neutral, there was no way of knowing without investigation whether their apparent identity, or that of their passengers or cargoes, was genuine or assumed. Some shipowners or masters attempted to maintain throughout hostilities trade routes pursued in peace. Others evidently hoped to take advantage of new trading opportunities created by the war. Whatever their motive, those that attempted to pass trade of benefit to the enemy through the British blockade had to conceal their purpose.

One well-known form of disguise was the flag of convenience. Perhaps typical of an enterprising master was that of a vessel described in a letter dated 11 February 1794, written by one Daniel Bomieter at Calvino, and passed on to Cockburn from Sir Hyde Parker. It brought to his attention the description of a vessel that had repaired at Calvino under a Spanish flag in June 1793. After wheat prices had soared in France, she had sailed to Ancona where she had hoisted Genoese colours, taken in a cargo of wheat and carried it to Toulon. She had then returned to Calvino under Spanish colours, by which means she had been able to load another cargo, even when there was 'a strict prohibition from the Court of Naples that no Genoese be permitted to load in His Sicilian Majesty's dominions with any kind of provisions'. Bomieter had represented these occurrences to the authorities at Calvino and, 'on enquiry being made into the matter, it could not be denied, yet from the corruptness of the underlings in office she was suffered to depart and will most probably carry the cargo to France as the best market'. Bomieter's description of the vessel was detailed: 'this vessel is ship rigged, is american built, about 250 tons, has a flush deck and railing, carried 14 or 16 guns, the stern a dirty white and yellow moulding, has america on her stern, a figure head, a woman with a lance in her hand'.[23]

The detection of such vessels without receipt of advance notice was the intellectual challenge of the war on enemy trade. Once on board a suspected vessel, the boarding party had to produce *proof* of attempted deception in order to detain it. Sometimes this was easy and the proof conclusive. On 2 March 1794 the brig *Seven Brothers* of Gibraltar was boarded and said to be bound for Barcelona, 'but finding false papers and false colours on board of her, took her off to the Admiral'. She was ordered to Leghorn for condemnation by the prize commissioners. Too often, however, the only evidence of possible deception was circumstantial or insufficient to gain condemnation. Thus on 9 March 1794 the *Meleager* boarded a Danish brig, said to be from Genoa bound for Algiers, 'but finding a quantity of money on board of her and supposing from her situation she was bound to France, sent an officer and 8 men on board of her to take her down to the Admiral'. This brig was released.[24]

With vessels being stopped every day, during 1794 and 1795 Cockburn gained sufficient experience and authority in the work to make judgements on proof of deception himself. He learned that the chances of penetrating disguises were improved by two factors. The first was surprise: to reduce the time available for a 'chase' to conceal her true identity and assume her disguise, British captains themselves raised false colours. The second was the thoroughness with which ships were examined. He was certainly instructed in where to search and what clues to look for, points covered by contemporary instructions.[25] Evidence was derived from two sources: the documents and the people on board. Both had to be painstakingly examined.

On boarding a vessel in all neutral or suspicious cases, it was recommended 'to be very particular in searching for concealed papers immediately on boarding with as much civility as possible, but without any respect to persons, passengers or others'. Papers found concealed had to be kept separate from the rest of a ship's papers, and a statement of their hiding place and the manner of their finding sent with the prize master. Meanwhile, the vessel's 'official papers' were minutely scrutinized: the ship's sea brief or title, her muster roll, clearance certificate from the last port of call, bills of lading, cargo manifest and mates' books, charter party and attested docket of clearance. Particular attention had to be paid to the name of the person who had made the contract for the voyage, and those upon whose account and risk the cargo was being shipped. Such details were checked against the dates of arrivals and departures at ports as represented in the log or journal. Dates were the 'great key' to the detection of frauds. 'Every word in every paper' had to 'be read again and again'. Where an inconsistency occurred, it was essential to 'follow the clue and search for other papers'.

As soon as possible after such searches and scrutiny, the master and any passengers were examined, noting their nationality. Where there was suspicion, individuals might be cross-examined separately. Passengers were likely to be supercargoes in disguise and consequently regarded both with suspicion and as good subjects from whom to tease out truth. Throughout these interrogations it was the owners' or subjects' place of residence, not their place of birth, that was borne in mind as determining whether property was liable to forfeiture (unless, that is, immunity was gained from a person acting as a consul or minister of state). But on no account were threats or bribery permitted, the information being rendered void by the means of obtaining it.

Cockburn possessed a number of advantages in prosecuting this work. He spoke French fluently, seems to have acquired an understanding of Spanish, and probably quickly learned enough Italian. Meticulous, perceptive and with a faculty for issues of a legal nature, he soon acquired sufficient experience to assess whether evidence of nationality of a ship or cargo was sufficient to achieve its condemnation. Serving under Nelson in the Gulf of Genoa in 1795–6, during the absence of Nelson from his squadron, Cockburn was left to act on his own judgement in sending vessels in to Leghorn for decision by the prize agents, Messrs Pollard, Udney and McArthur. Each vessel was accompanied by statements of Cockburn's opinion as to their liability to condemnation. Difficult cases included the cargo of a 'genoese brig, property of a Swiss residing in Marseilles', liable to condemnation in Cockburn's opinion on account of the owner's place of residence; and a French ship just purchased by an Algerian at Marseilles, which Cockburn thought would give rise to a law suit. The final decision was left to the agents. Nevertheless, by early 1796 he could confidently assert 'by the nature' of a Venetian brig's cargo of corn that it must have already been paid for by those to whom it was consigned, and that it *must* be condemned as it was said in the bill of lading 'to be at the risk of a merchant of Marseilles'.[26]

Characteristic of the explanation he sent to Messrs Pollard, Udney and McArthur was that relating to the cargo of the Genoese brig. Although ostensibly the property of the Swiss in Marseilles, Cockburn rather supposed the cargo was really the property of François Trayterrens and Company, the printed names in the bills of lading having been scratched out and the Swiss name inserted.

These cases of needles and casks of awls, though they sound but small are (I find by a person who understands the articles) of a very considerable value, there being 724 lb of the former and 5405 lb of the latter and are therefore well worth our contending for.

There are likewise two bales of cloth on board, which I believe will give you but little trouble as their bill does not even say they are for neutral account.

We found also 16 casks and 32 demijons of wine and 3 bales of leather on board her, of which there is neither any bill of lading or account whatever. To account for this the master says he smuggled them, but I suppose his saying *so* cannot clear this part of the cargo, which I suppose would be liable to condemnation for want of papers, if taken by the cruizers of any nation whatever.

It is very possible there may be more goods on board in [the] above predicament, but weather looking bad and it growing late, I have not time to search her minutely.

From the above, I have no idea that any part of this cargo will be claimed, but if it should, they cannot bring us in for damages, there being certainly just grounds for the detention. I would therefore have you immediately unload her and take all the merchandise on shore, paying the master his freight, which appears to be very small, he having told me it was only one hundred livres.

The master seems a kind of man who would answer any questions you might wish (for a small present). You must however be very cautious he does not prove you bribed him.

I would not have you give up anything whatever under the idea of it belonging to the passengers, except actually their wearing apparel, and I would have you send a trusty man on board till you unload her to see they do not smuggle anything away.

She has no manifest or other papers than those I have transmitted. . . . Although I always give you my opinion in full concerning the vessels I detain, you are nevertheless to consider yourselves at liberty to act differently when from mature deliberation it may appear to you necessary.[27]

In 1795 all the experience and judgement Cockburn and his agents could bring to bear was necessary, for the Gulf coast was a political minefield. The state of Genoa being technically neutral, French and British as well as neutral vessels entered its ports. The French vessels were to be seized, as were the enemy-owned cargoes of the neutral vessels. But at the same time, to placate the Genoese authorities, any appearance of a blockade was to be avoided. 'The disposition and acts of my cruisers will soon prove incontestably that Genoa is not blockaded', Nelson reassured the minister, 'as all vessels will arrive in perfect security which are not French or laden with French property'.

Nevertheless the Genoese, threatened by the French at their border, were foremost in trading with their powerful neighbour. To that extent they were also the subject of attentions from British ships, and principal victims of condemnations of prize goods by the British prize agents at Leghorn. There, rough justice was done. Condemned cargoes were removed from detained vessels to be sold, their owners receiving payment for demurrage and compensation for loss of freight. Even so, the Genoese had good reason to resent their harassment and detentions. Inevitably their merchants, shipowners and masters attempted to make good their losses by allegations of abuse of their neutral rights by the British.

In August 1795 Cockburn was obliged to defend himself against such an allegation. The necessity arose from an incident in the evening of 20 July. Cockburn sent a boat to examine several vessels inshore near Finale. A polacre ship attracted particular suspicion, and at nine o'clock, as it was getting dark, all the boats were manned and armed and sent to board her. At midnight one of the boats returned with the information that the ship was French, from Marseilles, was armed, and had French property on board including several chests of money. The ship had, however, cut its cables and was making for a French port. Meanwhile the other boats were in chase. Two hours later the polacre was boarded, the crew having abandoned ship and taken the money with them. Two men, who turned out to be passengers, were found on board. One of them was later able to provide a full account of the events of the night as seen from the French vessel.

> . . . on the 20th of July being off Finale, we saw a frigate which we supposed to be English, in consequence of which we hove too to see what course she would take; but seeing her stand towards us, the Captain appeared very much frightened and consulted with his brother, and the other passengers, the best method of escaping; at first we hove up to get under the French batteries at Alassio, afterwards the Captain altered his mind, and came to anchor at Finale close to the beach; after which he went on shore, carrying with him between 30 and 40 bags of money which he left at the house of a friend, and after having been up to the Austrian Commandant, he retook the money from the house and returned on board and put the bags of money on the quarter deck; after this I

observed him very much agitated, watching the motions of the frigate till it was dark; about 10 o'clock of the same night, a boat came from the frigate and said they were English and asked for the Captain; we answered them he was on shore, and all the crew armed with musquets said they would fire into the boat if they did not put off (the Captain was all the time upon deck but desired us not to fire); the boat put off immediately and we instantly cut our cable and made all sail towards the French batteries near Alassio; soon after which we saw some boats in chase of us which fired at us; about half an hour afterwards, seeing the frigate ahead of us and the boats still firing astern, the Captain and all the crew except another passenger and myself went into our boat carrying with them all the bags of money which had been kept upon deck and pulled in shore to the westward. Soon after this, the boats boarded us and took possession of the vessel.

This same passenger confirmed that the money taken by the crew as well as gold, ingots of silver and jewels later found in the cabin 'belonged to French merchants and was to pay for coin they had received from Genoa'.[28] However, two weeks later Cockburn had to supply a full circumstantial account of the seizure which had to go officially to Lord Grenville, the British Secretary of State for Foreign Affairs. The master of the polacre was Genoese and claimed his vessel had been boarded and rifled within gunshot of the city of Genoa—indeed while shots from the city were passing overhead. The Genoese Secretary of State claimed the neutrality of his state had been injured and demanded both redress and restitution of an illegal capture. Fortunately, Cockburn was able to defend his conduct with the depositions of the two passengers, pointing out at the same time the inaccuracies and inconsistencies in the story of the master. His own case rested on the conduct of the polacre appearing 'very unlike that of a fair trading neutral vessel'. By the crew threatening to fire into the *Meleager*'s boat and the ship then making off towards that part of the coast occupied by the French, it acted exactly as though it was an enemy. Maintaining that mistakes in the story of the master revealed his duplicity, Cockburn claimed that he had done no more than his duty and occasioned no breach of neutrality.[29] He evidently convinced the Genoese Secretary of State for no more was heard of the incident.

Serving a Superior: Nelson

In July 1795 Cockburn became the senior captain in the squadron commanded by Nelson in the Gulf of Genoa. Over the following winter

Figure 1. Nelson's squadron cuts out nine French ships in the Gulf of Genoa on 6 August 1795, by Nicholas Pocock. The ships were supplying the French army on shore. The attack was made at night with Nelson in *Agamemnon* and Cockburn in *Meleager*. (National Maritime Museum)

Nelson quickly came to rely upon him. By May 1796 he was leaving Cockburn in command of the squadron, 'resting perfectly assured' that His Majesty's service would be 'most punctually attended to, the particular nature of which you so well know'. The two evidently developed a clear understanding, for by October 1796 Nelson was reasoning 'we so exactly think alike on points of service that if your mind tells you it is right, there can hardly be a doubt but I must approve'.[30]

The confidence Nelson placed in Cockburn permitted him the freedom to absent himself in order to liaise with the Austrians and British main fleet. He consequently came to depend on Cockburn for the conduct of operations in the Gulf as well as for the management of administrative matters. In 1822 this was quietly emphasized by Cockburn to Edward Brenton for his forthcoming *Naval History*. To cut out ships carrying stores for the siege of Mantua from beneath a battery at the end of May 1796, Cockburn recalled:

> The commodore having determined to attack them desired me to lead in in the Meleager (as I was best acquainted with the coast). I run in of course as close to the battery and the armed vessels as the water would permit, anchored and commenced the action. The commodore, desirous to place himself if possible within me stood under my stern designing to luff in between me and the principal battery. But as I had taken as close a position as the depth of the water would allow he of course grounded under my stern, which gave us some inconvenience in the operation we were engaged in as of course our principal attention was then obliged to be given to get the Agamemnon off again.

Because the effects of the battery were 'trifling', the convoy was taken and the *Agamemnon* got off without damage. Nelson wrote to Jervis of the affair, complimenting Cockburn for his part. But, as Cockburn accurately recalled, Nelson's letter did not mention the *Agamemnon* grounding.[31]

For such practical help, by May 1796 Nelson already felt obliged to exert himself on behalf of his young deputy. 'He has been under my command near a year on this station and I should feel myself guilty of neglect of duty were I not to represent his zeal, ability and courage, which shine conspicuous on every occasion which offers'. An appropriate reward was *La Minerve*,[32] a 40-gun frigate captured from the French in June 1795. Sir John Jervis, the new commander-in-chief, had claims to meet elsewhere, but Nelson persisted in his own. 'I send Captain

Cockburn as I believe his anxiety to get into *La Minerve* is great'; and four days later—'I wish, Sir, that Captain Cockburn had the *Minerve*; he is worthy of her or a better ship'.[33] The pressure paid off. Cockburn transferred into *La Minerve* on 20 August 1796.

The reciprocity evident in efforts exerted to the other's advantage was an enduring feature of Cockburn's relationship with Nelson. In the long term, the interest Nelson exerted on Cockburn's behalf influenced the next decade of his career, although initially it was Nelson who gained more from his protégé, an advantage that was evident in two incidents that enhanced his reputation.

In December 1796, with the British fleet at Gibraltar, it was in *La Minerve* that Nelson raised a commodore's pendant with instructions to evacuate the remaining British vessels and the British garrison from Porto Ferrajo, Elba. While Jervis took the main fleet through the Straits for the Tagus, on 15 December Nelson and Cockburn sailed for Elba, accompanied by the *Blanche*, a 32-gun frigate under D'Arcy Preston. Four days later, off Cartagena, the two vessels encountered and engaged two Spanish frigates, both of 40 guns, the *Santa Sabina* and *Ceres*. The former was taken, but retaken next day by a Spanish squadron including two line-of-battle ships. The engagement is well documented;[34] but the extent to which Nelson relied on Cockburn is not.

While Nelson as commodore clearly directed the engagement, actual management of *La Minerve* was left to Cockburn. Nelson's public letters acknowledged his role: 'the enemy frequently within shot by bringing up the breeze, it required all the skill of Captain Cockburn, which he eminently displayed, to get off with a crippled ship'; his judgement, gallantry and the discipline of the *Minerve* did him 'the highest credit'. On returning to London in 1797 Nelson directed a gold-hilted sword be made for Cockburn which he hoped to present to him 'in the most public and handsome manner'. Being unable to do so himself, he sent it for Jervis to present.[35]

A second incident, seven weeks later, implies how much Nelson owed to Cockburn. Having reached Porto Ferrajo, Elba, on Christmas Day 1796, *La Minerve* was refitted and had both main- and mizen-masts replaced. Meanwhile, Nelson had the naval stores and officials on shore embarked in transports. Sir Gilbert Elliot, ex-Viceroy of Corsica, and his staff arrived on the 22 January 1797, to be embarked on *La Minerve*. General de Burgh, commanding the military force on Elba, declined to leave without written orders. Fourteen transports and storeships with five escorts accordingly sailed for Gibraltar on 29 January.

At Gibraltar Cockburn received back by cartel his two lieutenants, Culverhouse and Hardy, who had been taken by the Spanish in *Santa Sabina*. Nelson was anxious to reach Jervis and the British fleet off Cadiz. The Spanish fleet from Cartagena had, he learned, just passed through the Straits with the object of joining the French fleet at Brest, and Jervis was likely to be in its path. *La Minerve* thus remained at her moorings less than 48 hours. As she left the bay two Spanish line-of-battle ships also weighed and proceeded to chase her. The leading Spanish ship was the *Terrible*, from which Hardy and Culverhouse had just been removed, and was known by them to be a good sailor. Colonel Drinkwater-Bethune, a passenger in *La Minerve*, reported what, in his view, then happened. His account, included in a 'narrative' of the battle of St Vincent and published in 1797, added to Nelson's fame.

> Captain Cockburn, who had been taking a view of the chasing enemy, now joined the Commodore, and observed that there was no doubt of the headmost ship gaining on the Minerve. At this moment dinner was announced, but . . . the sudden cry of a 'man overboard' threw the dinner party into some disorder. The officers of the ship ran on deck: I, with others, ran to the stern windows to see if anything could be observed of the unfortunate man; we had scarcely reached them before we noticed the lowering of the jolly boat, in which was . . . Hardy with a party of sailors; and before many seconds had elapsed the current of the Straits (which runs strongly to the eastward) had carried the jolly boat far astern of the frigate towards the Spanish ships. Of course the first object was to recover, if possible, the fallen man, but he was never seen again. Hardy soon made a signal to that effect, and the man was given up as lost. The attention of every person was now turned to the safety of Hardy and his boat's crew; their situation was extremely perilous, and their danger was every instant increasing from the fast sailing of the headmost ship of the chase, which, by this time had approached nearly within gunshot of the Minerve. The jolly boat's crew pulled 'might and main' to regain the frigate, but apparently made little progress against the current of the Straits. At this crisis, Nelson, casting an anxious look at the hazardous situation of Hardy and his companions, exclaimed, 'By G-- I'll not lose Hardy! Back the mizen topsail.' No sooner said than done; the Minerve's progress was retarded, leaving the current to carry her down towards Hardy and his party, who seeing this spirited manoeuvre to save them from returning to their old quarters on board the Terrible, naturally redoubled their exertions to rejoin the frigate. To the landsmen on board the Minerve an action now appeared to be inevitable; and so, it would appear, thought the enemy, who surprised and confounded by this daring manoeuvre . . .

(being ignorant of the accident that led to it) must have construed it into a direct challenge. . . . the Captain of the Terrible suddenly shortened sail in order to allow his consort to join him, and thus afforded time for the Minerve to drop down to the jollyboat to take out Hardy and the crew; and the moment they were on board the frigate, orders were given again to make sail. Being now under studding sails, and the widening of the Straits allowing the wind to be brought more on the Minerve's quarter, the frigate soon regained the lost distance.[36]

Nelson here was the focus of attention. Yet several observations are necessary. Hardy and Nelson had sailed together only the four days preceding the *Santa Sabina* action. Hardy was far closer to Cockburn with whom he had worked since the latter's posting into the *Meleager* two years earlier; it was their understanding, and theirs with the crew, that made the rescue attempt almost spontaneous. The backing of topsails and lowering of a boat were routine. In these circumstances, Nelson's final order to back the mizen topsail can have been only a final direction. Cockburn's log states the ship was already hove-to when the jolly boat was lowered. There was, indeed, no immediate danger from the Spanish vessels. The distance probably looked close to a landsman, but according to the log, even when the jolly boat was hoisted in and all sail set, the *Terrible* was still three miles astern.[37]

Cockburn's role as captain in command of the ship was more evident in Drinkwater-Bethune's account of subsequent events. Having escaped from the *Terrible* and her consort, during the night *La Minerve* caught up the Spanish fleet. At about half past three, flashes were seen and percussions heard of eight guns. Drinkwater relates how he was awakened by Nelson entering the cabin which he shared with Sir Gilbert Elliot to warn the Viceroy that at that moment they were in the middle of the Spanish fleet. From their signals, he said he knew it was not the British fleet; that the night was foggy; that *La Minerve* was then between two very large ships within hail of each of them, and others were near on all sides; that he and Cockburn had little doubt of the strangers being Spanish; that Cockburn and his officers were all alert and every direction given to watch the movements of the strange ships and do as they did.[38] The remainder of the night was spent edging *La Minerve* out of the fleet. At seven she 'hove up to the northward' and 24 hours later joined Jervis and the British fleet.

The battle off Cape St Vincent developed the following morning, 14 February. For this, Nelson transferred back to his own ship, the 74-gun *Captain*. By the end of the encounter, which lasted just over six hours, the *Captain* was severely damaged, having been placed alongside and boarded the 84-gun *San Nicholas*, and through her the 112-gun *San Josef*. The two prizes formed half the total British captures, and after firing ceased the British line passed the *Captain*, each ship saluting her with three cheers. Cockburn sent a boat for Nelson, who hoisted his pendant in *La Minerve*, directing Cockburn to put him on board the first uninjured ship of the line. That night *Minerve* returned to take the *Captain* in tow, to be cast off two days later in the shelter of Lagos Bay.

For these services, Nelson continued to honour his debts. Cockburn became the standard by which others were measured. A week after the battle, on patrol around Lagos Bay, Cockburn came across the towering four-decked *Santissima Trinidad* carrying 136 guns. Though crippled, she was escorted by a frigate. *La Minerve*, accompanied by two other frigates, kept her distance and eventually lost sight of the Spanish ship. However, on hearing that the four-decker had been lost, Nelson's criticism still favoured his subordinate: 'Berkeley ought never to have lost sight of her, and to have tried her strength the first opportunity. I am sure Cockburn would have done so'.[39]

The elevation of Cockburn to the level of an ideal did not fail to influence Jervis. Early in 1797 attention focused on Spain's Atlantic supply routes. Jervis had intelligence that the Spanish Viceroy of Mexico was on passage from Havana to Cadiz under the protection of three ships of the line, with silver worth more than six million pounds sterling. Though expected in March, the specie ships had not materialized. In April, Cockburn, with Benjamin Hallowell in the 32-gun frigate *Lively*, was sent to find the vessels, possibly awaiting convoy off Santa Cruz of Tenerife in the Spanish Canary Islands. Had the ships been found, one frigate would go for help while the other tracked the treasure. Its capture would bring prize money in significant amounts; a share would have meant wealth even for a junior captain. Yet even without it, prizes were likely to be plentiful, for the islands were a landfall and watering place for vessels from Spanish America and the Cape of Good Hope. There is thus reason to assume Nelson's expression of hope—'I long for *poor* Cockburn and Hallowell to enrich themselves'— lay behind their selection for the task by Jervis.[40]

The Canary Islands were to be Cockburn's and Hallowell's station for almost a year, to be followed by leave from which Cockburn returned to the Mediterranean late in 1798. Between January and September 1799 he again worked under Nelson, who in March placed him in the Gulf of Genoa 'for service of head'. In September, when Nelson was left by Lord

Keith in command of the Mediterranean station, he dispatched Cockburn to its Lisbon division: 'marked proof of his continued recollection and consideration of him', because at that time that division was the only one upon which British ships still intercepted large numbers of vessels trading into Spanish and French ports.[41] This was to remain Cockburn's station until early 1801, maintaining a presence about Cape Finisterre, while keeping Ferrol and Corunna under observation. Though the identity and ownership of trading vessels and cargoes were the principal preoccupation, seven privateers were taken by *La Minerve* between November 1799 and September 1800.

Their respective shares in prizes remained a fundamental common interest to both Nelson and Cockburn. Since 1796, Nelson had left the management of their common concerns largely in Cockburn's hands: 'You know how to settle bills better than I do, therefore I shall say no more'.[42] Thus, having kept the names of ships in which they shared, and given instructions to their prize agent at Leghorn for the remittance of proceeds of sales to his own agent (Francis Wilson at the Navy Office), Cockburn remained the key figure in a group concerned with the distribution of prize money until 1802. In 1798, when he returned to England, he spent some time settling prize accounts and considering investments, some of this on Nelson's behalf. In 1802, between April and June, Nelson regularly met Cockburn and sometimes their prize agent, usually 'at Cockburn's' to finalize matters.[43]

Underlying mutual material interests lay a bond of real affection, at least on Cockburn's part. In 1797, when they were apart, long and affectionate letters made plain his pleasure in Nelson's company. 'Considering I was too late to be with you', he wrote in April 1797, the cruise with Ben Hallowell was 'the thing of all others most to my liking'; and in July, 'next to my own father, I know of none whose company I so much wish to be in or who I have such real reasons to respect'.[44] A cynic might claim Cockburn was simply maintaining a valuable relationship. This would not be untrue. But there is evidence to suggest his admiration and affection were real. Fifty years later, it was Nelson's humanity and the manner in which he treated Cockburn that the latter recalled. He told Croker in 1845 that Nelson was 'always a curious compound of weakness, with power of high exertions of intrepidity and talent whenever great occasions called for the exertion of the nobler qualities and subjection of the former, and blessed with a never failing kindness of heart'.[45]

Morality and Discipline

In 1796 the reputation Cockburn had been making for himself with Nelson was tested by the shipboard discipline of another captain named Charles Sawyer. He was seven years older than Cockburn, but a year junior to him as a captain. Sawyer commanded the *Blanche*, a 32-gun frigate, that had been operating with Cockburn in *La Minerve* throughout the summer. Early in June the latter learned Sawyer had been conducting himself with undue familiarity towards some members of the *Blanche*'s crew. The investigation resulted in Sawyer promising in future not to behave that way again.

However, on 8 September Cockburn received a request from Sawyer for a court martial on the first lieutenant of the *Blanche*, Archibald Cowan. On writing to Cowan to require him to prepare to answer the charges, Cowan returned a letter he had addressed to Nelson as commodore of their squadron on 24 August, but which Sawyer had refused to forward. The letter to Nelson requested he apply to the commander-in-chief for the court martial of Sawyer for several times having been seen in his bed with his coxswain, Edward Mullins; for taking no public notice of Mullins calling him 'a man fucking bugger and other names'; and for having 'frig'd', and been 'frig'd' by, two midshipmen, Thomas Rowe and Richard Pridham, and a black seaman, John Friday.

Investigation revealed that on 24 August and 7 September Sawyer had twice refused to forward to Nelson Cowan's requests for court martial on his commander. In August Sawyer had countered with the threat of court martial on 'very serious' charges against Cowan, and on 7 September threatened the same against all four of *Blanche*'s lieutenants, her master, purser and gun-room steward, 'unless in the meantime matters can be accommodated'. It was to convince these officers that his threat was serious that he made his request for a court martial on Cowan on 8 September and placed Cowan under arrest within the *Blanche*.

On 9 September, with both vessels in Leghorn Roads, an accommodation between Sawyer and Cowan did take place. Sawyer agreed that he would leave the ship. Both requested Cockburn to permit them to withdraw their respective charges, Cowan on account of the public exposure to which a court martial would subject the two midshipmen and Sawyer. However, at that stage Cockburn refused to agree to an accommodation taking place. It had become 'incompatible with the service'. The lengths to which Sawyer's indiscretions had run placed the reputations of too many people at risk, including Cockburn's own. Sawyer was informed:

Considering my rising charactor in the service I certainly went beyond the bounds of discretion by silencing the business when it came forward in June last, but in consideration of your respectable family and your promise that your future conduct (to use your own words) should give the lie to such a scandelous report, I took it on myself to settle it with the officers of both ships, and I verily believe owing to the promises they made me, it has hitherto gone no further; but what, Sir, must be my surprize when I understand that within a fortnight from that period you are accused of the same tenor of conduct, the truth of which you certainly allow if you agree to quit the ship to accommodate with those who (but yesterday morning) you told me were behaving in a most injurious and improper manner, and one of which (your principal prosecutor) you have accused of mutiny both by word and deed.

For Cowan also to withdraw would be 'highly improper and dangerous' to his 'future character'. As for Sawyer, the charges alleged against him were of such a scandalous nature that nothing, in Cockburn's opinion, but 'conscious guilt' should have induced him to agree to such an accommodation, in which case he deserved punishment. Yet if he was not guilty, he had an obligation to clear himself.

After the superior education you must have received and the exalted situation your Country has placed you in, if you are guilty of the crimes alledged against you, you certainly deserve every punishment that can be inflicted on you in this world or the next. But if on the other hand you are innocent (which for the sake of human nature I still wish to believe) you are certainly the most injured of men and you ought to prosecute to the utmost rigour of the laws, those who have made such daring attempts on your character and honor, and your former fears of wounding the ears of your relations should be overcome by the stronger ones, of being a disgrace not only to your profession and your country but to the human race.

It was Cockburn's own sense of duty to his fellow creatures that pressed him to settle the matter in a court of law. 'Was I again to be the sole means of stifling this scandelous business it would make me the most miserable of beings, as I should then conceive that my brother officers had a right to accuse me not only of insincerity but injustice.' Upon that, he was prepared to take advice. He would refer the whole business, that in June and at present, to the first officer of equal rank to himself that arrived. If that officer thought it possible to let the matter rest in silence in view of Sawyer's agreement to leave his ship, Cockburn would not object to it, even though he would regard it as a tacit acknowledgement of guilt.

Three more letters from Sawyer over the next two days attempted to persuade Cockburn to allow the accommodation. Cockburn was obliged to insist emphatically that things should remain as they were. Over these two days Sawyer came to admit both the accommodation and the attempt to withdraw charges had been mistaken. He came to trial for 'odious misconduct' and ignoring mutinous expressions on 18 October 1796.[46] He was sentenced to be dismissed from the service and 'rendered incapable of ever serving his Majesty, his heirs and successors, in any military capacity whatever'. Over the following two days, Cowan and his fellow officers were also tried on a variety of charges, upon all of which they were acquitted.[47]

The handling of this incident was marked by Cockburn's strength of moral feeling and determined rectitude. They were to form the foundation of his professional attitude throughout his career. For not only was the character or reputation of an officer dependent on his sense of morality and justice,[48] as Sawyer's difficulties demonstrated, so also was the respect and support he could command from his crew.

The Management of Seamen

The success with which Cockburn served his superiors during the Revolutionary War was underpinned by the loyalty and support he engendered from his crews. To the modern mind this may seem paradoxical when he himself was later depicted as a flogging captain.[49] Later he did not deny the regime he maintained, and simply acknowledged the 1790s as a period before the system of punishing seamen was reformed.[50] However, in examining the relationship Cockburn had with his crews, it would be wrong to focus simply on the aspect with which reformers were later concerned. This relationship had numerous elements, of which the power to impose summary punishment was only one. In this respect he acted, like the magistrate on shore, as the authorized head of his community.[51] But, just like that figure (invariably a land-owning employer), he had the means of providing employment, had a vested interest in maintaining order and subordination, and an obligation to care for the people who depended on his authority.

Loyalties

As a young captain, there is no doubt that he was fortunate. He learned his duties with crews that were stable. *Meleager* had been manned at the outbreak of war and her crew was virtually the same when he joined her in February 1794. Over the following two years her crew was depleted. Though possessing an official complement of 215, by February 1795 she had only 150 men on her books and mustered only 135. Nevertheless, that core remained intact until Cockburn left the ship in August 1796.

When he did so, 26 seamen voluntarily went with him into *La Minerve*. They were replaced by 18 'per order' from *La Minerve*. These 26 'followers' were all mature seamen or officers and provided the immediate means of controlling his new crew. Three were master's mates: Jonathan Knapp, aged 42, rated as an able seaman in March 1793, whom Cockburn had made second gunner in November 1794 and second master's mate in April 1795; he took the same post again on *La Minerve*. So also did Henry Morrison, aged 43. Charles Brady, aged 25, had joined *Meleager* in February 1795 as first master's mate, and transferred as such with Cockburn. Jonathan Evett, aged 33, had been made yeoman of the sheets in May 1793, a boatswain's mate in May 1794, and transferred in 1796 to become boatswain. Charles Fellows, 27, had followed a similar course: from able seaman to second gunner in November 1794, to ship's corporal in August 1795 (his predecessor in this post being flogged and reduced for drunkenness and neglect of duty). Fellows took the same post in *La Minerve*. Other key posts were taken by Thomas Johnson, 36, yeoman of the sheets; William Markey, 33, carpenter's mate; and Robert Taylor, 23, caulker.

While these men took specific posts, more at Cockburn's disposal for supervisory purposes were five midshipmen, all of long experience, aged 25, 33, 34, 35 and 36. Other experienced men included two able seamen aged 29 and 30, who would respectively become second master's mate in September, and midshipman in November 1796. In addition there was Richard Wilson, an able seaman aged 40, and Jonathan Fells, an ordinary seaman aged 18.

More personal was the relationship with a handful of other men. Robert Slaper, aged 28, was Cockburn's coxswain. Jonathan Renoux, 22, was a French seaman from Marseilles, possibly a refugee, entered as an able seaman in July 1794 and made captain's clerk in August 1794. There was an Italian acting as Cockburn's cook who would be discharged when the English evacuated the Mediterranean in December 1796; also four boys, aged 16 and 17, two of them Italian, at least one of whom was an officer's servant.[52]

Finally, there was Jonathan Culverhouse, *Meleager*'s first lieutenant, then *La Minerve*'s first lieutenant; and Thomas Masterman Hardy, who had been third lieutenant in *Meleager* since November 1793 and who became second in *La Minerve*. The latter, a larger ship, with potential for greater achievement, provided opportunity for officers. No doubt Cockburn's interest with Hood and Nelson also influenced their transfer. Hardy at this stage had no patron or interest and had only his own ability to commend him. As midshipman and master's mate in the *Hebe* in 1791, he had shared a mess with Cockburn when the latter was still a midshipman. For Hardy, Cockburn's friendship and knowledge of his talents probably provided the only foreseeable path to promotion.

Even after transfers from *Meleager*, *La Minerve* had neither completed nor trained her crew. However, three days after Cockburn took command, another 67 men were brought on board from a French cartel, exchanged for prisoners in British hands; and on 25 October another 42 were transferred from the *Ça Ira*, captured in 1795 and since then a depot ship. By February 1797 her complement had reached 220, though still far short of her theoretical establishment of 300. Following the Battle off Cape St Vincent on 14 February, prize duties reduced her crew to as low as 170. Even so, after seven Italians had deserted at Porto Ferrajo in December 1796, the crew was almost totally composed of young British volunteers, the core of which was to remain together until the end of the Revolutionary War. In April 1798 they totalled 241, excluding widows' men, and that number was retained until 1801.[53] Between May and September 1798, while *La Minerve* was refitting, they were housed in the *Prudent* hulk in Portsmouth harbour, a practice promoting both stability of relations, discipline and morale. Of 241 men still forming the crew by February 1801, only 3 were recorded as 'prest'.[54] But there were 102 entries and re-entries in *La Minerve*'s muster book in the summer of 1798, and 118 between then and 1801; and it was, of course, in the interests of seamen to volunteer when it was clear they could not escape impressment.

The crew that brought *La Minerve* into Portsmouth in 1798 was a competent one. Of the 241 men transferred to a new muster book, 126 were rated able seamen, 39 ordinary seamen and 19 landsmen. The construction of her crew from large numbers of previously experienced seamen certainly affected Cockburn's management, in particular his policy of allowing shore leave when in port. This in turn may have influenced the disposition of men to avoid desertion. Although others were successful in deserting, between 20 August 1796 and 20 February 1802 only two men were punished for attempted desertion, eight for going on shore without leave, and two for breaking or overstaying their leave.[55]

Punishments

The policy of allowing shore leave was affected by the age pattern of the crew. Of 241 men in 1798 only 26 were over the age of 40, 53 were in their thirties, while 162 were younger than 30. Cockburn himself was still only 26. In this high concentration of predominantly young adult males, there were occasions when relations between men were soured, as frequently between those who shared the crowded lower deck, as between the men and their officers. This is evident in the nature of the offences for which Cockburn awarded punishments over the whole period of his command of La Minerve. Of 212 known punishments for offences, 60 (28 per cent) were for drunkenness, and 51 (24 per cent) for fighting, quarrelling or theft, while 56 (26 per cent) were for neglect of duty or disobedience of orders, and 29 (14 per cent) for contempt or mutiny. Of these punishments, the majority (52 per cent) were for what may be termed anti-social offences, the minority (40 per cent) for those against authority.[56] This balance tends to suggest that La Minerve enjoyed greater harmony between officers and men than between the men themselves.[57]

The continuity of service for the bulk of the crews on both ships naturally created an atmosphere in which the frequency of offences diminished. In La Minerve between 1796 and 1801 they fell by 43 per cent per annum. Cockburn was quite particular in recording punishments, and the decline reinforces a view that the longer crews served together under the same captain the more they adapted to the standards he demanded. For the crew of La Minerve, in which the average number of punishments declined from nearly six a month in 1796–7 to four in 1800, and to little more than three in 1801, relations would seem to have become increasingly harmonious.

This of course overlooks strains, problems and breaks from the sea that naturally affected short-term patterns of punishment. There were seven calendar months in Meleager, and eighteen in La Minerve, in which no punishments at all were recorded. These periods invariably coincided with spells in port, though these were often of only a few days. Six consecutive months in 1799 passed without a single punishment, undoubtedly due to the relief from work at sea by a succession of brief breaks in Leghorn, Palermo, Port Mahon, Gibraltar and the Tagus. On the other hand, a significant increase in offences against authority was registered over the winter of 1797–8, before *La Minerve* refitted at Portsmouth, coinciding with the mutinies in the fleet and the end of long commission. Similarly, on a smaller scale at the end of the Revolutionary War, after anchoring at Spithead, punishments for neglect of duty escalated with the necessity to get the vessel round to Deptford to be stripped and paid off.

It would be wrong to generalize about the attitudes of a whole crew from the nature of offences committed by a few. Elsewhere, on the Leeward Islands command, during the Revolutionary War, only nine per cent of all seamen were flogged; on some vessels far fewer than that proportion were punished, while in others up to 18 per cent suffered.[58] In *La Minerve* certain men seem to have courted punishment. Within two months of taking command, Cockburn punished Theodosius Lawson three times: for disobedience of orders and 'aggravating insolence', for mutiny, and for quarrelling.

But regular individual offenders were uncommon, and then mostly for crimes such as 'uncleanness', 'indecent familiarity with some Portuguese boys', striking or drawing upon a superior officer. Such offenders probably possessed a predisposition to these crimes. This was perhaps the case with thieves, who were particularly heavily punished, receiving up to 200 lashes compared to the half to two dozen for fighting or quarrelling. But then these last offences were usually group activities where men were drawn in, sometimes drunk, carried by the spirit of the moment.[59]

Mutineers

Most men appear to have respected authority in *La Minerve*. In the five and a half years between August 1796 and February 1802 there were only 15 punishments for contempt, insolence or impertinence; and 14 for mutiny, mutinous expressions or language, countenancing the same or making a mutinous assembly. Nine of the latter were concentrated in the period June 1797 to March 1798 and were certainly associated, if only in Cockburn's mind, with the mutinies in the fleet at Spithead and the Nore. These eruptions of discontent had broken out in mid-April and their influence was communicated to the crew of *La Minerve* on the arrival at Madeira on 23 June 1797 of a convoy of 56 merchantmen under the protection of the frigate *Thames*. By then the concessions made to the mutineers at Spithead in May were already known.

The Spithead complaints had been the inadequacy of seamen's pay, the commission of two ounces in the pound taken by the purser from foodstuffs he purchased, the lack of fresh vegetables and meat when in harbour, the inadequate provision of 'necessaries' for the sick, the discontinuation of pay to the wounded, and the lack of shore leave when in harbour.[60] Parliament had made concessions on most points in an emergency Bill which had been passed by the House of Commons on 9 May. Its contents were immediately despatched to the fleet at sea, St Vincent sending on to Cockburn on 22 May a 'plan for the better encouragement of the seamen and marines serving on board His Majesty's Fleet'. The daily rate of pay for each grade of seaman, from petty officer to landsman and marine, was slightly increased; allowances of provisions were to be made without deductions for leakage or waste, otherwise short allowance money was to be paid; and the wounded were to receive full pay until they had recovered, were in receipt of a pension, or had a place at the Royal Hospital in Greenwich. St Vincent ordered that the plan be read aloud to all officers and crew.[61]

These concessions had done little to improve discipline in the *Thames* when she encountered *La Minerve*, accompanied by the *Lively* under Benjamin Hallowell, at Madeira. A month after the event, Cockburn recounted to Nelson:

I had heard before your letter arrived too much concerning the mutiny at home by the arrival whilst we were laying at Madeira of a large West India convoy under the protection of the Thames who was in such a state as I suppose no ship ever was before, especially at sea and with so great a charge, the men doing exactly what they pleased and the officers being absolutely afraid to control them. They endeavoured to persuade our people to act like themselves, telling them they turned all the officers they disliked out of the ships and that they did exactly what they pleased in the Channel ships and they even threatened if our people did not mutiny to write against them to the seamen in England; and on being refused leave to come on board of us, they swam under the bows to bring inflammatory papers, which were given up to me by our people. Indeed I had every reason to be very much pleased with the conduct of the majority of our ship's company (in the midst of temptation) who, on my turning them up on account of some suspicions about them, assured me of their firm attachment to their government and officers and offered to prove it by going alongside either of the other frigates that should behave improperly. In spite of this, however, since we have been out I have been informed that some few of them had been tainted by the Thames, but finding the generality of their shipmates against them they kept silent.

There is but one, indeed, who I have any proof against and he is at present away in a prize; when he comes back I shall certainly write for a court martial on him for endeavouring to persuade some of the ship's company to revolt and take the ship to England; he will have nothing to plead in defense but drunkenness so I expect he will be made an example of.[62]

Cockburn failed to mention the flogging for mutiny on 24 June (the day after joining the *Thames*) of a seaman who, after punishment, was discharged on shore; nor that four days later for mutiny and breaking leave on shore; or that on 10 July for 'making mutinous assembly'.[63] This was perhaps because conduct on board *La Minerve* differed materially from that on board the *Lively*. For, as Cockburn continued to Nelson:

The Lively, I am sorry to say, were not quite so quiet. They broke out one evening (when we [the officers of *La Minerve* and *Thames*] were all on board of her) by giving three cheers but they were almost instantaneously quelled and the only excuse they had to urge, or reason to give for their conduct, was that our people [*Minerve*'s] had leave to go on shore and they had not. The fact was Hallowell sent me in some days before he come in himself and according to my usual custom I gave a proportion of my people leave to go on shore; when the Lively arrived, what was at the same time as the Thames, Hallowell did not like to let them go on shore, but gave them leave to have some liquor on board, the fumes of which, added to what they had heard from the Thames, I suppose inflamed them so much they thought they might insist on obtaining liberty. They were however very much mistaken in the issue for most of the ringleaders were most severely flogged and one of them is in irons to be tried by Court Martial. Since this they have behaved with greatest attention and propriety and very much to Hallowell's satisfaction.

So Sir, as whatever mischief might have been instilled into our ships from the Thames is entirely subdued, I cannot but be very happy that we fell in with her, as I think it may be in a great measure the saving of the convoy and perhaps the West India fleet, for we (the Captains) held an enquiry on board of her, where things came out that Captain Lukin had not an idea of. It seemed that six or eight of his people had the rest completely under subjection, that they could do with the ship whatever they pleased; and one of these men had said at different times he did not know if he would permit her to go on to the West Indies, but if he did it would be only to make the fleet there mutiny, and he should then carry her home again immediately. These leading men we took out of her and sent on board a transport carrying out a detachment of foreign troops, in whose charge they are placed, and from whence they will most likely not be removed but to be tried by a Court Martial; and as we transmitted all the minutes of our enquiry, I hope they will have a different part to act in the West Indies to what they expected, as instead of inciting the ships there to mutiny, they will in all probability be a warning to them to behave with propriety. We kept company with the convoy for three days after they left Madeira and the last accounts I had from the Thames they were behaving in the most orderly manner possible and seemed all to be very happy they had got rid of the above mentioned *Terrorists*.

This view, that mutineers relied for their support on terror, was consistent with a belief that the great majority of seamen in the navy were reconciled, if never entirely content, with their situation. To Cockburn in *La Minerve* mutiny did not therefore seem a serious threat. On the voyage home, on 1 March 1798, six seamen accused of mutiny received but six or a dozen lashes each.

However, in England the mutinies in the fleet had deeply affected naval society, both high and low. In September 1798, at Portsmouth, Cockburn appealed to the commander-in-chief to request the Admiralty for a court martial on a seaman, William Nugent, for 'having declared himself to be a United Irishman with many other improper expressions' and then riotously opposing the acting Master at Arms who attempted to put him in irons.[64] Affairs in Ireland were closely associated in people's minds with events in the fleet. Cockburn himself was not immune from the same fears.[65] On his return to sea in June 1799 he awarded two heavy summary punishments for mutiny: one of five dozen lashes, the other of seven dozen for 'countenancing the same'. Perhaps the weight of these sentences had the desired effect, for these were the last and only punishments awarded for mutiny during the second half of Cockburn's command of *La Minerve*.

Paternalism

Why should most seamen in *La Minerve* have remained loyal, and why should Cockburn have believed that most seamen in the navy were reconciled to their lot? The reason may be found in Cockburn's official correspondence, which indicates that he attended to the financial and future interests of individuals, as well as to the collective physical needs of the whole crew.

Care for a crew's physical well-being was not well documented. Logs record the opening of casks of pork, inevitably several pieces short and sometimes inedible. However, records for an earlier period show the proportion of victuals that were condemned was small (less than one per cent of all but one item—stockfish).[66] Against that must be set a total provision that was as varied and nutritious as contemporary techniques of preservation and knowledge of dietary necessities permitted. In addition to provisions supplied by the Victualling Board, Cockburn, at the request of the surgeon, authorized the purchase of 'necessaries' that included onions and fruit.[67] Lemons were purchased in large quantities while the fleet occupied the Mediterranean, and *La Minerve* suffered no significant incidence of scurvy until serving on the Atlantic coast of Spain and Portugal in October 1799. Then Cockburn again took the advice of the surgeon and went into the Tagus to procure lemons and fresh provisions, these being 'absolutely necessary to check this disorder in its infancy'.[68]

Provisions for physical welfare included slop clothing and bedding. Allowances were discretionary, any excess in value beyond deductions from wages being chargeable to the captain.[69] Stocks of stores were bought in bulk. In May 1799 Cockburn purchased 300 pairs of shoes for the crew of *La Minerve*, drawing a bill on the Navy Board in payment. He also attended to the needs of the marines or soldiers serving on board.[70]

Attention to the financial concerns of seamen was more onerous than might initially be expected. The main task was the precise completion and submission of muster and pay-books, along with alphabets, sick, dead and remove tickets, remittance slips and allotment accounts. Five copies of the pay-books were necessary until May 1800, when the number was reduced to three owing to captains' 'multiplicity of business'. Most of the abstracting and copying was performed by subordinates and the captain's clerk, but the captain oversaw and took responsibility for the whole. Moreover, in addition to his authority in matters of pay, Cockburn was regarded by the crew as their advocate for claims that arose from service in previous ships. The task of representing individuals or small numbers of men evidently proceeded from personal approaches or notes to the captain. Thus, much of his administrative correspondence included requests for payments of bounty and back pay, some requests being revived up to three years after they were first made, owing to the intervention of service away from England.[71]

These appeals called for interest and confidence in the cases of seamen: for example, in the claims of ten men from two ships which had been lost (by foundering or capture) after they had left their vessels. On the return to England in April 1798, appeals were made to the master of the merchant ship *Weymouth* who still owed one seaman wages, and to a shipping company at Dartmouth by whom two men were due pay from the masters of two different ships. One of the men had lost the note of wages due; Cockburn nonetheless requested their remission 'if you find by the accounts of the said ship his statement is just'.[72] This interest in their financial concerns was intended to remove anxieties or grievances and promote contentment with life on board. It was not confined to a particular ship or time, but was part of a natural relationship with a crew.[73] In some ways it complemented the extra effort the crew itself occasionally exerted on behalf of Cockburn. This emerges in the cases of individuals: that of John Brady, for example, who acted as surgeon's second mate in *La Minerve* until 1798. He was of great use to the surgeon through his 'assiduity and attention, . . . although he did not feel himself equal to pass the necessary examination to retain the situation'. Cockburn therefore requested he be paid at the appropriate rate for the time he filled his temporary situation.[74]

Ensuring men received their just deserts for their good deeds as well as their bad worked to the natural advantage of both Cockburn and the men involved. Thus, after two years' service as acting warrant officers in *La Minerve*, Robert Galway and Robert Taylor, who had both come from *Meleager*, were the subject of Cockburn's request in September 1798 to have their warrants confirmed as Master Sailmaker and Caulker.[75] Patrick Mooney, the acting Master at Arms, was included in this request. Richard Hobbs, acting Boatswain in *Meleager* and in *La Minerve* since 1795, and John Henley, acting Cook, were the subjects of others.[76] These requests were always accompanied by commendations of conduct and sometimes by reference to supporting attributes, such as the presence of a son in the ship.[77]

Men who were no longer of service were recommended for Greenwich Hospital. John Thompson, late Boatswain of the *Meleager*, whose health had failed and who had to return to England to convalesce, was recommended on his recovery for an equal or larger ship on account of his activity, sobriety and long hard services.[78] Even for men Cockburn did not know, regulations were followed fairly. In spite of a shortage of men, foreigners without settlement in England and apprentices who had received no slops were regularly discharged on failing to volunteer.

Strict compliance 'with the forms of the service', consideration for the future welfare of deserving men, confirmations of promotion where due, attention to financial concerns, provisions for the health and physical welfare of the crew, together created a caring environment within which disaffection failed to flourish. All this naturally generated a burden of work which far outweighed that on behalf of men of the commissioned officer class. Of course, midshipmen ready for promotion were put forward for examination for lieutenant, while lieutenants were recommended when opportunities presented themselves.[79] However, even these recommendations were not unrelated to the interests of seamen, for good officers in Cockburn's mind were those who attended to the welfare as well as the discipline of their 'people'.[80]

Trade Protection

Confidence in his own seamen lay at the heart of Cockburn's success at sea. It gave him the freedom to respond flexibly, relying upon subordinates to act when necessary on their own initiative. Hence he was able to respond almost immediately when *La Minerve* lay stripped, ready for sheathing repairs, close to the dockyard at Gibraltar late on 5 November 1797, after a summer spent patrolling the Canary Islands. As darkness descended, a large convoy of merchantmen appeared, escorted by the frigates *Andromache* and *Emerald*. That evening a light contrary wind pressed the merchantmen towards the Spanish shore at the entrance to Gibraltar bay, the tide taking them towards Algeciras. From there about thirty Spanish gunboats were seen moving out alongshore to take whatever ships offered.

Cockburn at that moment was senior naval officer at Gibraltar. There were only three British gunboats in a state fit to be manned and the officers and crew of *La Minerve* were divided amongst them, Cockburn himself taking command of one. As he passed the *Andromache* he requested her captain to cover the gunboats as well as she might. It was dark, but Cockburn directed the gunboats pull for a position between that in which the enemy had last been seen and the ships of the convoy closest to the Spanish shore. Firing revealed the exact whereabouts of the Spanish boats, Cockburn's three eventually engaging them about nine o'clock. The firing of the English frigates at Spanish gun flashes appeared to deceive the Spanish as to British strength and to check their attack. Even so, under the fire of some Spanish batteries and an anchored frigate, the masters and crews of some merchantmen abandoned their ships. Although most of the convoy beat up to their anchorage, some vessels thus drifted—crewless—towards the enemy's shore. Most of these *La Minerve*'s crew repossessed. A brig (an army victualler) was lost but that on Cockburn's orders. He informed St Vincent:

the brig was lost having her master killed and being abandoned by her crew. I put some hands on board of her to endeavour to get her sails set again etc. but we found everything cut to pieces by the shot. I therefore took her in tow but the wind unfortunately springing up at SE, I could not keep her off. I kept her however in tow a considerable time in hopes of a change till she drifted close to Algeciras when, seeing no possible chance of getting her off, all the rest of the convoy having got clear and being myself nearly surrounded by the enemy's gun boats, I thought proper after withdrawing my people from her to make the best of my way after the rest of the convoy, all of which were safe anchored here by half past 4 o'clock.[81]

Control over convoys of merchantmen was crucial to their survival. For his first convoy as captain in command, Cockburn kept a more than usually full record of the measures he took to maintain the safety of ships and of his treatment of masters, possibly because he anticipated litigation. For much time was spent trying to keep the convoy together, while certain ships and masters absorbed a disproportionate amount of the escorts' effort.[82] He took command at Oporto on 11 March 1798. The 32-gun frigate *Meleager* and sloops *Kingfisher* and *Speedy* were also allotted to the convoy which eventually consisted of 40 ships.

On the day before sailing, 33 of the masters were called on board the merchantship *Weymouth*, where Cockburn distributed printed instructions.[83] The *Weymouth* 'I ordered to hoist a distinguishing red pendant to lead the convoy and carry a light for night, giving strict charge [to] the respective masters on no account whatever to go before her beam'. Emerging from the Douro next day, the brig *Favorite*, bound for Dublin, stuck several times on the bar, began making a great deal of water and, Cockburn assumed, was obliged to put back to Oporto that night. 'Excessive hard gales from the NE, which continued without intermission for three weeks' also began that night.[84] After a gale six days out from Oporto, the whole convoy was brought to after both pumps of the brig *Thurley* split. The master and carpenters were sent from *La Minerve*, a cistern pump from *Meleager* being fitted the following day. However, on that day the *Weymouth* sprang a leak and the same vessel, four days later, brought the convoy to a halt with a choked rudder. During the night of 25 March a Portuguese schooner disappeared and was presumed to have foundered.

Shots were being regularly fired at merchantmen which failed to comply with signals or went ahead of the *Weymouth*. On the 29 March:

> At 6 the Meleager hailed us and Captain Ogle informing me that the
> master of the Douro had behaved particularly insolent to him in con-
> sequence of the Meleager having fired a shot through his fore topsail after
> having fired both ahead and astern of him to no effect; asked Captain
> Ogle to come on board and sent a boat for the master who behaved so ill
> as to determine me to take the charge of the Douro from him; sent a boat
> therefore for the mate to give him charge of her; the master however in
> the meantime coming to his senses and begging pardon very submissively
> both of Captain Ogle and myself, allowed him to return to his brig
> acquainting him however that he might depend on my prosecuting him
> for his disobedience and insolence.

On 30 March a ship was supplied with provisions at the request of her
master. The next day the masters of the Lisbon packet and *Lady Bruce*
also came on board 'to beg provisions'. These were granted, but 'the
master of the *Lady Bruce*, who was intoxicated, was so impertinent (in
consequence of my reprimanding him for being short of provisions and
quitting his ship at sea) as to oblige me to keep him on board and to
send an officer and party of men to take care of the brig for the night'.
By the following morning the master had sobered up and after making
'ample written apology' was sent back on board his ship.[85]

The voyage lasted a little over three weeks. Off Cape Clear the convoy
divided, the *Meleager* escorting 'the eastern trade' up the English
Channel, while *La Minerve* continued north with the ships for the Irish
ports, Bristol, Liverpool and Greenock. On 7 April, Cockburn sent for
the remaining masters, 'enquired of them when they should consider
themselves perfectly secure from the enemy's cruisers', and appointed
hours for the ships destined for particular ports to depart. *La Minerve*
herself finally arrived at Plymouth on 14 April, sailing again shortly
afterwards for Portsmouth.

The Convoy Act of 1798 added to the size of convoys, and to the
frustrations of sea officers, by making convoy compulsory for British-
registered merchant ships engaged in foreign trade. The only shipping
excluded from the provisions of the Act were East Indiamen, ships of the
Hudsons Bay Company, vessels bound for Irish ports, and licensed fast-
sailing 'runners'.[86] Most merchantmen accordingly sailed in convoy,
while every possible naval vessel heading in the same direction was
employed as an escort.

Reasserting Command at Sea

In this same slow fashion *La Minerve* returned to the Mediterranean late in 1798. There the battle of the Nile in August 1798 had restored British naval supremacy. But it was supremacy that on a practical day-to-day basis had to be reasserted and held. Cockburn's operations defined the process by which British command at sea was reasserted until the preliminaries of the Peace of Amiens were communicated to him off Toulon late in 1801.

On his return to the Mediterranean, after some months back in the Gulf of Genoa, Nelson placed Cockburn on the Lisbon division of the station. There, on the Atlantic coast of the Iberian peninsula, the main enemy in winter were gales that took a toll on both ships and men. On 23 December 1799, attempting to see the prize Spanish brig *Volcano* into the Tagus, *La Minerve* met unremitting, strong south-westerly winds, against which it was 'with the utmost difficulty' that she got far enough south to get into the estuary on 5 January. Having taken the *Volcano* in tow, Cockburn successively lost three hawsers and a stream cable; and on the night of 4 January *La Minerve* sprang her fore topmast and split four sails, carrying away foot ropes or tackles with each. That night was an unending round of damages, repairs and new sails. Once in the Tagus on the 6th,

> I thought it prudent, it then blowing a gale of wind from the west, to anchor . . . for the night, during which we shifted our fore topmast and repaired our sails and were ready for sea again in the morning, but the gale continuing to the south-west it was impossible to get out, and excepting a few hours on the 10th which were moderate (and during which we got nearly to the bar, though forced by the old sea and gale to go back again) we have had incessant gale from SW to W till today [21 January 1800].87

The following January *La Minerve* was reduced to a similar condition. She limped into the Tagus on 7 January 'after a long and bad cruise off Cape Finisterre making about 16 inches of water an hour with rigging, sails, etc. in a very shattered condition'.88 Men exposed to these conditions naturally became exhausted. Scurvy broke out in October 1799. Occasionally men were discharged into the hospital in Lisbon, some invalided to England. Cockburn himself, from the deterioration in the writing and presentation of his journal, suffered some ailment in November 1800.

Though acting to a large extent alone, Cockburn formed part of a chain of ships in communication with the rear admiral commanding the Lisbon division of the Mediterranean station. This command depended on the accuracy of the information his captains raised about the enemy's readiness for sea. Thus from off Cape Finisterre in December 1799 Cockburn reported to Duckworth:

> I proceeded with the St. Vincent schooner to reconnoitre Ferrol and Corunna off which place I arrived last night and immediately sent my first lieutenant on board the schooner with orders to stand close in under the light house and at daylight to hoist American colours and endeavour to get a Spanish pilot on board of him, which he effected and by which he was enabled to run close into the harbour of Corunna, where there are only two French privateers, a ship and a schooner and some merchantmen; he then ran close past the entrance of Ferrol where he saw three sail of the line perfectly ready for sea, one of which had a Spanish flag at the fore and another a French [one]; the pilot informs me that one sail of the line more and two frigates ready for sea are likewise there, but shut in behind the land.[89]

When enemy ships escaped from port, accurate communication was essential to co-ordinate the search and unite searching ships. This was evident between February and April 1801 in the hunt for Admiral Gantheaume, who escaped from Brest with six sail of the line. Off the Portuguese coast Cockburn received information that the squadron was making for the Mediterranean. He promptly carried this information to Sir John Warren off Cadiz. Warren, with four of the line, stood towards Cape Spartel hoping to intercept the Brest force and, when it failed to materialize, made for Gibraltar. There he learned that the French squadron had already passed through the Straits. Cockburn was ordered to catch it, taking any frigates he met under his orders, to track it to its destination and to inform the British vessels at Port Mahon of its whereabouts.

Cockburn thus pushed on to Cartagena. Here there were only four frigates and those with no sails bent. The frigate *Constance*, met with nearby, was sent into Mahon to report, while *La Minerve* and frigates *Pearl* and *Santa Teresa* (which joined a few hours after Carthagena) again pressed north. The French squadron was sighted on 17 February and thereupon a game of chase developed. The French squadron, now of eleven sail, repeatedly sent back line-of-battleships which, as the British hauled off, were recalled to the main force. Each time, the frigates closed again until the French put into Toulon.

Cockburn remained off Toulon for three weeks. On 19 March the French squadron displayed exceptional activity. That night visibility fell; a violent north-westerly storm brought down the *Teresa*'s topmasts (though carrying no sails) and while it was 'thick and dark' the French squadron sailed, taking with it six merchantmen. Next morning one of the merchantmen was still visible from the masthead. She was taken and was able to provide detailed information. The squadron, under Gantheaume, was destined for Egypt, conducting 'succours' for the defence of Alexandria. With letters found on board the merchantman, *Pearl* sailed immediately for Lord Keith, commanding the main part of the Mediterranean fleet off Egypt where Abercromby commanded the army on shore. Cockburn himself made for a rendezvous with Warren in Naples Bay.[90]

There followed twenty days of anxious searching. A copy of Cockburn's journal, evidently supplied to explain delays, is preserved in the papers of Lord Keith. It records every move—each day with its particular frustrations. Naples Bay was made late on the 27 March. Yet here British neglect negated all of Cockburn's efforts. Warren had left Naples Bay without leaving notice of his course or destination and it was necessary to look for him. It was 9 April before he was found near Benghazi on 'the coast of Barbary'.[91]

There, Warren told Cockburn his squadron had itself caught sight of Gantheaume's force to the south of Sardinia. Yet, to keep his squadron together that night, he had reduced the speed of his faster vessels to that of his slowest, and by the following morning the French were out of sight. On 10 April Warren supposed Gantheaume to be still near at hand, yet later it was learned he had returned to Toulon after sighting Warren, some of his ships having already suffered mast damage in the earlier bad weather.[92]

Cockburn was deeply disappointed. Later he attributed Warren's failure to keep contact with the French to his neglect in leaving information of his intentions at Naples. Had he done so, Cockburn believed *La Minerve* would have joined Warren in time to act as a trail on the French. His poor opinion of Warren as an officer was to resurface when they worked together again in 1813 off the coast of North America.

If poor communication and co-ordination made for failure in the war at sea, the reverse enhanced the chances of overwhelming an enemy. These were the means Cockburn used in September 1801 to capture one French frigate and destroy another, even though both were sailing together. Returning to Minorca via the Straits of Piombino separating Elba from mainland Italy, *La Minerve* came across and spoke with the British 36- and 44-gun frigates *Phoenix* and *Pomone*. At first light next morning these two vessels were almost out of sight astern when two strange frigates were sighted heading directly towards *La Minerve* from Leghorn. They failed to answer the private signal and Cockburn tacked west, signalling and firing guns to recall the *Pomone*. Two hours later, with *Pomone* and *Phoenix* closing from the south, Cockburn tacked back towards the strangers, now recognized as French. They immediately turned north towards Leghorn. About 10.30 that morning the rearmost frigate, the *Succès*, dropping astern of the other, was overhauled by *La Minerve* and ran aground on a shoal off Vada. Later that afternoon the leading frigate, *Bravoure*, was cut off from Leghorn four miles short of her destination and also ran on shore. 'Bilged' and protected from fire from guns on shore she was abandoned next morning. The *Succès*, however, was refloated and taken prize.[93] Her capture brought Cockburn to public notice at almost the same time as the signature of the preliminaries of the Peace of Armiens.

CHAPTER 2

The Napoleonic War
1803–1812

When Cockburn took the coach for London in late February 1802, after paying off *La Minerve* at Deptford, he was still not quite 30. Already he possessed 16 years experience at sea: nine at war, eight as a captain. Yet this was only his second long leave; he had few, if any, friends apart from sea officers; he was virtually a stranger in society close to home; he knew almost nothing of that sophisticated life in London which many of his contemporaries took for granted. There was much upon which to catch up.

Certainly he must have followed naval affairs closely. St Vincent, his Mediterranean commander-in-chief, had been First Lord since February 1801 and was, by early 1803, putting in train an investigation into the efficiency and abuses of the civil departments of the navy. During the peace an Act appointing Commissioners of Enquiry passed through both Houses of Parliament. Of equal interest would have been the deteriorating state of relations with France: orders went to the yard by the night post of 10 March 1803 to fit ships for sea 'without a moment's loss of time'.[1] His appointment to a ship arrived dated 12 July. It was to the 38-gun *Phaeton* fitting at Deptford. She was ready a month later. By early September Cockburn was off Havre de Grace, at the mouth of the Seine, with 'a squadron of frigates' checking the report of French barges collected for an invasion of England.[2] However, on 13 September he was ordered to England to receive fresh instructions.

The United States Payments

Whether, in September 1803, Cockburn was advised privately at the Admiralty of the nature of the service for which he had been chosen or of the voyage to which it would lead is uncertain. For two months his letters carried only the official knowledge that his task was to convey Mr Anthony Merry, British envoy and minister plenipotentiary, to the United States. Sailing on 25 September 1803, the *Phaeton* reached Norfolk, Virginia, to land Merry and his suite on 4 November. Before landing, Merry acquainted Cockburn with at least the *general* nature of the service before him. Instead of heading south to join Admiral Mitchell at Bermuda, Cockburn was to sail north to New York to re-equip and provision. From there, on 10 November, he notified the Admiralty that he awaited orders.

Later, Mitchell was to reprimand him severely for failing to contact him as soon as he arrived on the American station, for failing to submit to him the need to refit, and for refitting at New York rather than at Halifax. Yet by then Cockburn was able to inform him of a ship coming from England to which the *Phaeton* was to act as escort, of further Admiralty instructions arriving with that ship, and that, because the *Phaeton* had eight months provisions on board including a great quantity of lime juice and sugar, he was 'convinced' she was intended 'for further and more distant service'.[3]

In fact by then Cockburn knew (but could not write, in case of interception by an enemy) that he had been directed to New York to receive there the first payment of compensation by the United States government for losses sustained by American loyalists during the War of Independence. He also knew that he was to be joined by a ship belonging to the East India Company which would take a portion of the specie and which the *Phaeton* would escort to India, where the bullion would be transferred to the charge of the Company.

Straightforward though they were, Cockburn's instructions had one area of difficulty. Americans in general remained hostile to Britain: an inheritance from the War of Independence, revived by Britain's war against Revolutionary France, by her check on neutral trade with French-occupied Europe, and the frequently alleged impressment of American citizens by the British navy. At New York this hostility quickly made itself felt, apparently provoked by the *Phaeton* anchoring only a mile and a half south-west of the city, where her captain purchased naval stores to refit the ship.

Within days of his arrival, Thomas Barclay, British consul to New York, protested vehemently to Cockburn at his ship's presence offshore. Without formal diplomatic sanction, Barclay argued, her presence would cause offence at the highest levels in the United States' government. He had therefore seen fit to write to Anthony Merry proposing he make a formal diplomatic request for *Phaeton* to refit in a United States port. Cockburn objected forcefully to the interference: 'Whatever nations are in a state of amity with His Majesty must afford shelter in their harbours, rivers etc. to his ships.' The employment of his crew in refitting depended on himself. Whether he should have procured naval stores from on shore 'may perhaps bear an argument' but he had done so with the permission of the chief magistrate of the place and 'it surely cannot be our business to investigate by what authority he acts'. In any case he was convinced of his right to purchase anything his ship might want.

> America having a commercial treaty existing with the present belligerent powers would permit the subjects of either of them to purchase at her public markets timber or rope, or in short any goods whatsoever, and load them on their own account on board ships of their respective nations, or neutrals, in which case if they are met with at sea by the enemy [and] they are captured . . . the Americans have nothing whatever to do with it; on the same principle I contend that I have a right to purchase here any thing publicly offered for sale & carry it away with me at the same risk.[4]

Very soon Cockburn had more than a consul to contend with. Americans were hired by Cockburn to assist in caulking the ship. On 14 November,

> no sooner . . . was the work of the day over and the people gone below than [one of the Americans] went down amongst them to induce them to desert and tell them how they might effect their escape from the ship. The Master at Arms, to whom he addressed himself by mistake, identified the same to me but not till after 8 men succeeded by the plan I suppose he laid down, which was for one man to jump overboard and pretend he was drowning and when a boat was consequently sent to pick him up, those men who were in the secret took care to jump into her, as if for the anxiety to save him, but as soon as they had got hold of him, instead of coming back to the ship they pulled on shore and landed.

Cockburn felt himself insulted by the American taken by the Master at Arms and wrote directly to the Mayor of New York, De Witt Clinton, to protest the 'villainy' of the transaction, request the American be punished and the eight men be apprehended.[5] Within a month six more men had deserted. But Clinton failed to provide information as to their whereabouts. Instead, on 9 December, he took up the case of a seaman on board the *Phaeton*, John Fetton, who claimed to be an American citizen impressed in London and detained against his consent. He also pressed the claims of three other men. Cockburn was co-operative, interviewing Fetton, and allowing the brother of an American alleged to be on board inspect his crew. Yet not one of the men in question could prove American citizenship.

Meanwhile Cockburn had been taking steps to retrieve his deserters. Convinced they were hidden in New York by crimps, he discovered where they might be concealed. 'After much discussion' with the Mayor, he obtained permission to search for and secure the deserters on condition they were then lodged in New York prison for their cases to be considered by the city authorities. During the night of 27 December, Cockburn himself, some officers, a few marines and trusted seamen from the *Phaeton* went armed to the crimps' haunts and, after brief resistance, took three of the deserters and deposited them in the city gaol.

However, antipathy to the British navy once again intervened. At the request for the gaoled deserters to be returned to the *Phaeton*, Clinton delayed for no apparent reason. Eventually Cockburn threatened to allow the issue to interrupt that 'good understanding now so happily established between our two governments'; Consul Barclay was contacted to prevent Clinton setting the deserters free; Merry was requested to demand the men be given up to Cockburn and to brief the British 'minister' in Washington.[6] The pressure carried the point and the men returned to the *Phaeton*. Later Cockburn claimed, though not convincingly, that every British captain who lost deserters to the United States ought to have persisted in demanding their return as he did. He claimed that one cause of later war would thereby have been removed, for there would have been less need to have stopped American vessels in search of British seamen.[7]

By 28 December the *Phaeton* was ready to sail and was joined that day by the East India Company ship *Sir Edward Hughes*. Only about half the specie destined for India was available in New York; the remainder was to be collected from a bank in Norfolk, Virginia. Consul Barclay detained the two vessels by insisting that their commanders inspect the contents of the treasure containers, and by fussing over the wording of the receipt they should give to him. Cockburn made matters worse by attempting to rush the loading, suggesting Barclay would be responsible for ill consequences should the delay in sailing permit news of the cargo to reach the enemy. Finally, the boxes were sealed in the presence of the first lieutenant, master and master's mate and stowed in the spirit room.[8]

The *Phaeton* and *Sir Edward Hughes* reached Norfolk in mid-January.

There the consul was less particular, being prepared to seal the containers before they were taken on board. By 28 January 340 boxes each containing 1,000 dollars, and 10 casks each taking 6,000 dollars were distributed between the two ships.[9] With a warning that a French squadron destined for the East Indies had last been sighted off the Isle de France, the two vessels sailed that day for Madras, where they anchored on 26 May 1804, four months after leaving Virginia.

The Governor-General of India

Cockburn remained in Indian waters almost a year, the second half of 1804 being spent off the Île de France (now Mauritius), then under blockade. For a while the *Phaeton* joined the blockade, at this time directed by Captain Jonathan Osborn in the *Tremendous*.[10] A major problem for British vessels was the lack of fresh vegetables. On 27 January 1805 the *Phaeton* reached Bombay with a hundred of her crew afflicted by scurvy.

Sir Edward Pellew, commander-in-chief in Indian waters, ordered Cockburn north to command a small squadron stationed in the upper waters of the Bay of Bengal for the protection of trade.[11] Early in June 1805, however, he was directed to transfer his responsibilities in the Bay of Bengal to Captain Peter Rainier, and to exchange command of the *Phaeton* for that of a 20-gun storeship, the *Howe*, in order to carry the Governor-General of India, Richard, Marquis of Wellesley, his suite of six gentlemen and 'many servants' back to England. The *Howe* was refitted in Calcutta at East India Company expense and sailed for England on 25 August.

At Calcutta, relations between Cockburn and the Governor-General did not begin well. As captain and host, Cockburn believed he should maintain the table for the voyage; he thus laid in wines, glassware, livestock and other foodstuffs at a cost that exceeded £4,000. At the time he believed 'that Government always allowed a very ample sum for the payment of any Captain who . . . conveyed the public officers from one country to another'. He therefore insisted on supplying everything himself, even though Colonel Shawe, Wellesley's secretary, waited on him to receive instructions as to the provisions the Governor-General should supply. Seeing the expense to which Cockburn was going, Shawe prevailed upon Cockburn to allow Wellesley to supply any further provisions from his 'private stores and cellars'—which could be done at a 'small comparative expense to his Lordship'—or to permit Wellesley to pay some of Cockburn's expenses. Wellesley's steward and a Mr Wynox, who was 'not in Lord Wellesley's family' and to whom Shawe thought Cockburn might speak more freely, were also sent to persuade him.

Yet under pressure Cockburn became more determined. He maintained that 'it was perfectly contrary to the rules of our service . . . for any body to keep the table on board one of HM Ships except the naval commanding officer'; furthermore it would 'be equally improper for any such commanding officer to receive money in consideration thereof'— from any individual, 'however exalted his rank'. He thus determined to suffer 'the whole weight of the charge' rather than allow anything 'derogatory' to his character as a captain in His Majesty's navy. He conceded only that Wellesley might send on board anything he might prefer or 'deem of superior quality' to what it might be in his own power to procure. In consequence, edible 'stores' to the value of £2,781, plus plates and dishes were sent on board.[12]

Two-thirds of Wellesley's edible 'stores' were eventually consumed: a graceful, if inevitable, concession on the part of Cockburn to an opulent lifestyle he could not hope to finance. The concession was matched by personal compliance and courtesy which pleased Wellesley. The Governor-General was well known for his arrogance; Cockburn himself was developing that strength of opinion which in time was to dominate the Admiralty. The relationship between the two, enforced through four months close proximity, could have been difficult. In fact Wellesley described his voyage as 'unbelievably fortunate', while Cockburn claimed an 'intimate acquaintance' arose between them.[13]

The relationship was cemented by conduct on Cockburn's part which placed him to some degree in the Governor-General's debt. On his arrival in England, he was mortified to discover that there was no official allowance for carrying officers of state. He found that, though expenses had been paid for the carriage of officers in other directions, he was the first captain to have been ordered to carry a Governor-General back from India; no precedent therefore existed for his reimbursement. The Admiralty recommended he be allowed £500. On appeal, the Court of the East India Company consulted the Society of East India Commanders through its secretary at the Jerusalem Coffee House. The Society expressed its unanimous 'opinion . . . that eight thousand pounds would be a very moderate compensation, and all above that a liberal one'.[14]

Whether Cockburn actually received that amount is unknown. Certainly he did receive a large sum, for two years later Wellesley suffered 'illiberal attacks' for having placed the expense of his voyage to government account. With Shawe's assistance, Cockburn thus placed on record at the Admiralty the cause of his large reimbursement.[15] The gesture was not to be forgotten.

The Taking of Martinique

From July 1806, when Cockburn returned from leave, his life at sea was interrupted as never before by requests to the Admiralty for 'leave of absence' and supersession owing to 'urgent private business' demanding his 'personal attendance' on shore. It coincided with his closer acquaintance with his third cousin Mary Cockburn, now 21, whom he was to marry three years later.

At the same time discontent with naval life emerged as never before. Appointed to the 74-gun *Captain*, he found her 'a very small and bad ship'. After moving her from Spithead to St Helens on 14 July, he demanded a court martial on her master who ran her aground in spite of a fair wind. In early August he was referred an anonymous letter 'purporting to be written by the petty officers and crew' of the *Captain* and was directed by the Admiralty to 'find out the author'. Lieutenant Thomas Hunloke was proposed for court martial for disobedience of orders and neglect of duty; the charges were withdrawn on Hunloke promising never again to commit a similar misdemeanour. Watering in haste to get to sea with a squadron under Admiral Thomas Louis, the final straw seems to have been the hijacking of the *Captain*'s launch by the officers of another ship. Almost in desperation he wrote in October to Lord Wellesley appealing for him to use his influence to gain for him either a better ship or a place at the Navy or Victualling Board.

The discontent generated by Cockburn during these months reflects not only the conflicts of personal and professional life, but the frustrations of growing ambition. At this time neither St Vincent nor Wellesley possessed influence and Cockburn lacked other connections necessary to promote his claims. There was consequently no alternative to routine service. The winter of 1806–7 was spent convoying troop transports and patrolling Madeira, the Canary and Cape Verde Islands. In June 1807 he did escape the *Captain*, but only to half-pay and unemployment.

It was March 1808 before he returned to sea. Appointed to the 80-gun *Pompee*, fitting at Chatham, he was despatched to blockade Rochfort. Almost four months were spent standing off on the coasts of the Île de

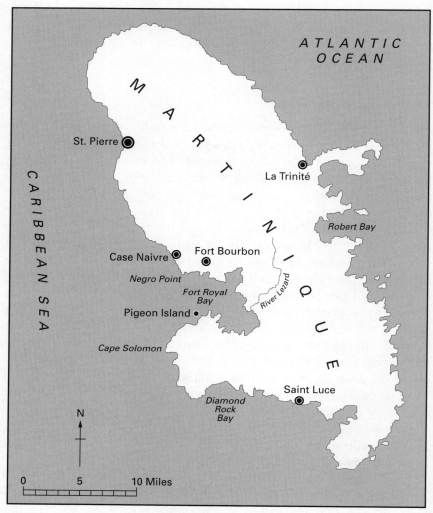

Map 2. The Island of Martinique

Ré and Île d'Óléron, watching the topmasts of French line-of-battle ships in Aix Roads. The coasts were lined with batteries, under the shelter of which small craft crept along shore, harassed occasionally by boats from English men-of-war and privateers.

The tedium was relieved early in September when he received orders to join Rear-Admiral Sir Alexander Cochrane in the West Indies. There,

British forces were taking the French colonies one by one. Delayed by adverse winds, the *Pompee* made Carlisle Bay, Barbados, on 22 October, from where she was directed to block French access to Fort Royal Bay, Martinique, while Cochrane arrranged an attack on the island with Lieutenant-General Sir George Beckwith.

Considered by the French to be one of their most important colonies, Martinique supported both a militia raised from the inhabitants and a sizeable regular-army garrison. The entrance to Fort Royal Bay was guarded by forts on Pigeon Island and Point Negro, while the bulk of the French professional force occupied two principal citadels, Fort Bourbon within the bay and Fort Deffaix further inland. None of the forts were amenable to assault from the sea; but the fortresses were not impregnable. The island had fallen to the British in 1794 and been handed back at the Peace of Amiens.[1 6] Now Beckwith was to land his troops some distance from the forts, approach them overland, concentrating his forces against each individually, and take them in the order that would best safeguard his rear.

Transported from Carlisle Bay, Barbados, the army landed in two divisions on 30 January.[17] In the east, about 6,500 men under Lieutenant-General Sir George Prevost landed at Robert Bay, marched seven miles through 'difficult country' to occupy a position on the banks of the Lezard River by daybreak on the 31st. From there they could take the heights which commanded Fort Bourbon. In the south a division of 3,000 men under Major-General Maitland landed near St Luce and Cape Solomon to take the heights commanding Pigeon Island and advance upon Fort Deffaix. After covering these landings, Cochrane and his squadron joined Cockburn on the 31st, anchoring the transports at the western end of Diamond Rock Bay. At the same time several vessels were detached to occupy the port of Trinité, lying beyond the range of the army's operations.

Within three days each division was within gunshot of their respective objectives, Fort Bourbon and Fort Deffaix. However in the south-west, resistance arose from French regulars securely established in the fort on Pigeon Island. Although by 1 February a 13-inch mortar was in place heaving shells into the fort, Cochrane was requested to land more guns. He turned to Cockburn, who later claimed he volunteered to command the seamen needed on shore to manhandle the guns. These had to reach 'a high and rugged point of land', previously deemed inaccessible by the French, who, as this work proceeded, concentrated a 'heavy fire' on the seamen landing and raising the guns. Two seamen from the *Pompee* were killed by French fire on the first day. Nonetheless on the next day 120 men from the *Pompee* were again on shore erecting batteries and getting the guns up to them. Altogether, nine guns—24-pounders, 13-inch mortars and howitzers—were raised into position, five by men from *Pompee*. Until Pigeon Island fell, Maitland's advance on Fort Deffaix was insecure to the rear.[18] The work accordingly went on without rest, 'notwithstanding heavy rains and most unfavourable weather'.

At sunset on 3 February the British battery opened fire; that of the fort on Pigeon Island gradually slackened through the night until it ceased entirely. By daylight most of the fort's walls had been destroyed, and just after dawn a white flag appeared. Of 136 people inside, five had been killed and nearly 40 wounded; 119 prisoners were taken on board the *Pompee*.[19] Many of her crew were employed throughout the day in getting down the howitzers and shells.

Only two days later the performance was to be repeated. Most of the squadron, including the *Pompee*, shifted to Case Navire Bay where guns were again disembarked in preparation for the assault on Fort Bourbon. On shore the two divisions of the army and the navy both worked to build new batteries. Cockburn, with three naval captains under his orders, again joined the work and was given command of a division of batteries to the right of the investing army, close to Fort Royal Bay.

Fire was opened simultaneously from all four batteries at 4.30 in the afternoon of 19 February. Twenty-eight mortars and howitzers and four 'heavy cannon' were brought to bear, the bombardment continuing for four days. Boats from the vessels in the bay plied constantly between ships and shore, ferrying shot and powder, men and provisions to the batteries, and returning with the wounded. Even while the bombardment proceeded, two naval captains with 400 seamen and marines struggled to haul four more 24-pounders and four mortars for another battery east of Fort Bourbon: a task 'of the utmost labour and difficulty owing to the rains and deepness of the roads'. The battery was finished by 22 February. But at midday on the 23rd the French offered negotiation under a flag of truce. General Villaret, the French commander, proposed his troops surrender on condition they return to France free of restrictions on their future service. Beckwith and Cochrane rejected the terms. At ten that night the bombardment resumed, to continue throughout the night. 'The next morning, a little past six o'clock, one of the magazines of the fort blew up with a great explosion.' At about nine, three white flags were seen, upon which firing ceased for good.[20]

With Sir George Prevost and Frederick Maitland of the army, Cockburn was appointed to meet three commissioners appointed by Villaret to negotiate the articles of capitulation. Twenty propositions drawn up by the French were presented to the British commissioners late on the 24 February in a tent erected for the purpose between the advanced picquets of each side. The terms were quickly granted or briefly qualified. The French garrison—14 senior officers, 141 ordinary, 1,827 subalterns and soldiers, and 242 seamen—were to receive the full honours of war, to march out with drums beating, colours flying and matches lighted, and to ground their arms outside the fortifications. They were to be embarked as prisoners of war within eight to fifteen days and escorted to Quiberon Bay for a formal exchange of personnel, rank for rank. Only General Villaret and his aides-de-camp were excluded from the exchange; they were to be released in France free of restriction.

On the 25th the French surrendered with honour. Fort Bourbon and the rest of the island was occupied by the British. Co-operation and co-ordination had brought operations to a close in just four weeks from the embarkation of the army at Barbados. In spite of 'incessant rains', the climate had not had time to exact its usual toll in deaths from tropical infections. Of nearly ten thousand men in the army, 819 had been admitted for hospital treatment of which only 416 were suffering from fevers and fluxes, 380 from wounds.[21]

Cockburn himself avoided both sickness and injury. Moreover his contribution was fully acknowledged. Beckwith offered him the appointment of Captain of the Port of St Pierre, a sinecure post he gladly accepted, arranging to execute the duties of office through a deputy.[22] Later he received the thanks of both Houses of Parliament.

Cochrane decided that Cockburn, as commodore, should command the convoy of transports carrying the French garrison back to exchange for English prisoners-of-war in France. For this purpose Cockburn shifted his pendant to the *Belleisle* and took on board the Governor of Martinique and principal French army officers to whom he gave up his own cabin. In all the *Belleisle* took in 210 French offices and men.[23]

They were ready to sail by 12 March. Distributed between nine vessels were over 2,300 French soldiers and sailors, 30 captains, a colonel, three lieutenant-colonels and two generals. By this time Cockburn was feeling the strain. The officers were particularly difficult to handle: they were treated as guests but were nevertheless prisoners. All went well until the eve of departure. About 10 o'clock that night three questions arrived from Beckwith and Cochrane which Cockburn had to put to Villaret and the French 'Prefet' or Governor of the island. Could they swear that no public money still remained under the control of the Prefet or any other public officer? Would the Prefet leave bills with a responsible person to meet any outstanding debts? Finally, if the debts warranted it, would the Prefet remain on the island as security that the bills would be met in France? To the first question the Governor must have answered No, he could not swear that no public officer controlled any public money. To the second, Yes, he would leave bills to meet any debts; but No, he would not remain as security—the terms of the surrender had not stipulated that he should. General Villaret, Cockburn reported, 'found no fault with the two first articles but . . . on coming to the third . . . he immediately altered his tone' and said that the demand was unjust and that if the British did leave the Prefet a prisoner he himself would immediately reland and share the Prefet's fate.

Cockburn was suddenly out of his depth, Villaret dictating the terms. As the hour turned midnight, he wrote to Cochrane:

I am sorry to inform you that on receipt of your last letter, the Captain General became furious, when, having asked me whether I considered him as a prisoner and being answered in the negative, he insisted on my putting him ashore. I represented to him the impossibility of my doing this without first consulting with General Beckwith and yourself but I could not refuse stopping for your answer to *this*, his request.

Cockburn was caught in a cleft stick. Cochrane and Beckwith required that he act on his interpretation of the answers to the questions. To guarantee repayment of debts, he should put the Prefet ashore. Yet article 12 of the treaty of capitulation explicitly permitted the French inhabitants of Martinique to share the fate of the garrison. To put him ashore would thus be a 'manifest infraction of the Treaty' and Villaret's determination to land with the Governor would draw attention to that infraction. Caught between duty and a diplomatic blunder, Cockburn argued that to take either action was of 'far too great consequence' without special instructions. At the very least, if only to manage Villaret on the voyage back to Europe, he had to maintain moral superiority. 'For God Sake,' he appealed to Cochrane, 'if you can prevent it do not let him be in the right at last—depend on it a breach of the Articles of Capitulation will be but ill received at home without very strong and solid grounds.'[24]

In the event, Cochrane and Beckwith allowed Cockburn to sail on 14 March 1809 without setting the Prefet and the General on shore. Even then, his instructions still left scope for misadventure. The articles of capitulation specified the garrison was to be transported for negotiation of a rank-for-rank exchange in Quiberon Bay. Cockburn was to ensure that French compliance with those terms was such as the British government should 'perfectly approve'. If the French complied, the British exchanges were to be taken on board before the Frenchmen were released; if they did not, the whole convoy was to sail for Spithead.[25]

From Quiberon Bay late in April 1809, Cockborn sent a letter to the French Minister of Marine to which an answer was received two days later. This came via Monsieur Redon, a ministerial official. Receiving Redon on board that evening, Cockburn became convinced the reply had been written for the purpose of deceiving him, 'with a hope of inducing me to land the French prisoners without having further explanation from him'. It appeared, in discussion with Redon, 'that instead of the full powers with which he declared himself to be invested, he was in fact only authorized to offer me in exchange for the Martinique garrison, a number of papers signed by masters and mates of English merchantmen or by English consuls, vice-consuls or agents, stating that a number of men as named in each paper had been released at sea or in different neutral ports after having been captured by French frigates or privateers'. Many of the men named could have been dead, or not released and used in other exchanges, especially as the dates on a large proportion of the papers were 1803 and 1804. The documents were fit only to be laid before the Transport Board who managed exchanges of prisoners. Moreover, even if the crews of the merchantmen had truly been released, their release was possibly only a convenience to permit their captors, French privateers, to continue their 'depredations'. In all, Cockburn reasoned, the documents were inadequate exchange for a delivery of 2,300 men who could be employed in military operations the very next day.

Further letters from Redon determined Cockburn 'to weigh without further hesitation'. The sick, Villaret and his suite of six were sent on shore and the convoy sailed for Spithead where it anchored on 15 May.[26]

The Walcheren Expedition

In London the Admiralty was preparing for an expedition of 40,000 men to take Flushing and Antwerp at the mouth of the River Scheldt.

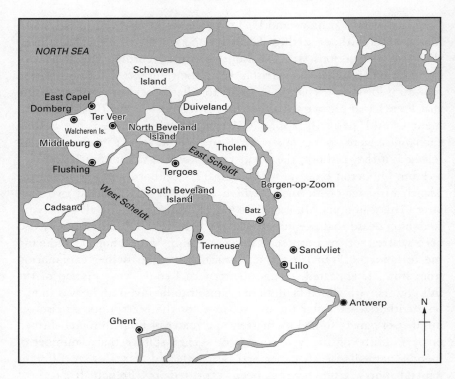

Map 3. Walcheren Island and the River Scheldt

Since the battle of Trafalgar, the river had become France's second largest naval arsenal (after Toulon) where Napoleon was rebuilding a navy with which to attempt an invasion of England. Intelligence, early in 1809, reported ten ships of the line afloat and three building at Flushing, with nine more under construction at Antwerp. The river could accommodate as many as ninety sail of the line; it had become 'a cocked pistol pointed at the head of England'. On 24 March 1809 the Secretary for War, Lord Castlereagh, had urged an immediate attack.

While the Cabinet considered the proposal, events in Europe reinforced the case for an expedition. Four years after its crushing defeat at Austerlitz, the Habsburg Austrian Empire was rousing itself for a new effort and on 24 April concluded an alliance with Britain. But in May the French army swept into southern Germany, occupied Vienna and drove the Austrian ambassador in London to plead for a British diversionary attack. Further south, although the British army in Spain had been evacuated from Corunna in January, Arthur Wellesley reached Lisbon in April to resume the campaign in Portugal which, it was hoped, would attract and tie down large contingents of French troops. A diversionary attack on the French in the north would help him and Austria.[27]

In May 1809 Cockburn was requested to accompany the expedition as captain of the 74-gun *Belleisle*.[28] By July he was at Portsmouth fitting the *Belleisle*, taking on board horses, barrels of powder and soldiers of the 71st Regiment. The vessels from Portsmouth, 23 of the line besides transports, sailed on 25 July to join Sir Richard Strachan commanding the naval forces in the Downs. There the assemblage of vessels was the most impressive ever gathered off British shores: 37 ships of the line, 27 frigates, 32 sloops, 170 other vessels including 82 gunboats, and 352 troop, horse and provision transports. Embarked on board, besides 200 pieces of ordnance, were nearly 43,000 soldiers, 1,888 officers and 4,500 horses. With more vessels joining all the time, the whole fleet weighed on the 28 July to anchor off the island of Walcheren the next day.

The enemy facing the expedition were considered to be relatively slight. With Napoleon's main forces in south Germany, it was anticipated that the largest Franco-Dutch force that could be assembled in five or six days would be 8,400 men.[29] The leaders of the expedition were thus optimistic that its objectives would be achieved. The instructions issued to Lord Chatham, commander-in-chief of the army, included the capture or destruction of the enemy's ships, either building at Antwerp and Flushing or afloat in the Scheldt; the destruction of the dockyards at Antwerp, Terneuse, and Flushing; the destruction of the defences of the island of Walcheren, and of the Scheldt as a waterway navigable to warships.[30]

Following the *Venerable*, the *Belleisle* pressed into the narrow Veere Gat channel to the north of Walcheren Island on 30 July, anchoring at 1.30 that afternoon in four and a half fathoms. To the south-west lay a 'fort called Fort Haak'. From about 4 o'clock troops were landed all along that north coast 'between Domberg and East Capel'.[31] Cockburn recalled landing 'with the army'. On 2 August a lieutenant and 80 seamen were sent to him from the *Belleisle*, perhaps to direct gun-hauling. There was relatively little resistance: enemy forces were thin. Fortified places and Middleburg surrendered as British troops advanced. By the evening of 3 August only Flushing remained to be taken on Walcheren. At the same time the whole of South Beveland Island had also been occupied. Only a third detachment to occupy Cadsand Island failed: the victim of bad weather on an exposed coast, confused communication and direction.[32]

Operations concentrated on the reduction of Flushing. By 7 August the town was completely invested by land and sea, with batteries ready by 13 August. At exactly 1.0 p.m. fifty British guns opened fire on the town's landward sides. Simultaneously two squadrons of gunboats, bomb-ships, brigs and sloops opened fire from the River Scheldt, one from the south-west and the other south-east. Cockburn commanded the south-eastern flotilla with his commodore's pendant in the sloop *Plover*.[33] The bombardment continued for one and a half days, only ceasing at 2.30 a.m. on 15 August when the French requested to surrender.

As at Martinique, by a process of selection Cockburn was singled out to represent the navy in setting terms of capitulation. Early in the afternoon of the 15th, in company with Colonel Robert Long, Adjutant-General of the army, he was taken blindfolded into Flushing. There, he and Long had 'much discussion'. The French wished the garrison to return to France on parole, not to bear arms against Britain for a year, whilst Cockburn and Long insisted that they 'must be prisoners of war and sent as such to England'. Cockburn and Long prevailed, emerging that evening with terms which Chatham and Strachen ratified at three the following morning.[34]

Chatham now turned his attention towards Antwerp. British troops had occupied South Beveland, including the town of Batz, only 13 miles above Antwerp. Chatham thus determined to force the river. Leaving a garrison of 6,000 men on Walcheren Island, the British army moved towards Batz, part overland, part by naval transport. Obliged to warp because of adverse winds, the transports had difficulties passing through Slough passage and, preceded by frigates and 74's, only made Batz on 24 August. Cockburn with his flotilla of gunboats and other craft advanced to Batz ahead of the main army, repeatedly engaging French batteries and defensive positions being built along the southern shores of the West Scheldt. Although for the most part thinly spread, Franco-Dutch forces were strong in places and, as Cockburn became aware, were rapidly increasing in strength.

On 3 August there had been only 20,000 Franco-Dutch troops spread along the 45 miles from Cadsand to Bergen-op-Zoom; within ten days there were 46,000. By 14 August a further 60,000 were under orders, half of them mobilized in immediate reserve. As British movements made their objective clear, both reserves and front-line forces were further increased. By 26 August, 100,600 were ready to meet any threat to Antwerp. Moreover, the river was obstructed by a log-and-cable boom, reinforced by a barricade of ships bound together by chains, a flotilla of gunboats and, finally, three ships of the line.

The intelligence received by the British left them in no doubt of the strength of the French position. On 25 August Sir Home Popham and General Brownrigg selected a site for landing the British army on the right bank of the Scheldt near Sandvliet. But two days later a council of British generals concluded that, while their army was capable of forcing its way along one bank, it was not strong enough to force both, and that, with soldiers succumbing to fever, withdrawal was the only alternative.[35]

The evacuation of South Beveland began on the 28th. Rapidly spreading sickness hastened the operation. On 1 September there were almost 5,000 sick; by 3 September, 8,914. Initially Strachan wanted time to sink block ships in the Scheldt near Batz. However Chatham refused to delay the evacuation. Cockburn's flotilla acted as the navy's rearguard, destroying batteries as they harrassed the retiring ships, and providing Strachan with a means of personally surveilling the enemy shore.[36] Cockburn left the gunboats at Flushing to return to the *Belleisle*. Meanwhile, she had taken on board 653 soldiers and 39 prisoners, most of them sick. On 8 September, in company with other vessels, she sailed for the Downs to be paid off at Portsmouth on 7 October.[37]

The garrison of 16,000 men left on Walcheren held out for two more months after the main army had left. Late in October, Lord Mulgrave, First Lord of the Admiralty, consulted Cockburn on the possibility of retaining the island, the force necessary to do so, and the advantages that would result from it. Cockburn estimated the island could be held with 9,800 soldiers and 3,720 seamen distributed in 60 bomb-vessels and 90 gun-vessels. But he argued the French would be better checked by a British squadron in the Downs in contact with frigates off the coast.

> I cannot but think that a French fleet being at sea is even more advantageous to us than the knowledge of its existence in a safe harbour. In the latter case it is a constant source of anxiety to us; in the former, it is impossible to describe the energy, spirit, and hope with which the chance of its destruction fills every breast, especially of those who have spent many a long and dreary night blockading them. It is also to be added that from the confused and hurried manner in which the enemy's squadrons traverse the seas, during the short periods of their escaping our vigilence, the damage they have ever done our trade has been comparatively very

small; but on the other hand, if any of our squadrons fall in with them, the result always has been, and I trust will ever be, both honourable and advantageous to our country.38

Cockburn's view coincided with others. By 1 October, 9,300 men of the garrison were sick and 1,728 dead. The decision to withdraw was taken at the end of the month. By 11 December the dockyard and defences of Flushing were destroyed, its harbour ruined, and a frigate, brig and dismantled ship of the line brought back to England. The human cost, however, was enormous: 4,000 of the sick died. A parliamentary inquiry in March 1810 exonerated both the policy and decisions of the King's ministers, but only against a heavy weight of opposition in the House of Commons.[39]

The Attempt to Rescue Ferdinand VII

Lord Wellesley became Foreign Secretary under Spencer Perceval in December 1809. Only three years before, Wellesley had been deterred from taking his seat in the House of Lords from fear of motions of censure of his administration in India. He had spoken for the first time in the Lords in February 1808, eloquently supporting the government over the seizure of the Danish fleet and revealing to ministers once again a figure of political ability and stature. The following year, with his younger brother, Arthur, appointed to command British troops in the Iberian Peninsula, Wellesley was despatched to Seville as ambassador-extraordinary to concert measures with the Spanish government for carrying on the war. Recalled in mid-October to take his place in the Cabinet, he was replaced in Seville two months later by Wellesley's other brother, Henry. The management of Spain and maintenance of political support for successive Peninsular campaigns consequently became a family affair involving a high degree of mutual understanding and confidence, and entailing numerous projects for the solution of Spanish problems.[40] These repeatedly called for a naval officer in whose professional conduct and political discretion Wellesley had confidence. Recalling the voyage of 1806, he asked for the services of Cockburn.

Britian's involvement in the Peninsula dated from 1808, though Portugal had long been an ally. In 1807, by the Treaty of Tilsit with Czar Alexander I of Russia, Napoleon sufficiently secured his rear to permit concentration on extending his empire southward. By March 1808 there were nearly 180,000 French troops in Spain. That month, in a palace revolution, Crown Prince Ferdinand deposed his father, Charles

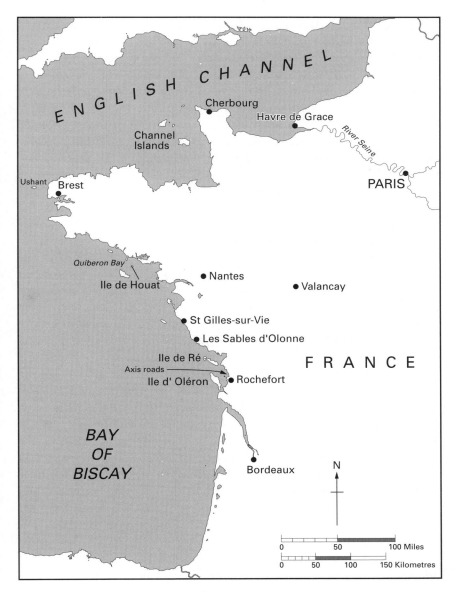

Map 4. The Atlantic Coast of France

IV, as king of Spain. Under the threat of force, both were summoned to Napoleon to whom each surrendered his right to the throne. Ferdinand, who did so unwillingly, was imprisoned in France, Joseph Bonaparte being named by Napoleon as his successor. It was the consequent rising in Madrid and defeat of a French army at Baylen that resulted in Sir Arthur Wellesley being sent with an army to bolster the Spanish cause. The defeat of the French again at Vimiero and subsequent convention of Cintra freed Portugal from French occupation but obliged Britain to repatriate the French army, giving rise to a public inquiry in London. Moore's advance, and his army's evacuation after Corunna, increased criticism of the campaign. In London, Castlereagh and Canning became increasingly disillusioned with a Spanish war, although the alternative— diversionary attacks like that on the Wacheren—clearly proved no substitute. This was the situation in which Wellesley was sent to Spain as ambassador.[41]

There he encountered the two main issues that were to dominate Anglo-Spanish relations throughout the ensuing three years. Spain expected unlimited monetary and material aid from Britain, but the latter expected Spain to open her colonies to British trade to make that aid practicable. However, Spain refused to open her colonies without a British commitment to a specified annual subsidy, and that, in Britain's inpecunious state, was a demand too exacting for her government to concede. As ambassador, and later as Foreign Secretary, Wellesley had to maintain relations with the Spanish government on the best possible footing, promising material—arms, stores, ammunition and clothing in large quantities—but stinting the monetary and military assistance as the British Treasury and War Office directed. A further difficulty, affecting opinion in London as to the value of providing aid, was the efficiency of the Spanish government in employing it. During the summer of 1809 Sir Arthur was starved of supplies; promises of logistical support were made by the Spanish government but with little effect. Two years later, Wellesley was mortified at troops, financed and equipped by Britain, being sent to suppress Spain's rebellious colonies, though such use of them was in direct conflict with Britain's war interests.[42]

As Wellesley appreciated, the government of that part of Spain still independent of France had its own interests to consider. In the absence of Ferdinand VII, following the battle of Baylen in 1808, the surviving political establishment in Spain had formed a Supreme Junta. It was intended as a stopgap government but postponed calling the representative assembly, the Cortes, and lacked public support. Above all, it lacked the authority to give satisfactory direction and impetus to the war. Taxes went uncollected; total mobilization was impossible;

ministers acted independently and collective energies were dissipated in internal party strife. In September 1809 Wellesley was informed of an intended *coup d'état*, but rather than be implicated, he informed the Supreme Junta that he was only interested in legitimate authority. Before leaving Spain, Wellesley was informed that the Cortes would be called on 1 January 1810. But that autumn France defeated the Spanish army at Alba de Torres and took control of all of Spain except Andalusia. With the Supreme Junta in disrepute, as Foreign Secretary Wellesley's first instructions to his brother urged the priority of finding a substitute government. Henry was to work for the assembly of the Cortes, for the formation of a regency and the dissolution of the Junta. Wellesley himself, meanwhile, attempted substitution by more dramatic means: one which would obviate the need for either the Junta or a regency.

It was for this scheme that, on 29 January 1810, he wrote to the Admiralty requesting the services of Cockburn. Mulgrave was promptly compliant, placing Cockburn—in command of the 74-gun *Implacable* and three smaller vessels—at the disposal of the Foreign Office. Cockburn was to carry to the coast of France two agents who would attempt the rescue of Ferdinand VII from his captivity at Valençay. The plan was proposed by one of the agents, Charles Leopold, Baron de Kolli, a disaffected French nobleman. Cockburn's instructions were issued to him on 2 Feburary. He was to land the agents in Quiberon Bay, arranging with them their later embarkation. Should they succeed in bringing Ferdinand back, Cockburn was to persuade him to sail to Portsmouth 'to concert with the British government' his return to Spain. If he was to insist on immediate carriage to Cadiz, Cockburn was to comply and land him by arrangement with Henry Wellesley. But he would 'render an important service by prevailing on His Majesty to visit England in the first instance'.[43]

The rest of the month was spent gathering the resources required for the mission. For their maintenance, bribes and other essentials, the agents were financed in currency not traceable to Britain. As well as £800 in cash, Cockburn thus received jewels to the value of £6,334 while still in London, and a further £1,093 worth on 27 February in Plymouth, carried by Messrs Albert and Graham of the Foreign Office. He himself was required to supply formal receipts and keep regular account of disbursements, the same being demanded of Baron de Kolli. In case Kolli should renege on the undertaking, his remuneration was to be determined by government on his return, according to the services he performed.

Kolli and his companion arrived at Plymouth in 'high spirits', apparently 'full of spunk and determination'. Kolli, however, quickly gave Cockburn a slight alarm, as he later informed Colonel Shawe, Wellesley's secretary:

> I presented the sword to the Baron with an appropriate speech when to my no small dismay he flew on me and *kissed me*; this was a mark of his regard and delight which I could have dispensed with; but I had sufficient command of myself to take it in good part rather than damp his ardor.[44]

He and his companion were landed in Quiberon Bay at about 11 o'clock on the night of 9 March 'without the least disturbance or molestation' and nearly at the spot suggested by Cockburn when in London. 'They were in high spirits at the facility with which they gained their first point and seemed very confident of further success.' Cockburn arranged with Kolli 'a cypher', only understood by the two of them, for communication between ship and shore through Baron de Feriet, whom they happened to find on the island of Houat in Quiberon Bay.

Feriet claimed to be a general of the Vendéan insurgents, that he had been in England a short time before, soliciting aid for his party, and had 'since been employed here smuggling British manufactures and colonial produce into France', a traffic which permitted him easy intercourse with the adjacent coasts. After a 'long conversation', in which Feriet produced a letter from Barrow (second secretary at the Admiralty), Kolli and Cockburn decided to employ Feriet as a courier, with the promise of a personal reward and recommendation for the Vendéan cause according to his 'zeal'. Feriet asked to be put ashore on the coast of Vendée where he was known to partisans, and promised to await orders at a private house at Nantes, with a *chasse marée* ready to bring messages to the *Implacable*. Feriet was consequently landed from the schooner *Nonpareil* between St Gilles and Sable D'Olonne on the night of 13 March.[45]

The *Implacable* and her consorts remained in Quiberon Bay throughout April and early May 1810.[46] About 12 May Cockburn learned 'from the continent' the disastrous new of Baron Kolli's apprehension'. Shortly afterwards a letter by cutter from Wellesley confirmed the report. According to the French *Moniteur*, the rescue attempt had been exposed because Ferdinand 'obstinately refused to have anything to do with the supposed agent of Great Britain'. It seemed his courage had proved deficient. Cockburn was furious: 'Had it not been for the unexpected and disgraceful conduct of Ferdinand and his minister, Amezaga, we had every reason to hope for a successful termination to our endeavours in his favour.' Orders were immediately issued for winding up the operation.[47]

A *chase marée* was despatched to Feriet at Nantes; the frigate *Imperieuse* and brig *Pickle* were left to await further news of Kolli, while Cockburn with the *Implacable* sailed for Portsmouth.[48]

For the Foreign Office, there were compensations.[49] There was little public or private reaction to the reports that appeared in the *Moniteur*. Little credit was attached to propaganda carried in the French press, and the story that appeared reflected more on Ferdinand than on the British government. The details of what had become of Kolli emerged only slowly and from sources that prevented public critics compiling the full story. This was not flattering to the Foreign Office. It appeared, as facts came to light, that through indiscretions the mission had been turned into a humiliating counter-intelligence coup.

Information about the mission had been leaked even before it left England. On returning to Portsmouth from London on 7 June, Cockburn found waiting a letter forwarded to him from Plymouth that seemed to prove 'what we always suspected, that Albert [the Foreign Office messenger] was not so discreet as might have been wished'.[50] It revealed too that Kolli and his accomplice had also been indiscreet. Contrary to Wellesley's instructions, they had gone to Paris to recruit support and arrange their entrance into Valençay. There they were careless in exposing their money. Not only had they been arrested but their papers had been seized, permitting the French authorities to use them for their own purposes.[51] Thereafter the rescue attempt had become a charade.

Five years later, on the voyage to St Helena, Napoleon took pleasure in describing to Cockburn the game that had been played. A French agent disguised as Kolli had been dispatched to Valençay where Ferdinand had been presented with a letter from George III attesting Kolli's identity and assuring him of the preparations made for his escape. Ferdinand's failure of courage was exactly what Napoleon had required. To embarrass the English, and dash every Spanish hope of a restored monarchy, Ferdinand's cowardice was proclaimed to the world.[52]

Mediation and Spanish America

Although temporarily reverting to routine Admiralty service, Cockburn was gradually drawn deeper into diplomatic relations between England, Spain and her colonies. The trade and wealth of the latter were a major asset to the prosecution of the common war against France, yet the

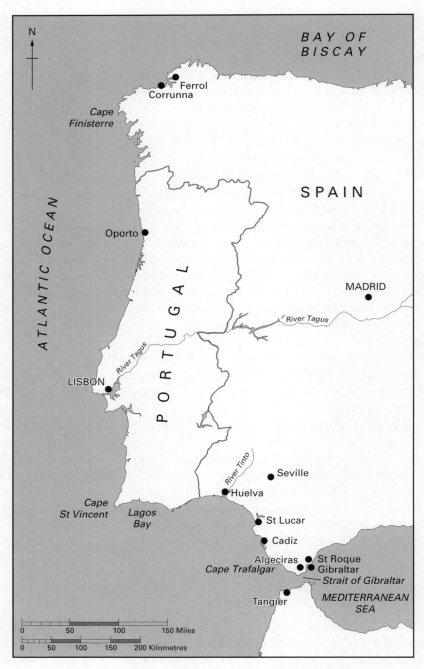

Map 5.   The Atlantic Coast of Spain and Portugal

colonies were taking the opportunity presented by Spain's weakness to seize their independence.

In July 1810 Cockburn was placed in the *Implacable* off Cadiz. By that time the city was all that remained of an independent Spain. Seville had fallen in February, Cadiz only holding out due to the injection of Spanish, British and Portuguese troops, and British arms and equipment. Once reinforced, however, it was relatively secure. Supplied from the sea the garrison could be maintained indefinitely; while the city, situated at the end of a long, narrow isthmus, was easily defended from land attack, especially with the ability to bring guns from the ships offshore to bear on any French attempt to advance.[53]

To divert French forces, the allied forces mounted attacks on the French along the coast above and below Cadiz. One such operation took place six weeks after Cockburn's arrival: Spanish troops were sent to the north for an attack on the town of Moguer on the River Tinto near Huelva. Cockburn accompanied them in charge of two brigs and some armed boats from the fleet, and was informed that about 1,180 French were driven from Moguer. He landed and inspected the field of battle, and was impressed by the Spanish; they remained cheerful and had evidently fought bravely and steadily, though without rest for three successive nights. They made him 'more sanguine than ever in the hope that such a people in such a cause must be ultimately successful'.[54] However, they failed to make a planned second attack on the French (at St Lucar, near to Cadiz) on the return journey because, to Cockburn's mind, the Spanish commander was set against it.[55]

His co-operation with Spanish forces earned him compliments from a new Spanish government.[56] The Supreme Junta's abandonment of Seville to the French earlier that year had ignited risings against it both in Seville and in Cadiz, and it was given no chance to establish itself in Cadiz where, on 31 January, a five-man Council of Regency was appointed. With the spread of French imperial power throughout the Peninsula, one of the new Council's main concerns was the security of a few naval vessels still under its command. Several remained in Cadiz harbour, including two 120-gun first-rates. By the end of August their equipment was sufficiently advanced for them to be evacuated to Port Mahon, Minorca, and to Havana, Cuba. Cockburn, on his return from Moguer, was given orders at the request of the Council to escort the two first-rates to Havana with the *Implacable*.[57] The small squadron sailed on 6 September.

From Havana, the *Implacable* was required to press on to Vera Cruz on the central American mainland and to return to Cadiz with two million dollars in Spanish-American specie. The carriage of specie to Spain was the only way of meeting the costs of maintaining Spanish armies in the field. It also supplied a means of redeeming bills of exchange issued to Spain in the place of loans by officials acting on behalf of the British government, a practice started in 1809.[58]

By mid-1810 the financial position of Spain's royalist government was desperate. Henry Wellesley had been pressed relentlessly by the Council of Regency for a loan. In July he had finally capitulated; but, instead of referring his intentions for approval to London, he had on his own authority granted a loan of one and a half million dollars. As suggested by the secretary to the Spanish Council, he issued bills of exchange on the condition that, if the loan was not approved in London, the amount would be repaid from the first specie received from South America. In the event, Spencer Perceval, the Prime Minister, was appalled. He feared paper currency to that amount would disrupt the money market in Cadiz and prevent Wellington making the purchases he required for his operations in Portugal. Perceval called for a strong reprimand; Lord Wellesley, protective of his brother, disagreed, their quarrel adding to strains in the Cabinet. But Wellesley did order Henry to demand repayment of the advance out of the first shipment of specie received from America. It was this specie that Cockburn was called upon to collect.[59]

The shipment was of extraordinary value to Cockburn himself. Since 1807 naval officers had been permitted to receive as compensation for their carriage of specie a gratuity equivalent to a percentage of its monetary worth.[60] This shipment was worth 43,500 dollars (above 2 per cent) to Cockburn, though subject to deductions for flag officers on the Mediterranean station.[61]

By February 1811 the situation at Cadiz had altered little. Armed boat operations—intended to 'harass and perplex'—had become routine. However, Cockburn's main interest focused on the diplomatic activity revolving about Henry Wellesley's residence in Cadiz. His recent acquaintance with the Spanish colonies of Central America gave his opinion special value in Wellesley's negotiations with the Council of Regency. Wellesley's confidence in Cockburn's knowledge led to his dispatch to London on 21 April.

The ostensible reason for the visit was to carry details of a new loan arranged by Henry, dependent upon repayment in further specie from Spanish America and an undertaking by the Council to expend this loan on the Spanish armies operating against the French. The ulterior motive was to concert with Lord Wellesley an attempt to persuade the Spanish colonies to remain loyal to the Council of Regency.[62] A colonial movement towards independence had begun almost exactly a year earlier. Shortly after receiving news of the fall of Seville, Venezuela, led by the city of Caracas, had declared her independence from executive authority in Spain on 19 April 1810. Chile and Colombia had followed suit, while Mexico was in popular revolt though still technically controlled by her Spanish governor.

The revolts bedevilled an already difficult Anglo-Spanish relationship. The colonies immediately appealed to Britain for support: for muskets, ammunition and naval protection. If Britain did not respond positively there was the probability they would turn to France or the United States. There was also the possibility of losing trade—the opening of the Spanish colonial markets had long been a British objective, especially as such trade would help finance the British armies maintained in Spain and Portugal as well as the subsidies made available to both allies. The colonists and the British commercial interest thus appealed for the lifting of trade restrictions. Yet Cadiz, dominated by her merchant community, opposed anything that would reduce their monopoly, defied the Council of Regency to concede it, and demanded a British blockade of the rebellious colonies.[63]

In London Lord Wellesley had to find a way of reconciling the interests of all concerned. Cockburn reached England in the frigate *Druid* on 5 May 1811. He immediately proceeded to London to lay before the ministers the dispatches and intelligence with which he had been charged.[64] The direct result was confirmation of a ten-point plan of mediation produced by the Foreign Secretary and received by Henry Wellesley in Cadiz on 27 May. As well as a termination of hostilities and general amnesty, the plan proposed measures of free trade and political representation for the colonies, but retained their allegiance to Ferdinand VII and their co-operation and assistance in the war with France.

Cockburn awaited the Spanish response in London. Lord Wellesley had in mind a three-man commission which would, if acceptable to Spain, tour the colonies arranging terms of reconciliation. He had suggested the same to his son Richard on 10 May, Cockburn being suggested for first commissioner, Richard for second, Charles Vaughan third, and with Hop Hoppner as secretary.[65] But the news from Cadiz was not encouraging. The Council of Regency refused to grant equal representation or redress grievances; Britain was condemned for surreptitiously encouraging the rebellions; and counter-proposals included the provision that Britain help Spain suppress the rebels should reconciliation not be achieved within fifteen months.

In London the Admiralty confirmed Cockburn's secondment to the Foreign Office. While negotiations in Cadiz dragged on, he had little to do but kick his heels. Indeed, the whole summer was to pass waiting for some Spanish sign of encouragement. By September the Council of Regency, far from concurring in mediation, had decided to send troops to America—troops equipped at British expense, in troop-ships refitted by the Admiralty. In London, Wellesley determined to force the issue. Three commissioners would be sent to Cadiz to offer mediation; either the Spanish would agree to sail with them to America to begin mediation on British terms, or they would refuse the offer altogether.[66]

Cockburn's role in this final determination is unclear. A memorandum existing in the papers of the Foreign Office in Cockburn's hand supplies the form of instructions the Prince Regent might issue to the commissioners. In November, when the commissioners of mediation were finally appointed, Cockburn remained the only survivor from the previous nominations. With T. Sydenham and J.P. Morier, he was created an envoy extraordinary and minister plenipotentiary. In preparation, two days later, he ordered from the Admiralty two chronometers and charts for the Jamaica and Brazil stations.[67]

Yet, just as the pace of events quickened, Wellesley's determination to send the commission weakened. He had become one of the British Prince Regent's intimate circle, and in the Cabinet had become a challenger for the premiership. The renewal of the regency bill was approaching and his attention turned to championing the Prince Regent's interests. In this hiatus, Cockburn conducted the diplomacy necessary to the commission, calling as Wellesley's representative upon the Spanish ambassador.[68] But by December 1811 Wellesley and Perceval were no longer on speaking terms, and the former was to resign in February 1812.

Nevertheless, still the commissioners waited on the point of departure: Cockburn's costs included over £300 for 'lodging, tavern and other expenses at Portsmouth' between December 1811 and April 1812.[69] By then events in Spain encouraged a more favourable view of the commission. Two new councillors, interested in co-operation with Britain, were appointed to the Council of Regency. Also, Wellington had driven the French from the Spanish frontier fortresses of Cuidad Rodrigo and Badajaz, permitting the British government to drive harder bargains with the Spanish Council.[70] In March 1812—a month after the appointment of Castlereagh as Foreign Secretary—Cockburn provided him with an appraisal of the grievances which the commission had to address. Using population statistics gleaned from the geographer Humboldt, he contrasted representation in the Spanish Cortes on behalf of the colonists to that of European Spaniards, pointing out the contempt in which the colonists held the idea of 'virtual representation' by 'deputies'.[71] He also dined with the Spanish ambassador, pressing upon Castlereagh the information he gleaned.[72] Cockburn's persistence paid off. The Prince Regent's instructions to the commissioners were finally signed in April 1812.

In Cadiz, however, the commissioners were to remain as inactive as they had been in London, though now nearer and more aware of the source of their inactivity. Correspondence about their proposed mission passed ceaselessly between Henry Wellesley, still ambassador, and the secretary to the Council. Yet the Council of Regency, reflecting opinion in the Cortes, which in turn largely reflected the views of Cadiz's merchant community, steadfastly refused to grant the necessary authority for mediation to proceed. Dominant opinion in the Cortes refused even to concede that the colonies were in a state of revolution. Hopes for approval were nevertheless sustained by a small number of 'American deputies'. In July Cockburn translated for Castlereagh's benefit the views expressed by three such deputies on mediation to Mexico. They refuted the claim that the rebellion there was not of a revolutionary nature.

> All the public parts and whatever intelligence has been received from that Kingdom prove beyond doubt that the insurgents aspire to a reform or innovation of the Government which can only be denied by those who are resolved to deceive themselves or to shut their eyes to what is acting before them . . ... The force which the Government has applied and can still apply against those hordes, as they call them, has proved insufficient by the experience of two years' continued warfare; notwithstanding they still continue in existence. They are like Hydra, which not only acquire new heads in lieu of those you sever from it, but likewise new bodies.

The deputies argued that the commissioners had no need to negotiate with representatives of a government but could seek out the fittest people, 'with whom you treat in the best manner you are able, as was the case with the citizens in the Revolution war'.[73]

In July Cockburn returned to London to advise Castlereagh whether Britain should undertake to send commissioners to those colonies for which the Council of Regency was prepared to accept mediation.[74] He was doubtful of any negotiations dependent on the Spanish government, and in any case immediate agreement on any offer could not be obtained from Cadiz for at least six weeks. Negotiations at Buenos Aires would take a further six months, the result of which would have to be submitted to Cadiz for approval. If the formula for peace was then also submitted to Mexico, at least a year would elapse. During that time the mines in New Spain, already flooded, could suffer 'incalculable mischiefs', while allied operations on the Continent might encounter 'insurmountable difficulties if not absolute destruction'.

To avoid such delays, Cockburn proposed a direct advance. He recommended advertising Britain's transactions with Spain on the question of mediation by manifestos throughout Mexico. If the colonists would acknowledge Ferdinand VII as sovereign and make contributions to the war in Europe, Britain would consider them friends and be ready to enter a treaty to use her influence with Spain to stop all further repression. A British squadron in the Gulf of Mexico would either persuade the Spanish government of the advantage of treating the rebels seriously or, by giving them protection, encourage the rebels to drive out the few remaining Spaniards. Thus Britain would permit the colonists to return to the mines and restore to the allies 'a decided superiority in pecuniary resources over France'.

Speed of action was of the essence. Mexico had formed a connexion with the United States which was growing stronger. The rebels were being supplied from there with arms and gunpowder, while 300 North American officers were serving with the rebel army. It now seemed possible that the United States Congress would invite Mexico to become an integral part of the United States, a union of strength and danger to Britain. 'The annual 24 million of dollars and other resources of New Spain being at the disposal of such an active industrious and intriguing people as the North Americans would leave us everything to dread, particularly a rapidly increasing navy, and a constant emigration from Europe of shipwrights, workmen of all other descriptions and sailors.'[75]

Cockburn's arguments were to no avail. Events on both sides of the Atlantic precluded further action. At the very time he wrote, the Spanish government confirmed its commitment to a military solution to its colonial troubles. On 2 September Castlereagh urgently appealed to the Spanish ambassador in London to intervene with his government and avert the 'calamities which threaten the Spanish monarchy in South America and, through its transatlantic dominions, the destiny of Spain itself'.[76] It was a forlorn hope. Castlereagh had already abandoned hope of sending commissioners. Cockburn's secondment to the Foreign Office was terminated early in August 1812.

CHAPTER 3

The War with the United States 1813–1815

For all concerned with Britain's war against Napoleon and its relations with the rest of the world, events took several new turns. In London they raised new hopes for peace in Europe. Until then, the Peninsular War had been waged in the face of heavy criticism and doubt as to its value. But in 1812 Wellington's achievements proclaimed that the French position was vulnerable, with the prospect of their eventual defeat as Spain began to rally her forces. To the north, Napoleon's invasion of Russia had proved his greatest mistake. By December he was back in Paris having lost 400,000 men and, of equal immediate importance, turned Russia from a British enemy into her ally. No longer theoretically confined to neutral ships, the Baltic was opened to British trade. Naval forces guarding 'neutral' convoys for Russian and Swedish ports could be reduced as the flow of Baltic naval stores—for some years in short supply—increased to meet commercial demand.

For Britain, these events were propitious, for they coincided with the demand for unlimited naval forces across the Atlantic and a check in the supply of those naval materials obtained from the United States. However, Britain's international situation had not become easier, nor its military commitments less demanding. Priorities remained the same. The war in Europe had to come first: since 1803 it had become a war to the death. Yet hostilities with a nation outside Europe raised logistical problems reminiscent of those forty years earlier. Following the American declaration of war on 18 June 1812, Britain had not only to defend its territories in North America and the troop convoys required to maintain that defence, but also its convoys to the Iberian Peninsula against American privateers. At the same time, it was expected of the navy that American trade should stop, that British naval forces would blockade American ports as they had done those of Europe controlled by France. Few in Britain appreciated the length of the coast and borders of the United States. Even less did many appreciate the naval and military forces necessary to control those fronts effectively.

So far as its naval forces were concerned, the 102 ships of the line and 519 frigates then in commission gave Britain the most powerful fleet any nation had ever put to sea. Nonetheless, most vessels were needed in European waters where Napoleon continued to build ships of the line in every port he could. At least for the time being, war with America was to mean unlimited demands to which the response had to be at the smallest possible cost to the British effort in Europe.

The Offensive under Warren

The logistical problems became apparent immediately. Vessels and troops had to be spared simply to defend British trade and territory. To professional military men, however, war meant offence as well as defence. The United States had declared war on Britain; she should be forced to withdraw that declaration and sue for peace. Yet, with the military forces available, quite how Britain should reduce the United States to submission was an open question. Wellington was as baffled by the matter as anyone.

> You may go to a certain extent as far as a navigable river or your means of transport will enable you to subsist, provided your force is sufficiently large compared with [those with] which the enemy will oppose you. But I do not know where you could carry on such an operation which would be injurious to the Americans as to force them to sue for peace, which is what one would wish to see.

The prospect', he concluded, was 'not consoling'.[1]

Operations by sea carried most promise—defence and offence could be served equally. In 1812 the United States lacked a significant navy. Indeed, a motion to build a bigger fleet had been defeated in Congress, preference being expressed for use of limited funds in a land campaign against Canada. The United States thus began the war with but 165 gunboats and 16 frigates, though the latter were admittedly almost equivalent to small ships of the line.[2] Instead American faith was placed in a privateering war, financed mainly by the mercantile community for commercial profit. A fleet so produced would be no match for the British navy, but it might do untold damage to its merchant fleet, now

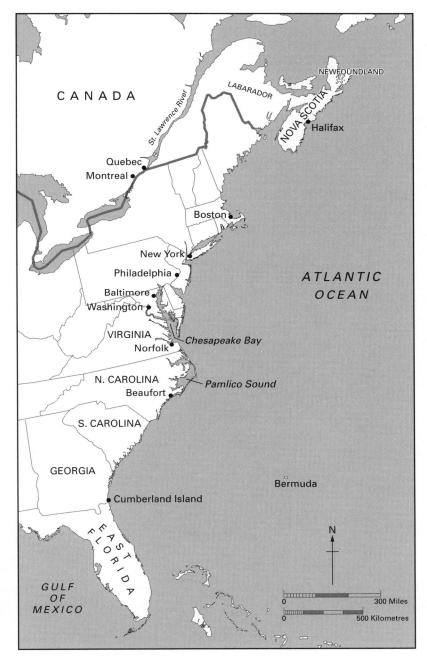

Map 6. The East Coast of North America

almost 2,000 vessels and a cornerstone of British financial strength. It could also damage the massive transport operation which was necessary in order to wage war against France in the Iberian Peninsula.

For the British government a priority was therefore the seizure or confinement of not only American warships, but all potential privateers as well. This was attainable by the blockade of all significant American ports, which had the advantage of confining American trade and thereby inflicting economic damage. It also minimized the problem of identification, search and seizure that materialized as soon as American merchant vessels reached the sea and took the opportunity, undetected, to change their ownership, nationality and papers.

Of this, Cockburn had first-hand experience. For a month, between 18 October and 23 November 1812, he had command at Cadiz where reports were received from all along the Iberian coastline of the interception of American vessels. Since the French invasion of Spain, the east coast of the United States had steadily increased its supply of grain to the Peninsula. Although Spain and Portugal were allied to Britain they were not at war with the United States; therefore American vessels could hope to gain a neutral Spanish or Portuguese port before being caught by a British vessel. British captains, however, were prone to ignore the neutrality of such ports and Cockburn was obliged to warn them to respect both Cadiz harbour and adjacent coastlines. Neutral Spanish purchasers had everything to gain from assisting American vessels into port—even purchasing the vessels to render them inviolate. 'All transfers of vessels from His Majesty's enemies to neutrals are deemed by us to be illegal', Cockburn informed the British consul at Cadiz in mid-November, 'and will be seized by our ships accordingly'. Only a transfer made prior to the American declaration of war would be considered a 'legitimate Spaniard' and be permitted to sail unmolested.[3]

Since 1807 the sale of licences to neutral vessels trading into enemy-occupied territory had become a feature of the British system of maritime control. In 1812 the demands of Spain and Portugal for grain required that some American vessels still be licensed to pass British vessels unchecked. Thus, from 13 October, United States vessels destined for Cadiz or Lisbon with cargoes of flour or grain and carrying official British passes were to be permitted to return with new cargoes of 'lawful merchandise'.[4] However licences simply undermined efforts to check American trade, their issue being open to abuse and their authenticity open to question.[5] Cockburn protested immediately to the Admiralty, and licensing became more tightly controlled soon after.

In London the fabric of regulations governing war with the United States was only gradually constructed. Vice-Admiral Sir John Borlase Warren had been appointed commander-in-chief on the North America and West Indies station in the summer of 1812. Cockburn received his orders to transfer command at Cadiz and join Warren at Bermuda on 18 November. The *Marlborough* sailed five days later, making Bermuda, after a difficult passage, on 17 January. Warren arrived shortly afterwards, having already installed ships off the Chesapeake. But it was 18 February before the *Marlborough* was ready for service again, when Cockburn sailed for the Chesapeake as the rear-admiral in command of that stretch of coast.

Warren has received little credit for his part in establishing the blockade of American ports. He had served with distinction in the Revolutionary War, but had seen little service since 1806 and, having reached the age of 59 in 1812, was weak in health. Under the strain of command, his vigour was to deteriorate, revealing by midsummer a lack of energy in both the development of ideas and the deployment of ships.

From the very beginning, however, he was in a difficult position. His command was a convenience for the Admiralty. Uniting five stations under his authority—Newfoundland, Halifax, Bermuda, Leeward Islands and Jamaica—it was intended that Warren would oversee the rear-admirals in command of each, and ensure that they had sufficient ships for blockade, escorts and reliefs. Yet he was never to be given enough ships and was never able to ensure his outlying rear-admirals had adequate forces. In February 1813 he had nominal command of 94 ships—15 of the line, 23 frigates and 56 smaller vessels. But that was to blockade a coastline of continental extent, and, on the whole, this force was to shrink. By December the command accounted for only 10 ships of the line, with 27 frigates and 54 other vessels. Correspondence between Warren and the Admiralty was consequently repeatedly punctuated on the one hand by appeals for ships, and on the other by criticism of their deployment.[6]

Yet Warren began the war with optimism and enthusiasm. In November 1812 he proposed to Lord Melville, now First Lord at the Admiralty, a programme of measures that would relieve pressure on the borders of Canada and Spanish Florida, while also creating alarm and despondency among the American people. He advocated reinforcement of the naval force on the Great Lakes; the seizure of New Orleans by a concentration of all available ships and troops, followed by a succession of raids by a 'flying army and squadron' to destroy all shipping and naval resources at Charleston and Savannah, in the Chesapeake and Delaware, and at New York; and an increase in the ships of the line and frigates at his disposal to permit the effective blockade of all east coast ports.[7]

His ideas were quickly checked. Melville's letter to him of 3 December laid out the Admiralty's 'intentions respecting the blockade of the enemies ports and the mode of the warfare proposed to annoy the enemy', with the number of ships he was to receive for employment. Being specifically limited by the Admiralty in London, he had little room for manoeuvre. Within two months he was already obliged to defend himself, his feelings hurt at reproaches for not having taken any American frigates: the ships that had joined him singly, he retorted, were in a wretched state and needed immediate refitting; 'the swarm of the enemies privateers in the West Indies rendered it impracticable to withdraw any ships from thence'; Boston and Rhode Island could not be blockaded between November and March owing to the severity of the climate; 'and before the orders of the board arrived it was impossible to institute a blockade of the enemies ports in the face of neutral licences and protections without number'.[8]

Warren's difficulties were to be exacerbated by the size of the station, the relative remoteness of shore bases, and length of his supply routes. With ships stationed the whole length of north and central America, his northerly squadrons could only resort to Halifax, the southerly to Port Royal, Jamaica, or if necessary to Antigua, while his inner east-coast squadron relied on Bermuda. These bases were not convenient. Bermuda, Cockburn's base, was over six hundred miles from the American coast; in February 1813, it had taken the *Marlborough* two weeks to make the voyage. Once damaged or weather-worn ships reached the island, there was a small refitting yard, ordnance store and hospital. But the yard mustered only about 70 artificers and labourers (as opposed to more than 4,000 in Portsmouth yard in 1812), while the hospital had to be extended to Ireland Island. To be effective, such shore bases demanded constant replenishing with provisions and equipment to be fed to ships as they were required. Yet such supplies placed further demands on Warren's ships. Convoys had to ply regularly between England, Halifax and Jamaica, most gathering and dividing at Bermuda.

Ease of communication with the Admiralty and with his rear-admirals would have helped the commander-in-chief considerably. Although Bermuda, in mid-Atlantic, was his fleet rendezvous, even from there reports to the Admiralty took an average of six weeks to reach Whitehall, while despatches by return could take up to ten weeks to reach Warren, especially when he was with squadrons on the coast. Within the station, reports and orders were exchanged more easily. Cockburn reported weekly to Warren when the latter was at Bermuda. Yet bad weather could extend the interval between letter and answer to three or four weeks.

These problems contributed directly to Warren's failure.[9] He was censured in June for allowing frigates to escape and for failing to establish effective stations for his ships. By July, following the failure of an attack on Norfolk, Cockburn was conscious of a clear lack of objectives, energy and motivation. He himself then took the initiative in proposing an attack on Ocracoke, North Carolina. Later he let it be known that he disagreed 'with Sir John Warren upon the best mode of carrying on the warfare against America'.[10] To Captain Barrie, who served under him, he hinted at more, 'especially at moments when my chief's conduct put me so much to my shifts'.[11] Warren was recalled on 4 November.[12]

The Chesapeake in 1813

Cockburn's squadron enjoyed a relatively privileged position under Warren. They agreed on the importance of that mid-Atlantic coastline, close to the United States capital, where local public opinion could do most to affect the will to prosecute the war.[13] But that coastline was not inviting. According to one new arrival, it was

> universally low and uninteresting insomuch that, for some time before the land itself can be discerned, forests of pines appear to rise as it were out of the water. It is also dangerous from the numerous shoals and sandbanks which run out in many places to a considerable extent into the sea, and which are so formidable that no master of a vessel, unless he chance to be particularly well acquainted with navigation, will venture to approach after dark.

Chesapeake Bay was more impressive, but only on account of its breadth. It was 'far too wide and the land on each side too flat to permit any but an indistinct glimpse of the shore from the deck of a vessel which keeps towards the middle'.[14] In March 1813 Cockburn did not penetrate far, anchoring in Lynhaven Bay near the entrance to the Chesapeake with the vessels Warren had already stationed there.

There, the most important target was the frigate *Constellation*, moored in the Elizabeth River below Norfolk. To test American strength in that

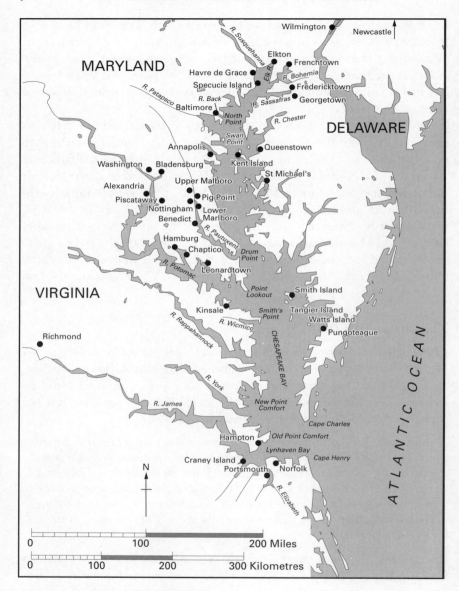

Map 7.   The Chesapeake Bay Region of the United States

river, Cockburn moved his three ships of the line, *Marlborough, Victorious*
and *Dragon* (all 74s), north into Hampton Roads. This apparently
simple manoeuvre turned out to be a real task: 'We were obliged to buoy

off the whole channel as we advanced, not having any person in the squadron who was in the slightest degree acquainted with it, and as we found it much more intricate and very different to our charts and directions.'[15] Sounding operations at the mouth of the Elizabeth River resulted in the *Constellation* being run up beyond Norfolk and three merchant ships being sunk to block the river channel. This was sounded at only three and a half fathoms over its first four miles. Several merchant vessels, seized by armed boats of the squadron in the James River, were thus converted for use as fire-ships. Cockburn hoped that these, with boats mounting Congreve rockets, would manage to destroy the frigate.[16]

Local inhabitants, fearing similar visits to other rivers entering the bay, came out under flags of truce to make their peace with Cockburn. 'An intelligent merchant of Richmond' told him that the outbreak of the war had been popular in that part of the world. But since then:

> the late measures of our government having . . . thrown back into the country an immense quantity of last year's produce, and caused an entire and complete stagnation of all commerce . . . there was now only to be heard from one end of the country to the other lamentations of individuals who were now beginning to suffer from the effects of the war.[17]

Cockburn was able to deliver the report into the hands of Warren himself who arrived in the *San Domingo* in Lynhaven Bay on 22 March. Warren's own letter to Melville a week later echoed Cockburn's words.[18]

To test for himself the resilience of the Americans, Warren accompanied Cockburn's squadron up the Chesapeake as far as Annapolis. From there Cockburn took part of the squadron—the *Marlborough*, two frigates, some brigs and smaller vessels—further up the bay to penetrate each of the tributary rivers in turn. On 3 April four large armed schooners were chased into the Rappahannock River; boats of the squadron pursued them for 15 miles and eventually seized them.[19] In the River Patapsco, having driven off a gunboat, the boats again brought out several vessels, though this time they found themselves bombarded from small guns and field pieces on shore.[20] At a flour depot in the Elk River (an army warehouse), army clothing, cavalry equipment and flour were burnt.[21]

The Americans had taken to building batteries to protect strategic points or buildings. Such batteries tended to attract Cockburn's attention, rather than to deter him. Thus, while anchoring off Specucie Island on 2 May, he noticed guns firing and American colours flying from a new battery at Havre de Grace, at the entrance to the Susquehanna River. Consequently, at daylight the following day, launches and rocket-boats closed with the battery, while 150 marines and artillerymen landed and took it. The Americans retreated into the buildings of the town, there maintaining 'a teasing and irritating fire from behind the houses, walls, trees etc' until driven into the woods.[22]

The guerrilla warfare practised by local inhabitants at first seemed dishonourable to Cockburn. He recalled that they 'took every opportunity of firing with their rifles from behind trees or haystacks, or from the windows of their houses upon our boats, whenever rowing along the shore within their reach, or upon our people when employed watering . . . in short, whenever they thought they could get a mischievous shot at any of our people without being seen or exposed to personal risk in return.' He thus repeatedly received reports 'of our poor fellows being killed in this dastardly and provoking manner', and consequently felt justified in adopting and publicising a policy of strict retribution. Those inhabitants who fired on the British 'from behind lurking places on their farms or from their houses' would have their property 'treated as a place of arms' and their persons as military prisoners of war.[23] At Havre de Grace he therefore set fire to the houses that had been deserted by their owners, presuming that they had 'formed part of the militia who fled to the woods'. He aimed to teach them 'what they were liable to bring upon themselves by building batteries and acting towards us with so much useless rancour'.[24]

Cockburn also despatched a division of boats up the Susquehanna to take or destroy whatever they found. They returned that evening having destroyed five vessels and a large store of flour. Cockburn himself meanwhile went north with the remaining boats in search of the Cecil or Principic cannon foundry, supposed to be 'one of the most valuable works of the kind of America'. Its destruction took the rest of the day, and included 'the complicated heavy machinery attached to it'. They returned to the ships that evening, 'where we arrived at 10 o'clock, after having been 22 hours in constant exertion without nourishment of any kind'. In all 51 guns were destroyed that day.[25]

By 5 May the squadron had entered the Sassafras, 'being the only river or place of shelter for vessels at this upper extremity of the Chesapeake which I had not examined and cleared'. In the evening boats proceeded upstream for Georgetown and Fredericktown, which were warned via local inhabitants against resistance. Although vessels and public property would be seized, provisions or the property of individuals required for the squadron would be paid for in full. Even so, at about a mile from the first town, around 400 men opened fire on the British boats with muskets and a field gun. With five men wounded, Cockburn kept his word. All the houses, except those still occupied by their inhabitants, were destroyed, along with stores of sugar, timber, leather and four vessels lying in the river.

Returning downstream Cockburn visited a small town that he had noticed a little way up one of the tributaries of the Sassafras. There, he was pleased to discover, his warnings had had the desired effect. 'The inhabitants . . . met me at landing, to say that they had not permitted either guns or militia to be stationed there and that, whilst there, I should not meet with any opposition whatever'. After a search for 'warlike stores', the town was left undamaged. Shortly afterwards Cockburn was to receive a deputation from Charlestown 'in the North-East River' to assure him that they too would permit neither guns nor militiamen there. He was assured, moreover, that all the towns in the upper part of the Chesapeake had adopted similar resolutions.[26]

On returning to Bermuda, Warren was to find that 'two battalions of marines' had just arrived and that sufficient ships were promised to close those American ports which were only under occasional observation. He thus issued a proclamation, dated 26 May, declaring New York, Charleston, Port Royal, Savannah and the River Mississippi in a state of formal blockade.[27] The troops were promptly ordered for the Chesapeake. Warren still dwelt on the idea of a 'flying army'. He really wanted 2,000–3,000 men to be 'superior to any force the enemy could bring to a given point in 68 [sic] hours'. But those now at his disposal would, he hoped, 'enable us to do something essential'. Norfolk, Baltimore and Washington were his immediate targets, each with stocks of naval stores, ships, dockyards or foundries. An attack on Washington particularly interested him. The river was navigable for frigates and was defended by but two batteries 'which, if they were carried, leaves the place open to insult from an enemy and would in such case oblige the American to withdraw a proportion of the regular force from the Canadas'.[28]

Warren's ideas were possibly based on a memorandum prepared for him by Cockburn. The latter had been deeply impressed with the freedom with which he could operate in the Chesapeake without significant interference from the Americans. After destroying the Cecil or Principic foundry, he observed that he had spent the whole day on shore 'in the centre of the enemy's country and on his highroad between

Baltimore and Philadelphia'.[29] Receiving news of the imminent arrival of the two marine regiments, he set about gaining more information on the 'various obstacles and facilities attending each mode by which an approach to Norfolk' might be made. [30]

The ships' companies left in the Chesapeake had, in large measure, to live off the land. Visits were made to Watts and Tangier islands, occupied by only a few people living in 'wretched poverty'. The water there was hard and brackish, but the inhabitants 'asserted that many of our ships watered there during the last war'. There was wood and a good harbour, and the visiting parties gathered provisions. On Smith's Island further north, local people were anxious to show assistance.[31] All the provisions —mainly cattle, and sheep—were willingly supplied and paid for, sometimes in cash, others by bills drawn on the Victualling Board in London.[32]

While preparing for the arrival of the troops, a floating mine was picked up by the boats of the *Victorious* on the morning of 5 June. It was 'one of the powder machines commonly known by the name of Fulton's, made to explode under water and thereby cause immediate destruction to whatever it may come in contact with'. It aroused in Cockburn a rare burst of indignation.

> This was no doubt destined for the Victorious or some other of our ships here, the American government intending to dispose of us by wholesale, six hundred at a time without further trouble or risk. But as it is not likely their laudable efforts in this way have been confined to *one* machine only . . . and as they will be as likely to come in contact with neutrals or indeed some of their own countrymen as with English, it may be right that in such case it be generally known by whom such infernal machines have been promiscuously turned adrift in the ocean, for otherwise it will scarcely perhaps be attributed to a Government, the head of which has in a public message to Congress so recently boasted of its '*invaried* examples of Humanity', and whose public prints and authorised documents are so constantly harping on the same theme, that it requires examples like these and such communications as we have recently received from its officers to prove the real spirit predominating in its councils.[33]

Warren arrived with the troops on 19 June. Commanded by Colonel Sir Sidney Beckwith, they comprised 2,650 men in all.[34] As planned, Norfolk, sheltering the *Constellation*, was to be taken first. Within hours preparations were in train for taking Craney Island at the mouth of the Elizabeth River—mounting an American battery that commanded the channel—and the west bank that commanded the island.[35] Soldiers were put on shore at a place called Pig's Point and briefly took possession of the nearby bank. However, an attempted landing on the island proved a fiasco. The boats carrying marines grounded on mud flats too distant from shore to permit a landing but within range of the island's battery. Two boats were sunk, whilst the remainder fell into confusion and were ordered to retire. Three marines were killed, 16 seamen and marines were wounded, and 62 went missing, presumed drowned.[36] Three days later Hampton, which commanded communications from the north with Norfolk, was taken. Cockburn accompanied the expedition, commanding the boats and naval contingent. The town's fortifications were destroyed but the troops were then re-embarked.[37]

Warren's hopes for the occupation of Norfolk as the first stage in the campaign of his 'flying army' were dashed. Moreover, it was evident from his private letter to Melville that he had no further ideas to sustain his campaign.[38] On 3 July Cockburn was permitted to take a force to attack Ocracoke 'at Pamlico Sound, the Emporium of the commerce and rendezvous of the privateers of North Carolina'. The operation, in conjunction with the army, went relatively smoothly.[39] One consequence was the discovery that the ports of Beaufort and Ocracoke were outlets, via inland waterways, for the trade of Norfolk, the Elizabeth River and the whole Chesapeake region. 'Immense quantities of goods . . . in numerous small craft' thus escaped the blockade and reached neutral shipping lying in open ports.[40]

By then the summer heat made refreshment on shore necessary to troops growing sickly in their transports. Kent Island in the upper part of the bay was now occupied, which, along with Watts Island, created bases from which the rest of the bay could be controlled.[41]

Cockburn, the subject of virulent abuse on the part of the pro-war American press, departed for Bermuda.[42] A reward was offered for his head. Yet from the first operations in the bay, he had consistently attempted to adhere to 'the principles of humanity and a sincere desire to lessen to individuals the hardships inseparable from war'. As usual, prisoners of war were exchanged, except that whenever 'partial exchanges' were refused, Cockburn threatened that Americans would be sent as prisoners to Europe. Non-combatants—passengers, apprentices, even seamen—not demonstrably participating in the war, also accompanied the cartels. Such distinctions were appreciated by civilians. Local inhabitants in the bay were in regular contact with his ships. Gentlemen were permitted to cross, also mail; fishing vessels could fish, though not carry their catch into Norfolk. Coals, one hundred tons, were permitted passage in June to supply a hospital at New York. The courtesies extended even to the return of runaway slaves, though Cockburn returned only those who were 'willing'.[43]

Of course some seamen, marines and soldiers who landed did behave with abandon. Reports of indiscriminate, comprehensive looting and destruction were manifold.[44] Yet there is evidence that Cockburn did attempt to check excesses, with a determination to punish offenders.[45] Moreover, he later claimed that the distinction he made between acts of war and those of peace had its effect on the whole tenor of relations in the Chesapeake by reducing acts of hostility on the part of Americans. He claimed that his boats ceased to suffer from sniping, and that he was able to carry on operations 'with less rancour and mischief towards the people of the surrounding country than otherwise would have been the case'. In consequence, local inhabitants 'suffered perhaps less real loss and inconvenience than ever was experienced by people inhabiting a country made the theatre of hostile operations'.[46]

The Offensive under Cochrane

After Warren's departure from the Chesapeake in September 1813, Cockburn was to see him no more. Warren's voyage to the north followed by his recall left Cockburn responsible for much of the convoying and administration of the command that focused on Bermuda.[47] In early January 1814 he was obliged to carry out Warren's duty of visiting the stations of ships off the United States coast to the north. On his return he learned that Warren was succeeded by Vice-Admiral Sir Alexander Cochrane.

Under Cochrane the naval war on the east coast was to prove very different from that under Warren. Experience, energy and ideas all favoured him. So also did the Admiralty, for it had come to appreciate the scale of the administrative burden he carried. Warren had failed to distribute his ships as effectively as the Admiralty required; Cochrane was not to have the same opportunity. Following the escape of two frigates from Boston, Rear-Admiral Griffiths had been ordered to direct the blockade of that port without deferring to the opinion of Warren, and to receive his orders directly from the Admiralty.[48] Warren had only to ensure Griffiths had sufficient ships to meet his needs. In addition, in November, when Warren was recalled, Rear-Admirals Brown and Laforey at Jamaica and the Leeward Islands were given their own commissions as commanders-in-chief with the independence of having a set number of ships attached to each of them for their disposal.[49] With official blessing, Cochrane was thus able to pay even less attention to the logistics of the squadrons to north and south than had Warren. Correspondingly more time and energy were to be devoted to the campaign of his Bermuda-based squadron.

Cochrane's arrival accordingly heralded a new, more vigorous direction of the war against the middle seaboard states. Hitherto Cockburn had made the running; limited in his own ideas, Warren had happily authorized suggestions. Now Cockburn was to find the steering hand much firmer. He was confined to the Chesapeake and even less favoured with ships. On the other hand, his efforts became a more integrated part of a concerted strategy aimed—with more determination than had before been the case—at forcing the United States to concede peace.

Strangely, Cockburn's dependence upon and subordination to Cochrane is much at odds with past representations of the war. Cockburn was to play a key role, and the post-war naval historians, James and Brenton, who were dependent on Admiralty (thus Cockburn's) goodwill, were not to understate it. In contrast they left Cochrane a shadowy figure. Yet in reality he was a man of bold ideas, strong enough to see them carried through, whose strategic thinking and organizing energy were crucial to the events in which Cockburn made his name.

Between the two of them there developed a strong accord. Cochrane, unlike Warren, had long experience of the North America and West Indies station. Aged 56 in 1814, he had served as a lieutenant and commander during the American War of Independence, becoming a post-captain in December 1782 while still in the West Indies, and recalled that he 'was at the taking of Philadelphia under Lord and General Howe'.[50] Acquaintance with the region was revived in 1805 when he became commander-in-chief in the Leeward Islands, where he took part in the battle of St Domingo in February 1806. He remained in command at the Leeward Islands until January 1810 when, after the capture of Guadaloupe, he became governor of the island. From there in 1812 he was able to contemplate from close proximity the strategy he would pursue, given the opportunity to wage war with the United States.

In April 1812, even before war was declared, he had decided that 'the places where the Americans are most vulnerable is New Orleans and in Virginia', both of which were to receive major attacks. New Orleans was the outlet for the trade of that vast interior tapped by the Mississippi and Ohio. Control of the estuary controlled the interior and, 'self interest being the ruling principle with the Americans, those in the interior will join the party that pays for their produce'. As the British would control both their outlet and their 'only market'—the West Indies—he had 'not a doubt but that they would separate from the Atlantic states'. As for Virginia, there were two targets: the black population and the cities. The black population was 'British in their hearts, and might be of great use if war should be prosecuted with vigor'. As for the cities, they were accessible to a moving force. The 'numerous rivers being navigable to a great distance leaves the interior—even Washington . . . not free from a surprise'.[51] These schemes had all been fully discussed before Cochrane left London.[52]

From the Chesapeake, Cockburn sent Troubridge to greet Cochrane with the local information and to explain his own views. Cochrane was permitted no illusion as to the problems he faced, in particular 'the inefficiency of force employed on the station for its extent, and the service necessarily required on it, of which nobody in England and particularly at the Admiralty seem to have the most distant idea'. On Cochrane's two principal ideas Cockburn was fully co-operative. He would establish posts for receiving negroes on islands in the bay. A corps of them to act against their former masters might be possible with the incentive of free settlements in the colonies and the example of a black regiment from the West Indies. And he concurred in thinking that the cities of the region were easy targets. With the exception of Norfolk, the shores of the bay were in their usual 'wretched state of defense', and, such was his confidence, he was sure the few soldiers already in the bay would be 'quite enough . . . to march to Washington if they like'.[53]

Cochrane was in a hurry. Without waiting for Cockburn's comments, on 2 April he issued a proclamation to all persons wishing to emigrate. All such people were assured they would be received on British ships or at military posts along the coast, and could either enter the British forces or go as free settlers to British territory in North America or the West Indies.[54] Cockburn's first move that month was thus to find an island accessible to absconding slaves. By 10 May Tangier Island had been occupied, and blacks had been landed to spread news that slaves would be welcome. Those that had enlisted as soldiers were 'getting on astonishingly' and were 'really very fine fellows'. Of greater success than the recruitment was the impact of its purpose on the Americans, which had 'caused a most general and undisguised alarm'. 'They expect Blacky will have no mercy on them and they know that he understands bush fighting and the locality of the *woods* as well as themselves and can perhaps play at hide and seek in them even better.'[55]

By 25 June the recruitment policy seemed successful, for recruits had behaved 'unexpectedly well' in several engagements. 'Though one of them was shot and died instantly in front of the others at Pangoteake [Pungoteague], it did not daunt or check the others, but on the contrary animated them to seek revenge.' Even then, they were kept in excellent order and committed no 'improper outrages'.[56]

Cockburn's principal interest over these weeks was the neutralization of a flotilla of gunboats built by the Americans under Commodore Barney. The effectiveness of shallow-draught, oared vessels had been demonstrated in June 1813 when 15 gunboats had attacked the 38-gun *Junon* in Hampton Roads and had only been driven off with the assistance of the frigate *Barrosa*. Barney had proposed the creation of the flotilla in July 1813, and as early as September 1813 Warren had become aware of a force of large schooners and 16 row galleys that would convoy vessels endeavouring to escape the bay.[57] By June 1814 a flotilla of about 30 vessels had been equipped at Baltimore. That month, off the mouth of the Patuxent in upper Chesapeake Bay the flotilla was suddenly encountered coming straight towards the 74-gun *Dragon* under Captain Barrie.[58] Only after ten days of manoeuvring was the flotilla confined in the Patuxent, when the opportunity was taken for vessels under Barrie to go as high in the Chesapeake as the Elk River 'to work our friends about Baltimore'.[59]

Meanwhile, Cockburn had been organizing raids from Tangier Island. 'This last month has cost the enemy around us more than a million of dollars', he claimed on 25 June, his excursions having resulted in the destruction or removal of large quantities of tobacco and other merchandise.[60] American militiamen who fired on the British were captured where possible and despatched to Halifax as prisoners.[61] Some local residents were complete cowed.

> One of them on the left bank of the river (about 40 miles from Washington) sent to me to beg I would give him permission to go from his property for a few days to visit relations ten miles distant, and another sent to ask leave to send a few of his young geese to another of his houses where part of his family resided. In short it is quite ridiculous the perfect dominion we have from the entrance of the river to Benedict. Mr Madison must certainly be either in confident expectation of immediate peace or preparing to abdicate the chair.[62]

The raids confirmed to him the total inadequacy of local defence. 'The numbers of their militia, their rifles, and the thickness of their woods still I believe constitute their principal, if not their only, strength.'[63]

Such assurances had the effect of convincing Cochrane to direct the first large-scale military reinforcements in the direction of the Chesapeake.[64] 'I hope you will be induced to push up towards the Patuxent or these islands without stopping in Lynhaven', Cockburn wrote to him on 25 June, 'that the armaments may arrive before the accounts of it. I am decidedly of opinion that about the seat of Government and in the upper parts of the Chesapeake is where your operations may be commenced to most effect, but the country is in general in a horrible state; it only requires a little firm and steady conduct to have it completely at our mercy.'[65]

The Burning of Washington

Without the army Cockburn's opinions were academic. Its imminent arrival made decisions imperative. In Europe the war had ended in March 1814 and the British government had not been slow in redistributing its forces.[66] On 1 July Cochrane had to delay his departure from Bermuda on account of news from England 'that a considerable body of troops' was under orders to join him: two regiments from Gibraltar, several from Sicily, Lord Hill and 15,000 men from Bourdeaux and 'several regiments from England and Ireland'. A total force of 30,000 men seemed likely.[67] Cockburn was requested to secure guides, people to serve as pioneers, pilots of every description (for the Delaware and New York as well as the Chesapeake), horses for 2,000 dragoons and artillery, and all the small craft possible. The landings Cockburn made, Cochrane urged, should be 'more for the protection and desertion of the black population . . . with them armed and backed with 20,000 British troops, Mr Madison will be hurled from his Throne'.

Cochrane assumed the troops 'must be pointed against Philadephia, Baltimore and Washington'. He preferred Baltimore to be first, for, by landing to the north, the city would be cut off from the resources and support of the country east of the Susquehanna. On the other hand it was 'worthy of consideration if we would not derive an equal advantage by landing at Annapolis and march direct either upon Washington or Baltimore', by which good roads would be secured for the artillery.[68]

Cockburn committed his opinions on these points to paper on 17

July, placing first his own preference for an attack on Washington via Benedict.[69]

> It is, I am informed, only 44 or 45 miles from Washington & there is a high road between the two places which tho' hilly is good; it passes through Piscataway, no near to Fort Washington than four miles, which fortification is sixteen miles below the city of Washington, and is the only one the army would have to pass. I therefore most firmly believe that within 48 hours after the arrival in the Patuxent of such a force as you expect, the city of Washington might be possessed without difficulty or opposition of any kind.
>
> As you will observe by my public letter of this day the ships of the fleet could cover a landing at Benedict, [where] the safety of the ships and the smoothness of the water in the river would render us entirely independent of the weather in all our projected movements, an object of considerable importance when we recollect how fast the season is advancing to that period when the weather becomes so unsteady on all this coast. The army on its arrival would be sure of good quarters in the town of Benedict, and a rich country around it to afford the necessary immediate supplies, and as many horses as might be wanted to transport cannon etc., which advantages might certainly *now* be obtained without meeting with the slightest opposition or requiring any sacrifice from us whatever; and as I have quitted the Patuxent and on this account do not intend again to visit it until you arrive with the army or I hear further from you, I trust and believe everything will remain till then in the neighbourhood of that river exactly as I have now left it.
>
> The facility and rapidity, after its being first discovered, with which an army by landing at Benedict might possess itself of the capital—always so great a blow to the government of a country, as well on account of the resources as of the documents and records the invading army is almost sure to obtain thereby—must strongly, I should think, urge the propriety of the plan, and the more particularly as the other places you have mentioned will be more likely to fall after the occupation of Washington than that city would be after their capture.

Cockburn proceeded to examine the other places mentioned by Cochrane in turn: Annapolis, Baltimore, Philadelphia. But none of them was so accessible, or offered the advantages of a strike at Washington.[70] Cockburn's confidence in his own views was emphasized in a second *private* letter to Cochrane, also of 17 July. He was delighted at the news 'as to the mode in which *my friend* Jonathan is likely soon to be handled. The sooner this sensible kind of warfare begins the better it will be for us & the greater will be the advatanges we shall derive from it.'[71]

Cockburn proceeded to follow a strategy he had outlined to Cochrane.[72] Leaving four vessels to maintain a presence in the Patuxent, he took the troops that had arrived, with marines from the ships and a division of seamen, into the Potomac. With this force—about 500 men—he began a series of diversionary raids intended to distract immediate attention from the Patuxent. Disembarking first on the Maryland side, then on the Virginian, the country was overrun in places up to ten miles inland. Intent on attracting attention, he caused the greatest havoc possible, destroying military stores, seizing merchandise, obliging the inhabitants 'to furnish him with everything required as the price of his forebearance'.[73]

On 19 July Leonardtown, Maryland, where the American 36th Regiment was stationed, suffered first; the American regiment withdrew quietly, leaving stores that were promptly destroyed. Nomini Ferry, on the Virginia side, suffered two days later; militia stationed there were dispersed, and 130 refugee slaves and two schooners brought away. On 24 July they were back in Maryland, in St Clement's Creek; four schooners were taken, one destroyed; the only resistance was the discharge of two musket-shots at Cockburn's gig for which property on the culpable party's farm was destroyed. Two days later they had returned to Virginia, parading along the banks and burning six schooners in Machodoc Creek. On the 28th the squadron moved up above Blackstone's Island from where, next day, boats went into the Wicomico River; landings were made at Hamburgh and Chaptico from where 'a considerable quantity of tobacco' was removed. Dropping down to the entrance of the Yeocomico River, Virginia, on 2 August, a landing on the next day encountered the strongest opposition yet. After an engagement, the Americans withdrew, Cockburn and his force following to find them gathered on the heights of Kinsale; after heavier fighting, the marines scaled the high ground and the Americans again withdrew; two schooners, two batteries and storehouses were destroyed, five schooners, tobacco and flour were carried away. On the 7th a battery in the Coan River, a few miles below Yeocomico, was destroyed; three schooners and tobacco were brought off. Finally, on 12 and 15 August, crossing again to the north, landings were made in the St Mary's River; being received peacefully, the party—also peacefully—left.

In all, nine raids were made in 25 days. Mobility, concentration of force, and speed of striking, frustrated attempts to engage the force with overwhelming numbers. Cockburn revelled in the raids. So, he thought, did the men he commanded. Among the lower ranks, he noticed a change in 'general feeling' towards the war; the rate of desertion from raiding parties dwindled to nothing. Although it was possibly from fear of reprisal, Cockburn attributed it to pleasure at their task.[74]

Meanwhile, at Bermuda. Cochrane received news of American atrocities on the Canadian border. On the 18th he issued orders to all squadron commanders 'to destroy and lay waste' all towns and districts accessible to them from the coast.[75] A week later the first instalment of the main force arrived from Europe in a convoy commanded by Sir Pulteney Malcolm. On the 29th another convoy arrived, bringing the troops available for a coastal campaign to 3,700 men. With them came Major-General Sir Robert Ross, a 47-year-old veteran of Wellington's Peninsular staff. He had power of veto over deployment of the troops, total command of their operations on shore, and orders cautioning him against 'extended operations at a distance from the coast'. Cochrane's ideas were still not settled, an attack on Portsmouth, New Hampshire, or on Rhode Island being considered. However, the arrival, two days later, of Cockburn's secret despatch of 17 July directed his thoughts to the west. By the 29th a decision had been suspended, the troops informed, and a course set for the Chesapeake.[76]

Cochrane and Ross joined Cockburn in the Potomac on 14 August, in advance of the main convoy. Cockburn immediately went on board the flagship. The meeting was critical. There was disappointment: Ross came with but a quarter of the anticipated troops. Furthermore, neither Cochrane nor Ross was convinced that Washington should be the immediate objective. Ross in particular was determined not to place the army in unjustified danger, and behind him stood his staff, intent on taking their own decisions. Both Cochrane and Ross thought their force inadequate to march far inland; Cochrane was still for going north.

Cockburn started afresh, setting out his arguments, convincing those present that an attack on Washington was viable, even with only 4,000 men. He cited his own excursions that last month with only one-eighth the force; the defenceless state of the country; the pretext of attacking the flotilla; the accessibility of Washington from Benedict.[77] Almost certainly he mentioned Captain Barrie's expedition from the *Narcissus* on 15 June: his landing at Benedict with 40 marines and 30 of the black colonial corps; his advance from there to Marlborough, only 18 miles from Washington, and the simple dispersal of 360 regular American troops plus militia by some marines on their return down river.[78] Gradually the army came round. It is uncertain what decisions were taken at that first meeting, yet we do know that even Ross's staff acknowledged Washington was the ideal target, preferred to Baltimore 'on account of the greater political effect likely to result'.[79] Certainly they discussed the possibility of a two-stage plan. The army might land at Benedict and march up the right bank of the Patuxent to clear the area of militia and cover a boat attack on the American gunboat flotilla. The decision to try for Washington could be finalized at the completion of this first stage.[80]

Before that, Ross had to be convinced of the state of defence of the country thereabouts. At 5 a.m. the following morning Cockburn landed with Ross and a party of marines, moved inland from the St Mary's river and destroyed a factory several miles from the boats. They returned to the ships 18 hours later without a shot being fired. Ross was impressed. The decision to try the first stage in the two-part plan must have been agreed next day. That afternoon—16 August—Malcolm arrived with the main convoy, approaching the Potomac that evening. His transports were directed to press straight on for the Patuxent.[81]

The fleet, about twenty vessels including seven transports, sailed soon after 9 the following morning. Two small squadrons split off—one up the Potomac, the other towards Baltimore—both to provide diversions, cut communications and, in the case of the first, clear an escape route. By 6.30 p.m. the main force was at anchor in the mouth of the Patuxent. On the 18th, after shifting troops between vessels, the frigate transports, brigs and boats began to ascend the river. Captain Nourse in the *Severn*, having for the last month maintained a presence in the Patuxent, led the way with the only accurate chart. At 2 in the morning of the 19th the disembarkation began at Benedict. Twelve miles downstream Cockburn left the *Albion* at 4 a.m., being pulled in his barge to reach Benedict about mid-morning. There, landings continued throughout the day, covered by a gun-brig with 32-pounders moored on spring cables to command the surrounding land. The last troops were not landed until early on the 20th. Even then they waited. Ross finally appeared about 4 p.m. Only then did they march, heading north for Nottingham, parallel to the river.[82] Three hours and six miles later they halted for the night. They reached Lower Marlborough about midday and Nottingham towards the close of the 21st.

Cockburn meanwhile had organized the naval boat force: a miscellaneous collection of barges, boats, cutters, gigs and captured vessels in three divisions. Moving upstream, he endeavoured to keep the boats and tenders as nearly as possible abreast of the army so that he might communicate with Ross as occasion offered.[83] At Lower Marlborough, while the army rested, Cockburn again met the General, and once more at Nottingham. There they found that Commodore Barney's flotilla of gunboats had withdrawn still further, beyond a bend in the river above Nottingham known as Pig Point. Next morning, after landing marines to encircle the Americans on land, the flotilla was found drawn up in line astern. Aiming for boarding and immediate seizure, the boats pulled hard for the leading vessel, a sloop bearing Barney's pendant. As they approached, however, the sloop was seen to be on fire, and proceeded to blow up as they drew near. Beyond the other gunboats were also abandoned and exploding, 16 in all. Just the last, the seventeenth, was left to be taken prize. Thirteen merchant schooners were also there, sheltering behind the gunboats. Some were taken, some burned.[84]

From Nottingham, Ross with the army started to move away from the river on the road for Upper Marlborough. To maintain contact, that afternoon Cockburn retired downstream with a division of his boats to anchor off Mount Calvert, from there the better 'to confer on our future operations with the major-general'. From there he reported the achievements of the day to Cochrane and it was there, that evening, that Ross's aide found him to report the safe arrival of the army at Upper Marlborough.[85]

The first stage in the two-part plan had been successfully completed. Ross was to hold the army at Upper Marlborough until 2 p.m. on 23 August. To have advanced further would have exposed the army's rear. At that point he needed to know whether the navy's boat expedition had been successful, and Cockburn cannot have failed to advise him of events at Pig Point as soon as the affair was settled. Next morning, however, the question remained: whether to advance or not. Ross has been accused of wavering.[86] But intelligence suggested an American force 'collecting in front was very strongly posted'.[87] Ross accordingly convened an army staff conference to examine each aspect of the situation. The staff conference was obviously split, the weight of opinion inclined towards discrete retirement.

At this point Cockburn again entered what was now an army matter. Two aides, keen on advance and hoping that Cockburn might repeat his previous contemptuous observations of the American army, set off to fetch him (one was the young deputy quartermaster-general, Lieutenant George de Lacy Evans). The river was only five miles back. 'Having submitted to him their views and wishes on the subject', the two aides proposed Cockburn 'should mount a led horse they had for the purpose brought with them in order to facilitate his getting to the bivouac, to

tender to the Major-General his services and presence on the occasion'.[88]
Cockburn promptly obliged. At the conference his comments had the
desired effect. Ross decided to advance. Cockburn offered to accompany
him, probably to command seamen and marines brought from the river.
The offer was accepted.

Later, in 1829, Evans claimed credit for the army in getting
Cockburn to the conference. He did so to counter the excessive degree of
responsibility being given to Cockburn for the capture of Washington.[89]
However, Cockburn was convinced that he had 'brought the Major-
General to concur with him', and was well aware that the plan followed
was in outline the one that he had proposed to Cochrane in mid-July. In
arguing for advance, moreover, Cockburn did so in defiance of the view
of his own immediate superior. A note from Cochrane reached Cockburn
while he was actually in conference with Ross. Congratulating him on
the destruction of the gunboat flotilla, Cochrane thought that 'as this
matter is ended, the sooner the army gets back the better'.[90] Yet—
perhaps intentionally—he failed to send a formal order. Cockburn chose
to ignore the note.

Nevertheless, it was Ross who commanded the army. Cockburn
accompanied him only as a volunteer. On 23 August Cockburn was
sharply aware of the difference. His letter to Cochrane, immediately
following the conference at Upper Marlborough, and written from the
army headquarters, accentuates his official subordination to Ross.

> Sir, I wrote you a hasty note from my boat yesterday as I thought it would
> be a great relief to you to know of the flotilla being actually disposed of. I
> learnt in the evening that the General had occupied the place. I came here
> this morning to consult with him and learn his future plans and I find he
> is determined (in consequence of the information he has received & what
> he has observed of the enemy) to push on towards Washington, which I
> have confident hopes he will give a good account of. I shall accompany
> him & of course afford him every assistance in my power.[91]

Cockburn's assistance with the navy was to prove of value. Most marines
from ships were left in command of Upper Marlborough. But the
marine artillery and seamen, providing human haulage for the guns,
accompanied the army. The rocket brigade of marine artillery, the
'colonial marines' (the former slaves) and a company of regular marine
infantry all played significant parts at the battle of Bladensburg.
Cockburn's presence, his radiant enthusiasm for the task in hand, must
have made a major contribution to morale. Ross, in his report to Lord

Plate 2. The Capitol building in Washington after the raid by the British army in 1814. A lithograph based on a sketch by the miniature painter Chittenden. (Library of Congress)

Bathurst, Secretary for War, later acknowledged his debt: 'to Rear-Admiral Cockburn, who suggested the attack upon Washington, and who accompanied the army, I confess the greatest obligation for his cordial co-operation and advice'.[92]

The march on Washington, the destruction of its key buildings, and the retirement to Benedict on 29 August are well known. From Upper Marlborough in the afternoon of the 23rd, the troops advanced another five miles, an American corps of about 1,200 men retiring as they proceeded. Twice that distance was managed next morning, to reach Bladensburg—a bridging point for the eastern branch of the Potomac—about midday. The American army was discovered in formation commanding the high ground across the river. In spite of considerable fatigue, the British troops coming up were arranged for an immediate attack on both wings and the centre. The Americans were in some strength, estimated at 8,000 infantry, 300–400 cavalry and over 200 pieces of artillery. Even so a flank was turned and the Americans fled.

Cockburn reported that only 1,500 British troops were involved. The rockets fired by the marine artillery seem to have created alarm if not damage. Supervising their launching only 140 yards from the enemy lines, which maintained a heavy fire on the launchers, he remained at the thick of the action. A musket ball is said to have torn off a stirrup without touching him or his horse. A marine attempting repairs was killed as he stood by the saddle.[93] Lieutenant James Scott, who stood beside Cockburn's horse and involuntarily ducked his head, recalled his reproof: 'Don't bob your head, Scott; it looks bad'.[94] Ross lost 250 men that day, killed and wounded; the enemy fewer, but including Commodore Barney who had commanded the flotilla of gunboats.[95]

A 'broad and straight' road led from the battlefield to Washington. Ross determined to push on with the minimum of rest. The army reached the city's outskirts by eight that evening, 24 August. Ross had no time to waste. While the remainder made camp at the end of the turnpike, Ross, Cockburn and about 1,500 men immediately pressed on to the Capitol buildings. One of the first houses sheltered snipers, but there was little further resistance. All but civilians had mainly deserted the city. As they entered, the Americans themselves set fire to their dockyard within which a frigate and sloop also burned. Other government buildings were simply abandoned. Parties of British troops were thus able to tour and burn unopposed the Capitol—including the Senate house and House of Representatives—the Treasury and War Office buildings, 'the President's Palace', the 'Arsenal', two ropewalks, and surviving buildings in the dockyard. A 'great fire in the direction of Washington' was seen that night from the mouth of the Patuxent.[96] Government property valued at one and half million dollars was destroyed; in addition over 200 cannon, 500 barrels of powder, and 100,000 musket cartridges were removed.[97]

A remarkable feature of the occupation was the respect paid to private property. Only government buildings and those sheltering snipers suffered. Cockburn himself would have burned the whole city, considering the total annihilation of Washington would have removed the seat of government to New York where it would have been more subject to opinion in 'the Northern and Federal States' which were adverse to the war with England. He was certainly present at the destruction of the Capitol Building and President's Palace, and particularly desired the destruction of the buildings of *The National Intelligencer*, the government newspaper, whose type and printing materials he had destroyed.[98] Ross, however, sanctioned only the burning of public buildings.[99]

Within twenty-four hours the British army had begun it withdrawal. Taking the same route by which it came, after a forced march the army made Upper Marlborough late on 26 August. Next day Cockburn, the seamen, marines and walking wounded went on board the boats and tenders in the Patuxent near Nottingham.[100] Meanwhile, the troops marched for Benedict where they began re-embarkation in the evening of 29 August. Although deserters and scavengers looted in its wake, the officers of the army met no opposition throughout the withdrawal. At 6 a.m. on 31 August the squadron weighed anchor and began moving down river. Between 2 and 4 September it paused under Drum Point. The greater part then sailed for Tangier Island, the troops to recuperate, the vessels to replenish.[101]

Jubilation reigned among officers in the squadron those early days in September. In April 1813 the Americans had symbolically burned the parliament buildings at York, capital of Upper Canada. Now the British had proved the fabric of American government was also open to violation. As Cockburn later pointed out, the expedition had been made with only 4,000 to 5,000 men in only nine days in the heart of enemy territory; that 'for the extent of ground passed over, the importance of its objects, and the mischief done the enemy—ashore and afloat—in so short a space of time is scarcely perhaps to be paralleled'.[102] The Prime Minister, Lord Liverpool, informed Cochrane that 'nothing could have been more complete & brilliant'. The Secretary for War, Lord Bathurst, complimented him on his 'active and enterprizing spirit'.[103] But in the long run it was Cockburn's name that was made. 'Full justice is done by the whole country to the judgement with which you suggested, and the activity and gallantry with which you co-operated in, the movement on Washington', Croker wrote to him on 30 September, 'an exploit which for moral effect both in America and in England has never been excelled'.[104]

The Attack on Baltimore

Recovering quickly from the fatigue of the march, Cockburn was keen to attack Baltimore where there was also a dockyard and ships being built. A 'dash against that place' would, he argued, take that city as much by surprise as it had Washington. Cochrane was less sure, being still interested in assaults elsewhere. However, at Tangier Island Cochrane was to learn that the approaching equinoctial new moon (and its related tides) made it unsafe for some vessels to navigate the mouth of the Chesapeake immediately. He and Ross reconsidered. On 7 September Cockburn was summoned to hear their revised view. Although sufficient time had elapsed for defences to be strengthened, it was nevertheless agreed that an attempt against Baltimore should be made.[105] Cockburn would accompany the expedition in overall command of a brigade of 600 seamen, a battalion of marines (those from the ships) and the colonial black marines.

Retracing its course, the expedition made the mouth of the Patapsco on 11 September. Cockburn, in the leading vessel with Ross, chose 'North Point' for the landing. That night, troops were ferried up to the vessels close to the landing place, where they disembarked at first light on the 12th. Frigates, sloops, bomb-vessels and a rocket-ship passed by on their way to bombard the fort commanding the water approach to Baltimore. Cochrane was to join them later.

Cockburn landed with the army on the 12th. There was no opposition, but it was evident the Americans were 'in a state of activity and alarm'. Some light horsemen were cut off, taken by the advancing troops, and some freshly made entrenchments were discovered simply abandoned. About five miles from the landing place, Cockburn and Ross with the advance guard of 50 to 60 men were some way ahead of the main column. Cockburn recalled pointing out to Ross that their forces had become separated. On his own excursions in Virginia and Maryland he had always concentrated his force and had skirmishers spread along the flanks of the main column. Within a hundred yards his fears were realized. At a wooded turning in the road, an ambush occurred. Unsupported by the main force, 'there was . . . nothing left for it but to dash forward against them, returning their fire as quickly as possible to induce them to suppose our whole force to be at hand'.[106] The charge had the desired effect, the Americans breaking and running. Ross had turned back to order up more troops when one of the last 'straggling shots' hit him in the arm and entered his chest. He died on a stretcher on the way back to the river.[107]

Cockburn carried on, with Colonel Brooke in command of the army. No further opposition was encountered until within five miles of Baltimore. But there, an estimated six thousand men with six pieces of artillery and some hundred cavalry were drawn up in dense order across the road, partly sheltered by a wood and lining a strong paling fence about chest high that stretched either side at right angles to the road. Both flanks appear to have been protected by creeks and inlets of the Patapsco and Back rivers which approach each other at this point. Brooke made the necessary dispositions under cannon fire, and ordered an immediate advance. Some light troops were ordered to encircle the American left flank. As soon as the range became possible, the advancing troops came under heavy musket fire but maintained their impetus, eventually breaking through and over the palings. Within fifteen minutes, as at Bladensburg, the Americans had been routed. Seamen with small arms and the marines formed the whole left flank of the British army. The slaughter was particularly heavy. Brooke estimated American casualties at above 500. British losses were almost as bad: 41 killed, 261 wounded from the army; 14 killed and 92 wounded from the naval contingents.

The army camped that night in the wood from which they had just driven the Americans. Within the trees a 'Meeting House' had formed the American headquarters. Brooke and Cockburn now made it theirs. Next morning, 13 September, leaving a guard at the Meeting House, they advanced further. American cavalry showed themselves occasionally, hovering about, watching the line of march. About 10 a.m. they reached Baltimore's outer defences, about a mile and a half from the city. Brooke, accompanied by Cockburn, was able to reconnoitre at leisure. The city was surrounded by a series of hills upon which a string of palisaded redoubts had been constructed, each one connected by breastworks. Chinkapin Hill, which lay directly in front of the advancing army and over which their road passed, was the most strongly fortified. Overlooking the palisades and double ditches were batteries of artillery from which advancing troops would find little protection, the hill's slopes being clear of any cover. Moreover, Chinkapin Hill, so they were informed, was defended by at least 15,000 men, including all the seamen from the ships in Baltimore harbour and militias from Philadelphia and Washington. To Brooke and Cockburn there seemed no immediate likelihood of an attack from the Americans. On the other hand, the only chance of their 4,000 men storming the hill was by surprise attack at night. Hoping for diversionary movements from Cochrane, they planned to storm the hill at midnight.[108]

Cochrane, meanwhile had himself run into difficulties with the frigates and bomb-vessels. On that morning of the 13th the British ships began their bombardment of Fort McHenry which protected the entrance to Baltimore harbour. The fort stood on the western point of the entrance and shells from the bomb-vessels appeared to be successful in hitting their target.[109] Yet there was also a battery set on the eastern point, at the Star Fort, which was also returning their fire. Even if both forts were silenced, there seemed little prospect of penetrating the harbour, the mouth of which behind a shallow bar was 'entirely obstructed' by a barrier of sunken vessels. Behind them, moreover, was a squadron of gunboats, with the harbour sides fortified, the left one bearing a battery of 'several heavy guns'. By the evening Cochrane had therefore abandoned hope of reaching the city, still two miles beyond the harbour mouth, and could offer little hope of helping Brooke and Cockburn.

That night was extremely dark with torrential rain. To provide what diversion he could, Cochrane sent off 20 boats for an attack up the 'Ferry Branch' of the Patapsco. In the darkness and rain, eleven boats pulled by mistake for the harbour mouth, only to discover their mistake and return in confusion to the ships. The other nine, including a rocket-boat and launches, opened fire on the shore some distance above Fort McHenry and drew American troops to the beach. With only 128 men, however, they did not land.

The token attack was in fact unnecessary. Still with thoughts of moving elsewhere, Cochrane had sent warnings to Cockburn and Brooke. 'It is impossible for the ships to render you any assistance', he informed Cockburn, 'the town is so far within the forts'.

> It is for Colonel Broke [sic] to consider under such circumstances whether he has force sufficient to defeat so large a number as it is said the enemy has collected, say 20,000 strong more or less in number, and to take the town. Without this can be done, it will only be throwing the men's lives

away and prevent us from going upon other services; at any rate a very considerable loss must ensue, and, as the enemy is daily gaining strength, his loss, let it be ever so great, cannot be equally felt.[110]

Before Chinakapin Hill, the rain was just as heavy. Brooke and Cockburn knew that their attack would incur losses, probably heavy ones, and Cochrane's letters made clear 'the onus of preventing other services was to be thrown upon any such loss'.[111] Brooke took the logical decision: to retire immediately. Next morning Cochrane also called off the bombardment of the forts at the harbour mouth.

The retirement was steady and dignified. The first of the British troops began their march back to the Meeting House at 1.30 that morning. There, the American prisoners were sorted, Brooke taking about 200 'persons of the best families in the city'. After resting through the heat of midday, they marched another three miles late in the afternoon, only reaching North Point to re-embark early on 15 September.[112]

Cockburn regarded the expedition as a military failure. Having hoped to go straight from the Patuxent into the Patapsco, his reminiscences harp repeatedly on the week's delay at Tangier Island. In his view, it was the indecision of Cochrane and Ross which had given the Americans time to prepare their defences around Baltimore. He was impatient of Ross's lack of confidence in the Americans' disorganization, impatient too of the time taken for an army to make ready for such expeditions. Whereas the navy was accustomed to preparing for battle in a matter of hours, the recuperation and preparations of an army took days if not weeks.

However, Cochrane, Melville and the British government judged it by other standards. 'Though the attempt against Baltimore did not succeed to the full extent of what the General appeared to have contemplated', Melville complimented Cochrane on 25 October, 'I wish that the accounts you have sent of our proceedings in Canada were of the same description. They are neither honourable to the character of our arms nor creditable to the commander as was so conspicuously the case at Baltimore'.[113]

In London, indeed, operations were judged not so much for the achievement of the objectives set by their commanders in the field, as by their contribution to the achievement of the requisite peace settlement. Cochrane was aware of this. He termed the Baltimore expedition a 'demonstration', and stressed the defeat of the American army at the

Meeting House, the alarm and disturbance created throughout the area of Baltimore, and the Americans' destruction of their own shipping, public buildings and a ropewalk. 'Demonstrations' of this nature were assumed to undermine public support for hostilities in a democracy supposedly the source of the government's determination to prosecute war.[114] And in September 1814 such demonstrations were highly desirable. Peace negotiations had been under way at Ghent since early in the year. Seen from London, the Baltimore expedition reinforced the Washington effect, creating a pattern of incursions of which the government approved. It was this approval which hastened Cochrane's withdrawal from Patapsco: he had received assent from London for his long-projected attack on New Orleans.

Cumberland Island

From the first, an attack on New Orleans had a high priority in Cochrane's strategy for undermining the United States' will to wage war. At the end of July 1814 Melville talked of sending 7,000 men from England specifically for this attack.[115] Off North America this information made immediate preparations essential. To speed the construction of flat-bottomed boats for the new expedition, Cochrane sailed for Halifax on 19 September. Sir Pulteney Malcolm remained in the Chesapeake to command the blockade and troopships until 14 October, when he departed with the troops for a rendezvous off Jamaica. Cockburn meanwhile sailed for Bermuda,[116] where he received news of 'the sensation' which had been 'created at home by our Washington operations'.[117]

From London, in August, Melville warned that troops in large numbers were still not available. The home militia had been disbanded; a large force, including Wellington's army, was still in Flanders; and 'the experience of twenty years of war on an extended scale has taught the government of this country to have no more irons in the fire than what we can continue to keep red hot'.[118] But by October the news in America was more promising; in any case, in North America preparations were too far advanced to simply abandon; Cochrane was determined to go ahead.[119]

Gathering what men he could from the Chesapeake, Cockburn was to make a diversionary attack on the coast of Georgia, help stimulate a rising by the Indians of the Creek confederation, recruit negroes into a military force, and raid along the coast disrupting trade and

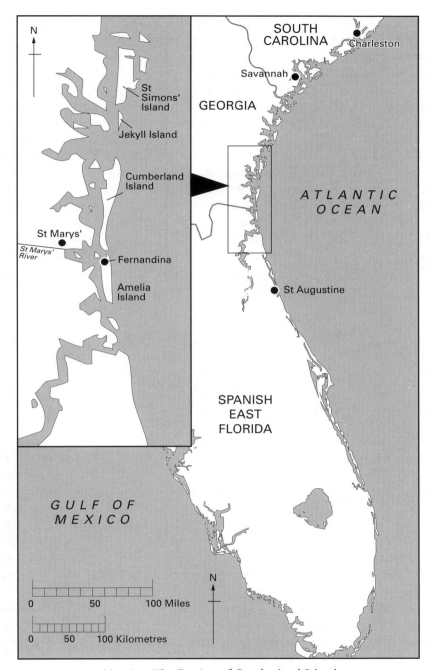

Map 8. The Region of Cumberland Island

communication. As a base for these operations he was to occupy
Cumberland Island—the most southerly territory of the United States
off the coast of Georgia, conveniently close to Spanish East Florida where
official interests opposed United States expansion. In conjunction with
the expedition to the Mississippi, there were hopes that Cockburn's
diversion might also favour a rising among the Gulf coast Indians. The
United States might be expelled from the Gulf coast region
completely.[120]

Cochrane's plans were not to work out because his strategy was too
grand for the forces at his disposal. Men for Cockburn's minor diversion
were scarce. For his initial armed force he had to collect marines from
the ships in the Chesapeake, and the colonial black marines—the
refugee slaves trained into a regiment. It was thus 14 January before
Cockburn in the *Albion* reached Cumberland Island.[121] Captain Philip
Somerville as senior officer had occupied the island on 10 January. Three
days later 600 men had crossed to the mainland, captured an American
battery at Point Petre and that night occupied the town of St Mary's.[122]

A key port for the south-east of Georgia and North Florida, St Mary's
stood at the mouth of the St Mary's River which marked the border with
Spanish East Florida. An entrepôt for the Spanish as well as the
American hinterland, the town's main trade commodities were cotton
and slaves. An American law of 1808 had prohibited the import of
slaves. Even so, they were now smuggled, St Mary's remaining 'the most
important distribution centre for smuggled slaves on the south-eastern
American coast'.[123] It was therefore considered the best place for
securing refugee slaves seeking freedom.

Taking charge on the 14th, Cockburn sent ships to blockade
Charleston and Savannah, and boats up the St Mary's River—later to
bring down a new gunboat and an East Indiaman, the *Countess of
Harcourt*, hidden some thirty miles upstream.[124] They also started
shipping off 'great quantities of cotton and other goods'.[125] In all,
Cockburn found he had 900 men: the remnants of two battalions of
marines from Canada, the corps of refugee slaves from the Chesapeake,
two companies of the 2nd West India Regiment (black recruits with
English officers), some marine artillery, and a division of armed seamen.
They had little to fear in St Mary's; it had only about 600 inhabitants
who had organized their own surrender, disregarding their military
defenders. But the American army grew steadily stronger on the outskirts. It was Cockburn's intention to hold the town for as long as
possible, to draw American reinforcements in that direction.[126]

However, about 20 January he learned from Cochrane of the defeat of the main expedition against New Orleans—a 'reverse so little expected'. There now seemed little reason to risk being overrun or driven from the town. Removing cannon, blowing up fortifications, the British marines and seamen withdrew to Cumberland Island on 23 January.[127]

In spite of the reverse at New Orleans, the grand strategy for war in the south remained the same. Cockburn still expected to co-operate with Indian risings in western Florida, southern Alabama and Louisiana. 'I expect to be joined by a body of Indians', he wrote to Croker at the Admiralty on 28 January. 'As yet however there is no appearance of them. I think the *savage* Cockburn, as I am termed among my Yankee neighbours, when joined by the Indians will create no small consternation in the country. . . .'[128]

Some such assistance was now essential. 'To be sure my force is not very respectable, having only a few hundred marines and the rest blacks'; but these, he claimed, were 'good enough to oppose the Yankees' especially as 'we now understand bush fighting as well as him'.[129] For the time being operations were small scale. Three vessels were sent to attack St Simons and Jekyll islands up the coast. The main camp was made to the south of Cumberland Island, Cockburn taking over the principal building, Dungeness House, for his headquarters. This was fortified, surrounded by an entrenchment with a large breastwork, over a quarter of a mile long, between the house and the coastal marsh. Partly to occupy the men, but also in expectation of quantities of prize goods, 'an immense wharf' was begun at Dungeness Place. The aim was to hold the island for the rest of the war 'for a safe depot, and a position from whence to carry on operations against any part of the southern states of America'. First Savannah, then Charleston, would be attacked. Meanwhile Cockburn awaited more troops and an influx of refugee slaves with whom to swell the ranks of the black colonial corps.[130]

These hopes were not disappointed. On the contrary, the influx of slaves seeking freedom far exceeded expectations. Cochrane's proclamation of 2 April 1814 inviting slaves to desert to the British had been posted here in the south too, even in Fernandina on Amelia Island, Spanish East Florida territory, immediately south of Cumberland Island. Now the British had established a military post, the slaves took advantage of it. By 4 February Cockburn was inundated; he needed more marine clothing and to ship as many refugees as possible off to Bermuda. By the end of March, 1,483 black supernumeraries were registered on the books of ships in the squadron. With more than 280 deaths, the total inflow was possibly more than 1,700 persons. Of these, 702 were said to have come from Cumberland Island itself, 'the scene of one of the most extraordinarily effective mass military emancipations ever seen in the United States'.[131]

Cockburn was now accustomed to the practical problems of managing such refugees. Since Cochrane's proclamation, whole families had arrived together; now, whole plantations were enticed to the island. Inevitably, as well as able-bodied males, they included females, the young, the old, the sick and infirm. Weakened by their journeys, sickness spread easily among them and deaths were common. On Cumberland Island about four died each day; over two months, perhaps ten per cent of the total.[132]

On top of debilitating infections was a frustrating maladjustment to their new situation. At Bermuda Cockburn had tried to treat them as English subjects, encouraging them to earn money with which to purchase their needs. Yet the women in particular assumed they would be fed and clothed just as they had been by their owners. That their new freedom placed upon them a new obligation to earn their keep did not occur to them. Such adaptations took time. Meanwhile, discontent due to thwarted expectations gave rise to disturbances, at which Cockburn despaired. 'These foolish and ever discontented people . . . appear not to understand the advantages of, nor indeed what comforts they can buy, with the daily pay.' He was obliged to feed and clothe most of them on ships as supernumeraries, subject if necessary to military discipline. At Cumberland Island, from 4 February, all arrivals not willing or fit to serve as soldiers or seamen were immediately sent to tenders lying near the camp. As opportunities presented themselves they were transferred into line-of-battleships off the island; from these they were discharged into vessels sailing for Bermuda.[133]

In spite of such attendant problems, to swell the colonial corps Cockburn had parties of men visiting estates along the coast reminding slaves of Cochrane's offer of service in the British forces or emigration to a British colony. Early on, possibly by mistake, a party visited Amelia Island, which was Spanish territory. In consequence Cockburn received a request, dated 31 January, from the Governor of East Florida for the return to their owners of Spanish slaves. Pointing out that the Spanish owners had to look after their own property, Cockburn assured the Governor that his officers would not actually assist Spanish slaves to escape, that very few such people had in fact appeared on Cumberland Island, but that he would not return those by force against their will. He maintained that Cumberland Island was now governed as a British possession and that the laws of Great Britain did not recognize slavery.[134]

A legal argument thereupon developed. The Governor, Dr Sebastian Kindelan, maintained that the refusal to return refugee slaves was worse than an act of war, being a failure to respect the property of passive farmers. 'That they may take back such as are willing to follow them is the same as a refusal to deliver them up. What slave, when it is left to his own choice, will voluntarily return into slavery?'[135] Although the Governor threatened to elevate the 'theft' to the status of an international incident, Cockburn declined to explain his position further.[136] Nevertheless, the next six days were spent developing his case, delving into his own experience and law books to produce a statement of precedent, practice and belief which he submitted to Cochrane for approval as policy for all captains of ships serving on that coast.[137] Later at Bermuda, from where most refugee slaves were sent to Halifax, those from East Florida were kept together to facilitate an equitable settlement, but their number was far exceeded by the number of claims. Cockburn accordingly believed that slaves had taken the opportunity presented by the British presence to flee in all directions, and that the Spanish incorrectly supposed they had all gone to Cumberland Island.[138]

Cockburn's quarrel with the Spanish was quickly overtaken by another with the Americans. The Treaty of Ghent had been ratified on 24 December 1814. Although Cockburn learned of it from an American officer on 25 February, he continued loading and sending off prize goods, receiving Spanish and American refugees and training recruits.[139] Not until 1 March did he acknowledge receipt of orders to cease hostilities. Four days later two United States commissioners arrived to negotiate the return of American public and private property. The first article of the Treaty of Ghent agreed the return of all territory, places and property seized by either party during the hostilities or following the treaty. It specifically required the return of property belonging to places occupied by the enemy at the date of exchange of ratifications, on 17 February.[140] To prove the truth of their claims, the commissioners showed Cockburn the terms of the treaty as printed in *The National Intelligencer*. First, Cockburn challenged the status of the newspaper as an authoritative document. In the absence of an official document, he could only suggest the commissioners make a transcript, certifying it was in their opinion a true copy of the original treaty. The commissioners then demanded the return of all public and private property taken or received on Cumberland Island. Again, they were challenged. Cockburn considered the first article of the treaty to refer only to property belonging to place of occupation on the date of ratification. Cochrane arrived on 8 March and approved Cockburn's narrow interpretation. In consequence 81 slaves were all that was left to their owners on the island.[141]

The evacuation was completed by 18 March. At Bermuda, regardless of his rebuff at New Orleans, Cochrane remained confident of the correctness of his southern strategy. 'Had the war continued . . . by following such active operations upon the vulnerable part of the enemy's shores, he [the enemy] would have been soon obliged to sue for peace.'[142]

Cockburn's own benefit from the war was more honourable than material. Although many American vessels were taken prize,[143] as his brother observed in January 1815, 'so many flags have to share with him that his portion will be little worth having. On this station (loaded as it is with junior flag officers) it is almost impossible that any pecuniary advantage can be reaped by any admiral except the commander-in-chief.'[144] Cockburn became a trustee for the distribution of prize monies in which he had a share. Such were other claims, litigation was still going on in 1821.[145] Yet, as Cockburn's brother continued, 'in point of fame, George, thank God! has had a good harvest'. His decisiveness was later compared to that of Nelson.[146] Public acknowledgement of his achievements was marked on 2 January 1815 by his nomination as a Knight Commander of the Military Order of the Bath—it was a title he had long desired. He sailed for England on 8 April 1815.

CHAPTER 4

Napoleon and St Helena 1815–1816

Napoleon's escape from Elba marred the peace to which Cockburn expected to return in May 1815. His flag was retained in commission at Portsmouth and, though he himself returned to his house in Cavendish Square, London, there was every prospect of immediate service. Waterloo on 18 June seemed to settle the war, but on 15 July Napoleon surrendered to Maitland in the *Bellerophon* off Rochefort and, soon after, Cockburn learned of the task to be his. On 21 June he had been made commander-in-chief at the Cape of Good Hope. This, as much as his known 'energy of character', accounted for orders issued to him at the end of July. St Helena, to which the British government determined to exile Napoleon, was within the Cape station. Cockburn was the appropriate officer to convey and secure him there. Yet on this occasion Lord Bathurst, as Secretary of State, and the Board of Admiralty laid more than normal stress on the personal qualities necessary for the task. The Prince Regent required Napoleon's confinement to be no more severe than was necessary to his perfect security; indulgence, on the other hand, could permit no betrayal 'into any improvident relaxation' of duty. There could be no repeat of the Elba escape. Precision of judgement was at a premium, and the 'zeal, ability and discretion' revealed by Cockburn on earlier occasions were 'the best pledges that can be given for the due performance of the Prince Regent's intentions'.[1]

Bathurst's instructions were conveyed to Cockburn by the Admiralty on 31 July. He was to hoist his flag in the 74-gun *Northumberland* at Spithead, take in convoy two troopships carrying a battalion of the 53rd Regiment and a detachment of artillery, and to rendezvous with the *Bellerophon* in Plymouth Sound where he was to take on board Napoleon

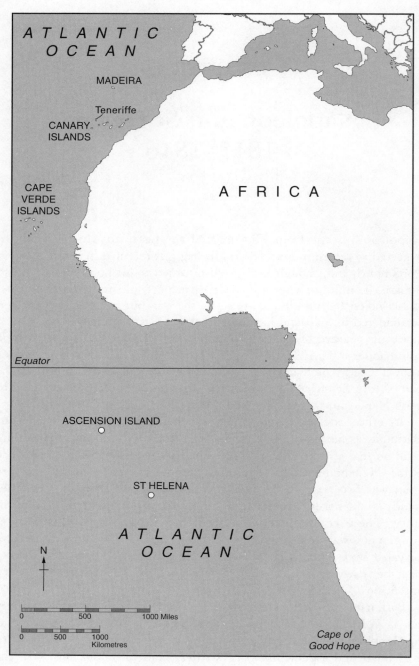

Map 9. The South Atlantic

and his suite. From there, in company with seven more vessels and a storeship, he was to convey the former emperor to St Helena.[2] Memoranda from Bathurst detailed the precautions Cockburn was to take regarding the luggage, valuables and money of the whole French party; measures for the security of Napoleon once at St Helena; and the channels along which correspondence with Napoleon was to pass.[3]

These instructions were to shape Cockburn's management of Napoleon and his entourage. However it was the enforcement of compliance with the spirit of these regulations that was to be the real test of Cockburn. Napoleon was an emperor defeated, yet still regarded as emperor by his followers, treated by them as such, and accustomed to the servility due to one. To check his pretensions, reduce him to submmission and control his conduct—all without losing his co-operation—demanded a confidence amounting to an insurmountable sense of superiority. For from the first, Napoleon posed repeated minor, but important, problems of personal control. For him the battle was now one of wits—conflict at a psychological level. But it was conflict at a level at which Cockburn also excelled. Speed of thought, word and deed were his strength. At no time on the voyage did Cockburn lose control, and on no occasion was he reduced to discourtesy or emotion. At St Helena, though at times indirect conflict revived, it was quickly checked. The successful internment of Napoleon at St Helena was thus as much the product of Cockburn's capacity for managing the man, as of the government's list of instructions.

Mastering 'The General'

Management was essential even before the voyage commenced. The *Northumberland* had been at Portsmouth only 48 hours when Cockburn arrived from London on 2 August. Stores and equipment were still being loaded, the crew being obliged to work through the night to stow them away. Next morning, when Captain Charles Ross[4] ordered her to be unmoored, the crew grumbled with discontent at a new commission, and six men were confined. After the first anchor was raised, Cockburn addressed them, pointing out that the ship would be relieved when peace was arranged; but in the meantime he would consider any applications men might make in the proper way for exchange on grounds of ill-health, wounds or long service. He then sent them to their duties, to which they went 'cheerfully and properly'. Even the six in confinement protested their innocence, assured him of their readiness,

Plate 3.   Napoleon on board the *Bellerophon* in 1815 with Grand Maréchal
Comte de Bertrand and Captain Pointkowski, by C. Eastlake. Based on
one of Napoleon's occasional appearances for the public.
(National Maritime Museum)

loyalty and inclination to do as required. He had them released and they resumed their duties in the 'best manner possible'.[5]

In Torbay, on 6 August, the *Bellerophon*, *Tonnant* (carrying the flag of Lord Keith, commander-in-chief in the Channel) and the frigate *Eurotas* were unexpectedly sighted off Berry Head. It transpired that Keith had hurriedly removed the *Bellerophon* from Plymouth to Torbay to avoid the threat of a writ of *habeas corpus* taken out to require Napoleon to appear in evidence at a trial in London.

After conferring in the afternoon, Cockburn and Keith went on board the *Bellerophon* to inform Napoleon of his removal to the *Northumberland* next day. Napoleon protested, challenging the right of the British government to dispose of him as they wished. Keith and Cockburn simply insisted on the necessity for them to obey their orders. Cockburn returned next morning and (as required by Bathurst) examined the baggage of each member of the French party to remove arms and valuables that might be used to purchase assistance;[6] 4,000 napoleons were transferred to Captain Maitland to be sent to the British Treasury. Finally, about midday Cockburn and Keith again waited on Napoleon to accompany him to the *Northumberland*. Popular interest in him was intense. The waters about the ships were crowded with boats from shore carrying sightseers. After a long wait, he eventually appeared on the deck of the *Bellerophon* where, as he took his departure, dead silence prevailed—so 'deeply the attention of every man must have been rivetted'. Descending to the *Northumberland*'s barge, he took his place between Keith and Cockburn. The 28 members of the French party which accompanied Napoleon to the *Northumberland* included Grand Marechal Comte de Bertrand, General Comte de Montholon, both their wives, Comte de Las Cases, General Gourgaud and also fourteen servants and five children.[7] They posed an immediate accommodation problem; all were found quarters, but not without difficulty. The ladies and their families received adequate space and privacy, but each of the other members of the suite also asked for, and expected, a separate cabin. For a day the party settled in, the *Northumberland* lying-to while a squadron of one frigate, six brigs and sloops joined her. On 9 August they sailed for St Helena.

Occurrences on the voyage concerning Napoleon were fully documented by Cockburn in a diary. This, including minutes of his conversations, were copied by his secretary, J.R. Glover, who himself kept a diary embellished with information derived from Cockburn's. The latter's diary has been published twice, Glover's three times, but none of these printed versions are entirely trustworthy.[8] Words vary between the two publications of Cockburn's diary; and doubt must always attach to the accuracy of Glover's account as Cockburn himself observed that Glover copied minutes of his conversations and other documents inaccurately. These printed versions can, however, be checked against copies of both diaries that have survived in manuscript, and these with copies of minutes corrected by Cockburn after he discovered Glover's inaccuracy.[9] The latter were sent to Melville and survive in the National Library of Scotland.

Cockburn compiled his minutes and diary partly, as a naval man, out of habit, partly to keep Melville and other members of the government informed of events. He simply requested that his account 'not be made so generally known as to risk its getting into the public papers', particularly while he was still at St Helena. Cockburn was aware that he had an opportunity, unique to an Englishman, to record the impressions and news of a man who had kept Europe in a state of war for two decades. Others appreciated this opportunity too. Warren Hastings observed that it was worth Cockburn's while 'to keep a log of all the Napoleonisms, good, bad and indifferent (for all are character), that escape from his passenger during the voyage'.[10] It became Cockburn's determination 'to note down . . . every particular this extraordinary man tells'. He did more than this, adding his observations on Napoleon's behaviour, attitudes and state of mind, and occasionally his own opinion of Napoleon's credibility. His charge was thus treated as a subject of study; the diary was a report of his findings. From it emerges the relationship Cockburn formed with Napoleon, the tenor of which was marked by the periodic checks Cockburn placed on his charge's conduct. From it we thus appreciate the means by which Cockburn came to manage Napoleon, and obliged him to accept the new terms of his existence.

Cockburn can have had no illusions as to the challenge this management problem presented. He was well aware of the ruthlessness of the man: in 1813 he had described him as 'a despot who has deluged the world with blood and invariably caused misery and desolation wherever he has been enabled to infuse his . . . influence'.[11] He quickly learned his arrogance. As an emperor, Napoleon did not think he should be confined at all: their first encounter, at which he had learned his fate, had generated anger, the examination of baggage, extreme indignation. On the *Bellerophon*, Cockburn, Keith and Ross waited nearly an hour for Napoleon to appear for transfer to the *Northumberland*; only Keith calmed Cockburn's impatience, desiring he 'be put in mind'.[12] Galling too that day was Napoleon's condescension in pinching Cockburn's ear!—a practice he employed to ingratiate himself with subordinates.

For the methods he used to reduce Napoleon to subordination, Cockburn has been accused of lacking fine feelings, chivalry, magnanimity, and consideration for the situation of an ex-emperor.[13] He certainly took the role of custodian seriously. 'You may depend on my taking care of the common disturber', he assured Croker on the day they sailed, as long as Croker attended to Cockburn's claims for expenses.[14] For beneath the banter lay a common understanding that the British government intended to incarcerate Napoleon for good, and, above all, Cockburn was concerned to win the psychological duel for intellectual supremacy which constituted the critical element in physical control.

An adroit campaign to check Napoleon's pretensions began as soon as he stepped on board the *Northumberland*. The first priority was to limit Napoleon's claims to living space. To prevent any possible dispute, he was allotted a sleeping cabin (12 feet by 9, with a passage leading to the quarter gallery) of which Cockburn had the identical copy on the opposite side. But on being left to talk to would-be followers in the after or great cabin, he promptly assumed an 'exclusive right' to that as well, as had been the case on the *Bellerophon*. Cockburn countered by taking in and introducing his lieutenants, along with Sir George Bingham, Lord Lowther and the Hon. W.H. Lyttelton, begging the latter three sit down once the lieutenants had left and leaving them to establish a British presence while he himself found Bertrand to explain that the after-cabin was common space.[15]

During the first day Napoleon maintained a polite, sociable facade, and seemed reconciled to his fate. At times, however, especially when reminded of his increasing distance from Europe, he became dejected. Adding to these moods was a repressed anger—a sulkiness—that followed checks on his claims to special treatment. As Cockburn was responsible for these checks, the moods added to difficulties of management, especially in the first week when Napoleon tried on several occasions to exact from English officers the deference to which he was accustomed.[16]

All had gone well for the first three days. Cockburn was pleased. On government instructions he addressed his charge and treated him with no more respect than would have been accorded an army general. 'It is impossible for people to conduct themselves better or with more propriety than General Bonaparte and his followers are doing', he advised Melville on 9 August. 'The General has descended from Emperor on board the *Bellerophon* to be prisoner on board the *Northumberland* with wonderful flexibility of mind and I am very much mistaken if I shall have any further difficulty in performing the task your lordship has confided to me.' However, that same evening, as Cockburn recorded in his diary:

> After dinner he went upon deck and persisted on keeping off his hat as he walked up and down, evidently with a view to inducing the English officers on deck also to continue uncovered (as his French attendants did, and as I am told the officers of the *Bellerophon* used to do whilst he remained on the deck of that ship). Observing this, I made a point of putting on my hat immediately after the first compliment upon going out, and I desired the officers to do the same, at which he seemed considerably piqued, and he soon afterwards went into the cabin and made up his party at vingt-un, but he certainly neither played nor talked with the same cheerfulness he did the first night . . ..

This Cockburn attributed to 'downright sulkiness', but, as Glover observed, it 'produced no alteration in our manners towards him, neither was he paid more respect to than any other officer present'.

This lack of response prompted Napoleon next day to demonstrate his contempt for the code of conduct expected of him. Immediately after dinner, having swallowed his coffee and before anyone else could be served, he got up 'rather uncivilly' and went up on deck. Cockburn intervened: 'this induced me to request particularly the remainder of the party to sit still and he consequently went out only attended by his Maréchal without the slightest further notice being taken of him'. Indeed, to give Napoleon the opportunity to repeat his incivility every evening should he so wish, the steward was requested to 'serve coffee to the General and such of his followers as chose to take it immediately after the cloth was removed, whilst we would continue at table and drink our wine'. 'It is clear he is still inclined to act the Sovereign occasionally', Cockburn noted, 'but I cannot allow it, and the sooner therefore he becomes convinced it is not to be admitted the better.'

Napoleon seems to have realized he would gain no concessions by such behaviour. He was low in spirits for several days, and Cockburn allowed the mood to take its course, deliberately refraining from unnecessary contact. On 13 August 'owing to his appearing inclined to try to assume again improper consequence, I was purposely more than usually distant with him, and therefore, though we exchanged common salutations and *high looks*, nothing passed between us worth noticing'.

Such deliberate disregard was conspicuous, especially when Napoleon demanded the attention that was withheld. In the evening of Sunday, 13 August, when he and Madame Bertrand wished to play cards—though he was informed it was customary for the officers not to play cards on Sundays—he told Glover to send for Cockburn and Sir George Bingham, observing that, as upper circles in London played, presumably Cockburn would not dislike it. Yet neither Cockburn nor Bingham appeared.

Napoleon had now been on board a week. From this time relations gradually improved, and on the terms set by Cockburn. On the 14th, they 'were again distant and high with each other, though perfectly civil'; on the 15th Napoleon seemed more sociable and at ease. It was his birthday and Cockburn made him 'compliments upon it and drank his health, which civility he seemed to appreciate'. That evening after dinner they had a long conversation, walking together on deck. Next day Napoleon seemed better in spirits and behaviour. Cockburn thus reciprocated: 'I am always ready to meet him half-way when he appears to conduct himself with due modesty and consideration of his present situation'. By 24 August Cockburn felt sufficient confidence to advise Melville that he had 'every reason to believe we shall not have any further difficulty or even unpleasant occurrence during the remainder of the voyage'; finding he would not be allowed to resume the status of emperor, he had 'fallen again into his proper place'.[17] On 27 August so confident was Cockburn of Napoleon's stability, he caused the whole squadron to steer between Gomera and Palma in the Canary Islands simply to gratify the latter's curiosity.

Such confidence was perhaps premature. On 6 September Cockburn was surprised to have Napoleon getting up after dinner for his usual walk, though it was pouring with rain. Cockburn had no doubt Napoleon 'intended this dash of his should give us a great idea of his hardiness of character'. But 'the General' was quickly wet through, the walk soon over, and 'no further particular notice was taken of it by any of us'. There was one further incident. On crossing the equator, the Comte de Bertrand attempted on Napoleon's behalf to gain permission to distribute 'one or two hundred napoleons' among the seamen. Cockburn 'considered this to be an attempt of the General's to avail himself, with his usual *finesse*, of a plausible excuse to distribute such a large sum amongst the seamen solely with a view of rendering himself popular with them'. He 'pointedly prohibited it', permitting the distribution of no more than five napoleons. Bertrand argued vehemently. 'The rhetoric, however, as usual' had not 'the slightest effect towards changing my determination'. Napoleon let the matter drop, showed no sign 'that he was hurt or piqued', but did not send even five napoleons.

One factor helping to stabilize relations was the invariable routine into which meetings between French and English fell. The patterns of their respective lives coincided only in the evenings. At dinner Cockburn always sat beside Napoleon, their places requiring observance of essential courtesies. At table only some of the English officers spoke French: Captain Ross, for example, spoke little. Cockburn's fluency on the other hand permitted him to communicate at will, his conversations with Napoleon commanding the attention of all diners. Cockburn was able to draw him out, sometimes prompting with questions, so that his reminiscences became the main accompaniment to meals. This was followed by exercise on deck, in which Cockburn and Napoleon usually walked together, mostly out of earshot. These conversations—ranging between 'free and pleasant' to 'a frank strain'—were vital to the understanding they developed. Both gave equally: Cockburn flattered by his questions; Napoleon rewarded with his confidences. It was during one of these conversations that Napoleon gave his side of the events surrounding the attempted rescue of Ferdinand VII in 1810. Finally, evenings were completed by an hour or more of cards.

The relationship so formed was to prove of long-term value to Cockburn. Its remnants were still evident in 1816. But it did entail a risk. By becoming so intimate, there was a chance of slipping under Napoleon's influence; that he did not was due to his objective assessment of his charge. Within three days Cockburn had taken particular note of Napoleon's manners: 'uncouth and disagreeable and to his *French friends* most overbearing if not absolutely rude'. At chess with the Comte de Montholon, 'he appeared to me to play but badly and was evidently inferior to his antagonist, who I observed nevertheless was quite determined not to win the game from his ex-majesty'. Later Cockburn commented on Napoleon's geographical ignorance, his hypocrisy, untruthfulness and malicious hatred of England. By the end of the voyage, he had even come to question the man's capacity to reason dispassionately and apply his own logic to his own situation. The questioning of Napoleon's rationality was a common practice among contemporaries; Cockburn did so, however, only after close acquaintance over two months.

By studying and humanizing him, Napoleon diminished in

Cockburn's estimation. In contrast, Cockburn seems to have risen in respect among the French party, especially for his professional competence. On the day when St Helena was sighted, numerous suggestions were made as to when they would see land. Glover records that Cockburn 'decided we should see it at six o'clock, and so correct was he in his calculations that the time we saw it did not differ a *minute* . . . at which Bonaparte and all the French party seemed much astonished'.

The end of the voyage on 15 October was a welcome release from a passage of 67 days, the later part of which Napoleon suffered with more patience than his followers. Yet sight of the island was discomforting. 'Nothing can possibly be less prepossessing, nay more horribly forbidding, than the first appearance of this isolated and apparently burnt-up, barren rock, which promises neither refreshment or pleasure'. Its 'terrific appearance' and 'stupendous barren cliffs' seemed 'to but ill accord with the feelings of our guests'.[18]

Cockburn immediately found them rented accommodation in Jamestown, to which they disembarked on 16 October. Cockburn also visited Longwood, the house of the Lieutenant-Governor of the East India Company who managed the island. Repeating the visit with Napoleon on the 17th, it was fixed as the house which, after extension and renovation, 'the General' would occupy. On his return journey, about a mile and a quarter from Jamestown, Napoleon noted the Briars, a cottage housing the Balcombe family. Rather than return to the lodging house, Napoleon wished to occupy a small outhouse close to the Briars. They stopped to discuss this with the Balcombes and it was promptly agreed. Until the improvements at Longwood were completed about mid-December, Napoleon accordingly lived at the Briars, with most of his followers in Jamestown. Meanwhile, Cockburn lived on board the *Northumberland*, later moving to the castle in Jamestown.

Governor of St Helena

The problems Cockburn now faced took several forms. He remained in sole charge of Napoleon, and would so remain until the arrival of the new Governor in April 1816. He not only had to make Longwood habitable for the French party, but the island habitable for the troops placed there to guard him. In addition, he had to establish and maintain a system of regulations around Napoleon that would prevent any repetition of the Elba experience. Both tasks interacted and not to advantage. Security restricted the sources from which building materials, furnishings and provisions could be obtained quickly; and while such supplies were limited, neither army nor French party could be settled into permanent quarters; the French party could not be reconciled to their new habitat; and a lasting system of security could not be established around their permanent residence.

Security was nevertheless Cockburn's first priority. Lord Bathurst had laid down minimum measures. The boundaries of Napoleon's residence were to be posted with sentries; his outings beyond those bounds were to be accompanied by an English officer and orderly, except when strange ships were in sight, when outings had to be discontinued, and communication with islanders forbidden. Letters to Napoleon had to be read by Cockburn before delivery; those from outside the island had to go first to the Secretary of State in London. Letters out were to be similarly treated. Complaints or any other representation as to treatment had also to go to London accompanied by the comments of Cockburn or the new Governor. These same regulations applied to his followers as well as to Napoleon.[19]

On the island, Cockburn and his successor had sole responsibility for all matters affecting security. From the troops stationed there, he was authorized to weed out all foreigners or others of untrustworthy character or disposition and send them to the Cape, from where replacements and reliefs were to be ordered. Foreign civilians could also be sent there.[20] The whole coast and even boats frequenting landing places were considered under Cockburn's control. Troops were to be stationed at landing places, and the arrival and departure of every ship closely observed; their intercourse with the shore was to be only as approved. Bathurst took upon himself to issue orders preventing foreign ships, both merchant and naval, from calling there.

These regulations effectively sealed St Helena from the outside world and brought the whole island under Cockburn's control. Interpreting Bathurst's instructions in his own way, he eventually had guard boats patrolling to windward and leeward of the island.[21] Sea-going vessels were permitted to land only if in want of water or provisions; even then a guard was put on board. Along the shore every private boat was secured at sunset and given an armed guard. Inland every bridge and gate, bar one, was closed and locked at sunset, and no person allowed outside Jamestown without a signed pass after 9 p.m.[22]

Security increased in stringency the closer Napoleon was approached. Detailed instructions were issued to each officer responsible for part of

Cockburn's system. Those, for example, to the officer stationed at Napoleon's house required him to obtain certain knowledge of the captive's presence twice every twenty-four hours. Cockburn was to be informed at 8 a.m. and at sunset the exact time when his sure presence was established. Without permission, the whole of Napoleon's household had to be indoors by 9 p.m. Any extraordinary or suspicious movement such as the packing of trunks was to be reported immediately. The officer stationed at the gate in the boundary marked by sentries was given specific instructions as to who could be allowed through without a pass. The officer at the lodge gate, when Napoleon moved to Longwood, received another even shorter privileged visitors list.[23]

Initially, dragoons on orderly duty carried all the messages Cockburn required. Later, after the move to Longwood, a signalling system was established by which an officer on duty could send secret signals to or from ten signal stations around the island. Cockburn then required to know whenever Napoleon passed through the cordon round his house; the code included messages indicating whether Napoleon was within or beyond that perimeter, properly attended or not, well or unwell.[24] It thus became possible for an officer to raise the alarm promptly even had his charge escaped him while out riding.[25]

Yet the establishment of this system depended on the occupation of Longwood. The morale of the French party depended on this too. Only three weeks after their debarkation Count Bertrand began a series of complaints to Cockburn, recounting events since Napoleon's surrender, and deploring his master's confined quarters, lack of amenities, exercise, and adequate company. At the Briars, Bertrand complained, he occupied 'the pavilion' which contained 'but one room in which he is obliged to dress, eat and walk and to remain all day'. It was impossible for him to take a bath; there were no saddle horses available for riding; he was surrounded by sentries; his companions—except Count de Las Cases and his son who lived in a small room above the Pavilion—were all lodged at a distance; and when they visited him were accompanied by a British army sergeant.

> It were much to be wished that the conduct observed toward the Emperor should be such as to remove from his thoughts the remembrance of the horrible position in which he is now placed. It is such that one may dare to affirm that even barbarians would be affected by it and would treat it with consideration.[26]

The complaint obliged Cockburn 'officially to explain' (as he was to do on repeated occasions) that he had 'no cognisance of any Emperor being actually upon the island or any such person possessing such dignity having . . . come hither with me in the *Northumberland*'. He had already pulled back the ring of sentries, but it was 'incompatible' with his instructions to dispense with the accompanying sergeant or officer. Even so, it was Cockburn's 'most anxious study' to render the situation of the French party 'as little irksome and disagreeable as possible'.[27] To Bathurst, Cockburn observed 'their requests and complaints (particularly those of M. de Bertrand) but increase with every favour or attention shewn them'. But to Croker at the Admiralty he admitted he could hardly hope for reconciliation to their destiny until he had them established at Longwood, to which object his 'principal attention and efforts' were therefore directed.[28]

The house took more work to put in order than Cockburn had anticipated. The materials available for doing so were less than expected and the island's whole stock of suitable timber had to be purchased at a high price. Repairs and additions were made with the aid of the *Northumberland*'s carpenters and crew, and completed about mid-December. Then house frames were required, and artificers to create accommodation for the 53rd Regiment that otherwise had to live under canvas half a mile from Longwood.[29] Planking too was needed, and not just to house people. The increased military force on the island required a larger stock of cattle; they were usually brought from the warmer African coast and sheds were therefore necessary for their pastures. As American traders were excluded from the island, Cockburn supposed England was the best source of these materials, but two months later he also requested planking from Rio de Janeiro along with mules to carry everything the five miles to Longwood.[30]

Building materials were not all that was lacking. Initially even basic provisions for ships' crews were short. By 11 November the *Northumberland* was down to half rations of bread and flour with only four days' supply left. More was available from the East India Company stores but at an 'exhorbitant price'. A naval storeship was expected. So also was a collier, equally in demand. The Company's stock of coal was small and real inconvenience was anticipated on that account. Good wines were short. Wine was the staple drink of children as well as of adults in the French party, and at every meal including breakfast. For Croker to judge demand, he was sent an account of consumption on the voyage: 20 dozen of port, 45 of claret, 22 of madeira, 5 of malmsey, 13 of champagne and 7 of sherry—1,344 bottles in 70 days. As wines at St

Helena were poor in quality and expensive, Cockburn suggested that ships heading for St Helena put in to a French port for a quantity.[31]

The problem of food supply was apparently resolved with the return of the vessels taking foreigners to the Cape. The Governor informed him that that settlement could supply bullocks, sheep, poultry, salt pork, wheat, forage, soap, salt, candles and fruit—all 'to any *extent*', being the produce of the area. Moreover, the Cape overflowed with British manufactured products.[32] In December Bathurst was attempting to hasten the shipment of furniture for Longwood, and in March there was a request for books—to be selected with the advice of M.Barbien, the former librarian to the emperor, and of the Council of State at Paris.[33]

After extension and repair, Longwood consisted of more than forty rooms. As accommodation Ross thought it 'very good'; Glover described it as 'an English gentleman's country seat'. Napoleon was initially satisfied,[34] and entertained enthusiastically for a fortnight, until the novelty wore off. With house-room for almost all his followers, and stabling for twelve horses, a carriage and phaeton, he had company as well as provision for exercise. At 1,750 feet above sea level, the site of the house was cooler—about 65°F—than the lower valleys and coast. It was surrounded by a park of about four miles circumference, partly cultivated as a farm by the East India Company. Its perimeter marked the first line of sentries; a second some way beyond formed an enclosure about twelve miles in circumference. Within this area Napoleon and his followers had free movement; beyond, they were accompanied by an English officer.[35]

Cockburn's hope that the French party would become reconciled to their fate after moving to Longwood was not soon realized. The move itself on 10 December brought forth a tirade against the British government and, more particularly, against the regime exercised by Cockburn. He had been prompt in forbidding Dr O'Meara, the naval surgeon placed at Longwood, from acting as a British officer and accompanying French residents beyond the sentry line, the doctor having gone with General Gougaud to see the island's Governor on 17 December.[36] At Longwood this prohibition was received as 'an affront, as insulting to him as to us'.

On 21 December Montholon gave vent to the range of grievances the decision provoked. To the injustice of sending Napoleon to St Helena was added 'that of relegating us to the most savage part of the island', lacking 'convolutions' of which British ministers would not have dared deprive them. 'Yet every day those communications with the inhabitants, which are authorised by such of your instructions as you have made known to us, are additionally restricted.' Visitors to Longwood were obliged to receive their passports from Cockburn. Thus the French party could 'not freely see' even the island's inhabitants. Anything wanted from town had to be ordered in writing. Yet errors had given rise to a 'multiplicity and continual variation of orders'.

> I appeal to you, Sir, whether every day does not bring about a change in our position, or whether we are only subject to fixed rules.

They were in want of everything: 'the little furniture placed at Longwood appears to have been composed of articles grown old in waiting rooms'. General de Montholon had been charged to buy articles from the 4,000 napoleons given up before leaving the *Bellerophon*, but Cockburn had ordered the Jamestown shopkeepers not to deal with them. For shooting, they wanted fowling pieces; this was permitted, but only if returned each night. The scenery around Longwood consisted of barren rocks which they could only 'contemplate with horror'; the gum trees gave no shade, and the water was scanty and of bad quality. 'The Emperor is ill off at Longwood and is much incommoded by the smell of oil paint; the climate is here more disagreeable than in all the rest of the island: one lives in the circle of clouds and in a very damp atmosphere; the health of the Emperor is deranged, and we all of us suffer'.[37]

In reply, Cockburn refused to acknowledge Napoleon's title of emperor, and as to the letter itself:

> The very uncalled for intemperance and indecency of the language which you have permitted yourself to use to me respecting my government I should not perhaps, Sir, condescend to notice, did I not think it right to inform you that I shall not in future consider it necessary to answer any letters which I may receive couched in a similar strain of unfounded invective; and to assure you how much you are deceived if you really believe the Government of Great Britain have not 'dared' (as you have been pleased to express it) to give every requisite order for authorising whatever measure may be deemed necessary; as well as for the furtherance of the purposes for which you and the other French officers and persons . . . have been sent here or for insuring a continuance of due tranquillity and security to the island; although I have the satisfaction to add that the instructions hereupon breathe throughout the same moderation and justice which has hitherto characterised the whole conduct of my Government towards you; and which (notwithstanding your individual assertions to the contrary) will, I have no doubt, obtain the admiration of future ages as well as every unprejudiced person of the present.

Cockburn stood by his orders: changes in them were only made to suit the convenience of the French party; Longwood was 'beyond comparison the most pleasant as well as the most healthy spot of this most healthful island'; Napoleon had expressed himself satisfied with the house; Cockburn had given no orders to tradesmen in Jamestown; and it was not for him to explain to Montholon his grounds for finding fault with O'Meara.[38]

Even so, there is evidence that Cockburn was influenced by Montholon. Following the move to Longwood, he had made every effort to mitigate the harsher features of Napoleon's captivity. Thus, for example, at half past eleven one Saturday night Captain Poppleton, the officer on duty at Longwood, was informed by Glover that the Admiral was 'much annoyed' that afternoon to learn Napoleon had not been allowed to pass the sentry at Huts Gate. Poppleton had to explain to Napoleon that it was 'entirely a mistake either of the officer at Huts Gate or of the orders given him'; at the same time he had to 'state that General Bonaparte and all his suite (including servants) have the liberty of passing and repassing anywhere within the [outer] cordon of sentries'.[39] Aggravated by the sight of the guards, Napoleon requested they be allowed to wear civilian clothes; Cockburn accordingly directed the officer on duty at Longwood not to wear uniform.[40] Six days after Montholon's tirade, Cockburn allowed Englishmen and the inhabitants of the island working at Longwood to have passes and periods of leave to visit other parts of the island. Another four days later, Count de Bertrand was allowed to grant passes to people wishing to visit Longwood and to those who were invited—the passes simply to be deposited with the sentry at the lodge gates and sent to Cockburn next morning. Later, he facilitated purchases from the 4,000 napoleons confiscated on the *Bellerophon*, and did courtesies like passing on French newspapers even before he had read them himself.[41]

Such measures indicate a degree of flexibility. On the major issue however—Napoleon's ability to exercise beyond the outer cordon of sentries unaccompanied by a British officer—Cockburn remained firm. As both knew, a concession on that point would have rendered control of Napoleon's movement next to impossible. His determination not to concede it was certainly reinforced by his distrust of Napoleon—on the voyage out he had noticed behaviour that disqualified his captive, to his mind, from being a gentleman. Being no gentleman, in Cockburn's view, Napoleon lacked the honour to keep to his word.

His distrust increased after the move to Longwood when Napoleon's domination of his followers again became apparent. In a private conversation with Montholon, Cockburn discovered that the letter of 21 December had virtually been dictated by Napoleon: 'written in a moment of petulance of the General (who has been subject to paroxysms of such nature)'. Montholon 'was aware of the reproach to which he subjected himself by writing it'; indeed he 'considered the party to be in point of fact vastly well off and to have everything necessary for them'.[42] The sarcasm with which Cockburn denied Napoleon the status of emperor fuelled the captive's frustration.[43] The 'paroxism' produced by Cockburn's insistence in December that all visitors to Longwood carry passes, was reported by O'Meara to an Admiralty friend: 'He [Napoleon] sent for me in great haste and with considerable emotion' and demanded Cockburn's orders be rescinded.

> It is, added he, an insult and one of those which are daily offered to myself or some of my followers. I will never receive any person coming with a Pass from the Admiral, as I will immediately set down the person receiving it as like the donor and a 'spy upon me'. Tell him that his sending to inform me that the sentinels are placed in order to prevent people from annoying me with visits is only adding wrong to insult. I will chuse myself what kind of visitors I like . . ..

> Was the Admiral to heap every kind of benefit on me, the manner in which he does it would make me conceive each and every one an insult— everything is given to us as if we were demanding alms.

Yet face to face, Cockburn and his captive still seemed capable of reviving that rapport they had established on the voyage. O'Meara added that Cockburn had an 'audience' with Napoleon a few days later and was able to satisfy him that 'several of the things he had imputed to him had been misrepresented, and they parted better friends than I expected'.[44]

Cockburn's resolution to enforce regulations hardened as the duration of Napoleon's captivity lengthened and the likelihood of fraternization between captives and captors increased. In February he had to investigate the occurrence of a 'highly improper communication' between a naval officer and Bertrand, and in May, a 'suspicion' that an army officer had been asked to carry letters for Napoleon. He was as rigorous with his own subordinates as with the French party in insisting that written communications to or from the French were read first by himself. From February, permission to visit Longwood and even spoken communication with detainees had to receive his sanction.[45] The insulation of Napoleon and his followers from their captors soon seemed justified. In April the consul at Rio de Janeiro wrote to warn Cockburn of the arrival of a number of Frenchmen and their families who had emigrated 'chiefly from motives of disgust at the Restoration'. One was alleged to have been a member of Napoleon's 'secret police'. It was therefore probable that attempts would 'be made by some of them, or at any rate by their means, to open a secret correspondence with General Bonaparte'.[46]

Such fears were given substance by the interception of proposals for Napoleon's escape. A letter intercepted in St Helena's post office, written by a Frenchman in English to escape suspicion, spoke of preparations for Napoleon's escape by rope down a cliff and then by boat drifting before the wind to a ship 14 miles to leeward. The writer described the boat— 'a masterly contrivance'—as shaped like an old cask and painted the colour of the sea. It was 'so ingeniously wrought inside (being steel) that it will render and stretch to 4 times the length it appears to be with a clever graplin at one end that will spring out with pressure of the thumb'. He also spoke of 'the most cordial fraternal reception' Napoleon would receive in the United States, and the support he would obtain from Americans as well as from people in France and Spain.[47]

In London fears of such a rescue turned ministers' thoughts towards the need for a trained engineer to inspect the island and propose improvements in the physical barriers to escape.[48] On 13 March Cockburn received Bathurst's instructions to occupy Ascension Island in order to remove 'the facilities' it would provide to people planning Napoleon's escape. Late in April, HMS *Havannah* was accordingly sent from St Helena with a detachment of soldiers to occupy the island.[49]

By this time, Cockburn had been relieved of his custodial duties. Major-General Sir Hudson Lowe arrived in mid-April to become Governor of the island with special responsibility for Napoleon. Cockburn remained commander-in-chief of the Cape station for a while longer but had transferred his custodial responsibility by 17 April when he went with Lowe on the latter's first visit to Longwood as Governor. It was to prove a humiliating experience, for Napoleon took the opportunity to revenge himself on his gaoler by adopting 'some rather unpleasant points of etiquette'.

Lowe had made an appointment for them both. When they reached the house, he informed Bertrand that he and Cockburn would 'go up' together. From the outer reception room, Lowe was immediately shown into Napoleon's apartment and only after half an hour—on turning to ask Cockburn if he had brought with him a copy of the Regent's speech—did he discover that his predecessor in office had not followed him into the room.

> On going out I found Sir George in the anti-chamber much irritated. He told me Bertrand had almost shut the door in his face as he was following me into the room; that a servant had put his arm across him. He said he would have forced his way, but that he was expecting I would have turned round to see if he was following me, when he supposed I would have insisted on our entering the room together . . ..

Napoleon was ready to receive him after Lowe went in search of him. But Cockburn would not go in.[50] Both Bertrand and Montholon visited him later to make apologies, but he remained affronted.

Cockburn was relieved as commander-in-chief on the Cape station by Sir Pulteney Malcolm in mid-June. He sailed for Ascension Island and Spithead with Glover on the 19th. According to Glover, his departure caused a 'general regret . . . testified on the crowded beach as we embarked'; his 'hospitality' had made him a 'univeral favourite'. But Napoleon was glad to be rid of him; indeed had occupied his time in drawing up a memorial against him. According to Napoleon, Cockburn's behaviour had been 'rough, overbearing, vain, choleric and capricious'—an opinion strikingly similar to that which Cockburn had suggested of his captive in his diary on the voyage.[51]

In London, Cockburn's balancing act between gaoler and host was already appreciated. The Prince Regent deigned to notice his conduct. Bathurst observed that he had 'discharged a very delicate trust with great zeal and judgement'. He had not been imposed upon by an authoritative tone, deceived by misrepresentation or cajoled by flatteries; at the same time he had been mindful 'of that tenderness and respect which adverse fortune, however merited, has ever a right to claim from the generous and humane'.[52]

Cockburn's achievement gains in perspective when compared to that of Sir Hudson Lowe. After an angry exchange in August 1816 Lowe never met Napoleon again, though he remained Governor of the island until after his captive's death in 1821. To those who also remained on St Helena, he appeared to lack drive and organization as well as tact. At Longwood progress in building works fell off. According to Major Barnes, who wrote to Cockburn late in July, the means were abundant, 'but the system, the energy and the soul of the thing' was wanting. Little was done to alter Cockburn's security arrangements: new regulations simply recapitulated those already established.[53] And Lowe himself admitted a reluctance to alter arrangements for supply. 'The subject of the general provisioning of this island for the navy, the inhabitants, the East India Company's troops is one of very complex consideration', he advised Bathurst on 21 April 1816; the island was then 'pretty well supplied', so he would not be 'too hasty in making any change'.[54] Instead, Lowe tired the French party 'to death with volumes of trifles'. Things were 'not well managed', Malcolm informed Cockburn on returning to England in September 1817; 'I sincerely wish they had left you Governor and Ministers would now be better pleased'.[55]

CHAPTER 5

Parliament and the Admiralty
1818–1830

'George Cockburn is come back in good health and spirits; he gives us no hopes of Buonaparte's dying. He eats, he says, enormously, but he drinks little, takes regular exercise, and is in all respects so very careful of his carcass that he may live twenty years.' John Wilson Croker's comment to Robert Peel aptly reflected contemporary interest in Cockburn on his return from St Helena.[1] His recent close association with Napoleon made him a source of first-hand information about the fallen emperor, which the Russian ambassador as well as British ministers wished to tap.

The convivial consultations that followed his return reinforced Cockburn's re-entry into society surrounding the departments of state. Those who determined even junior membership of these departments were already familiar, through his reports and copies of his correspondence, with his management at St Helena. This, and his record in North America, opened the way to his appointment as second naval commissioner at the Board of Admiralty in April 1818. His connections with Peel undoubtedly helped; as did first-name familiarity with Croker, with whom in March 1818 Cockburn was already in 'secret and confidential' correspondence about the qualities of the other intended junior Lord of the Admiralty before he was 'irrevocably fixed upon'.[2]

The concern about his intended colleague reflected the small number and interdependence of office-holders in central government. The Crown had long since ceased to govern except in the appointment of ministers whose duties were limited to key functions of state: taxation, diplomacy, war, order and justice. Sustained by the confidence of the King, and by the confidence they commanded in the House of Commons, in 1818 the principal ministers had been in position for six

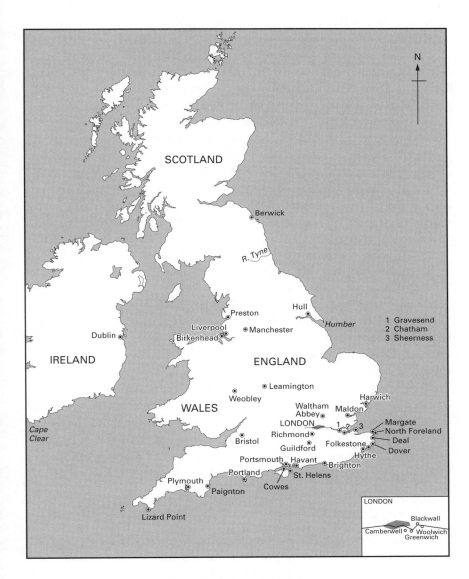

Map 10.   The British Isles

years: Liverpool at the Treasury, Castlereagh at the Foreign Office, Sidmouth in the Home Office and Melville at the Admiralty. Professional politicians, they managed through small departments of dependable subordinates.

The Admiralty in 1818 consisted altogether of 60 persons—this, however, included 51 assistant officials, clerks and housekeepers.[3] Decisions stemmed from only seven commissioners, including the First Lord, assisted by two secretaries, whose orders maintained over 120 vessels in commission, more than 430 others in ordinary or reserve, 20,000 men on sea pay and a corps of nearly 5,800 officers.[4] Beneath the Admiralty, to be sure, the Navy Board managed the workforces and contracts of the dockyards, while the Victualling Board was responsible for the victualling yards and hospital service. Even so, the small group of men at the pinnacle of naval administration carried responsibility for the efficiency of an organization of immense public expense: over six and a half million pounds, or eleven per cent of gross national expenditure in 1818.[5] It was a situation that remained basically unchanged until 1832.

Responsibility for this scale of public finance made the role of an Admiralty commissioner a political office. While John Barrow as Second Secretary at the Admiralty, and Sir Thomas Byam Martin, the chairman or Comptroller of the Navy Board, held posts with permanent tenure, that of an Admiralty commissioner changed as necessary with the Cabinet. Closely in touch with ministers, Cockburn quickly adapted to the political dimension of his new office. Henceforward, meetings and dinners with Melville, Liverpool and later Sidmouth introduced an element of statesmanship into the routine of managing the navy.[6] His family connection with Peel, who succeeded Sidmouth at the Home Office in 1822, continually reinforced this bond with the politicians, while the affinity of one military man for another made Wellington a professional friend as well as his political leader after 1828.

Champion of Liberty

Cockburn's compatibility with these politicians derived partly from his own experience in life and partly from his pragmatic conservatism. Having seen at first hand the social chaos and suffering caused by the revolution in France, he well appreciated the Tory determination to deter sweeping political change. As a sea officer, he believed the British constitution was but part of the larger geographical environment that gave the British seaman a motivation superior to any other. In

Plate 4.   Cockburn in 1817, after his return from St Helena and before taking up his appointment at the Admiralty. Note the riding boots and breeches, and the burning buildings of the United States Government in the background.
By J. J. Halls. (National Maritime Museum)

November 1818, for example, he was able to encourage Sir John Gore, who despaired at the reduction in guardships, to

> believe with me that so long as our *Island*, our *Climate*, our happily blended *Constitution*, and consequently our *men* continue the same, whenever another War may call for them, our ships will be as readily brought forward as has ever heretofore been the case, the Topmasts and Top Gall[t] Masts, Flags and Pendants will tower as high and they will be as gallantly as ever carried alongside the Enemy to the honor & advantage of old England . . .[7]

Working alongside Croker, it was natural for him after April 1818 to absorb much of the thinking of the ultra-Tory secretary. Cockburn was never quite so pessimistic as Croker, even in the depths of the Reform Bill crisis of 1831. Yet he too came to fear the excessive demands of radical reformers who threatened to sweep away the 'happily blended' constitution of England. For him, as a lifelong servant of the Crown and adherent to the Anglican faith, the constitution preserved these two elements that gave his life purpose. In his view the law rightly safeguarded the private property of the middle and upper classes, while the lower orders were protected by it. Even though they were not proportionally represented in the House of Commons, the latter were virtually represented by members for such constituencies as Westminster. Moreover, in his view, they were the benefactors of a Christian society in which privilege had its obligations in charity and paternalism. Having witnessed oppression, degradation and impoverishment, Cockburn was to argue that the maintenance of a constitutional framework was productive of greater freedom from such evils than anything radical change might bring.

Cockburn's sympathy with Tory ideology was certainly recognized by Croker who also foresaw the use that could be made of his ambition and energy. Since Trafalgar and the death of Nelson, the navy had lost ground in public popularity compared to the army and the Duke of Wellington—the role of the navy in establishing the recent peace demanded recognition.[8] On 22 February 1818 Cockburn was nominated a Knight Grand Cross of the Military Order of the Bath, and there was opportunity to exploit his public character for the benefit of the navy. Admirals with outstanding achievements had traditionally been identified in the popular mind with patriotism and liberty from foreign domination.[9] Cockburn, in consequence, made an ideal candidate for a parliamentary constituency in which popular appeal mattered.

Almost certainly, Croker had Cockburn in mind for the borough of Portsmouth. An Admiralty borough, so-called because of the high proportion of the local population dependent for their livelihood on work or contracts provided by naval establishments, it had nevertheless slipped out of government control. With a franchise limited to about a hundred freemen of the borough, the strong Independent party in the corporation (most of them religious dissenters) had since 1783 regularly elected a member of the Carter family to one of its two parliamentary seats. Since 1801 the other seat had been occupied by the Whig Admiral John Markham, who had served on the Admiralty Boards of Lord St Vincent, the later Lord Grey and Thomas Grenville between 1801 and 1807. In 1816 Croker himself had been induced to canvass the borough because 'no other person connected both with the naval administration and the government' could be made available. Croker found he had no chance, but had staked a claim with his supporters and planned an Admiralty effort for the next general election.[10]

A general election occurred a month after Cockburn's appointment to the Admiralty. On 30 May 1818 he accordingly presented himself as candidate for the borough of Portsmouth. Mr John Carter was expected to take one seat and Markham to contest the other. However, having reached Portsmouth before Markham and ten days before the election, Cockburn began an 'active canvass' of the borough which lasted four days. Markham arrived just as Cockburn completed the task. Seeing himself forestalled 'by prior solicitations, and being unwilling to cause a schism or unfriendly feeling among the members of the corporation', he decorously withdrew his candidature.

After a few days in London, Cockburn returned to Portsmouth on 15 June to a traditional welcome.

> The probable time of his arrival having been anticipated, the populace, anxious to express their gratification which so generally prevailed at the prospect of Sir George being returned one of the members to represent the Borough, met together about two miles out of town, with a view to intercept Sir George's carriage and draw him into town. On arrival at the spot Sir George was reluctantly compelled to submit to have his horses taken from his carriage. They drew it (the carriage being surrounded by a very large concourse of people) through the principal streets of Portsea, St George's Square, through those of Portsmouth to the George Inn in the High Street, where Sir George Cockburn alighted amidst the acclamations of an immense assemblage of persons who had waited a considerable time in expectation of his arrival. Sir George, immediately

after he reached the Inn, which he accomplished with difficulty, the
pressure being so great, presented himself at the window and, as soon as
silence could be obtained, expressed the gratification he felt at the manner
in which he had been received, and said that he had given orders for the
distribution of beer to those who were disposed to partake of it, which
having been given in much profusion, all pleasantly separated to their
homes.

At the subsequent hustings, Cockburn stressed his independence and
lack of a political past. He was not a 'party man'; his life so far—'during
the most arduous and unprecedented war that the world ever knew'—
had been devoted to the service of his country. Yet, having been called to
the Admiralty, he would serve the interests of Portsmouth as well as the
Crown. His line of conduct generally was to agree with the measures of
the present ministers, but he would neither support them nor keep his
place should their conduct in his opinion not be conducive to the public
good.

> I trust my character is too well known that it can be supposed for a
> moment that I will become the tool of any party man. I have sufficient
> sense of my duty, I trust, to know when to resign my seat at the Board
> . . . to preserve such conduct as will enable me to face my constituents
> and ask again for their suffrages.

Cockburn was duly elected with Carter. A round of dinners followed,
one for the corporation at the Fountain Inn, another for the new
members at the Assembly Rooms, concluding with a ball for the ladies
of the local towns and neighbourhood which attracted 400 people.
Cockburn gave the ball and shared in the cost of the first dinner. It was
capped by a ten-guinea donation and annual subscription to the
Portsmouth Charity School, a similar donation to the district committee
of the Society for Promoting Christian Knowledge, half as much to the
Garrison races and 20 shillings to each debtor confined in Portsmouth
gaol. As one toast made clear, it was generosity in aid of Admiralty
popularity.[11]

However, popularity was as easily lost as won. Another general
election following the death of George III brought Cockburn to
Portsmouth again in March 1820. By then he was associated with the
government's controversial Six Acts aimed at controlling public
meetings and suppressing insurrectionary movements. His candidature
was nonetheless required by a petition of some 2,376 householders.
Markham too received a petition and offered himself in opposition to

Cockburn, for whom local radicals ill concealed their hostility. While placards reviled his personal character, an address admonished his supporters 'for activities aimed at influencing the votes of the corporate body in their choice of representatives'. At the hustings Markham simply coupled opposition to the Six Acts with the traditional Whig naval-town cry against an 'enormous standing army' and reduced navy. Cockburn, on the other hand, expressed partiality for the government's policies since 1818, intended, in his opinion, to preserve law and order.

> The word 'liberty' was dear to every English heart and he would ever stand forth as its advocate and defender; but it was not the liberty which is connected with the rights and reciprocal duties of civilized society which was so vehemently vociferated in our public meetings, but a liberty closely allied to a lawless intention of depriving by brute force all the upper classes of society of their just rights and property.

Cockburn received only 27 votes, with Markham 37 and Carter 53. It was as well that the day before, in his absence, Cockburn, with Lord Bentinck, had been quietly elected member for the pocket borough of Weobley in Herefordshire.[12]

Cockburn nevertheless fought the Portsmouth result by demanding a parliamentary committee of inquiry into Carter's use of non-resident voters. The initiative for this arose from Cockburn, the consequence of complaints registered during the poll at Portsmouth. But late in May 1820, he complained bitterly to Croker that 'the Treasury have treated me scurvily about it and left me quite to myself and my own efforts'. Even convincing the committee to consider his case was a long-winded procedure. Croker was not available to represent his case and he had to rely upon a good-hearted but less able advocate, Fitzgerald. By September the costs to bring the appeal to a conclusion amounted to £500. Cockburn thought the cause worthwhile.

> I think the government owe it to the Portsmouth loyal people (after the struggle recently made by them to free themselves from the yoke of the radical party which have so closely held the borough of late years) to make some effort in their favour. I should therefore be ready to sacrifice £200 towards making up the sum required if Lord M[elville] agrees with us in attributing importance to establishing an Admiralty influence in the borough and would therefore interfere with the Treasury folks for getting the remainder of the sum you have mentioned made up. But should he take a different view of the subject to us, I think we had better let the matter drop in its present stage, however much we may lament over the hard lot of our Portsmouth friends. . . .

Melville gained the support of the Treasury for pushing on with the appeal, and Croker agreed to represent him. All hinged on the voting rights allowed under the borough's charter and whether non-residents voted in 1795. However over a year later the election had still not been ruled invalid and Cockburn let his case drop.[13]

The House of Commons

The Portsmouth experience was salutary. Although in 1837 Cockburn was to respond again to an invitation from the Portsmouth inhabitants to stand as a candidate, never again was he tempted to invest in a contest more than his basic election expenses. This arose partly from disenchantment with parliamentary politics in which he was now inevitably immersed, for after 1818 he was regularly obliged to attend debates in the House of Commons and when necessary give his support to ministers. This was facilitated by the provision of accommodation at the Admiralty and the proximity of Whitehall to Westminster. While the Board met at eleven each morning, dividing after midday, debates began in the afternoon and ran into the evening. Parliamentary sessions ran only from January to July, with a break over Easter, but demands in that time could be intense. In May 1821 he was kept from his 'regular work' for a week 'by a tiresome election committee'. In March 1822 he maintained that no individual 'could without injury to his health attend at his office from nine o'clock in the morning until four in the afternoon, and then be in his place in this House from four in the afternoon until two in the morning to answer such questions as might be put to him'. By the end of the decade he openly admitted finding the duty of attending the House of Commons 'very trying and irksome'.[14] It was nevertheless a task in which he persisted to maintain the interests of the navy, to the extent permitted by government policy and public opinion.

The functions of the House were limited to debating and voting amendments. Whigs and Tories had identities, but parties were still little more than groups of collaborators, while the opposition was sufficiently disorganized to be incapable of generating policy manifestos or imposing ministers.[15] Yet the House could refrain from supporting government measures, and ministers were especially careful to respect its right of approving the expenditure of public revenues. The naval estimates were thus submitted annually, if only in outline, for the approval of the House. Cockburn's main constitutional role was to assist in justifying the amounts annually anticipated as necessary.

Tailored to be acceptable, these amounts were never a major political issue because the roles performed by the navy had cross-party agreement. Debate upon the estimates thus generally ranged widely over naval matters upon which prompt answers to questions and explanations of a technical nature damped down objections usually raised by radicals. Between his election at Portsmouth and the resignation of the Wellington ministry in November 1830, Cockburn thus spoke about sixty times, over half of these occasions in debates on the naval estimates. The subjects of other debates included petitions, the reduction of the number of Admiralty junior lords, the prevention of smuggling, the conduct of Queen Caroline's funeral, piracy in the West Indies, the merchant vessels apprentices Bill, promotion and manning in the navy, the management of Greenwich Hospital affairs, Codrington's conduct in the Mediterranean, and the office of Treasurer of the Navy. Over the whole period, Cockburn participated in three or four debates each session.

The burden created by these contributions to debates varied according to the issues. Specific topics called for precision: preparation for the debate on Queen Caroline's funeral demanded despatches from Croker two days beforehand.[16] But usually the level of expertise necessary to satisfy even experienced protagonists, like the renowned Hume, was not great. Points that required answering generally drew upon basic professional knowledge. Cockburn's contributions thus consisted of fair statements of matters as he saw them. Largely spontaneous, especially during wide-ranging discussions on the estimates, Cockburn's speeches were intended to appeal to, and allay the fears of, the conservative backbencher.

Out of their element, most naval officers in the House were wretched speakers. Cockburn himself was no orator: workmanlike and straightforward, without particular appeal to ear or intellect, he was nevertheless articulate, lucid and authoritative. His strength was his speed of response, collecting together opposition points, dismissing irrelevances of interpretation, and insisting upon the naval necessities of which the government case was comprised. In debates on the naval estimates, this ability to answer the opposition usually placed him second spokesman after a civil commissioner like Sir George Clerk had presented the Admiralty case. Here, his courtly courtesies ill-concealed a sharpness and strength that was rarely risked. The respect with which he was received can be judged by the contempt with which colleagues were sometimes treated. After nine years as an Admiralty commissioner, Sir

George Warrender was said by Sir Joseph Yorke in May 1821 to get 'up a speech indeed every year and let it off with all due flippancy; but, besides that, he never said a word about the naval service unless it might be in St James Street or any other place where he took the air'. Warrender was removed from the Board at the beginning of the subsequent parliamentary session. Cockburn, on the other hand, brooked no disrespect. In 1830 Yorke felt obliged to compliment him on 'the tone and temper' of his response to Lord Althorp who 'thought proper to call upon me [Cockburn], and to call upon me in no very delicate terms, in a manner in which I should be extremely sorry to address myself to his Lordship . . .'.[17]

Important elements in his appeal to the House of Commons were the presentation of himself both as a distinguished member of the naval profession, who had achieved his position through the merit of his own exertions, and as a fellow member of the gentry. Indeed, from about 1822, after his acquisition of High Beech House near Waltham Abbey, Essex, his claim to be a country gentleman carried authenticity. These appeals were coupled with a direct, ingenuous manner that conveyed a sense of complete integrity: 'I will not trouble the House further about myself and my merits. I have explained exactly the situation in which I stand; and if it shall be the pleasure of Parliament to pronounce that "the labourer is not worthy of his hire", I shall retire without hesitation . . .'.[18] Sharpened by points of a legal or naval nature, his appeals for support commanded respect and understanding.

Familiarity with Cockburn, and his familiarity with the attitudes of backbenchers, promoted a working relationship. After ten years in the Commons, in which he had consistently maintained the principle of promoting young officers, he could take the support of backbenchers for granted: 'he would not argue the question by reference to the feelings of the House because he knew by experience that he could carry them with him . . .'.[19] This experience of the House was important, for Cockburn and his colleagues relied upon backbenchers' sense of national duty and loyalty to the Crown, even during periods of difficulty. Indeed, in spite of the country's economic problems, from which few country gentlemen escaped untouched, it was their support for national interests that permitted the numbers of men voted for the navy to rise steadily from 19,000 in 1817 to 29,000 in 1824. Even the growth in this last year by more than 4,000 men raised virtually no opposition,[20] for most backbenchers were prepared to accept on trust even relatively extravagant demands.

The same trust, coupled with conservative disinterest, prevented radicals from making difficulties for the government over social conditions in the navy. Between 1824 and 1829 they managed to make impressment and flogging the subject of four debates. Divisions were forced in the first two, yet the government proportion of the vote in March 1824 on impressment was still 73 per cent of the House, and in June 1825 on flogging, 67 per cent. This was little less than the usual 74 per cent commanded by the government on naval matters between 1821 and 1828. In consequence, reformers looked upon the navy 'as a kind of forlorn hope'.[21]

The security of this support for the navy permitted ministers to virtually ignore naval matters in the Commons until 1828. Lack of controversy also reduced the numbers of members attending debates. More than 180 voted in divisions in 1822 and 1823; less than 70 between 1825 and 1828. Various factors affected interest. One was obviously the distraction of greater issues. In 1829, when the trickle of debates on social aspects of the navy temporarily ceased, the House was preoccupied with the Roman Catholic Relief Bill. In 1830, on the other hand, the insecurity of the government superimposed political interest on naval issues, and attendance at debates rose to an average of over 230. Indeed in March 1830, when the government faced defeat for the proposed provision of pensions to two naval commissioners, attendance rose to as many as 260.[22]

Political instability for the navy and its administrators, as for other branches of government, commenced with the death of Liverpool. Melville declined to serve under Canning and was replaced at the head of the navy by the Duke of Clarence as Lord High Admiral. To Cockburn, in May 1827, Canning's administration appeared 'to be as strong in the House of Commons as the former government ever was'. However, Canning's death in August—'so sad a blow'—threw the Tory government again into confusion. His decease, the failure of Goderich as Prime Minister and of Clarence as Lord High Admiral, took Wellington to the head of government and Melville back to the Admiralty. Yet, with the resignations of Huskisson and other Canningites and consequent reshuffles, Croker at the Admiralty was still half expecting a new office in June 1828. Cockburn himself may have had like thoughts, for Melville advised him in August 1829 that the clubs in London had selected him for the government of Bombay: 'no bad thing' in Cockburn's view, 'and they are therefore entitled to my thanks for their gossip taking a kind turn rather than otherwise'.[23] But by then, unsettled by shifts and weaknesses in leadership, backbenchers had begun to heed the views of reformers, and ministers to feel a need for concessions.

The Defence of Naval Interests

The process of political change that begain in 1828 revealed Cockburn as the principal professional defender of naval interests in the House of Commons. It coincided with his appointment as first naval lord at the Board of Admiralty, and with the earliest recollections of his main historical detractor, Sir John Briggs. But already, of necessity, he had long since assumed a defensive role in conflicts between the Admiralty and other departments of government, within the Admiralty during the administration of the Duke of Clarence as Lord High Admiral, and in the representation and control of the officer corps.

That he should have been cast in this role was due primarily to changing circumstances. After 1818 the British navy needed all the resources it could muster. The assumption that it had so convincingly defeated its enemies and was without potential opponents is without foundation. Old enemies, the American, French, Russians and Algerians, remained a cause for concern, the first growing in influence in the 1820s, the defence of Canada and Gibraltar becoming matters of official consideration proportional to the perceived threat. The period was one of considerable instability in Latin America, Italy and Greece, and the navy was called upon to exert influence in Portugal and Turkey, while defending British trade and interests in South America and the Mediterranean in particular. In consequence, the battle capability of the British fleet had to be maintained, its ships rebuilt or replaced with larger vessels more strongly constructed and more powerfully gunned.[24]

In the 1820s the British navy appeared at the height of its international power. Yet, paradoxically, within British politics it was in relative decline. Until 1823 economic recession, mass demobilization and unemployment created Cabinet preoccupations that, in the absence of hostilities, made naval matters secondary in importance. The influence the Admiralty possessed and the resources it could command consequently continued in decline. As late as December 1826 the Comptroller of the Navy Board could complain with justice that 'year after year everything is sacrificed in order to pull down the estimates'.[25] This meant fewer ships maintained fit for service, tighter limits on the numbers kept in commission, and rationalization of the administration.

Plate 5. The exterior of the Admiralty Buildings in the late 1820s. A screen separates the courtyard from Whitehall. The post for the semaphore projects from the roof. (National Maritime Museum)

This in turn threatened Admiralty authority, officer morale and the efficiency of organization and training.

This relative decline in the standing of the Admiralty was illustrated by an explanation given by Cockburn in March 1820 in response to a charge of supineness for failing to obtain from the Cabinet a decision on Sir Robert Barrie's discretionary powers on the Great Lakes in Canada. The failure was due, he explained, simply on account of the 'important occurrences which have so followed each other during the last six or eight months': 'the Manchester and numerous other radical efforts to produce internal anarchy and civil war, the death of our late good king, the changing of parliament, the affairs of Spain and her colonies, the late infernal assassination conspiracy, with other pressing circumstances.' The problems had kept 'the Cabinet so anxiously and so constantly occupied that they have been prevented from fully considering the whole of the Canada question'.[26]

At this time, domestic problems included clashes between smugglers and the navy's 'coast blockade' forces. In November 1818 the Admiralty had to refer to Lord Liverpool, as first Lord of the Treasury and Prime Minister, a full account of events at Deal where local officials were intimidated and the crew of a naval vessel stationed in the Downs physically ousted from the scene of smuggling activities. The Board requested steps be taken for 'such a system of police' as would protect persons on naval service. A party of seamen, from the *Severn*, on patrol on shore had been attacked by people assisting the smugglers and one of the seamen had been shot and killed. Although the murderer had been identified, the mayor of Deal would not issue a warrant for his arrest. He did not dare to attempt it himself 'where so great a population have not only separated themselves from the law of the country, but treat it with contempt and derision'. Several local people 'publicly and openly extolled the murderer for his conduct'. Later, the *Severn*'s look-out men on shore were again attacked 'with large stones along the beach opposite the town where some goods were prevented from being seen'. Such incidents were not isolated. In December 1820 Cockburn signed a request to Liverpool to consider the conduct of magistrates at Folkestone over whom the Secretary of State was 'unable to exercise any control'.[27] In 1821 a south-coast fisherman was killed in a struggle to inspect his boat.

Admiralty commissioners like Cockburn could not avoid involvement in domestic problems. In 1821 the likelihood and danger of popular demonstrations against an 'unfaithful' George IV required the funeral procession of Queen Caroline go overland to Harwich on its way to Brunswick, rather than proceed down the Thames. The route was altered 'on the representation of Melville who brought . . . Cockburn with him to a small Cabinet at which the Chancellor, Westmorland, Vansittart' and Liverpool were present.[28] One reason advanced for the change was the danger to crowds in river-boats that might be jammed between the piers of a bridge by the ebb tide. The navigation of the Thames was a naval concern and Cockburn maintained liaison with the New London Bridge Committee throughout the 1820s. Later in the decade he also advised Croker on the role the navy might play in the event of an insurrection in Ireland.[29]

The Board of Admiralty to which Cockburn was appointed in 1818 was well equipped to deal with such civil concerns. Its civil members were experienced and distinguished. Lord Melville, the First Lord, had held office since March 1812 and was to remain First Lord (except for 16 months when the Duke of Clarence was Lord High Admiral) until July 1830, when Cockburn also retired from the Board; two other civil commissioners had also been at the Admiralty since 1812. Supplementing their experience was that of the First Secretary, John Wilson Croker, who took office in 1809 and was also to remain until 1830. In addition, there was John Barrow who (apart from a year's absence in 1806–7) had held the office of Second Secretary since 1804 and was not to retire until 1845.

In contrast, its naval commissioners, though good sea officers, possessed neither long administrative experience nor professional distinction. When Cockburn joined the Board in 1818, Sir Graham Moore had been there two years and was to retire in 1820. He was replaced by Sir William Johnstone Hope, who could claim two years previous service at the Board between 1807 and 1809; he remained at the Admiralty as first naval lord until 1828. Sir Henry Hotham joined with Cockburn and retired in 1822; an amenable colleague, he was to rejoin in 1828 when Cockburn became the first naval commissioner. Among these relatively undistinguished naval officers, Cockburn stood out—even more so after 1822, when Board membership was reduced from seven to five commissioners, its naval members from three to two.[30]

The duties of these commissioners were loosely specialized. Melville, as a member of the Cabinet, convoyed government policy to the Board as it concerned naval strategy, expenditure and patronage. He kept 'much in his own hands, the accountant business and the erasing from or restoring officers to the List'.[31] The first sea commissioner (Moore, then Hope and after 1828 Cockburn) specialized in the management of the dockyards; the building, equipment and choice of ships for particular services; and advising on the choice of officers for ships. As second sea commissioner Cockburn was not excluded from some of this, but was expected to concentrate on the other naval business. In March 1819, after a year's experience, he described in the House of Commons the range of these duties: correspondence with over 8,000 naval officers distributed around the world; the investigation of grievances; the consideration of proposals for improving hulls, guns, ropes, rigging, astronomical instruments etc; the maintenance of measures to provide protection to British trade and to enforce observance of treaties by other powers; dockyard visitations and decisions on details of management for the guidance of the Navy and Victualling Boards.[32]

Loosely defined, overlapping duties and a collective system of board management gave Cockburn a wider influence in the business of the Admiralty than his own particular responsibilities. At Board meetings the commissioner with the best grasp of a subject and most convincing exposition of a solution invariably carried the day. Here Cockburn excelled. John Barrow recalled his 'possession of a rigorous understanding, of thorough professional knowledge in the military, civil and judicial departments of the service, and of indefatigable perseverance in the execution of the laborious duties of his office. For clearness of intellect, for ability in making himself master of the most intricate and complicated cases', Barrow 'never met his equal'. In view of Barrow's service to the Board of 41 years, this was a considerable compliment.[33]

His domination of naval matters should not be overstated. At times he did differ in opinion with the other commissioners. Also, much of Board business was matter of small importance. Many of its letters were from the subordinate boards, especially the Navy Board. The majority were routine, requesting instructions relating to the construction, equipment or paying off of ships, the supply of guns or tenders, physical improvements in the yards, the provision of pensions for artificers or their widows, and so on. Some answers—concerned with details of procedure or requesting reports—were simply signed by Barrow.[34] Others were the product of an individual in the privacy of his office. Melville himself drafted many documents, especially instructions of political importance, and also the estimates after discussion with Byam Martin, the Comptroller of the Navy Board, whom he consulted on most matters concerning the material of the navy. On such drafts there would be some debate at the Board before Croker had the final letters drawn up and signed in triplicate.[35]

Nonetheless there was a key factor that, when present, made Cockburn's opinions almost insuperable—it was the partnership in ideas and arguments with Croker. Already friends, they were concerting over Board membership even before Cockburn was appointed; thereafter they maintained a close relationship. Croker's experience already gave him a formidable knowledge; he contributed regularly to the *Quarterly Review* and often on naval subjects. But his principal distinction was as a speaker in the House of Commons, on more than just naval matters. With equally strong personalities and speaking together as necessary in debates, the two operated naturally in tandem, and sometimes also with Barrow. Sir Thomas Hardy was said to observe 'that he could not argue against Cockburn, Croker and Barrow, for they carried too heavy a broadside for him. They would prove him wrong in two minutes, though he knew he was right for all that'.[36] The success of this team stemmed as much from close co-operation as from like minds. Within the Admiralty they talked through problems together, arranging how to handle them. While Croker obtained Cockburn's professional opinion, the latter secured a place for his interests in Board agendas.[37]

A major duty which brought the two together was the drafting of regulations and instructions. John Barrow noted that Cockburn had 'acquired so complete a knowledge of naval and military law that the Board were seldom unsatisfied with his opinion; and the office of Counsel to the Admiralty was all but a sinecure, a solicitor alone being required'. Briggs too observed how Cockburn could 'dispute a point of law with almost the ability and acumen of his talented nephew, Sir Alexander Cockburn'.[38] He was capable of expounding as well as analysing regulations. In 1822 he was thus employed to revise the Admiralty's general printed instructions, assimilating suggestions both of Croker and of Melville. In this his main concern was that the instructions would 'at last be clear and decided on every point mentioned and not be liable to be misinterpreted even by sea officers'.[39] He also drafted instructions for particular voyages, for example for Parry in 1824 at the time of his expeditions in search of the north-west passage.[40]

Croker and he came together again to judge infringements of regulations and instructions. Croker was specially familiar with accounts referred to the Admiralty for clearance due to some irregularity. Over a decade later, Cockburn recalled being called to Croker's office in connection with an incorrect certificate given in by a purser. Croker had been 'desired to see the purser himself to know if he could give any satisfactory explanation regarding it'. The purser defended his conduct and Croker was convinced no fraud was intended. Even so, Cockburn was called to explain to the purser 'the more serious light in which it had been viewed by Lord Melville and the Board with reference to the article of the instructions bearing upon it'.[41]

Croker and Cockburn naturally consulted over cases for courts martial, a business which involved them wading through all the relevant papers. Croker, as Secretary to the Board, sometimes had to give evidence at these trials, especially those which placed the Admiralty in conflict with other departments of government. This was the case in 1823 when Captain Harris of the *Superb* was court martialled for not keeping to his instructions when carrying Sir Edward Thornton to Portugal for the Foreign Office. Ships were frequently employed on duties requested by the Foreign Office, or officials acting for it, and their captains were sometimes subject to requests that conflicted with their Admiralty instructions. Harris evidently acceded to a request from Thornton that seriously interfered with Admiralty intentions for the *Superb*. At his court martial Canning, the Foreign Secretary, as well as Croker was called to give evidence—a situation which Cockburn found annoying as he foresaw that Harris would automatically be acquitted. Even so, he advised Croker that he should give a 'full and clear state of the case' as the Admiralty saw it and 'not be turned aside from the straight path' they had pursued. In the event, it was not so much the acquittal as Canning's evidence which damaged relations. At a late stage he produced an extract of a letter previously unseen by Croker specifically intended to exculpate Harris, though it completely contradicted other official letters.[42] 'A grand quarrel' developed between Canning, Croker and Cockburn. Indeed, Cockburn was 'so highly offended that when he received Canning's invitation to the usual dinner meeting of the members of Government previous to the opening of Parliament to read the speech, he sent immediately refusal'. Croker was 'equally offended' but went. That did not prevent Canning issuing an order, or so W.H. Fremantle heard, 'at the Foreign Office *not* to correspond through the *Secretary with the Admiralty*'. Cockburn and Croker were 'sorely hurt'. Fremantle nevertheless took Cockburn 'to be an ungovernable man, . . . his head turned by the dominion he holds at the Admiralty'.[43]

However, it was not just for the sake of discipline that Cockburn was concerned about obedience to Admiralty instructions. The refitting, repair and maintenance of the navy depended on a proper circulation of ships. In August 1824 Cockburn was still complaining of the diplomat Thornton who, in combination with 'the meddling wife of the captain of *Windsor Castle*', attempted to insist that that ship remained in the Tagus. Cockburn required Croker to contest the issue with Canning if necessary: 'they ought certainly to be satisfied at the foreign office if we place the *force* asked for at his disposal, without leaving to him the selection of particular ships. . . . There were many reasons which made me desirous to have *Windsor Castle* home in preference, and I trust when *Superb* arrives in the Tagus there will be no more of this petticoat counterworking of our orders to prevent again the return of the former'.[44]

Interference from diplomats and 'meddling wives' was aggravating on account of the shortage of ships in commission. Indeed, had that interference been tolerated, the confidence with which the Admiralty could plan the allocation of vessels to stations and tasks throughout the world would have been undermined. The huge effort of gaining finance and men, commissioning and deploying vessels, would have been dissipated. As it was, vessels surplus to immediate requirements were scarce. Cockburn spent mid-September 1819 'rummaging' vessels for troop transports out of Portsmouth harbour![45]

Naval efficiency was also threatened by parliamentary economies. In 1818 Cockburn joined the Admiralty at perhaps the most difficult stage in the post-war peace reduction. Opinion in Parliament demanded that both army and navy expenses be severely reduced; the impression was 'that if the thing was not done *bona fide* and to a very great extent by the Government, the House of Commons would take it out of their hands and do it for them to a still greater amount'. Consequently, in June 1818, Lord Liverpool informed Melville that the naval estimates for 1819 should not exceed six millions, a small reduction on the sum granted to the navy for 1818.[46] Cockburn was obliged to examine the potential impact of this reduction and argued that the economies should not be allowed to reduce the number of officers maintained in commission and training.

At the Admiralty, on this occasion, the choice lay between reducing the number of vessels in service at sea or cutting the men on board guardships at each of the major naval bases. The latter carried the flag of their respective Port Admirals who maintained them as showpieces. To

Plate 6. The Admiralty Board Room in the 1820s. The First Lord sits at the near end of the table, the other commissioners on either side, with the Secretary at the far end. (National Maritime Museum)

many they were symbols of the Royal Navy's standards and standing, and as such carried strong emotional attachments. Yet they were the obvious economy. Cockburn later explained to Sir John Gore:

> had we allowed the weight of the reduction to have fallen in any material proportion on the seagoing ships, we must have put entirely *out of commission* the greater number of the young officers rising in the profession who are now gaining *necessary* professional practice *afloat*. But by turning as we have done the guard ships into hulks or rather into mere store houses for their own armaments and residences for their captains and officers, we have managed to reduce the number required of us without giving up a single cruizer or putting one captain or admiral out of *full* pay, points of no small importance when it is considered how very *few* situations are opened to naval officers to offer them aught beyond their *half* pay and yet how numerous is the list of them and great their claims.[47]

At the same time Cockburn wanted these guardships to serve as training establishments. Thus, when Melville suggested that two extra guardships might be provided if all the guardships did without jolly boat, gig and tender, Cockburn argued forcibly against dispensing with the latter:

> by every guardship having a tender in constant activity, if the captains send the officers and mids in them in rotation as they ought to do, these gentlemen will be rather gaining than losing professional knowledge whilst belonging to these guardships, and the contrary certainly would be the case if they were confined to the ships as merely hulks.[48]

Meanwhile, the danger of a shortage of seamen seemed less threatening. Pensions had been granted to 35,000 men at the conclusion of the last war on condition of their return to the navy if called upon. In addition there was the possibility of resorting to the press. 'Whilst we have such extensive commerce we may be able always to put our hands on a sufficient number of seamen from our merchants ships to commence a war with.' Impressment was questioned in the House of Commons from 1821, but it still seemed the only practicable method of manning the fleet in an emergency. Cockburn defended it as a necessary evil. His only concern at this time was to improve the existing means of recruitment through 'rendezvous' at the main ports, for, except in the Thames, raising the required number of seamen was slow in peacetime.[49]

The facility with which Cockburn argued these and other points reinforced his ascendancy at the Board. His thinking had a natural logic which defended both the authority of the Admiralty and its resources: its strength in commissioned ships, its officers in employment and training, and its means of manning the navy. Throughout the 1820s the frequent absence of Melville in Scotland and at the Cabinet, and the occasional absence of Croker in the holiday season, gave him experience in overseeing Board business.[50] By May 1827, after nine years in office, he had developed an almost proprietorial command of the conduct of naval affairs. It was this that the Duke of Clarence encountered on his appointment to the office of Lord High Admiral.

Defying the Lord High Admiral

At the beginning of May 1827 Lord Melville resigned his post. Lord Liverpool, Prime Minister since 1812, had been found unconscious after an apoplectic fit and George Canning had formed a new government in which Melville declined to serve. To replace Melville, Canning grasped at an idea proposed by Croker, to make the 62-year-old William, Duke of Clarence, the third son of George III, Lord High Admiral.

Croker had probably not advanced the idea too seriously. The last Lord High Admirals had been the Earl of Pembroke and Prince George, Duke of Denmark, between 1703 and 1709. The subsequent neglect of the office reflected the opinion that it was better placed in commission. Qualities possessed by Clarence did not recommend the arrangement either. He had been a professional sea officer between 1779 and 1789, rising quickly to post-captain on account of his birth. He had achieved a basic competence, but his conduct as an officer had been marked by brutish, bad-tempered self-indulgence. Refused further employment at sea in spite of twenty-two years of warfare, he had come to detest the Board of Admiralty. At Brighton in 1815 Clarence had given Croker 'provocation beyond all endurance by abusing Lord Melville, George Hope and the rest of the Board' even though Croker had 'begged of him' to recollect his situation.[51] In 1827 there were thus some who did not think Clarence's appointment the *coup de maître* Croker and Canning did. Knighton, the King's private secretary, called the appointment a 'sad and foolish act'.[52] And so, for Admiralty administration, it was to transpire.

Cockburn in 1827 was regarded by the Duke as 'an upstart'.[53] George IV nevertheless made him a Privy Councillor and, with the other commissioners of the former Board, one of the Lord Admiral's council. The secretaries too remained in position. But the council now performed a different role to that of the former Board.

The patent appointing the Lord High Admiral and his council was 'substantially' the same as that granted to Prince George in 1702. In appearance the Lord High Admiral alone had direction of naval affairs: he was in fact vested with all the power and authority formerly possessed by the Board. So powerful was that position, indeed, that Wellington was able to assure Clarence in 1828 that he knew of no other office under the Crown of Great Britain of which the holder had such power.[54] However, he was subject to checks. The patent was followed by an Act of Parliament (7 & 8 Geo. IV, cap.66) which constituted the new arrangement in law. Under this Act, the nomination of the council remained with the King. Clarence had to accept the advisers whom the government recommended to the King and with whom the latter agreed. Secondly, the patent deliberately set out to relieve the Lord High Admiral 'from all pecuniary and official responsibility'. He had always to have 'two men skilled in maritime affairs to assist and advise' him 'in all things and business appertaining or belonging to that office'. Thus:

> the Lord High Admiral while in London and acting with the knowledge of his council and without objection on their part has all the power that the Board of Admiralty possessed. But if his Royal Highness should be afloat or otherwise at a distance from his council, it will be necessary that he should be attended by one or more of his council, or transmit his orders to his council to be carried into execution.

Without the advice and consent of two members of his council, the Lord High Admiral could not be relieved from official and pecuniary responsibility, and if he attempted to act without them he was acting in contravention of the new Admiralty constitution.[55]

For the first few months Clarence and his council worked in harmony. The Duke, full of enthusiasm for his new role, applied himself eagerly. One of his first self-imposed duties was to lead a visitation of the dockyards where his days were spent personally examining ships, accounts and storehouses. His interests were catholic and his orders unstinted.[56] The young clerk Briggs in the Admiralty office could only marvel at the novelty of the Duke's orders. He recalled how Clarence gave orders for the exercise of guardships, the commissioning of the first steamship on the list of the navy, a check on the use of the cat, the employment of commanders instead of first lieutenants in ships of the line, a quarterly return of gunnery exercises performed on each ship and a half-yearly report 'of the state of preparation for battle' from each ship on every station.[57]

At the Admiralty, Cockburn and Croker soon began to tire of the degree to which Clarence could impose his own personal wishes.[58] The council met regularly with Clarence just as the Board had met before. But measures now depended more on the opinion of one man than on concensus. The existing system of minutes enlarged: proposals were put up on paper which the Duke would sign 'Approved, William'; more would come from the Lord High Admiral's office, 'His Royal Highness wishes an order to be issued . . .', which Cockburn would initial with 'orders accordingly'. Accustomed to Melville's experience, confidence in their own expertise, and the use of board meetings for discussion, Cockburn and Croker began to realize the new arrangement was not operating to their liking.

There were two particular problems. First, responsibility for the direction of the navy remained at the pinnacle of the hierarchy. Whereas Melville had been content for many routine decisions to be taken by his fellow commissioners, now every decision had to receive the Duke's approval. Cockburn, Croker and the others still had to manage the business—consulting with the Foreign Secretary and executing orders for the deployment of ships—but now there was no credit or final responsibility in it. Whereas previously the Lords Commssioners had issued orders collectively, now only the Lord High Admiral commanded. Secondly, although his councillors were supposed to advise him, Clarence was unaccustomed to receiving advice and resentful when his councillors insisted on offering it. Though earnestly intending to improve the service he loved, he refused to become accountable to his social inferiors. Had he not been inexperienced in administrative matters, his leanings towards independence might have been conceded. But his councillors quickly learned that Clarence was not the man in whose hands they could trust the navy in time of crisis.

The greater the council's experience of Clarence, the greater grew their distrust. It was soon scarcely concealed. As all *official* communications from the subordinate boards to the Admiralty *had* to receive the answer of the Lord High Admiral, proposals or information requiring tactful handling were now communicated by personal note to Croker or members of the council.[59] Perhaps Clarence became suspicious that he was being deprived of knowledge by such means. At all events, by the end of July Cockburn was adopting a new rule not to mention official matters in private correspondence. To sea officers like Codrington, off the Greek coast, the new rule was bewildering; he could neither answer the points just mentioned to him in a private letter nor express those professional worries which most troubled his mind.

> Your letter of the 31 July was delivered to me yesterday [he replied to Cockburn on 31 August]. How was I to understand that we were not to write privately on official matters, I know not. Nothing to that effect ever passed between us; but I should say quite the contrary by your desiring to know in all respects how the ship answered under different circumstances, particulars I imagine not to be expected from me to J.W. Croker. However, you have a clear right to make this decision, although as my experience goes your predecessors have found the other practice most convenient. I will not therefore discuss the matter further, tempted as I am to shew the unsoundness of your reasoning on it.[60]

Clarence decided that he alone should determine appointments within the civil departments. On 15 September he thus declared his intention 'to take to himself the appointment of clerks on their first entry in the several naval departments'. The Navy Board then felt they were 'forbidden to receive any other nominations', a fear which the Lord Admiral did not dispel. Cockburn was well aware of these uncertainties: his brother James was Paymaster of Royal Marines and he too proceeded warily.[61] In the civil departments the selection and appointment of clerks by their principals was a much guarded traditional prerogative.[62] At a time when those departments were pared to the bone, the Duke engrossed the whole of civil patronage for himself.

Cockburn and Croker were also disturbed by Clarence's personal selection of officers for reward and promotion. The council's lack of involvement was evident following the Battle of Navarino. Sir William Dillon noticed that:

> the honours distributed to the naval officers present at the battle . . . surpassed in proportion those given to the heroes of Trafalgar: and many comments were the consequence of that act. The fact was the the Duke of Clarence . . . upon receipt of the account of that victory, repaired instantly to his royal brother, the King, and they settled quietly between themselves the honours to be awarded without consulting the [prime] minster.[63]

The officer corps at each rank was still inflated by the greater numbers needed before 1815. Promotions were kept to the minimum necessary. Yet, by September 1828, Croker was forced to observe to the Duke of Wellington, then Prime Minister:

> Your Grace must recollect that First Lords on going out have been generally in the habit of making a promotion with a view to satisfy either

private friendship or claims to which they may have pledged themselves and have not been able to satisfy in the ordinary course of service; Lord Melville, for instance, made eight captains, eighteen commanders, and fifty lieutenants. But these were *all* made with concurrence, and in the majority of instances by the advice of my confidential Sea Lord; for instance, of the fifty lieutenants, thirty were made from the *head of the list* of those who had passed their examination for that rank prior to the year 1815.

The promotions which his Royal Highness now makes are without any advice with his council; they have already (except in the minor article of lieutenants) greatly exceeded Lord Melville's amount, and they will, of course, go on during the existence of the present state of things; and what Sir George Cockburn fears is, that they will be still followed (when the day of retirement shall come) by a list similar to those which First Lords have been in the habit of making.[64]

The difficulty of managing the Duke of Clarence was common knowledge in the government by October 1827.[65] The Duke's jubilation at the destruction of the Turkish fleet at Navarino—in stark contrast to the government's dismay and private condemnation—was the final straw. Croker noted in his diary on 19 March 1828:

The king, that is Huskisson, has directed that Codrington shall receive orders direct from the Secretary of State. There are many precedents; even as late as the last Copenhagen expedition; and if it had been done in July last, no one could have objected, but doing it now does look like disapprobation of the conduct of the Lord High Admiral and he so feels it . . .'[66]

In the council, the task of placing a check on Clarence fell to Cockburn. From March 1828 he succeeded Sir Willaim Hope as first naval councillor. Of particular concern to him was Clarence's appointment of an admiral and six captains to be his personal aides de camp.[67] Having selected these officers himself, they expressed political and professional views more representative of the liberal Lord Admiral than of his Tory council. Moreover, they had an influence with Clarence and brother officers which rivalled that of the council.

The occasion for Cockburn to take the Duke to task occurred in July 1828, over the institution of another body which threatened to rival the council's authority. While Cockburn was away, Clarence proposed the establishment of a 'standing commission' of officers to consider naval gunnery. On his return, the council modified the plan, the alternative being accepted by the Duke. Shortly afterwards, however, Clarence 'sent for Sir James Cockburn and complained to him in very strong terms of his brother, the admiral's conduct, in respect to this commission'. Sir George consequently had an audience with the Duke, when he explained 'that his objections, in common with those of the council, generally applied to the permanent establishment of the commission, and to the extent of the objects of their enquiry (which in fact embraced all the duties of the Admiralty) rather than to the commission itself for enquiry into any particular branch of the service'. The discussion ended amicably.

Yet on 9 July the quarrel suddenly revived.[68] Without the knowledge of his council, Clarence hoisted his flag as Lord High Admiral on board the yacht *Royal Sovereign* in the Thames. Soon after, without consulting his council, he sent an order, dated 10 July as if on board the *Royal Sovereign*, to the members of the committee on gunnery, then sitting at the Admiralty, for them to proceed to Portsmouth to meet him there and to remain there for so long as he saw fit. A copy of the order was sent to Cockburn who immediately wrote to Clarence pointing out

> that such an order (even if its form had been unobjectionable) so given on board of a ship, separated from, and without the knowledge of, the council . . . is neither in accordance with the spirit of the Act of Parliament regulating the appointment of the council, nor consistent with the real nature of the high office your Royal Highness has condescended to accept; for if your Royal Highness can, whilst so separated from the council, issue orders involving questions of important official regulations, or of public policy, or involving (as in this instance) expense to an indefinite amount, the responsibility of the council would be ideal rather than real and our continuance in that station under such circumstances would only tend to mislead the public, which might suppose us to be parties to occurrences in which in point of fact we have had no share whatever.

Cockburn went on to suggest that for Clarence to hoist his flag was to misinterpret the nature of his office, which was 'that of a high and important department of the State, rather than that of the first flag officer of the sea service'. In point of constitutional form, he argued, Clarence could not assume the role of a sea officer without instructions from the King and an order in council defining the portion of the fleet he was to command.

Predictably, Clarence did not concur. He responded to Cockburn:

> Your letter of this morning does not give me *displeasure* but *concern* to see *one* I had kept when appointed to this situation of Lord High Admiral, *constantly* opposing what *I* consider *good* for the King's service. In this free country every one has a *right* to have *his* opinion, and *I* have therefore to have *mine*, which *differs* totally from *yours*.
>
> The *only* part of *your* letter which I *can* approve, is where *you* mention *expense*, and being now underweigh I have only to say I shall, *for the present*, leave the order *you* so *improperly* object to in your hands till I return, when I shall talk the matter over with you deliberately. But I cannot conclude without repeating *my* council is *not* to dictate but to give advice.

In addition, at four the following morning from off the North Foreland, he wrote to the Duke of Wellington:

> Finding by the *continued* and *serious* difference of opinion there is between *me* and *Sir George Cockburn*, on points of the utmost consequence concerning his Majesty's service, it will not be to the advantage of the public good that *Sir George* should continue *one* of *my* council. I am to request your Grace humbly to submit to the King, in *my* name, that Rear Admiral the honourable Sir Charles Paget may be appointed . . . in the room of Sir George Cockburn.

Wellington was aware of the correspondence that had already taken place. His advice had formed the basis of Cockburn's first letter to Clarence. He now informed the King that Clarence's proposition was 'impossible to . . . be carried into execution without causing public discussion, and doing his Royal Highness the utmost injury'. The King, though brother to Clarence, was 'entirely in unison' with Wellington. Indeed he believed it necessary 'not only to settle this immediate question, but to put the extinguisher upon *all* and *every* future attempt which might (other and at some most unexpected moment) hereafter arise, or rather recur, if not *now*, and *immediately* (but with good humour and firmness), stopped *in limine*'. Clarence accordingly received a frank letter from the Duke of Wellington at every point supporting Cockburn.

By then, however, Clarence had received a second unrepentant letter from Cockburn and come to believe the admiral's removal was the only alternative to his own. He considered 'this answer of Sir George Cockburn's, if possible, more *disrespectful* and more *impertinent*, if *possible*, than my *first*.'[69] The crisis had reached its height. Each of the other three councillors expressed their intention of following Cockburn should he be forced to retire. Wellington declared a necessity to 'consult the Cabinet as to the advice to be given to his Majesty upon this occasion'. George IV conceded his brother nothing. He wrote privately to Clarence late on 15 July:

> It is with feelings of the deepest regret that I observe the embarrassing situation in which you have placed yourself. You are in error from the beginning to the end. This is not a matter of opinion, but a positive fact; and when the Duke of Wellington so properly calls your attention to the words of your patent, let me ask how Sir George Cockburn could have acted otherwise?
>
> You must not forget, my dear William, that Sir George Cockburn is the King's Privy Councillor, and so made by the King, to advise the Lord High Admiral.
>
> What becomes of Sir George Cockburn's oath, his duty towards me, his Sovereign, if he fails to offer such advice as he may think necessary to the Lord High Admiral? Am I, then, to be called upon to dismiss the most useful and perhaps the most important naval officer in my service for conscientiously acting up to the letter and spirit of his oath and his duty? The thing is impossible. I love you *most truly*, as you know, and no one would do more or go further to protect and meet your feelings; but on the present occasion I have no alternative; you must give way, and listen to the affection of your best friend and most attached brother.[70]

Wellington followed with another private letter to Clarence asking him 'to take a different view, not only of the case itself, but likewise of the conduct of Sir George Cockburn', whose letter, he argued, contained not 'a disrespectful word or intention in it'.

Clarence became stubborn. To his brother he observed 'that Sir George Cockburn *cannot* be the most useful and the *most important officer* in your Majesty's service who never had the ships *he* commanded in *proper* fighting order'. He travelled to London and demanded that Cockburn retract. Cockburn of course would not:

> he would repeat as often as was desired his respect for the Duke, his personal regret at having displeased him, and his disavowal of anything like personal disrespect; that on *all such* points he was willing to go as far as could possibly be suggested; but that as to the *principle* involved in the discussion, *that* he must abide by, and could retract nothing of *that* kind.

On 18 July Wellington saw Clarence twice. He again had Cockburn express in writing his regret at causing displeasure, and then effected a meeting between the two in his presence. Clarence was not 'entirely satisfied' with Cockburn, but Wellington was hopeful that business would thereafter be carried on as intended.

Yet the reconciliation was short-lived. Clarence returned to Portsmouth to resume his inspection of the out-ports and 'to exercise for a few days with the three-deckers'. On the last day of July, he hoisted his flag and sailed to join the manoeuvres. Separated from his council, the Admiralty was without power. On Cockburn prompting Wellington, and him the King, George IV posed the alternative for Clarence to 'obey the law or resign'.[71] Still he resisted, insisting that he would defer to his council only on matters of finance. 'Unless it is clearly understood between your Grace and myself that I am to be *in future* the judge, *except in matters of expense*, on what matters I shall consult my council, *I must resign*'. Coming to London on 7 August, he 'behaved very rudely to Cockburn; in short, laid him aside altogether, sending his orders to the council through Sir Edward Owen'. Wellington saw Cockburn and Croker: 'both agreed in stating that the machine could no longer work'. After consulting the Cabinet, Wellington so informed Clarence who promptly submitted his resignation.[72]

On 12 August, in the presence of the Lord Chancellor, the King explained his ultimatum to his brother. 'The truth then came out that his Royal Highness would not remain in office unless Sir George Cockburn was removed.' He had no reason to complain of the King or Wellington 'but . . . of Sir George Cockburn he did complain, and that he must be removed'. His obsession with Cockburn settled the matter. Wellington spoke to the King after dinner, re-emphasising the monarch's inability to remove from office a gentleman who had performed his duty, and for no other reason than that he had remonstrated against a breach of the law by the Duke. As he later observed, 'the sacrifice of Sir George Cockburn would have been a gratuitous degradation of government'.[73] For his part at the Admiralty, Cockburn 'felt it to be due to himself' to have Clarence informed 'that he did not stand alone', that the whole council would have resigned had he been obliged to go. There was an immediate change of heart. On the 16th the Duke 'begged to shake hands'. This gave rise to hopes in the royal family of the resignation being withdrawn.[74] But they were ill-founded hopes, for by then Cockburn was already hard at work arranging with Melville the composition of the next Board of Admiralty.[75]

Managing the Officer Corps

As both second and first sea commissioner at the Admiralty between

Plate 7. Cockburn as an Admiralty commissioner, about 1824. Note the equipment of office—the chart, documents and bound volumes—at his right hand. By Sir William Beechey. (National Maritime Museum)

1818 and 1830, Cockburn performed four roles for the officer corps. He interested himself in their welfare; he acted as an intermediary through whom officers and their patrons pressed their claims for appointments; he attempted to manage the ill feeling generated among officers by Cabinet or Admiralty decisions; and he participated in decisions necessary to promote discipline.

Welfare

At the time Cockburn joined the Admiralty, the officer corps was only just coming to terms with the end of the French wars. Economies posed problems of morale and welfare, and Cockburn took a paternal interest. Of those who wrote, the senior and the distinguished received personal replies. These, a mixture of philosophy and sentiment, hoped they would set sacrifices and difficulties 'at nought'.[76] When possible, he took up their cases, especially those of a financial nature. Expenses were secured for attendance on committees or courts martial, and battle was waged with other departments. Thus Sir Charles Morice Pole was told:

> You cannot do better than remain quiet and leave me to fight the battle about the Bath fees. I have had a similar letter to yours from Mr. Harries. Lord Melville says I am *not* to pay; the Treasury seem inclined to require it of me, but you may depend on our making a stout and very decided stand about it.[77]

Junior officers too were represented: 'I fought a hard fight for the Lake pay for the officers employed under you', Sir Robert Barrie was informed in 1820, 'but I was beat, the rage for economy was too much'.[78]

The representation of all officers was performed by Cockburn as a matter of principle. 'No person from the highest to the lowest ever asked to see him', he maintained in the Commons in 1826 'that he did not see and whose business he did not hear'.[79] Underlying this attitude was the belief that the navy should take care of its own, a scheme of things in which even widows and children had a place. For example, Cockburn wrote to Pole in December 1823:

> I had, previously to receiving your letter, drawn Lord Melville's attention to the sad case of poor Lady Minds and we had, I trust, secured the admission of the children in the compassionate fund list. I was glad to learn from you that two of the boys are already in the Service and the Admiralty must with regard to them (as has been done regarding others) become Fathers to the fatherless when they have served their time. I wish

it were in my power to do more for the poor unhappy widow but I fear there is no chance of getting anything for her beyond the regular pension of a captain's widow.[80]

Sir John Briggs, Cockburn's best known critic, noticed the humanity with which the latter took the part of officers in trouble or difficulty.[81] In Cockburn's own view 'he paid less attention to a man who had family interest than to one who was without it'.[82] And indeed, privately and publicly, officers did acknowledge the 'kindness and consideration' they experienced from him.[83]

Interest

Parallel to the problem of morale accompanying the reduction of the navy, was a necessary adjustment to the opportunities available to members of the officer corps. In November 1814 Cockburn well knew 'the great value of its being generally [known] in the profession that those who distinguish themselves in any particular enterprising undertaking against the enemy are the individuals likely to reap the advantages which may accrue from its successful termination'.[84] During war honours, appointments and promotion were the currency of reward; at every level petty, warrant and commissioned officers could and did achieve advancement. The navy in wartime was a means of social mobility.

However, between 1818 and 1830, with an officer corps of around 5,000 men, only approximately thirteen per cent of commissioned officers were able to obtain employment at any time;[85] and even in employment the navy in peacetime presented few opportunities for distinction. Moreover, to maintain an element of youth at each rank, it soon became necessary to give priority in affording experience to younger officers. The majority of wartime veterans accordingly felt themselves neglected. 'Not only have I not received honorary reward', Robert Maunsell wrote to Cockburn in October 1830, 'but my earnest and repeated applications for employment have been unattended to for sixteen years, and being now more than eighteen years a captain, I fear their Lordships will ere long tell me that my seniority precludes me from the command of a frigate and thus blast for ever the only hope which has buoyed me up for so many years . . .'[86] It was not just the old who felt neglected. In September 1822 Robert Fitzroy observed to his sister on the death of Lord Londonderry: 'it will, I am afraid, retard my promotion; at least I shall not get promoted as soon as I otherwise should, for promotion goes entirely by interest now . . .'[87] This was a charge that, if wholly true, seriously affected the efficiency of the navy. For it naturally affected the extent to which merit obtained its just reward.

Within the procedure that sifted candidates for naval appointments and promotions, Cockburn occupied a key position. But the opportunities available to an Admiralty commissioner to assist anyone in particular obtaining employment for himself or his nominee were limited. There was at least one vacancy at Greenwich upper school at Admiralty disposal, while Cockburn and Croker were able, through their influence with captains, to secure places for a few midshipmen and (until 1830) first-class volunteers. They could also prevail upon commanders-in-chief on foreign stations to fill vacancies for lieutenants with their nominees. These vacancies were invariably committed.[88] They thus fell back on the patronage available to the Admiralty.

Here, to avoid criticism, inconvenience, imposition and above all political inconsistency, the First Lord retained control of all key appointments. The Cabinet approved the names of commanders-in-chief, for they had specified powers of appointment, subject to approval, within their station. Captains were appointed by the First Lord and, although captains could request particular subordinates, so were the lieutenants. Marine officers, dockyard commissioners and officers of divisions of ships in Ordinary—those laid up in reserve—also came under the Admiralty. Indeed centralization increased during the 1820s after the Lord High Admiral claimed power of appointment of all clerks, which thereafter remained with the Admiralty. By 1830 the appointment of first-class volunteers was also transferred from captains to the Admiralty. With the abolition in 1832 of the Navy Board, the Admiralty came to control the majority of subordinate civil appointments as well as the issue of warrants to non-commissioned sea officers.

At the Admiralty, clerks to the First Lord entered the names of recommended applicants for appointments in the respective 'Admiralty lists'. The Board commissioners could and did recommend individuals to the First Lord, often simply annotating the original application and passing it on. Sometimes unknown applicants were researched; for example, Thomas Hoskins who offered himself in 1830 for a Master Attendant with the observation that 'my relative Lord Hood and my worthy old officer Captain Parker will highly appreciate the obligation'. His application was annotated: 'nothing is known of Mr. Hoskins for the last 14 years. The last ship of war in which he served was the Venerable in 1808 after which he was employed for a considerable time in a storeship. His general character is good.'[89]

Such a system was obviously necessary, for even royalty, peers and prominent politicians, who were frequently seeking appointments for those whom they owed or with whom they wished to curry favour, were unaware to whom they should apply. Peel, for example, in 1826 had to request Cockburn point out to him the way in which he should proceed.[90] The bulk of the applications went to the first naval lord, but even as second Cockburn frequently received applications. In reply he was able to explain the system without embarrassment to himself, sometimes also explaining why Melville was unable to assist without personally involving him in the correspondence. A potentially difficult case occurred in 1823 when Lord Wellesley applied on behalf of a Mr Greene. As a former patron of Cockburn, Wellesley had every reason to expect assistance from him. Yet the latter was able to reply:

> Your Lordship is of course aware that everything relating to promotions is *wholly* in Lord Melville's patronage as the *First* Lord of the Admiralty and therefore (although from the anxiety I always feel to meet anything I know to be your Lordships wish I have several times pressed Lord Melville for Mr. Greene's advancement) the decision must be entirely with his Lordship, whose scruples to giving Mr. Greene immediate promotion at home arose from that officer's name being as yet so low on the list of lieutenants, and the want of anything in his professional services to bear out so strong a measure as it would be considered by the public generally.[91]

A letter identical in form was written in January 1830 to HRH the Duke of Sussex who was concerned to have Captain William Dillon appointed to a ship.[92]

Nevertheless, within this system, from the labour committed to recommendations by the sea commissioners, it is evident that their opinions were considered by the First Lord. This is confirmed by the appointment of their own nominees. Sir Robert Barrie, for example, Cockburn's subordinate in the Chesapeake in 1814, was made commissioner at Kingston dockyard, Canada, in 1818.[93] Cockburn's old secretary, John Glover, too, became storekeeper at Kingston in 1824.

The opportunties for influencing the First Lord occurred as frequently as requests for patronage were received. Cockburn received most opportunities while first naval lord between 1828 and 1830. His letterbook for the 23 months between January 1829 and November

1830 records replies to 80 requests for entry, employment or promotion.[94] Forty of the applications that he passed on to Melville between 4 December 1828 and 9 October 1830 survive in one cache of the Melville papers. They concern 39 candidates for places. Only 13 letters were from naval officers, of which 10 were requests for themselves, the others for their sons; 21 were from civilians, written on behalf of officers (11 of these were from people with social standing, often with a title, or mentioned one or more officers of reputation). Thirteen (approximately one third) were written from naval constituencies, the boroughs of Portsmouth and Plymouth, by the first of which Cockburn had been elected in 1818, and by the latter in 1826.[95]

What influenced Cockburn to forward these applications to Melville? All of them had bargaining power of one form or another that it was necesssary to take notice of. Even officers without patrons sometimes had the credit of a good wartime record to call upon. Senior officers who wrote, or allowed their names to be used, brought into balance the weight of their own credit, while also hazarding their own reputations as judges of military character. Civil patrons too sometimes had credit. Hence Cockburn wrote to Melville in August 1830 after an interview with the Dower Lady Nelson who wished to gain employment for Commander Blanckley, who was married to a niece of Lord Nelson and her Ladyship:

[She] pressed it upon me as the *only favour* she has asked of me since her husband's death. I own therefore that your Lordship would gratify me very much by obliging the old lady on the point, and I will with your permission put you in mind of it when any ten gun sloops are to be commissioned.[96]

Inevitably some applications called upon political credit or offered political influence. Mr Padwich of Havant unashamedly referred to the part he took in promoting Cockburn's views at Portsmouth. A former naval surgeon, writing from Plymouth on behalf of his son George Hughes, claimed his influence with his 'borough friends' would be useful in the future.[97]

Precisely how much notice Melville as First Lord took of such political interest is unclear. Undoubtedly some, for in July 1820 Cockburn himself responded to three young men supported by aristocratic patrons—Lord Lynedock, Lord Prudhoe and Lady Ardin—who were all quickly placed as a school master and extra midshipmen; and in May 1821 he sent on to Sir Alexander Cochrane a letter from 'one of our parliamentary friends' with the observation that if Cochrane could 'manage to take the gentleman he is anxious about into the Impregnable, you would much oblige us'.[98]

Yet most letters Cockburn wrote prevailing upon captains to take such gentlemen did not mention political factors, and to Melville he equally frequently stressed service qualifications. One 'fine young man' was 'an excellent scholar'; Commander Blanckley had 'distinguished himself' during the Burmese affair; Lieutenant Taplen had 'commanded a Spanish 74 as a battery in the war'.[99] He did, therefore, ensure that professional competence received its due. Nevertheless, to the naval profession outside the Admiralty, the edge that competence provided cannot have been strongly apparent. Too many other personal and political factors appeared important, and in a few appointments heavily outweighed the professional ones. Thus Cockburn knew, for example, that the application of Lord Melville himself, when out of office, on behalf of his son Richard was a foregone conclusion.[100]

There were of course complaints. From the early 1820s appointments made through influence came under criticism in the press.[101] Cockburn had to defend them, and did so by reference to fate: a person's fortune or misfortune. The importance of fatalism in his thinking emerged clearly in an interview he had with Lieutenant Joseph Nias in February 1825. He refused to allow comparisons between the claims to appointment of individuals: they were invidious. Only proof of meritorious service mattered. As Nias recorded, although he had been selected by Captain Parry for a voyage,

> He [Cockburn] said . . . I was ill and could not go and could I expect the same for lying in bed (although it was an affliction) as those who were out employed on service undergoing all the hardships of it. And then [he] stated a long story about Captain Fitzgerald having lost his promotion by not being employed although it was not his fault, for he had repeatedly asked for a ship but he had not been fortunate enough in obtaining one and neither had I, but it was not my fault but I had not been fortunate. Then again he quoted the instance of one of the youngest commanders in the navy, Captain Graham, being so fortunate as to get a ship and shortly afterwards to fall in with and take a pirate for which he got again promoted; that, said he, was his good fortune, where perhaps many old Commanders were serving many years and were still so, but it was not their fault, but that they had not been fortunate.[102]

For Cockburn, fate, be it good or ill, operated equally in peace and war. But while in wartime its operation largely arose from opportunities of service, in peacetime its operation was as much affected by other factors; and of these interest was clearly one.

Discipline

Most officers accepted this philosophy in the making of appointments, even if they were not favoured by it, because they accepted the discipline of the service which was also administered from the Admiralty. In maintaining this discipline, Cockburn frequently reiterated two principles: first, the impossibility for a junior officer always to be aware of the views that induce a senior officer to give particular orders; and secondly, the necessity for officers of every rank to set an example to the officers and men subordinate to them in every point tending to the good of the service.[103]

Because, from 1818, Cockburn often drafted orders for issue, he also frequently noticed their violation. Often he was the first to request Croker to demand an explanation and, when this proved deficient, to propose a court martial. Trials were ordered to support officers in the enforcement of regulations, to punish offences appropriately, to deter others from so offending, and to establish a code of conduct for 'the general good of the service'. These objectives demanded the application of consistency in considering and authorizing trials, regardless of the effect the outcome might have for any third party. 'You can see that I quite agree with you', Cockburn wrote to Croker in July 1827, 'in thinking Lieutenant Whitfield's punishment ought to be of the severest description, and I care not about the triumph to the Dover smugglers. We cannot so effectually keep them in order as by doing in every case exactly what is right.'[104]   Minor misdemeanours or disapproved conduct were in some cases punishable by the Admiralty itself, by the removal of officers from active employment to half-pay. Even there, officers were subject to Admiralty authority. They had to receive permission to take employment in the merchant service and, because they were liable for active service at any time, leave of absence to travel abroad. Failure to obtain such leave was itself sufficient to demand their return. Serious displeasure was marked by the complete removal of officers from the list of the navy. Melville retained final authority over the removal and restoration of officers' names from the Navy List. But removals were considered by, and ostensibly were the responsibility of, the Board as a whole.[105]

Marines were equally subject to such sanctions, although in

consultation with their chief officers. Their terms of service contained some differences to those of the navy: the possibility for sale of commissions for example. But, just as for naval officers, Cockburn consulted with Croker over regulations governing their conduct, while Melville marked displeasure by removing offenders to the half-pay list, decisions implemented by act of the Board.[106]

Politics

To mark displeasure with the conduct of an officer was 'a painful point of duty' for Board commissioners. Longer lasting and ultimately more painful were protracted disagreements with officers over differences in interpretation of instructions. These disagreements were invariably aggravated by political differences, for the navy was no less divided politically than the rest of society. Added to this ideological division was the natural timeless tendency for officers to sit in judgement upon one another, and upon those who drafted their instructions. These unseen rifts, antipathies and loyalties set officers for and against one another. They were revealed during the administration of the Duke of Clarence, and were deepened between 1828 and 1830 by the enmity for the Tory Board of Admiralty of the difficult Whig admiral, Sir Edward Codrington.

He had been given command of the Mediterranean station in February 1827, and soon revealed his discontent with Admiralty provision for his squadron.[107] He complained, for example, of the failure to allow him an interpreter—though he was obliged to communicate in French, Italian, Greek, Turkish and Russian—and of his inability to refit his vessels without fleet caulkers, shipwrights and carpenters.[108] In their official roles, he and Cockburn exchanged private letters in which Codrington made no effort to conceal his impatience with his correspondent and the Board.

> If I had ten times the ability and energy of mind with which you smooth me down, believe me I have plenty of demand for their entire occupation without having my career checked by the sixpenny difficulties which have been thrown in my way by economical arrangements. Although those impediments to the better execution of the service come not within the focus of your optics, they seem pretty evident to all the parties more immediately concerned in them, I assure you.[109]

The necessity under the Lord High Admiral to exclude public matters from private letters hampered informal discussion of difficulties. Codrington's private recommendations for appointments did not get answered. 'It is evident that in these cases', he reproached Cockburn, 'the only unfairness is towards the writer, who has a claim . . . to an answer in writing similar to what could be given him verbally if personally present . . . if you were serving afloat you would feel the limitation of patronage in such matters as fully as it is felt by the rest of our officers'.[110]

Initially, after the battle of Navarino in October 1827, along with the King and Duke of Clarence, Cockburn offered Codrington his congratulations. Yet by December relations between Turkey and Russia were on the verge of war and, both to salve Turkey's honour and preserve the balance of power in the eastern Mediterranean, the British government decided it should publicly disapprove of the naval action.[111] On hearing that a letter containing an ultimatum had not been delivered to the Turks before the allies had opened fire, the government withdrew its approval. The change of view soon reached the Mediterranean. 'I cannot help saying', Codrington complained to Clarence on 26 February 1828,

> that I think it somewhat unfair that persons seeming to have authority should let slip doubts and insinuations which give rise to torrents of coarse abuse on the part of public writers, hardly admissible in describing acknowledged criminality. In Blackwood's Magazine I am depicted as a disgrace to H.M. Service, quoting as a fact a statement in the Morning Post which was fabricated for mere party purpose.[112]

Debates in the House of Commons in March and April, from which Cockburn remained aloof, evoked both hostility and approval for Codrington's conduct. The government deplored the hostilities; others recognized their inevitability. In Whitehall his supersession was agitated. In mid-March the Duke of Clarence was required to relinquish to Canning, as Foreign Secretary, the authority for furnishing Codrington with instructions.

Meanwhile, Codrington awaited clarification of his instructions. Having requested this on 5 February, he heard nothing until superseded in July, accused of failing to prevent Ottoman vessels from sailing with impunity between Egypt and the Greek archipelago.[113] For this hiatus of five months the Admiralty was not responsible. Cockburn disapproved of the handling of Codrington's supersession. He wrote to Croker on 24 May: 'We have nothing yet from the Cabinet about

Codrington, but his recall is the common talk in the streets. This is a bad way of going on, but I suppose the recent state of the Cabinet is the excuse to be offered'.[114] Yet Cockburn was the obvious target for Codrington to blame. He believed his supersession was a 'blow . . . aimed at the Lord High Admiral through me whom he so nobly protected', and that Cockburn, with Croker, was playing an entirely political game:

> As to your Sir G.C.'s and your J.W.C.'s, I pray not only to leave them in ignorance, but to encourage their floundering in the mire of their own wishes, that I may have the satisfaction of seeing them sticking there by and bye when I, according to the prevailing fashion, come to have my little explanation. You think these men in office are not personally hostile to me! Now, if they are not, their conduct is. I have no reason to believe the public good at all enters into their consideration.[115]

His eventual meeting on 10 October with Cockburn and Sir Henry Hotham was a tense affair. The former reported to Melville:

> The interview with Sir Edward was not, as you will readily believe of a very pleasant character. In the first place on his card sending in his name, he added "to wait on the Board" to mark that he had not come to call on any individual; to meet this Hotham and I went to the drawing room to receive him where we found him looking much agitated and very angry. Having, however, entered with him into the general state of affairs as regarded the fleet in the Mediterranean, he by degrees entirely recovered himself and although occasional expressions fell from him showing that he considered his own services to have been most valuable, and the orders sent him so vague that they could not be understood, yet nothing at all violent or disagreeable passed between us, and after an interview of considerable length he took his leave, apparently in rather better temper than he arrived but still evidently angry and distant with me, though abstaining altogether from any expression of intention to ask for court martial or take any hostile measure.[116]

The Admiralty's determined maintenance of an uncompromising silence on the subject of Codrington's interpretation of his instructions simply sustained the latter's desire to vindicate his reputation.[117] He consequently requested an official statement on his conduct from the Admiralty. This was passed to the Foreign Office which did not feel itself obliged to express an opinion. A second request specifically to the Admiralty met the same response. A third gained no more.[118] In January 1829 he turned to the Duke of Wellington, now Prime

Minister, who flatly denied either hostility or difference of view on Codrington's instructions. Sensing ambivalence, Codrington was prompted to print for private circulation a 'Narrative' of his proceedings in the Mediterranean in the hope that opinion in Parliament would force Wellington to acknowledge the injustice of his recall. Whether it was this that drew forth a conciliatory gesture is uncertain. But in May 1829 Wellington informally offered Codrington a pension of £800 for life, an offer Codrington immediately turned down on the grounds that the head money of his seamen had still not been paid.[119]

Charges and counter-charges, aired publicly, obliged the Admiralty by August 1829 to bring before a court martial Captain Dickinson who had assumed command of the *Genoa* during the Navarino action on the death of his predecessor, Captain Bathurst. At this, Cockburn wanted the Judge Advocate to offer to produce all the Admiralty correspondence with Codrington. As he urged Croker:

> their being produced in some way or other is essentially requisite to shew the whole transaction in its proper light and sure I am that if that explanatory letter of yours . . . were once published it would take from Sir Edwad the little mount he is endeavouring to raise for persuading the Court and the public that this has been forced upon him by the Admiralty unjustly and unnecessarily.[120]

Dickinson was acquitted by the court maritial.[121] Even so, questions regarding the conduct and treatment of Codrington were still being raised in the House of Commons the following year.[122]

Codrington himself entered the Commons in 1831 as member for Devonport and brought about debates on Navarino in March 1833, April and June 1834. Only in July 1834 did the House finally vote the seamen of the battle their head money. This, in its way, was a vote of approval for the battle and for Codrington's conduct. By then, however, there was no disguising the clear division in the personal and political affiliations of the officer corps, a division exacerbated by undercurrents affecting the whole of naval adminstration.

The Beginnings of Reform

In 1828 the movement for reform began to gain concessions. Those elements of the administrative and political system most vulnerable to change were the laws restricting civil liberty on grounds of religion. In March 1828 the Test and Corporation Acts of 1673 and 1661 were repealed, formally allowing Protestant dissenters from the established faith to hold posts in government, the judiciary and armed services without the necessity for an annual Act of indemnity. In June of that year, along with Sir Thomas Byam Martin, the Comptroller of the Navy, Cockburn fought a by-election at Plymouth, where he was pressed on his view of Catholic emancipation, for which there had been demand especially in Ireland since the political union of that country with the United Kingdom in 1801. Cockburn was for supporting the measure, arguing that the 'purity and beauty of the established religion' was in no way threatened by 'the mummery and mockery of the catholic religion'; there was therefore no necessity to maintain laws 'owing to which 300,000 people were only kept from open rebellion by the point of a bayonet'.[123] This was not to say he trusted non-conformists in influential posts: over a decade later he was still ready to support the removal from a dockyard of a chaplain with Puseyite propensities.[124] Nevertheless, in public in 1828, when Wellington and Peel were ahead of opinion outside the House of Commons, Cockburn could be counted among their moderate supporters.

From 1828 political necessities more than ever governed his conduct in matters directly affecting the navy. For, embodying in its management the apparent abuses and injustices of contemporary society, the navy was a natural target for an opposition intent on revealing the weaknesses of the government. In 1828 pressure was most immediately felt in the realm of naval finance, which, for all the debate generated by the estimates, still remained largely free of control from the Commons. The estimates were organized under headings that had existed for a century and a half—the Ordinary, Extraordinary and Sea Service, the latter consisting of Wages, Wear and Tear and Victualling—logical to naval adminstrators but baffling to the layman. Accounts permitted the Navy Board to check the Treasurer of the Navy, but provided no explanation of detail and were regarded as unintelligible to the uniformed observer: 'no man not officially educated in the existing plan would know how to set about the detection in it of an error or fraud'.[125] Even to ministers the traditional organization of naval finance obscured the effectiveness of their own policies. In 1824 the cost of over 2,300 seamen to maintain the coastal blockade in aid of the customs service was concealed within the total costs of manning the navy; it was consequently impossible for an analyst to differentiate the cost of collecting the revenue from that of naval defence.

Throughout the 1820s lack of information had the effect of keeping critics in check, while maintaining the freedom of manoeuvre of administrators. This was particularly evident with respect to funds voted on the estimate for Sea Service. This was calculated by the Cabinet on behalf of the Crown according to the number of seamen needed each year; the House of Commons was simply expected to vote the sums required to maintain the number needed at the established rate for each man. But for not one of the estimates were details provided of the manner in which the sums voted were proposed to be expended; actual expenditure sometimes exceeded the sums voted; and the Admiralty, on its own initiative, transferred sums from one heading to another according to demands and expediency. Cockburn later explained 'it had always been the practice to consider that the gross sum voted was applicable to all purposes indiscriminately in detail, provided the total amount of the vote was not exceeded'. The precise costs of keeping the fleet in commission were not disclosed either, partly to keep secret the force maintained, and partly because the costs were difficult to anticipate. Indeed, it was claimed the vote for 'wear and tear' was 'in some degree a vote of confidence to government'.[126]

Having, since 1821, protested vehemently at the lack of detail in the estimates and the inability to hold the Admiralty to account, by 1828 some, like Hume in opposition, were intent on checking 'the unlimited power of the Admiralty'. Early that session a parliamentary Finance Committee was conceded and in anticipation of its recommendations only half the annual naval supplies were requested and granted. Its predecessor, the 1817 Finance Committee, had merely been an aid to the implementation of government policy. But in 1828, on being reminded that it was the province of the Crown to recommend the number of men wanted for naval defence, Hume promptly retorted that though the sovereign might recommend, it was for the Commons to decide whether to acquiesce in that recommendation. He reminded the House that the members' responsibility to their electors was as important as the ministers' responsibility to advise the sovereign.[127]

Cockburn as first naval lord, was called twice before the Finance Committee where he was required to explain why more seamen were needed in 1828 than had been necessary in 1792. He was able to emphasize the navy's peace-keeping role between the hostile forces of Greece and Turkey following Navarino, and the dependence of British trade upon the suppression of piracy in the Mediterranean and West Indies. He was able to indicate the growth of the American and Russian navies, but also forced to acknowledge the relative decline of French,

Spanish and Dutch sea power relative to that of the British. The Comptroller of the Navy Board, Sir Thomas Byam Martin, did the navy least service by revealing his positive jubilation at its wartime success and current relative strength.[128] The Committee was chaired by the able opposition backbencher, Sir Henry Parnell, who was later able to maintain that the 'new posture of public affairs' permitted a large reduction in naval expenditure.[129]

The evidence heard was much cited in the debates on the naval estimates in 1829. Most was made of that given by John Barrow, who had been Second Secretary at the Admiralty since 1804. He claimed too much was wasted in the manning and supervision of the Royal dockyards. The observation struck a sensitive chord, for critics repeatedly contrasted the expense and quality of products of civil establishments with those of private contractors. Cockburn conceded the number of supervising quartermen and clerks at the dockyards and in London might be reduced, as could the functions performed by the eastern yards: Woolwich and Chatham would be confined to building, Sheerness to become the principal fitting port.[130]

In the Cabinet and at the Admiralty, the means by which critics of naval administration could be assuaged was the source of serious consideration. To improve cost and quality control, in January 1829 Wellington persuaded Melville to improve the individual reponsibility of commissioners at the Navy Board: to have a Comptroller and deputy for the general direction and management of business, a surveyor for ship construction and repairs, a commissioner for stores, another for accounts, and a sixth for transports. As Master General of the Ordnance, Wellington had found the organization to work at the Board of Ordnance. By April 1829 the arrangement was also established in the Navy Office.[131] In February the Admiralty also required the Navy Board to produce for the first time an annual balance sheet and statement of receipts and expenditure for 1828. Intially, from January 1829, it also required monthly statements of receipts and expenditure, although these were subsequently reduced to quarterly (to comply with the timing of existing returns from the dockyards).[132]

Further than this it was difficult to go. As Comptroller, Sir Thomas Byam Martin was a stout defender of the Navy Board's management of its responsibilities, and, like other comptrollers before him, he had a grasp of technical and procedural business that Admiralty commissioners could rarely rival. After more than a decade of regular investigations of dockyard business, Cockburn was closely acquainted with these operations. But, like Byam Martin, he was reluctant to impair the efficiency of the dockyards by too zealous a reduction. He could recall the difficulty St Vincent had caused in 1804 by his severe reduction of the shipwright workforce during the Peace of Amiens. In 1829, rather than reduce their number further, he was persuaded to reduce their cost by having them work one day less a week.[133] It was a method of reducing costs that was prudent, in case of a sudden emergency, and avoided heavy dependence on contractors who, according to tradition, would hold the navy to ransom. It was a logic, moreover, that appealed to the paternalism of both Byam Martin and Cockburn.

In the Commons, in April and May 1829, the Admiralty was able to demonstrate its will to improve efficiency with the introduction of two Bills remodelling the management of Greenwich Hospital. With four to five hundred governors and 24 directors, 'there was too heavy a mass of management to make it possible to work well'. One Bill accordingly reduced these directors to five, operating under the supervision of the Admiralty. The second Bill transferred responsibility for some of the hospital's finances to the Treasurer of the Navy, a measure 'imperatively called for'. The hospital's own deputy treasurer had walked out with its funds and been brought to court, but 'it was found impossible to make out whether he was the officer of the King or of the Admiralty, or of the treasurer of the hospital, so that they could not take the money from him, though he was now living in Greenwich in possession of his spoil'.[134]

These demonstrations of good intent temporarily staved off further criticism of naval administration during the remainder of the 1829 session. However, late in February 1830, seemingly to coincide with the debates on the naval estimates, the chairman of the 1828 finance committee, Sir Henry Parnell, published a pamphlet *On Finance Reform*. This covered the whole of government finance, and was inaccurate in some respects, being based on evidence and impressions gained at the 1828 committee. Yet it claimed that the efforts of the Admiralty Board to obtain reductions in cash expenditure within the responsibilities of the Navy Board 'were so much opposed as to be able to accomplish in the department only some trifling reductions'.[135]

The reaction of Byam Martin was dramatic. On 26 February he suddenly detained the House from converting to a committee of supply and furiously accused Parnell of unfounded imputations condemning the conduct of a whole body of men without allowing them to defend themselves. The ensuing debate developed into a row. Parnell argued the situation had altered little since the Navy Board had blocked the Admiralty's attempts at reform in 1803–4. Cockburn defended the Admiralty's relationship with the subordinate board. Peel proposed an 'honourable reconciliation' of Byam Martin and Parnell. Only 102 members were subsequently present to vote in a division on the estimates, and only 17 supported an amendment proposed by Hume. But those present could not avoid the conclusion that, even if the allegation of the Navy Board's 'obstruction' was untrue, the strength of Byam Martin's commitment must have made the policies he maintained difficult to influence.

The estimates were presented in unprecedented detail that session. With social distress and discontent throughout the country, debates were characterized by pressure to reduce the costs of bureaucracy. A continuing preoccupation was the alleged 'solid band of placemen and pensioners out of which the majorities voting away the public money, and voting it into their own pockets, had that session chiefly been formed'.[136] As a placeman himself, Cockburn was not sympathetic to the view that he sat in the Commons for mercenary motives. So far as he was concerned, Admiralty commissioners sat in the Commons to represent the interests of the navy. In 1822, when the number of Admiralty commissioners was reduced to five, he had refused to think of their political role in the Commons: 'as to the influence which they afforded in that House, it was a subject with the consideration of which he meddled not: it was immaterial to his reasoning'.[137]

In March 1830 a natural target for criticism was the office of Treasurer of the Navy. Sufficiently few duties were attached to the post for it to be held nominally with another and primarily for the high salary attached. In 1828 Cockburn admitted he thought the sinecure nature of the post wrong, and that the Treasurer ought to be 'an efficient officer', rather than having the work of the post executed by the Paymaster of the Navy and his clerks.[138] Admiralty plans thus intended to increase the duties of the Treasurer and abolish the post of Paymaster. The reorganization of Greenwich Hospital management in 1829 had accordingly transferred the supervision of out-pensions to the Treasurer, and established him as the president of the hospital's new board of management. The proprietorial rights of the Paymaster still prevailed: the government could not simply 'turn off the gallant officer . . . until an opportunity occurred of otherwise providing for him'. In 1830 the government's reasoning gave them a majority of 98; but the opposition motion of condemnation and censure was still supported by 90 members.[139]

Two weeks later the government failed to survive a motion of censure. In a vote on the superannuation allowances for former employees of the naval departments, pensions of £400 and £500 were refused to the Honourable Robert Dundas and W.L. Bathurst. Both had held their offices about four years and lost them on account of economies and reductions in their departments. The pensions were appropriate in proportion to their salaries and were only for so long as they were without other civil offices. Both, it was argued, had abandoned other professions to enter government service where they had accepted appointments for life during good behaviour. Yet the naval boards had long been regarded as places of patronage and training for young politicians. Dundas and Bathurst were both sons and grandsons of noblemen who had, and still held, high offices of state. The government was accordingly defeated by 139 votes to 121.[140]

The defeat served to reveal the limited breadth of reliable support for the government. In April the beginning of the King's fatal illness dissipated that support further. With the possibility of a dissolution, members began to concentrate on conduct that would recommend themselves to constituents.[141]

In May 1830, in a debate on the emoluments of Privy Councillors, Cockburn himself had to justify his income. Cockburn had become a Privy Councillor in 1827. A titular rather than a functional post, the office was held for honour rather than profit. The holders of the title nevertheless usually held other offices of profit. Cockburn himself, for example, received £1,000 a year as an Admiralty commissioner and £593.2s.6d. half-pay, with £1,037.5s.0d. a year since 1821 as a Major-General of Marines.[142] Before that, his income had been supplemented for a decade by the salary of a Colonel of Marines. He maintained that the income from such sinecure posts was a reward for past services and 'entirely independent' of his situation at the Admiralty, but nevertheless essential to the maintenance of the status of an officer in his position. For, 'endeavouring late and early' to do his duty, he made virtually nothing from his post, while others in the same profession 'on different stations' made five or even ten times as much in the year as his whole salary.[143]

The justice of these claims was not contested. Even so, there could be no mistaking public interest in a thorough overhaul of government bureaucracy. With respect to the navy, there was clear dissatisfaction with the inability of the Admiralty to manage the Navy Board, and the lack of public control over expenditure. As the power of the Tory government to manage the Commons slipped away, the reform of the system of naval administration became a prime political objective.

CHAPTER 6

Opposition and North America
1830–1840

The end of the Tory government came with the death of George IV late in June 1830. Having himself had dealings with William IV, then Duke of Clarence, Cockburn viewed the ceremonies surrounding the new king's accession with a sceptical eye. On 25 July he wrote to Croker:

> We have been going on in London since you left us in a continued state of agitation and excitement, with reviews, levees, breakfasts, dinners, etc., etc., but in the main I learn that the ministers are satisfied; they consider that they possess the king's confidence and that he is heartily with them and will leave to them the management on all important points, as well as the essential part of the patronage. You and I however know how uncertain all this must be.

No more certain was the future for himself and Croker, to whom he went on: 'I am told the king continues as angry with you and me as ever...the other day at a levee he turned his head from me and would not speak to me. This perhaps will wear off with time and though unpleasant is not of any importance.' Ministers assumed an air of optimism, even regarding the outcome of the election necessary following the accession. About a quarter of the constituencies in England and Wales were to be contested, but 'the Duke of Wellington at our Fish Dinner yesterday was in high spirits, and said he trusted we should meet there again next year with renewed confidence in each other. In short, as far as I can judge, we are rather "looking up" as they say of the Funds than otherwise'.[1]

However the result of the election was disappointing: Cockburn was returned for Plymouth, having held a seat there since 1826, but Croker lost his seat in Ireland. Exceeding anything known in previous elections, electors made clear their wish for reform of one sort or another. Coming to terms as best they could with these demands, many members returned to Parliament with a commitment to support improvements in government.

In November the new parliamentary session began against a background of disturbances throughout southern England, in Belgium and France. Early that month 500 armed marines were ordered from Chatham, Woolwich and Deptford to St George's Fields to reinforce the troops guarding the capital against rioting reformers.[2] Attempts to recruit support for the government were doomed to failure. At the opening of the new session in November 1830, Wellington made his celebrated declaration against even moderate reform of Parliament. Defeated in the Commons, Wellington and his ministers resigned and their political assistants with them.

The new Whig Board of Admiralty received their patents on 25 November 1830. Somewhat relieved to be out of office, Cockburn could observe with amusement the 'official caution' now adopted by his successor, Sir Thomas Hardy, towards administrative issues. His own first lieutenant thirty-five years earlier, Cockburn felt reasonably content with him. 'As I really believe he means well and will endeavour to effect what appears to him to be right in such matters, as far as his influence and abilities enable him, we must be satisfied or rather thankful that in the late shuffling of the cards a worse professional leader of our governing body has not fallen to our lot.' But the remainder of the Board left him dissatisfied. He confided to Barrie on 9 January 1831, 'it is evident our royal master has had a principal hand in the arrangement and, I apprehend, intends to take the chief management of the general duties of the service. We may therefore look for many changes and have only to pray that they may prove for the better.'[3]

Resisting Revolution

In March 1831 the Whigs' first bill for the reform of Parliament passed its second reading in the Commons by a majority of one, but was defeated by amendment at the committee stage. Earl Grey decided to appeal to the country with a general election. At Plymouth, Cockburn's seat was contested for the Whigs by the Honourable Captain George Elliot, the new First Secretary to the Admiralty. With only a quarter of the seats in the country being contested, the prospect of removing Cockburn from Plymouth excited much interest in the Whig Cabinet and throughout the west of England. Having voted with the Whigs in the two divisions on the Reform Bill, and holding an office that did not change with ministers, Byam Martin, the Comptroller of the Navy Board, was requested to join with Elliot against Cockburn. However, opposed to such alliances, distrustful of the Whigs, and as an old friend and colleague of Cockburn's, Byam Martin refused. Willing to resign as Comptroller if necessary, he determined to stand on his own account.[4] Elliot for the Whigs and Cockburn for the Tory opposition were consequently matched against one another.

As the poll approached, the excitement at Plymouth became intense. Elliot was the clear favourite among locals, while Byam Martin was 'very favourably' received. Having voted against the Reform Bill, Cockburn was the main target of abuse. 'Most of the squibs and anonymous addresses which have covered the walls of the town, many of which were of the most virulent description, were pointed at him and what was supposed to be his principles.' However, the result remained an open question. In spite of a population of 16,000, the franchise was limited to about 260 freemen, of whom only three worked in the dockyard. *The Plymouth, Devonport and Stonehouse Herald* reported a great number of electors went to cast their votes 'unshackled'.[5] Their uncertainty enhanced the potential influence of the unenfranchised, especially within the Guildhall where votes were declared verbally.

On the first day of the election, 5 May, a part of the Guildhall was full of voters by 9.45 a.m. when Elliott, Martin and Cockburn took their places. At ten the mayor, Captain Nicholas Lockyer, arrived and took his place on the bench between the candidates. At a signal the doors were thrown open to the general public and in a tremendous rush that part of the hall railed off was completely filled. The hostility in the crowd for Cockburn was palpable. Proposed as a candidate, the address was 'followed by groans and hisses and the most discordant cries, interspersed with cheers and applause'. Dr Bellamy, seconding the proposition, was obliged to speak over hisses which the mayor was unable to quell, though he demanded 'the cowardly persons come forward and speak' and threatened to clear the hall. There were shouts instead of 'sit down Bellamy'. The same clamour persisted throughout Cockburn's speech.

He was not, he claimed, the enemy of all reform. He had not only supported Catholic emancipation but also a Bill in 1828 to extend the elective franchise of Plymouth. Yet, as an advocate of virtual representation, he maintained there were objections to the current Whig Reform Bill. First, in towns it limited the vote to one class of people. It was right, he thought, for the lower orders to have a voice in the Commons; he was thus for maintaining Preston, Westminster and other places where they had substantial shares of the vote. All classes should send representatives to Parliament to be heard. Yet if the bill was passed, the number of £10 voters was so large that they, by and large, would return members of Parliament; the votes of other classes would be swallowed up and their opinions would not therefore be represented. Secondly, so far as individual constituencies were concerned, he believed existing voting rights should be protected and maintained among all classes of people. The Reform Bill actually proposed to lessen the number of voters for some places: at Maldon, for example, the voters would be reduced by half; it would become a closer borough than before. Thirdly, he objected to the proposed reduction in the number of members returned for English constituencies. Catholic emancipation had brought in 100 Irish MPs. That number had posed no threat to the English Church, but the Reform Bill would further increase the number of Irish members, at a cost to the English.

Several prominent local residents followed Cockburn, declaring their support for him. Elliot and Martin had their turn. Polling followed. Martin mentions voters sent down by the government to support Elliot against him: three members of the naval establishment—Admiral Sir William Hargood, Captain Sir Michael Seymour and Mr Joseph Tucker, ex-Surveyor of the Navy. Nevertheless, local loyalties prevailed. Martin emerged at the end of this first day with 94 votes, Cockburn with 85, and Elliot with only 54.

This result provoked determined reformers in the town. Martin believed that the crowd was organized; next day it quickly became a 'mob' bent upon intimidation. At his hotel Elliot was provided with a 'handsome chariot' and dragged to the Guildhall, preceded by a band and surrounded by 'thousands'. The people lining the streets applauded as he passed. Cockburn by contrast left the hotel with one of the local magistrates and several gentlemen. On the road he was 'most grossly attacked by a crowd of miscreants' throwing 'mud, stones and other missiles . . .. On their arrival at the Guildhall they were literally covered with dirt and mud'.

This was a prelude. The mayor had not arrived and the doors of the Guildhall were still closed so the crowd proceeded to break the glass in the east window. The door was opened but 'the hall was no sooner filled than the most discordant yells, accompanied by groans and hisses intermixed with expressions of the most violent and disgusting kind, resounded from amongst the crowd'. With the arrival of Martin and the mayor, polling resumed, though with repeated interruptions. 'Before scarcely a vote had been polled, stones were flying in every direction . . .. The gentlemen around the table wore their hats to protect their heads from the stones.' Various people called for order and, in brief periods between disturbances, the poll went on.

As the day advanced the crowd became increasingly impatient of non-reformers. About three o'clock a 'tremendous rush' took place, the barrier dividing the hall gave way, and a general surge followed. 'The professional gentlemen and those around them leaped on the table and a scene of general confusion continued for some time.' Persuaded by Elliot, the crowd retreated and business resumed. But at about four o'clock another rush took place which completely overwhelmed the platform party. Even Elliot could gain no response. Fighting, noise, confusion reigned throughout the hall. Eventually the Riot Act was read. Yet this only tended to increase disorder. The crowd was reinforced from outside; the authorities had insufficient strength to force it back. 'It was impossible to give anything like a detailed account of proceedings', the *Herald* reporter apologized, 'we were obliged to put our note book in our pocket for two hours before the Mayor left, all idea of writing out of the question'. 'The table was crowded with persons standing on it and nearly all distinction of persons appeared to be lost.' At last, with no hope of order being restored—'amidst a scene which beggars description'—the poll was closed for the day.

In spite of the disorder, voting that day still left Martin at the head of the candidates with 98 votes, Cockburn with 89, and Elliot with 62. After leaving the public hall, Cockburn retired to a back room in the Guildhall. Owing to the violence of the crowd, he took advantage of protection offered by the magistrates who decided to send for a military escort. Between 5 and 6 o'clock two companies of soldiers arrived with whom Cockburn and his friends set off for the hotel. Though they took a back route, 'unfortunately, as they were passing the square an immense crowd, principally boys and persons of the lowest class, attacked Sir George, the magistrates and their friends and, notwithstanding the military, they pelted them with stones, many of which struck them'. Cockburn was cut in the ear and was escorted to the hotel with difficulty. That evening crowds continued to parade the streets, and the windows of several people who had voted for Cockburn instead of Elliot were broken.

Better order prevailed on the final day. Cockburn was persuaded not to attend the poll, while a large number of 'respectable tradesmen' were sworn in as constables. The result simply confirmed the preceding days' polls: Martin 101 votes, Cockburn 91 and Elliot 63. In spite of the disorders, Martin and Cockburn were duly elected. Even then the town remained quiet. Elliot was drawn to the turnpike gates in the 'chariot', 'surrounded by thousands', while Martin and Cockburn were able to tour the town paying their respects to voters. 'As soon as the Government candidate left the place, the mob and the excitement disappeared', Cockburn wrote to Croker; 'I afterwards visited every hole and corner of the town to thank those who had voted for me, and to solicit the new freemen for future occasions, without meeting with even a disagreeable observation from a single individual'. He remained at Plymouth for a week after the election dining with and paying attention 'to those gallant fellows who so nobly stood by me against every influence and exertion of the Government and menace of the Government mob'.[6]

Cockburn was naturally jubilant at this apparent victory of restraint over revolution, especially as no voters he met wished to be associated with the 'mob'.

> I think what passed at Plymouth has done much good to our cause and of course harm to the revolutionists; the most decided reformers in Plymouth were anxious to assure me they were ashamed of the proceedings of the mob (which seemed only to have been defended and countenanced by the *Government* Candidate) . . .. I was generally told (and of course pretended to believe it) that the mob was not composed of Plymouth People but of the lowest description of persons from Devonport and the adjoining neighborhood and the workmen of the government works at Cremall Point . . .. I enclose to you an anonymous letter received by Captain Wise, a magistrate and chairman of my committee, to shew you . . . the state of terror which has been operating.

The injuries Cockburn had received he considered of no consequence compared to the success achieved. 'The Admiralty and even a higher quarter' felt greatly annoyed at it. Yet it did little to console senior Tories. Wellington saw nothing but revolution in parliamentary reform, which he felt the election results encouraged the Whigs to pursue. Cockburn had difficulty resisting the gloom.[7] He took little part in debates on the two further Reform Bills in the following months, although he did oppose a proposal to disenfranchise impressed seamen on account of their non-residence. He claimed it was bad enough for them to lose their families without losing their civil rights too.[8] In

March 1832, when the King refused to create new peers to pass the third Bill and asked Wellington to form a new ministry, he only hoped that Wellington could do so: 'I care not much about anything else'.[9]

In the event Wellington's failure and the withdrawal of sufficient Tory Lords from the Upper House to permit the Reform Bill to pass on 4 June was something of an anticlimax. The redistribution of 56 seats and extension of the franchise to 300,000 new voters left many features of the old electoral system intact. Indeed, by effecting the minimum change necessary to quell discontent, it was a measure with which Cockburn, with many other Tories, was later able to feel reconciled.

It was, however, but part of the Whig programme of change. To complement reform of Parliament, the Whigs undertook almost concurrently to satisfy the agitation in the Commons for reform of naval administration. Overshadowed, and almost ignored by those concentrating on the greater issue, the Whigs' navy Bill effected change in naval administration greater than anything known since 1660. Achieved on the strength of the 1831 election, and embodying a new administrative ideology, the Bill was as revolutionary to naval administrators as the Bill to reform Parliament was to officials of the former Tory government.

Administrative Reform

Cockburn may well have anticipated the 'Navy Civil Departments Bill' introduced in the Commons on 14 February 1832. For there, Hume had continued to maintain that the Navy Board practised 'systematic deception' in its accounts, by spending more than had been voted—for example, on Woolwich dockyard or the number of marines maintained. In 1831 he challenged the new government to bring the Navy Board to account before the end of the session.[10] In response, and to reduce naval expenditure, the new First Lord, Sir James Graham, began a campaign to discredit Navy Board management in the eyes of the King and the House of Commons. On more than one occasion, provoked beyond self-control, Byam Martin rose to demand Graham retract an imputation that public monies had been misappropriated. His refusal to stand against Cockburn in the May election, in spite of his high office under the Whig government, demonstrated his alienation from his new masters. Appointed by Letters Patent under the Great Seal, his removal had to be approved by the King. But on 17 October 1831 he was summarily dismissed as Comptroller.[11]

The new Prime Minister, Lord Grey, was firmly behind Graham. Secure in the result of the May election, and with Sir Byam Martin gone, he encouraged Graham to dismantle the bureaucracy beneath the Admiralty. As First Lord himself in 1806–7, Grey had found the civil business of the navy difficult to control through the subordinate boards. In 1806 he acceded to the Whig view of apparent obstruction suffered by St Vincent in his attempts to alter Navy Board policy three years earlier.[12] Graham was to act on these apparent lessons. By December 1831, with the help of John Barrow, he had drawn up 'proposals for a great change in the administration of naval affairs' which were subsequently approved by Hardy at the Admiralty, by Grey and Althorp, Chancellor of the Exchequer, and by the King.[13]

The grand object of the exercise was to achieve sweeping economies both through savings in salaries from dismantling naval bureaucracy, and by the removal of powerful subordinate post holders whose views were invariably opposed to reductions in yard establishments or alterations in fleet maintenance policies.[14] His object necessitated a direct attack on the efficiency of the board system, and consequently upon the administrative reputations of the Tory officials who maintained it. Indeed, on 14 February Graham claimed that the 'subordinate boards had at all times continued to divide the power and thwart the views of the Board presumed to be set in authority over them'; moreover that he had 'pregnant evidence of the mismanagement of the subordinate boards and of their successful opposition to the Board of Admiralty'. He proceeded to allege five cases of monies expended in excess or in the absence of estimates, two instances of disobedience of Admiralty orders, and three cases of long-term managerial failure: failures to prevent fraud and embezzlement, to reduce prices from their wartime level, and to achieve the precise costing of ship construction.

For the Tory opposition the removal of slurs on their credibility as administrators was a precondition to convincing backbenchers of advantages in the traditional system. Cockburn, Croker, Byam Martin and Sir George Clerk consequently consumed the first two debates on the Bill in refuting Graham's allegations, and arguing that Graham knew virtually nothing, compared to themselves, of naval adminis-tration. Together they represented almost sixty years of experience in central government. Their testimony on the workings of naval administration was almost incontestable. By contrast Graham's allegations were superficial and contrived.[15] He nevertheless possessed several advantages over the Tory veterans.

Firstly, the latter had for their preparations only published works and personal copies of the official Admiralty papers.

> I transmit to you herewith my gleanings from the books you sent me and which I now return [Cockburn wrote to Croker about 20 February] . . . I send also Martin's answer to me about the copper, the surveys etc. When I get his further explanations, I will send them to you. I have not been able to get you 'Derrick's history of the Navy' but I think you have quite enough to work from and you may refer to Beatsons Index to ascertain if the changes in the Admiralty have been as I have stated.[16]

Secondly, the Tories were working against established prejudices. Opinion over the previous three years had demonstrated a decided inclination in the Commons towards redefinition of administrative responsibilities, the eradication of unjustified expense, and greater accountability to Parliament. Thirdly, for all their detail, the Tories' explicit administrative explanations were lost on the majority in the Commons. Towards the end of the two and a half hour second reading—of which Croker alone filled one and three-quarter hours—Clerk admitted despondently 'how difficult it was to fix the attention of gentlemen upon a subject which did not interest them particularly'. In this circumstance, speakers who were technically correct were less appreciated than those who stuck to basic and appealing themes.

And this Graham did. His knowledge of naval administration was shallow but his arguments were simple and straightforward, with a Benthamite logic that appealed to tax-paying gentlemen. He proposed to abolish the Navy and Victualling Boards and divide naval administration into five great departments with a principal officer set over each. These officers—the Surveyor General, Accountant General, Storekeeper General and Superintendents of the Victualling and Medical departments—would, unlike the previous board commissioners, be appointed by Admiralty warrant, and be individually responsible to five Admiralty commissioners, each presiding over a separate naval department. He reinforced his arguments by claiming that the reduction of five commissioners, 54 clerks and 38 other officials would save £49,800 annually. Above all, the Navy Bill required the accounts of the navy not only to be checked by the Admiralty but to go before the Board of Audit which would submit 'any discoveries of improprieties' to the House of Commons. This report would, he argued, provide the House with the information necessary to question and make the Admiralty really accountable for naval expenditure.[17]

Cockburn was not entirely opposed to these proposals. He fully appreciated the frustrations of an Admiralty commissioner unable to impose his will on politically dissident subordinate officials. In 1820 he himself had concluded the only means of deterring the son of a secretary to the Navy Board from canvassing a constituency against government will was to make the secretary's tenure dependent upon his son's conformity.[18] As an officer he had also reacted against 'the harsh and dictatorial behaviour' of Navy Board officials in their inflexible maintenance of rules and procedures, an intransigence defended by reference to precedent and long experience.[19] In February 1832, his own defence of the subordinate boards was consequently ambivalent.

> He had frequently thought some change in the civil and administration of the navy must ultimately take place. He was ready to admit that the Admiralty had not always found the Navy Board ready to act as the Admiralty wishes . . . but the Navy Board, which he might call the Board of Detail, being composed of men who had risen principally from the various departments in the service, was generally opposed to any sweeping change . . . and it had . . . by that part of its constitution prevented a great deal of mischief.

To retain this advantage of the existing structure, the Tory amendment to Graham's Bill, proposed by Cockburn on 6 April, was for the five principal officers subordinate to the Admiralty to be organized into a single new board. Cockburn maintained that if the individual officers did not sit at a board they would be acting unchecked, except by Admiralty commissioners who in wartime would be too overwhelmed by business to provide close supervision. It was a mild amendment. But even that was convincingly defeated, 118 votes to 50.[20]

The defeat was accepted with resignation. Most annoying to him was the lack of support from former colleagues. Graham's defence of his Bill during the final debate made reference to support from Lord Melville as well as Barrow. This was news to Cockburn. Only on inquiry did he learn that Melville had contemplated an arrangement similar to Graham's. 'With respect to your observation regarding Lord Melville', Cockburn told Croker on 12 May,

> I own I am much dissatisfied with him, for I find that when he was at the India Board during the time of our Royal Lord High Admiral, he drew a plan for bringing all the naval detail under the different members of H R Highness' council, something like Graham's present measure, without having ever mentioned it either to you or me or any other Admiralty

person. I take for granted that his son Robert [at the Navy Board] must have known of it and mentioned it to Sir James Graham, as Sir James wrote to Lord Melville to ask him to let him see it and it was in answer to that letter that Lord Melville said he thought the principle of Graham's was better than his own and he therefore did not think it necessary to send his to Sir James. His Lordship however told Clerk he knew nothing of the details of Graham's plan and his approbation of it therefore cannot in my opinion go for much.[21]

As First Lord between 1812 and 1830, Melville was the only speaker in the Lords who could seriously have opposed Grey in 1832. A son at the Navy Board, the subject of 'kindness' and confidential communications from Graham, certainly influenced his failure even to take part in the debate.[22] The Bill thus passed the Lords without division and received the royal assent on 1 June. A week later, boards that had been in existence since the seventeenth century simply ceased to exist.

Divided Loyalties

Among former administrators, the Act of 1 June 1832 caused deep concern. There were serious fears that war would combine with changes of ministry in which Admiralty Board membership would revolve and the navy then lack a council of experienced men capable of managing the minutiae of business. Cockburn's proposed amendment was recognized to obviate this difficulty.[23] His role in proposing it, and simultaneously opposing severe reductions in the finance of dockyards, marines, coast blockade and guardships, reinforced his place as the leading Tory officer in the Commons.[24] As the session passed, however, it became evident this parliamentary role was capable of achieving little. 'What a mess the government seems to have got into', he confided to Croker in November, 'but the overturning system has gone too far to leave any chance of bringing matters right again by any change of our rulers'.[25]

After fourteen years preoccupation with Admiralty administration, Cockburn was looking for a change. The formal offer on 3 December of command of the North America and West Indies station was thus welcome.[26] Although he was a Tory, the government was short of Whig admirals, and Cockburn at sixty was still one of the youngest men who had received their flags in the Napoleonic War. His appointment had already been mooted to Peel who responded favourably. Accordingly, when Sir James Graham made the offer 'in a particularly flattering manner, as well on the part of the *King* as of the Government', Cockburn accepted promptly. In doing so, he explained to Peel, it was clearly understood that he did 'not swerve one iota' in his political allegiance. He would 'of course zealously endeavour to carry into successful execution every wish and intention of the Government', however much he differed from their views, but should events in England take a turn in which he would 'be useful towards effecting or maintaining a total change of men and measures', he would resign the command to resume his political position under an administration formed by Peel and Wellington.[27]

Following dinners for political allies and professional colleagues at the Carlton Club and the Admiralty, Cockburn, his wife, daughter and their female companion joined the *Vernon* in January 1833 and, after several false starts and a good passage of 26 days, reached Bermuda on 16 March. There Cockburn took charge of a command stretching from the Arctic in the north to the Windward Islands in the south, a region through which Cockburn would voyage as the seasons dictated. Considering it 'more easy to make a house warm in extreme cold weather than to make one cool in extreme hot weather', the cooler latitudes had the preference. The Caribbean hurricane season was spent in Nova Scotia, departing again for the tropics before the severe cold set in, with 'winter' being spent touring the southerly divisions, visiting island governors and consuls. Barbados, Trinidad, Jamaica figured regularly on the itinerary, even Belize where Cockburn's brother, Francis, was Governor of British Honduras. Bermuda, where there was an admiral's house and dockyard facilities, was a pivotal point on these voyages. During the American war he had considered it 'a detestable place'—now it became the place of which he was most fond. Time was also spent at Jamaica where he selected a site for the construction of an admiral's house, and at Halifax from where there were visits inland and down the St Lawrence.

From the beginning, relations with the Whig First Lord and the Admiralty's First Sea Lord were cordial. Although Sir Thomas Hardy had been one of Cockburn's lieutenants during the Revolutionary war, the latter made the transition to subordinate without difficulty, accepting without complaint the negligible amount of influence he was permitted in the choice of officers and ships. Appointments were strictly controlled by rules laid down at the Admiralty that kept patronage almost completely in Whig hands. So too in the choice of ships: even his flag ships were selected for him, the transfer from *Vernon* to *President* in

1834 being 'settled at the Admiralty' without any communication with Cockburn.[28]

Communication was the key to the maintenance of working relationships between the Admiralty and commanders on foreign stations. Between officials of conflicting politics it was even more important. As soon as he was on station, Graham invited Cockburn to write freely and privately to him on any subject he wished, and within limits the invitation was accepted.[29] Cockburn also wrote to Hardy on purely professional subjects, such as the conduct of disreputable officers and aspects of naval duty needing new or altered instructions. The limits to this correspondence were set by the political sensitivity of the subject matter. In only one area did these limits conflict with naval interests, in that of ship architecture. This was not owing to lack of effort. Cockburn put himself out to give the desk-bound Graham and Hardy as much information as possible about the sailing qualities of the *Vernon*, constructed by the new Surveyor, Sir William Symonds. But the *Vernon* was a symbol of the new Whig administration and his criticisms of her qualities aroused defensive feelings, as much for the Surveyor's appointment as for the design, based as it was on yacht construction. It was eighteen months before Cockburn heard how his reports were received, and he then took offence. But by then changes in the Whig ministry had brought Melbourne to the Treasury as Prime Minister, and Lord Aukland to the Admiralty instead of Graham.

Initially Cockburn observed the political changes in England with despondency.[30] During 1833 both the domestic and the foreign policies of the Whigs seemed to herald ignominious decline. The only consolation Cockburn could draw from them was their progressive approach to a point at which

> the mass of those possessing property in the United Kingdom will see the necessity of uniting hand and heart to save what may then be remaining to us of constitution and property, and with that view to effect an entire and decided change of measures and rulers.[31]

In prospect of such a reaction, officers out of employment were consoled in their enforced residence on shore by encouragement in the duties of a country gentleman and magistrate. Much did it seem to require at this time 'the exertions of *good* men and *true* . . . to check and keep down the spirit of mischief and anarchy' in England and Ireland.[32]

The resignation of Graham and Stanley from the Whig ministry in 1834 was 'the first bright gleam that has broken through the dismal black threatening cloud which has for the few past years been hanging over us'. It opened a hope of 'fairer weather and better days'. But Cockburn was in no hurry for the formation of a new Tory or Conservative government. 'On the contrary, I consider the longer and stronger the folly of the present course of misrule is exposed the more it will insure support and strength to those who shall be called upon...to endeavour after such a reckless storm to right the good old vessel, now so shattered and on her beam ends, and to save her from entire destruction'.[33]

Graham's replacement by Aukland raised a groundless fear of recall, while an offer of transfer to the Mediterranean was gently declined. But the changes at the Admiralty in mid-1834 were prelude to the return of a Tory ministry in November. Cockburn hoped this would rally all who desired the preservation of monarchy, just as it appeared to stimulate the 'whole commercial community' in the West Indies.[34] Cockburn was named as first naval lord in the new Conservative government, but he emphasized to Croker his reluctance to become 'one of a board where everything appears to me to be now wrongly or inefficiently conducted'.[35] The disappointment of a general election, with Peel's defeat in the Commons and resignation, seemed to afford proof of the near 'impossibility of any government now preserving its existence if it will not run . . . hand in hand with the destructive radical combination'. Cockburn continued to hope for a reaction, the return of 'a more sober feeling', so that 'after a few more struggles like the last, the cause of the King, of Right and of order' would gain triumph.[36]

It was not to come while he remained on the North American station. Succeeding Whig First Lords retained him for his full term of four years. It was service he found pleasant compared to the 'office fag' of life in London.[37] At the same time he managed his officers and international affairs with the impartiality of one for whom professional duty was separate from the politics of his masters. However, a commander-in-chief on a foreign station was never really independent of the administrative politics of the Admiralty, as he found to his cost in the *Vernon* affair.

The *Vernon* Affair

Cockburn attempted to contribute to administration in London through his reports on the *Vernon*, his flagship in 1833–4. The practice of naval architecture was fundamental to Britain's defence, yet, as a science, it

Plate 8. HMS *Vernon*, the large frigate designed in 1831 by Sir William Symonds, the Surveyor of the Navy appointed by the whig Admiralty of 1830. Cockburn was deeply critical of her sailing performance to windward. (National Maritime Museum)

was still in its infancy. Consequently practical experience of ships under sail was regarded as equally important to the pragmatic alteration of designs as schooling in theory and practical construction. Sea officers were thus considered as capable as master shipwrights to propose and complete designs. As a naval lord of the Admiralty in the 1820s, Cockburn had been closely involved in the institution of sailing trials of experimental ships and in the commissioning of new designs by Captains Hayes and Symonds, as well as by the navy's own professional designers, the Surveyors of the Navy.[38] One of the results was that naval architecture assumed a strong degree of personal rivalry. After 1830 it also gained a political overtone.

Under the Tories from 1813 there had been three surveyors, Sir Henry Peake, Joseph Tucker and Sir Robert Seppings; from 1822 only two, and in 1831 the Whigs reduced this number to just one. Because he held his post by Letters Patent under the Great Seal of the King, the surviving Tory surveyor, Seppings, had taken some time to remove, but had finally been replaced by Sir William Symonds in June 1832. Symonds was appointed as much to bring his patron, the Duke of Portland, into the Whig camp as for his ship designs. But these designs had been generally successful. Sponsored by the later Lord Vernon, he had built the yacht *Nancy Dawson* on experimental lines in 1821. The Admiralty had then permitted him to build the brig *Columbine* in 1825, another brig *Philomel* from 1827, and finally in 1831 the 50-gun frigate *Vernon*. In general, Symonds' vessels possessed greater beam and more wedge-shaped bottoms than usual; under suitable conditions they achieved greater speed and stability; but, substituting beam for ballast, they tended to carry lighter armament than their tonnage formerly did.[39]

In 1832 the *Vernon* was still under trial, as indeed was the appointment of Symonds, who was the first Surveyor not trained to his profession by traditional dockyard apprenticeship. Not unnaturally the Whigs were sensitive to criticism of both the vessel and the appointment. To Cockburn fell the opportunity to assess the *Vernon* in varying oceanic conditions over a protracted period.

Though a quick passage of 26 days, the voyage out to Bermuda consisted of about 9 days of constant gales of secondary strength, then a fair following wind and calm sea to 29 degrees north, after which a moderate breeze and smooth water was sometimes crossed by a north-westerly swell. While the sea was calm and the breeze moderate, the *Vernon* went astonishingly fast 'at eight or more knots'. But in the same breeze and a swell on her beam, the difference was 'very striking'. She took to pitching heavily and her speed slowed to about three knots. However, it was the early stormy weather that revealed her worst qualities. Cockburn could think of no other ship in which he had ever been that would have suffered at all under similar circumstances. Consequently he reported his observations after relieving her of her foresail, the sea running more on her beam than ahead. In three successive pitches the whole of her forecastle hammock netting, bowsprit and jib boom were dashed completely under the sea, scooping in and sending into the main deck vast quantities of water. In short, it was 'impossible to fancy anything more uncomfortable than all the movements of the ship and their effects'. Her rolling and jerking so strained the vessel that, though caulked at Plymouth, she became leaky in every part, especially along her decks and waterways, the pitch even being squeezed out of seams along her gangways. Such was the damage, especially to the knee of the head, that on completing this voyage the ship had to be repaired while Cockburn contemplated sending her back to England.

These observations were returned to Graham and Hardy immediately on reaching Bermuda. To Graham he discreetly concluded that the *Vernon*'s good qualities would permit her to shine on a fair-weather station, like the West Indian, but that in the North Atlantic or other stormy latitudes he would prefer 'any other frigate in the service'.[40] But to Hardy her 'merits and demerits' were detailed at length. He was particularly concerned with Symond's refusal to believe reports contradicting the 'idea that the breadth of this ship's bows and the waterline must protect her from pitching deeply'.

> . . . but after what I have seen, I can assure him he is greatly mistaken on this point, and I should hope that in any future ships he may build he will endeavour to remedy this defect; indeed afer noticing the manner in which the *Vernon* falls into a sea forward and after, I should think a small vessel on the same lines scarcely safe in a real gale of wind, especially if obliged to carry sail against it or scud before it.[41]

Eight months passed before Cockburn could again observe *Vernon* under a similar range of conditions. On her return voyage from Halifax to Bermuda 'she again carried away the whole of the rails and frame work of her head'. This was 'of no further consequence than the trouble and expense of repairing it so often'. But, he added pointedly to Graham, he 'should not like to be kept in her in more stormy seas'.[42] Accompanied by the sloop *Fly*, he once again noted the superiority of *Vernon*'s speed in smooth water under topgallant sails over single-reefed topsails. Yet on the passage from Bermuda to Jamaica, they met westerly winds accompanied by a southerly swell. The *Fly* was reduced to her topsails but still beat the *Vernon*, as did a schooner tender. So badly did she sail, Cockburn was convinced that 'any common merchant vessel in existence would have beaten *Vernon* that day'. Yet that night the southerly swell went down and the tables were suddenly turned. The *Vernon* could easily have outpaced *Fly* and the tender, and did so when it was decided to leave them. 'Now' Cockburn concluded to Graham,

> if I have at all succeeded in conveying to you sufficiently clearly these details as they occurred, it will give you a better practical proof of what *Vernon* really is than anything deduced from theory that can be written or said. I firmly believe that in smooth water and a good breeze she will beat any that swims upon the sea, especially to windward, but the moment she is opposed by a sea ahead, whether she be going by or large, she becomes worse than can be believed by any that do not witness it, and I can compare her to nothing but a child's rocking horse constantly moving up and down without advancing a step. It is certainly curious that a small sloop and schooner should obtain advantage by the presence of a head sea over a ship of such magnificent size and length as *Vernon*, but such is the fact from the difference of the form of their bodies under water.[43]

Cockburn had no intention or need to return to this subject of correspondence with Graham and Hardy. In June 1834 he received news that he was to transfer his flag to the newly built and significantly named *President*, modelled on the United States frigate of the same name. But, naturally enough, friends of his own political persuasion were also interested in his experience of these new vessels—Sir Robert Seppings more than most. By coincidence, Cockburn answered Seppings' questioning letter of August 1833 on the same day in December as he wrote to Graham from Jamaica. He had not previously written to Seppings, being 'disinclined to take advantage of the situation my political enemies have handsomely placed me in, to discover and to make known what may appear to me erroneous in their proceedings, especially on what must naturally prove to them tender points'. Notwithstanding Seppings' promise of secrecy, he would therefore say no more about *Vernon* 'than that it is impossible for a more practical proof to be accorded of the correctness and soundness of the observations you have forwarded to me than that ship'.[44]

Cockburn's reluctance to say any more on the subject to Seppings was prudent. In England, Symonds' ship designs became a matter of public debate. Even before the *Vernon* had sailed for North America, the young Walter Devereux, who also sailed in her, was amused 'to hear of the various reports in circulation at Plymouth respecting' her.[45] Even then, it was said she was 'a Tory ship' and 'therefore faults have been found with' her. By early 1833 the subject had reached Parliament where Hume had criticized her construction. Naturally, professional sea officers had taken serious interest, the impassioned Captain Hayes addressing a letter to the Admiralty 'relative to the probable disastrous consequences' of persisting in building warships similar to *Vernon*. Reacting strongly, the Board commissioners had begun to feel deeply defensive. Hayes, who was initially granted permission to build a frigate on design principles opposite to those of the *Vernon,* now met an 'apparent disinclination' to forward its construction, a lack of interest Cockburn regretted 'as of course Constance cannot well be tried until Inconstant shall be ready to contend with her'.[46]

Across the Atlantic, Cockburn was only gradually to learn of this reaction at the Admiralty. When in mid-1834 he learned from his ex-flag captain, Sir George Westphal, of 'the time taken by Sir Thomas Hardy and the other sea lords' to forward his own reports on the vessel to Graham he was surprised. He expected his own genuine aim of improving naval architecture would be reciprocated at the Admiralty. It was not so much the apparent prejudice against him at the Board that hurt, it was the tendency to assume he was attempting to discredit Symonds. He thought they impugned his professional honour. Cockburn responded to Westphal:

> if they have such little minds as to suppose I could have been actuated by any unworthy feelings towards Captain Symonds in giving my opinion on a matter of such national importance they lower themselves sadly in my estimation and oblige me to lament their being placed in situations where more honourable and liberal sentiments should prevail, and it is quite clear they neither do nor can they know me.

Symonds too was a target for Cockburn's wrath. He could understand the Surveyor 'feeling sore at his favourite child being found fault with and being anxious to attribute it to any thing rather than real defect'. But he wished that Symonds 'also had shewn a higher feeling than to have supposed I could have any personal prejudice against him individually'. If he had seen Cockburn's letters to Graham—'which I cannot help thinking he ought to have done'—he would have seen that he was spoken of 'in the handsomest manner'.[47]

Not unnaturally, Cockburn's reaction was to dissociate himself from both *Vernon* and Whig architectural thinking. Now they had 'got this pet ship home . . . they may do as they like with her and think as they please, it will be wholly indifferent to me'. The reaction was regretable, a product of poor communication and the delicacy with which ship design was being handled at the Admiralty. Cockburn was not to learn until much later that his letters resulted in the recasting of the bow of all Symonds' ships.[48]

Management without Patronage

By 1836 Cockburn commanded 26 vessels on the North American station. The force represented more than 16 per cent of the commissioned British navy. As well as his flagship, it included four frigates, ten sloops and five steam paddle vessels. Officering this fleet there were seven captains, two appointed commodores, 14 commanders, 52 lieutenants and 24 masters. The management problems they presented were numerous and probably representative of those faced on other stations. They included potential insubordination; the need to check the pecuniary impulses of those wishing to profit from their commands; the necessity to maintain harmony between officers and men within ships; and the problem of how to maintain morale at a time when opportunities for higher appointments and promotion were limited.

Cockburn's response to these problems was affected by the peculiar political situation in which he found himself. As a Tory serving a Whig Board of Admiralty, the authority and influence he could command was significantly less than if he had been of the same party. His power to appoint officers to new posts was particularly affected, as the Whig government kept in its own hands all the patronage available to it—and the officers within his command were well aware of this. In consequence, to maintain motivation and discipline, Cockburn was thrown more than was usual upon his own resources. His efforts reveal that the power of patronage was not absolutely essential to the management of a foreign station in the early 1830s.

Initial difficulties arose from Commodore Sir Arthur Farquhar, a captain with seniority dating back to 1805. The previous commander-in-chief on the station, Sir Edward Colpoys, had died in post and, as the most senior officer on station, Farquhar had instituted himself as a flag officer. Cockburn heard, however, that even before Colpoys' death an 'improper kind of opposition' had been shown 'by many of the captains of the station to the late Admiral'.[49] On Cockburn's appearance, Farquhar seemed ready to lead this opposition against a new commander-in-chief. Though expected to resume his former post as a divisional commander, Farquhar refused to haul down his flag, claiming that he was entitled to remain a flag officer as long as he remained on the station; indeed, so long as he remained in commission. So determined was he to 'adhere to own sentiments about it' that in a public letter, 'respectfully though not perhaps very regularly', he questioned Cockburn's order to change his pendant; such was his behaviour, Cockburn was obliged to quote to Farquhar his own Admiralty instructions. He 'did not at any time . . . refuse to obey my order to him to change his pendant but the manner in which he expressed his complaints . . ., the questions he thought proper to put regarding it, and the excuses he made to put off carrying it into execution (nearly 24 hours) gave the whole the character' of 'considered and determined opposition'.

To Hardy in London, Cockburn stressed the obligation of the Admiralty to support him.

> I feel entire confidence that in the answer I will receive from Sir James Graham or the board, the propriety, I had almost said the necessity, of upholding your commander in chief so long as he is in the right will not be lost sight of and you may I hope trust to my steadiness very quickly to put an entire stop to . . . [this] . . . improper kind of opposition.[50]

And steadiness was indeed necessary. Other captains on the station got up an address in support of Farquhar. The latter had sent home two vessels, one of them via Vera Cruz to pick up specie, and he had dispersed, on detached duties, all the schooners on the station 'under a mistaken notion . . . that whilst they were acting under his particular orders he would have a claim to share in any capture or freight they might make'. Cockburn responded by sending Farquhar to act as senior officer in the Windward Islands, reminding the Admiralty that the commodore was due for replacement. He was confident that without Farquhar he and the other officers would 'all very soon understand one another'. So events proved. By November 1833 he met 'nothing but cheerful obedience and ready compliance' with his wishes; 'such is the change of a few months under a due degree of steadiness aided by your support at head quarters'.[51]

A key factor behind Farquhar's determination to fly his flag for as long as possible was the income the command-in-chief gained from a principal share in earnings made by ships on the station from the carriage of specie and from prize and head money for captured slave ships. Earnings from the carriage of specie were considerable. A regulating Act of 1819 limited freight money to 1.5 per cent of the value of the treasure carried within a station in peace, 2 per cent in war. For carriage from Europe to a foreign station 2 per cent was permitted in peace, 2.5 per cent in war. Of these percentages, the captain of the vessel concerned obtained half the earnings, the admiral one quarter, the fourth quarter going to Greenwich Hospital.[52] Between 1839 and 1843 the North American commander-in-chief's annual share averaged over £4,300.[53] It is not surprising, therefore, that, though having consented to strike his red broad pendant, Farquhar raised an argument for their 'mutual right to share as flag officers' between the time of Cockburn's arrival within the limits of the station and Farquhar hauling down his flag. Settlement of this question extended Cockburn's difficulties with Farquhar for another year.[54]

Disputes of this nature reflected the persisting view that naval officers could be expected to profit from the perquisites of their post. Cockburn himself shared this view, observing to Sir Richard King in May 1834 that, although the command was 'no longer the profitable thing it was, it still nevertheless does rather more than cover my mess and establishment which is so far good'.[55] Yet the profit motive was not always an appropriate incentive to efficiency, especially for younger officers anxious after money. Cockburn was obliged to lecture Captain Strono for resenting Commodore Pell's refusal to allow him to proceed to Jamaica to land money and passengers from England.

> Freight money, although it may be very acceptable to an officer when it comes in his way in the course of his duty without detriment to the service, is, and must be always deemed, a very secondary consideration and must not for a moment be brought into competition with or be permitted to interfere with the more important duties required for the squadron in the extensive station under my command.[56]

Cockburn kept a close eye on all arrangements for the conveyance of specie. There were Treasury rules pertaining to the receipt of payments for freight, as well as Admiralty rules for their distribution, and Cockburn was fastidious in ensuring they were observed.[57]

The opportunity to convey specie did not fall to all ships. Nevertheless, it was so regularly available that when the merchants at

Vera Cruz 'determined not to send any treasure by ships of war so long as the charge for the freight continued higher than that of the packet', the voyage of the *Columbine* to England without freight was noted as unusual. For Cockburn, the authority to select the ships that should convey specie provided a form of patronage. As he noted to Captain Wise, transferred to the Mediterranean in 1834, he had little opportunity of placing him 'in the way of doing any grand deeds of arms' but he might have managed to put some dollars in his pocket'.[58]

The indulgence of carrying specie was a reward for services rendered. In March 1833 Lord William Paget in the *North Star* was sent back to England by way of Vera Cruz, because he 'had a kind of promise from the late admiral for some such indulgence in reward for his general officer-like and good conduct during his services in this station'.[59] A like desire to reward his officers motivated Cockburn in June 1834 when he was considering the carriage of 'compensation money' to pay the owners of slaves that were to be emancipated. He thought it would be 'an act of justice to the squadron employed here' to raise it 'either at Vera Cruz or wherever it can be obtained *within* the station rather than sending it from England' which would subject it to additional charges for carriage.[60]

From officer-like and good conduct Cockburn naturally excluded motives which placed private gain before public service. Otherwise criticisms for behavioural deficiencies were suffered most frequently by young men undergoing training and being considered for promotion. Captain Charles Ross was urged to write a letter of parental advice to his son pointing out faults that required 'early and determined attention and correction'. These included 'foolish extravagance, consequent idleness, and inattention to his professional studies and duties so as to prevent his being a favourite with his Captain or superior officers, and a sad carelessness (either affected or real) both of *manners* and *dress* as would convey an impression to those not knowing who he was that he has been more accustomed to low company than the society of gentlemen'.[61]

Good officers, in Cockburn's view, had been brought up to possess manners that blended smoothly with those of their class. In May 1834 Lieutenant Charles Pears was found wanting in his conduct and language at the mess table that 'was at times *unmanly* and disgusting such as to call forth expressions of deep indignation from those officers present who possessed the mind and feelings of gentlemen'. Trustworthiness and a sense of personal honour were important. Pears' fault was his failure to rebut a statement about him by Lieutenant

Seymour during an argument after a game of cards before leaving Portsmouth. Seymour asserted 'that if his character was as well known there as it was to him no one would associate with him, and that he was a damn'd blackguard and swindler, and ought to be kicked out of society'. His submission to this denigration became a subject of such general notoriety on the North American station that, to Cockburn's mind, it rendered him 'unfit to be forced by military authority upon any mess of gentlemen objecting to associate with him'.[62]

A sensitivity for culture was thus as necessary as intellectual ability. Cockburn accordingly enjoyed meeting Sir Colin Campbell's brother, 'he being evidently a correct and intelligent officer with excellent open and agreeable manners and no nonsense about it'. A special quality for a young man was to have the ability to make himself a 'favourite with everybody'.[63] But that depended on their adoption of an approved style of dress and behaviour. 'For depend on it', Captain Ross was told for the benefit of his son, 'the officer who, in addition to a perfect knowledge of the duties of his station, has the appearance, manners and feelings of a gentleman will always be far more respected not only by the world in general but by the sailors whom he has under his command'.[64]

This emphasis on cultural accomplishment made sense. It made for harmony between officers within the confines of a ship. Responsibility, rank, authority, earnings, living expenses, messing arrangements, appearances and conduct were all inseparably linked, and Cockburn was concerned to reinforce by social means the gradations in authority between officers in a ship's hierarchy of command.[65] For, as commander-in-chief, he could interfere personally in the discipline between officers only to a limited extent.[66]

The model gentleman was, of course, Cockburn himself. In relationships with younger officers within the flagship he was 'much too exact and correct an officer' to show any form of familiarity. To 24-year-old Lieutenant Walter Devereux, he was 'the only man I have yet seen who comes up to my idea of perfection as an officer'. It was 'delightful to serve under him'; one was 'always quite certain that justice, and the most impartial justice too, will be done to every individual'.[67] It was equally important to inspire respect from the seamen of a crew. Here the dispensation of impartial justice was a sound beginning. Yet the age of enlightened reforms demanded more from such justice than simply a quiet and obedient crew. In encouraging a voluntary subscription for a seaman maimed by an accident on board the *Vernon*, Cockburn commended the 'liberal and considerate feeling' of the seamen towards one another.[68] It was the task of the officer to encourage compassion and thoughtfulness, and this, it was maintained, could not be done by brutality.

An excessive number of punishments in any particular ship was now considered due to an officer's want of attention 'in not taking sufficient active precautions to prevent crime on the part of the men'.[69] Quarterly returns of punishments were made to the Admiralty via the commander-in-chief. The captains had been urged since 1830 to exercise 'a safe forbearance' in the number of lashes awarded in individual cases. More than two dozen were forbidden without court martial, detailed explanations of cases being required with the returns.[70] As an alternative to heavy punishment, Cockburn preferred malefactors to be 'discharged the service with disgrace', the descriptions of such men being reported to the Admiralty. He studied the returns, compared numbers of punishments to size of complement, contrasted vessels of similar size, and demanded explanations for excesses.

Cockburn's principal problem, the *Scylla*, upon which Commander Edward Carpenter seemingly exercised neither restraint in punishment nor adequate supervision of his crew, was sent home ostensibly due to the ship's leaky state, Cockburn's letter outlining Carpenter's failings preceding him to the Admiralty.[71] Lieutenant Charles Pears was quietly posted into a vacancy on a ship bound for England, also preceded by a letter to the First Sea Lord. He would, Cockburn predicted, 'fall back in due course (and without any appearance of authoritative interference) to the half pay list . . . until he shall have cleared his character from the stain thus publicly standing against it'.[72] At least two other young men, serving in the *Vernon* under Cockburn's eye, also went home, both having proved unsatisfactory to their officers. In these two cases Cockburn arranged that they should return 'in the manner least hurtful' to them, by allowing them to apply for discharge to attend urgent family business.[73] Commodore Farquhar was also smoothly replaced through the normal process of replacement.[74]

To what extent could Cockburn replace them with men of his own choosing? We know that he had the choice of his own immediate 'instruments', some of the officers of his flag ship, and was able to influence the selection of his two commodores. The other vessels on the station, however, all contained officers who carried Admiralty commissions. For how many of these commissions could Cockburn claim some responsibility? There can be little doubt that his powers of appointment would have been greater had he been of the same political party as the government; for, to the government, the navy was part of its patronage, the Board of Admiralty its agent, making appointments of political as well as professional value. And so much more numerous were the requests for appointments than the places available to it, that an allowance of this patronage was only made to a commander-in-chief in the confidence that he would use it to the government's advantage.[75] As a Tory, Cockburn could not be so trusted. Indeed, as he explained to Mrs Brane of Gosport, 'situated as I am with reference to politics I have no right to ask favours . . . from any branch or individual members of the existing government, nor would it be of the slightest use to you if I did, but on the contrary might prove detrimental to your husband's efforts through other channels . . .'.[76]

This distrust of Cockburn was unfair insofar as he faithfully performed his duty both as confidante of Whig parents and as impartial superior to officers appointed through influence with the Whigs. Thus, for example, among his official communications to John Backhouse, Under-Secretary at the Foreign Office, he assured him of the good health and behaviour of his son, who was among the midshipmen on board the *Vernon*, promising Mrs Backhouse that her son should 'be taken every possible care of that our somewhat hardy service will admit of'. He urged those with Whig friends to exert influence with them to obtain the promotion they sought for their sons.[77] While to Captain William Hamilton of the *Comus*, who despaired of Sir James Graham thinking of him, Cockburn loyally argued that Graham had not '(as you and I are aware) the means of giving always, when asked for, suitable employment to officers of your rank and standing'.[78]

The main problem certainly was the shortage of employment for those who sought it. Lieutenant vacancies occurred infrequently. Cockburn had a number of 'fine young officers' come out with him as supernumary mates 'pleasing themselves with the indulgence, if not unnatural hope, that some chance might offer for their advancement', but most were destined to return as they came.[79] Midshipmen vacancies rarely arose either. Cockburn's flagship usually carried three or four supernumary volunteers awaiting such vacancies. They received no pay, not being borne on the ship's books, and had to pay their own victualling and mess bills, as well as pay the cost of clothes and of their washing. Vacancies did exist for volunteer midshipmen from the Portsmouth naval college. But to applications on behalf of men in all other ranks Cockburn could only 'grieve to say that naval promotion seems to be now almost entirely put a stop to'.[80]

Initially, Cockburn did attempt to influence the Admiralty's choice in appointments. In April 1833 he provisionally apppointed 'young Sir Peter Parker' an acting commander; the choice was based on the impression that Sir James Graham would wish to advance Parker when the opportunity offered from 'claims on the service from his great-grandfather, grandfather and above all from his gallant father who fell advancing against the enemies of the country leaving his orphan to our care'. Young Sir Peter was, moreover, 'a fine, honourable, well-disposed young officer and an universal favourite with everybody'.[81] Yet the posting was not confirmed, an omission that was especially galling to those who hoped to benefit from Cockburn's favour. Walter Devereux, a lieutenant on the *Vernon*, explained to his parents in August 1833:

> We are very happy here, except in the example we have just had of the determination of the Whig Admy to give Sir G.C. no more patronage than is strictly his beyond their control—viz—death and ct martial vacancies, for Sir P. Parker who was . . . made into the Gannet by Sir Geo. C. is superseded altho his father's services and death entitle him to rapid promotion, certainly from a Govt. who are so liberal and make a point of rewarding *merit* only, from which good notice Ld Galloway's youngest son was made Lt 3 days after he passed.[82]

Political influence still mattered as much, if not more than, merit. In February 1834 Devereux tartly observed that Lord Grey had 'very nicely furnished his family jobs, by appointing his son to a line of battle ship—it smells rank to heaven'.[83]

In this situation, Cockburn had few opportunities to advance his subordinates. Vacancies from court martial occurred infrequently; illness and death were a little more common, especially on the Jamaica division. In such cases, opportunities were taken to shuffle officers between ships, principally according to the wishes of the commodore, but also according to the seniority of the officer concerned, how they would fit in relevant vessels, and the degree to which they had become adapted to the climate.[84] Geographical proximity to a vacancy and the convenience with which an officer could transfer, added an element of chance, operating for some and against others.

With so few opportunities available to him, Cockburn was cautious to avoid commitments.[85] He often talked of an order of claims upon him. This order was never disclosed but it was evidently in part a chronological one—earlier undertakings took precedence—and fell into four categories: those with political overtones;[86] requests from professional colleagues;[87] Cockburn's own private connections;[88] and those due to past naval services on the part of the applicant or the father. The credit earned by a father to whom Cockburn felt a personal debt, gained the strongest response. Thus the ungentlemanly son of Captain Charles Ross—Cockburn's flag captain between 1812 and 1816— obtained the first of the lieutenant's death vacancies. Even then, however, the appointment was grudging: 'had it depended on *his own* merits instead of his father's, he most certainly would not have obtained the boon from me this early . . .'.[89]

To young men like Walter Devereux the reward of past services, especially those of an earlier generation, added to their frustration.[90] How then did Cockburn maintain the motivation of his officers? He encouraged them in four ways. First, he took communication with them seriously. As well as touring the divisions of his command each session, he maintained regular correspondence with his commanders and commodores. Although the official correspondence was purely administrative and formal, with his commodores there was also a private correspondence that, he confided, placed him at his ease as to affairs within the divisions.[91] Secondly, he did not fail to praise and encourage his officers, not only in the management of specific responsibilities, but even on the routine submission of blank returns of punishments— giving 'the best practical proof' of their officers' 'constant, due and temperate attention' to their respective duties in the supervision of their crews. Such commendations he communicated to all officers.[92] Thirdly, Cockburn fostered loyalty by hosting regular social events at his own expense. In August 1833 at Halifax, Walter Devereux noted that there were 'very good parties every Friday—small ones', while there was 'a grand 250 touch about every month'. Two years later, Cockburn was still holding 'two or three large dinners weekly and frequent balls'. Primarily on this account, Devereux suspected, 'very little of his income' stayed in his admiral's pocket.[93] At Bermuda in October 1833 he even staged a regatta for seamen as well as officers. Of the principal donors to the prize purses, the Cockburn's together (Sir G., Lady and Miss C., and her companion Miss Sims) subscribed 56 dollars—almost twice the amount of the other principal donor, the Governor (32 dollars), or Lord Valentia (12 dollars).[94] Finally, of course, the commander-in-chief had the selection of the vessels that carried specie, and the authorization of their course home. Of all the favours that could be conferred as a reward for service on the station, this was the principal one. For Cockburn, it compensated to a large extent for lack of more conventional patronage.

North American Affairs

Throughout his command between 1833 and 1836 Cockburn insisted that captains in no way interfere in the internal political arrangements of foreign states.[95] But, 'under pressure of unusual circumstances' and 'trusting for vindication to the necessity and the general national feeling as to the propriety of the course adopted', he was prepared to overstep the limits of international law. Priority assistance was to be given to British subjects where popular insurrection was spreading violence, confusion and destruction in defiance of every law and treaty. Captains were instructed to remonstrate with local authorities in the first instance, and then to receive British subjects on board and protect their ships and cargoes. They were to interfere only if British lives were theatened.[96]

Unusual circumstances included incidents of piracy. On the whole, reports of pirates always seemed to be mistaken, or else traceable to slave runners. But in January 1836 the capture, plunder and murder of the crew of an English brigantine *Clio* prompted the dispatch of a vessel in search of the culprits in the River Para near the mouth of the Amazon.[97]

Elsewhere, a discreet naval presence was necessary. For example, at a potential confrontation between a French naval force and the Columbian authorities at Cartegena where the French consul had been insulted;[98] and in 1835–6 at an insurrection in Venezuela, where opponents of the government fitted ships in ports under their control. Cockburn demurred from interfering so long as their operations were restricted to the political struggle.[99] This policy of non-interference was pursued in liaison with local consuls and with reference to the Admiralty. Most of the new states in South America had factional conflicts still going on; Cockburn thought they would be a considerable time before they worked 'themselves down into sufficiently fixed and permanent government to afford happiness and quiet to their inhabitants'.[100]

British interests were rarely threatened. In October 1835 settlers 'garrisoned' and raised the Spanish flag on Cay Sal in the Bahama Bank where there was agreement with Spain for a lighthouse and for sovereignty to remain 'as before'. Cockburn simply referred the matter for settlement to their respective governments in Europe.[101]

The United States—'My Friend Jonathan'—remained 'very quietly and friendly disposed *towards us*'. However Cockburn remained wary and quietly pleased that 'Jonathan' was:

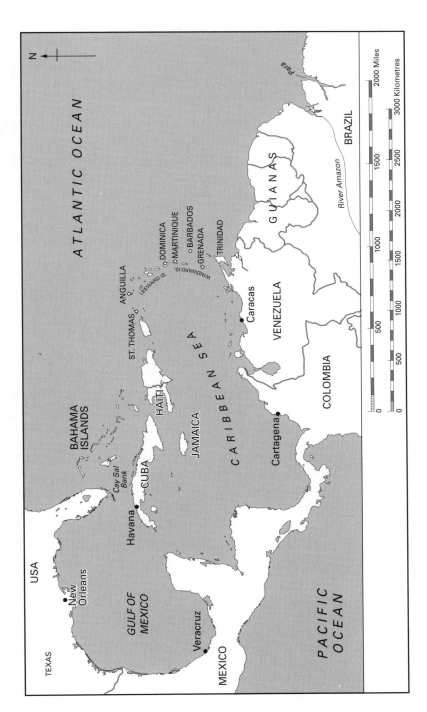

Map 11. The West Indies and South America

involved in some difficulty in his domestic policy in consequence of some late arrangements of the President regarding the currency which has occasioned many bankruptcies and much momentary inconvenience to their commerce. They are therefore open-mouthed against their hitherto favourite President—the devil relieve them.

His own shift into the *President* in 1834 was no coincidence. The name of the 52-gun ship and his own presence off the American coast were strong reminders to the United States of the war of 1812. Britain was deeply conscious of the growing power of their old enemy, and Cockburn was carrying toward completion the dock and ordnance yard on Ireland Island at Bermuda in order to strengthen British naval capability on the station. Yet his only disturbance from that quarter was the revolt in Texas early in 1836 which caused alarm among British merchants operating in the Gulf of Mexico.[102]

The principal problem was the continuing slave trade, conducted by the Spanish, Portuguese, French and Dutch. Cuba was the main destination but Cockburn had insufficient small cruisers to surround the island closely enough to prevent traders getting through. He obtained some intelligence of ships fitting in Europe, but was aggravated by reports of slavers receiving supplies from small cays and islands in the British Bahama group.[103] Agreements with European powers—Spain in 1835 and France in 1836—enlarged the geographical area and powers of search.[102] Yet these came at a time of apparent growth in the number of slavers and a comparable success rate in the 'havoc' achieved by British cruisers.[103]

This increase in activity coincided with the emancipation of slaves in British colonies. This was being debated in colonial assemblies at the time of Cockburn's arrival in the West Indies. The main concern was the premature promulgation of emancipation precipitating a general slave revolt which British troops would have difficulty putting down. A revolt also seemed likely if slaves were expected to work after emancipation as before. Cockburn was conscious that the collapse of the plantation economy would ruin West Indian trade and shipping. The announcement in July 1833 of compensation payments to the amount of 20 million pounds damped owner opposition, while the suppression of a minor slave revolt in Jamaica encouraged the military authorities. By November Cockburn was consequently predicting a smooth transfer to free labour.[106]

As the date for emancipation approached, British naval forces were concentrated off the coast of Jamaica to give support to her Governor, who addressed the slaves as to the 'apprenticeship' that would be required of them afterwards. Owners who attempted to resell slaves before emancipation were deterred by the detection and prosecution of one at Anguilla who shipped some girls to the Danish island of St Thomas—the culprit was discovered through undercover work performed by a purser whose expenses were refunded from secret service money. With these preparations, emancipation on 1 August passed peacefully, though some former owners remained 'fretful and obstinate' to the plans of the 'imperial government' and predicted their labour force would abscond as soon as their terms of apprenticeship had expired.[107]

Cockburn was in the northern half of his station at the time of emancipation. On the mainland in that area cholera was sweeping through the lower classes of larger towns—Halifax was losing 25 to 30 people a day. Local people were concerned that the navy should police a three-mile belt of territorial water around Labrador, Newfoundland and Nova Scotia against infringements by French and American fishermen. Americans were also suspected of small-scale smuggling into Nova Scotian ports. However, Cockburn believed infringements of treaties to be insufficient in scale to warrant an increased naval presence.[108] His response to these appeals reflected his conviction that the navy was not present to settle local affairs. British subjects and their commerce could call on its protection, but his force was a final resort in the enforcement of law, both British and international.

His enthusiasms were those which would benefit all seafarers. In 1833 he praised Captain Beaufort, the Hydrographer of the Navy, for his new edition of the *Nautical Almanac*—'now for the first time worthy of our leading maritime nation'. He speculated on the discoveries made possible by the expeditions of Captains Ross and Back, and enthused over the employment of naval vessels surveying 'those parts of the ocean not yet sufficiently well known' but still 'too extensive'.[109] Assistance was supplied to Royal Engineers erecting lighthouses in the Gulf of Florida, and the Governor of Barbados was encouraged to have one placed on rocks east of the island where two ships were wrecked in December 1834: 'to afford security against similar losses must very soon fully repay the cost of the required light houses'.[110]

Such work contributed to the increasing pace of change in maritime affairs. British technology and commerce were gradually altering the naval world. Cockburn's mails were brought to the West Indies by steam packet, and to Halifax by Messrs Cunard and Company. Though conscious of the wear and tear on steam engines, he claimed these arrangements worked 'extremely well'. It was this experience of a changing world that he carried back with him to England on being relieved in May 1836.

Leadership without Office

On his return from the North American station, Cockburn entered a political world significantly different from that which he had left behind in 1833. In 1835, in spite of his absence, he had again been invited to stand for Parliament at Plymouth, now the constituency of Devonport. The extension of the franchise there had strengthened the radical vote, making it unlikely that an absent Conservative candidate would succeed without a contest, and he had firmly declined the invitation. However, in 1837, following his return to England, he received an invitation to stand once more for Portsmouth, and this time accepted without hesitation the opportunity 'to fight the good cause'.[111]

At Portsmouth the Reform Bill had enlarged the electorate to more than 2,200. There was now a possibility of new voters overcoming the radicals and corporation interest, especially if Cockburn gained support from seamen, dockyard artificers and naval pensioners. And indeed, from the 'weather-beaten countenances' of many who drew his carriage to the hustings on 26 July, he did gain the support of many naval men—his opposition to the new poor law, introduced by the Whigs three years earlier, directly appealed to their vote. He maintained it was a cruel and tyrannical law that reduced poor rates, enlarged demands for charity, and sent people to a distance to be separated man from wife and shut up in a poorhouse. He was also opposed to the introduction of the secret ballot, preferring voters to exercise their right 'boldly and fearlessly'.

At Portsmouth, ironically, it was the open vote that militated against him. The Carters still dominated the corporation: 'no person was allowed to hold any situation under the corporation unless they promised to give their votes to Mr Carter and his friend, Mr Baring'. The secretaries of the Treasury and of the Admiralty also had some influence against him, the former through patronage in the Customs, the latter by ordering an Ordnance vessel to sea and through the muster of the warrant officers of the ships in Ordinary. Cockburn possessed 'not the slightest doubt that much active unfair influence was exerted by the government' but could not sufficiently substantiate any allegations to lay charges. The larger part of the dockyard vote nevertheless went to

Cockburn and against the Government. He recieved 519 votes, his Conservative ally Lord Fitzharris 439, but Carter and Baring each received over 630.[112]

Cockburn turned to professional matters. A commission for inquiring into naval and military promotion and retirement was appointed in May 1838, and he acted both as a commissioner and as a witness. Lord Minto at the Admiralty referred to him for his opinion on recommendations for the Navy's medical arrangements, and for changes in the office of purser.[113] A range of voluntary services involved him. He became president of the Shipwrecked Fishermen and Mariners' Royal Benevolent Society; chairman of the committee for the establishment of a United Services Benevolent Institution; vice-chairman of the committee for the erection of a column at the junction of Whitehall and the Strand as a 'memorial' to Nelson[114]; and he took up the cause of a school in Camberwell for the sons of naval officers, attempting to have the Admiralty accept their two best scholars as first-class naval volunteers.[115]

All these activities reflected Cockburn's persisting role as a leader in his profession. To Wellington, about the United Services Benevolent Institution, he lamented that other 'superior officers of the two services so unhandsomely' kept aloof from the project.[116] These projects were not just charitable pastimes. Some of his contemporaries—Henry Hotham for example—had already died. To men such as he, Cockburn felt debts of honour still unpaid; he thus took upon himself the moral duties of his generation.

Such activities had the advantage of maintaining contacts within his profession, with the Admiralty, and with public figures. At the same time, for friendship and family reasons, contacts within the Tory party resumed. Croker remained in intermittent correspondence, and Peel in regular touch, especially about his son who in 1838 entered a naval career. Cockburn provided guidance and encouragement on the course of his initial experience, and the relationship blossomed into family visits to Drayton, the Peel home.[117]

In August 1839 Cockburn reached his sixty-seventh year. Newspapers that December proposed him for the Mediterranean command, and he remained ready to assist the Conservative cause, especially as hopes of regaining office rose. In July 1841 he stood against two government candidates in the election at Greenwich. The Royal Hospital, Deptford dockyard and the adjacent Victualling yard granted the government extra influence. But, as one blue silk banner proclaimed, Cockburn stood

as 'the Friend of the Poor and an Enemy to the New Poor Law'; another
was inscribed 'Cockburn and Independence'. But he continued to oppose
the secret ballot, and now too the repeal of the Corn Laws, both
supported by radicals. Noise and violence in the crowd, pushing and
shoving on the platform, made the hustings an ordeal. Cockburn trailed
third in the poll with a little over one quarter of the vote.[118]

Yet his physical and mental robustness did not go unnoticed. In
September 1841 Peel requested he act once again as first naval lord at
the Admiralty, on a board led by the Earl of Haddington. Cockburn
readily agreed. At the end of that month, he was brought into
Parliament through the safe Conservative seat of Ripon which he was to
represent for the next five years.[119] At the age of 69 Cockburn
consequently resumed administrative and political duties at the
Admiralty where he was to remain until July 1846.

CHAPTER 7

The Early Victorian Navy in Transition 1841–1846

As first naval lord between 1841 and 1846, Cockburn concentrated on the technical problems of managing the navy. Management of these problems was initially made more difficult by the subjection of the Board of Admiralty to a Cabinet led by Peel, who was determined to reform the country's finances. In 1841 Peel was heir to a succession of Whig budget deficits. In consequence he prevented the naval estimates from rising significantly until after the defence scares of 1844. Only then, assisted by the introduction of income tax in 1842 and a balanced budget in 1843, did spending rise, funding investment in screw and iron ships, and in 1846 a retirement scheme for elderly captains.

These changes did not attract a great deal of public attention. On account of tight financial control, the naval estimates usually passed without the scrutiny that had characterized the last years of the Tory administration of 1828 to 1830. Since that time the Whigs had attempted to provide greater detail of budget allocations, although there were still grumbles of inadequate explanation.[1] Otherwise the Conservative Board of Admiralty was viewed from the Commons with confidence. This was due in some measure to a complaisance inspired by Lord Aberdeen, the Foreign Secretary,[2] and by Cockburn—who tended to generate a generally pacific view of the world, which even the 1844 invasion scare did not long unsettle. Cockburn's confidence in the navy's defensive capability diffused debate on questions about its effectiveness in checking the slave trade, and about the abolition of impressment and flogging. But his part in these debates waned as the years passed. From participation in nineteen debates in 1842, his contributions dropped to twelve in 1844 and seven in 1846. He remained as commanding, knowledgeable and persuasive as ever, but there was an increasing softness about his manner that denoted increasing age. Indeed, in 1843 he was advised not to attend the Commons on account of illness.

It was not just age and illness that reduced Cockburn's participation in debates in the Commons. The invasion scare and increases in expenditure on the navy after 1844 speeded the pace of naval change under the Conservative government. Cockburn was obliged to concentrate his dwindling energies on challenges at the Admiralty fuelled principally by technological innovation, affecting the recruitment of seamen as well as the construction, propulsion and equipment of ships. Moreover, management of these matters from the Admiralty was not facilitated by the changes wrought to the constitution of the naval departments in 1832. These changes not only made Cockburn's managerial task more difficult by increasing his workload, but enhanced his isolation at the Admiralty. To a large extent, he fought a lone battle for the navy he wished to create, a battle that inevitably affected the reputation he left behind on his retirement.

As his difficulties grew more challenging, so, of necessity, Cockburn took an increasingly detached view of the government's situation. He deplored the hostility of all but two of the public newspapers and their power in unsettling the Conservative party, within which there were strains over Ireland and Free Trade. But he remained confident until 1846 that moderation on these issues would hold the party together. Differences between the Whigs and radicals in 1844 seemed to reinforce that security, a position maintained by parliamentary majorities in 1845. But after January 1846 he could only lament 'Peel's uncalled for conversion to Cobden and free trade' with its consequent 'disruption of our hitherto powerful and influential Tory party'.[3]

For the division of the Conservative party in 1846 marked the end of an era for the British navy as well as for the mercantile view of the world. It brought a change in attitude, not just in economic ideas, but also to the role the British navy was expected to play in this new commercial theory. It implied changes too in the nature of that navy, for the new liberal thinking sat uneasily with institutions like impressment. However, these were changes which Cockburn foresaw and with which he was already grappling before 1846. They were changes for which, in several respects, he prepared the ground.

The Admiralty Reformed

The Admiralty to which Cockburn returned in 1841 was a department of government reduced from its pre-1830 standing. Reorganization had reduced the assurance of those who presided at the Board; its officials were not the public figures they had been, and the principles upon which the office operated were still under review. Having lost its subordinate boards, the naval departments no longer rated so highly as an area of patronage; time had also influenced the weight carried by the First Lord in the Cabinet. The persistence of peace for twenty-five years had reinforced the hold of both the Treasury and the Foreign Office, a grip which only the influence of the Prime Minister released.[4] In consequence the navy performed, more consciously than had ever previously been the case, a subordinate service role: the Admiralty simply 'did the best they could with the funds allowed them in order to carry out the views of the Cabinet'.[5]

More evident was the change in its relations with the navy's civil departments. The abolition of the Navy and Victualling Boards in 1832 had left this civil business dependent on the management of five 'principal officers' at Somerset House, each responsible to a super-intending Admiralty commissioner: for the dockyards and shipbuilding, for naval stores, for victualling and transports, for medical provisions, and for finance. Partly in compensation for the removal of the expertise that had existed among subordinate board officials, the number of Admiralty commissioners had been increased from five to six, among whom the number of Admiralty lords experienced at sea was increased from two to four. In 1841 Cockburn became the senior of these four naval lords.

Individual responsibility was the guiding principle of this arrangement. Yet clear vertical lines of accountability reduced horizontal communication between otherwise heavily loaded Admiralty commissioners, encouraging individual commissioners to conduct their branches without reference to board colleagues. It demanded that subordinate principal officers undertake much of their branch business, though not formally vested with responsibility for it, and matters were not always co-ordinated fully with related operations in separate branches. Cockburn found the system pernicious. On leaving the Admiralty in 1846 he set his opinions on Admiralty administration to paper. The principles of the system he considered 'to be the most unsatisfactory and least efficient for its purpose, that could have been devised':

> In the first place, it is most inconsistent and inconvenient that one member of the Board should without any communication with his colleagues, issue orders at Somerset House, in the name of the Board, for

the governance of the whole fleet, dockyards, &c., provided it relates to the branch of the Admiralty business he is selected to superintend, such orders being issued in the name and under the authority of the Board, without any other member thereof being aware of such order, and often only learning its promulgation from the newspapers, or from questions asked about it in Parliament.

He objected to the Board remaining 'wholly ignorant' of such general orders or the grounds for them, unless the commissioner responsible for them mentioned the matter to his colleagues. But this, in the latter part of the administration, was 'very rarely done', especially by one of his colleagues. As a result, 'the business could not but be carried forward in an unconnected and disjointed manner, the fault being with a system admitting of, and indeed leading to, such evil result'.[6]

In 1837 the former Comptroller of the Navy Board, Sir Thomas Byam Martin, had objected to the arrangment which, he claimed, would 'entirely break down' during war. He proposed the formation of a single subordinate board, incorporating the 'principal officers' and headed by a comptroller who would be a member of the Board of Admiralty.[7] In 1841 this proposal was considered by Peel and Haddington but was rejected as too expensive in salaries, and politically impractical in that a non-political and permanent comptroller would have been a member of a political and non-permanent Board of Admiralty.[8]

At this decision neither Cockburn nor Haddington, the First Lord of the Admiralty, were perturbed.[9] They were perhaps reassured by the experience of the resident principal officers, all five of whom had held their posts since the earlier reorganization. But within six months Haddington was claiming to Lord Melville that the burden was 'far more laborious' than in the latter's time, not only due to the changes wrought under Graham but from 'having 13,000 seamen and marines and a war or two on our hands, to say nothing of the pressure on a Tory Government after eleven years of Whig rule. Except at the time of reducing the fleet in 1814–15 you can have had no pressure upon you at all equal to what has weighed upon me ever since I have been here'.[10]

Cockburn was equally burdened. On leaving office, Lord Minto, the previous First Lord, had pointed out the onerous duties that attached to the post of first naval lord.[11] Moreover, the responsibilities of that post were growing. Between 1835 and 1845 the number of sailing vessels in commission rose only from 155 to 159; but the number of steam vessels increased from 12 to 75. And Admiralty business increased in proportion. The number of officers' appointments issued from the

Admiralty increased by almost 1,000, from 1,736 to 2,701; the number of letters received at the Admiralty grew from 25,973 to 39,275; and the complement of the home dockyards rose from 7,884 men to 12,194.[12] With only a small increase in the size of the Board, much of this growth in business pressed upon the first naval lord.

In addition, Haddington's ignorance of naval matters had continually to be accommodated. This very ignorance encouraged the First Lord to concentrate on his political role within the Cabinet. But, as a result, he left almost all naval matters to Cockburn, who nonetheless had to keep him informed.[13] Cockburn later pointed out that nothing could be more contrary to reason and common sense

> than for a person to be selected to preside at such professional Board, who is totally unable and admits his inability to understand three-fourths of the professional statements or even expressions contained in the various documents read on such occasions to the Board, and which, therefore, the professional members of the Board become obliged to occupy time in explaining and endeavouring to make him comprehend, which, nevertheless, cannot be always sufficiently effected.[14]

Even so, Cockburn patiently supported Haddington. Before taking office the latter had been alarmed at the prospect of working with Cockburn. But in March 1842, after six months' experience, he admitted that his first naval lord was 'invaluable'. It was 'perfectly impossible for two men . . . to go on better than we do'. He had seldom known a man he liked better. Cockburn's frankness assisted him, his confidence reassured him, and his bluntness and occasional 'buntades' he cared 'not a chaw about'.[15]

For Haddington there was a price to be paid for this dependence. In the Commons, if only in flattery, Cockburn was addressed as the head of the Admiralty by both officer and civilian alike. Mistaken though this was in a strict sense, in matters of naval management it was close to the truth.[16] At the Admiralty he had oversight of all naval arrangements. Specific responsibilities included the dockyards, the selection of vessels for particular duties or stations, the recommendation of appointments to the First Lord, and preparation of the estimates.[17] Matters in which he had a dominant influence included policy on manning, experimentation and design in shipbuilding. Deliberation upon such matters demanded not only political judgement and technical knowledge, but readiness of communication with the First Lord of the Treasury and the Foreign Secretary who he advised on matters of naval strength and deployment.

In response, Peel used Cockburn to achieve his objectives at the Admiralty as freely as he used Haddington.[18] On matters of naval defence this was natural. Thus in April 1845 Peel informed Cockburn that he had written to Haddington about the policy of taking unostentatious precautionary measures for strengthening the fleet in consequence of 'the inaugural speech of the President of the United States' and the discussion on that and the Oregon Question in the Commons and Lords; but that he trusted Cockburn would 'suggest to the Board whatever can be done without exciting suspicion and what reasonable caution may justify'.[19]

Accompanying these concerns were the distractions of routine Admiralty life. Initially he was 'always easy of access' to anyone who went to him on public business, and by reputation ready to give 'free attention to any representation'.[20] But parliamentary business was time consuming. Naval matters seemed regularly to run into the night, anything up to two or more in the morning; in consequence, office duties sometimes ran into the evenings at weekends.[21] Much Admiralty business was conducted by minutes drafted by commissioners and circulated to whomever necessary. Often they were the basis for appointments and instructions issued by the Secretary; or they provided advice for others within the Admiralty or at the Treasury or Foreign Office. As the senior commissioner, such minutes invariably originated with or received annotation from Cockburn.[22]

The principal means of executing business was through the meetings of the Board. Until 1846 these were held on alternate days and were attended by as many of the commissioners as were available and by the First or Second secretary. Here, in debate, Cockburn encountered his greatest frustrations. Consistent with practice, as the most experienced professional officer, the first naval lord generally proposed how a letter should be answered, others either agreeing or differing as they saw fit.[23] Yet Cockburn frequently encountered such opposition that he found the Board more of an impediment than an aid to business.[24]

> . . . the Board, consisting of six persons, and the professional members, or a portion of them, being selected with reference to political considerations and their having seats in Parliament, and without regard to their knowledge of each other or how far they might be likely to act cordially together, much valuable time becomes consumed in fruitless and sometimes irritable and unsatisfactory discussions, interfering greatly with the necesary advancement of the numerous professional and other matters almost daily brought for decision before the Admiralty; and the

evil of such check to business may be well conceived when it is considered that matters of almost every possible description, from the building of ships of war and ordering the movements and discipline of our fleets, down to the deciding on the details and eligibility of railroads, are now brought either for decision or opinion, before the Board of Admiralty.[25]

It has been suggested that Cockburn managed these difficulties by ruthlessly dominating the Board.[26] Certainly his experience, ability and personality permitted him to manage these difficulties. But he had too much respect for the niceties of constitutional practice to be deliberately domineering. His conclusion to a long minute on the service of naval officers in the coastguard aptly reflected his attitude: 'Having thus freely stated my impressions on the whole subject, whatever Lord Haddington and the majority of my colleagues deem to be the best course to be adopted under the existing circumstances . . ., I shall not hesitate to accede to, feeling that the points I have submitted will have received due and impartial consideration and that the decision of the majority is the most likely to prove right on the whole.'[27] And he did concede points, concessions later depicted with a malicious pleasure by J.H. Briggs: 'He [Cockburn] argued . . . with an ability it was difficult to gainsay. Still he found it at times almost impossible to resist the strong representations made to him by Mr Herbert [first or 'political' secretary] and Mr Corry [civil commissioner]. It was very amusing to see one on one side and one on the other rather persuading and coaxing rather than arguing the question. Yet you could perceive he was gradually giving way and conceding the point against his will and professional judgement.'[28] According to Briggs, Corry and Herbert, who were both members of Parliament, supported the 'movement party'. It was therefore perhaps these two civilians, with their limited professional knowledge, whom Cockburn found irritating to deal with.

Inevitably the management of the navy appeared to suffer. With the 'want of concert' at the Board, Cockburn

experienced frequent annoying checks and obstructions in carrying forward those objects which appeared to me essentially required and called for, and some of which I was obliged to abandon from the opposition of one or other of such disjointed ruling body, and such opposition, in some instances, springing from parties having no real knowledge on the professional matters under consideration, but objecting to them in consequence of something that may have been said to them by some irresponsible person out of doors.[29]

Undoubtedly his deepest distresss arose from the opposition of two professional colleagues, Sir George Seymour and Captain William Gordon.[30] Supported by Haddington's private Secretary, Captain Baillie Hamilton, and by the civilians Corry and Herbert, these two officers had the odds on their side.[31] Cockburn was supported by Vice-Admiral Sir William Gage, but Board meetings were evidently an ordeal. 'Unworthy jealousies', annoyances and debates kept him 'in a continual state of anxiety and difficulty' and required from him 'the strongest exertion of forbearance' to enable him 'to remain in a situation so truly unsatisfactory' to his view of efficient management.[32]

A fleeting glimpse of the conflicting attitudes of the Admiralty commissioners was obtained in November 1845 by Edward Pearn, the master of the transport *Atholl*. He was given an order to embark more passengers than he could accommodate and was ordered to appear at the Admiralty with the plans of his cabins and with one of the master shipwrights. The difference in the way he was received by the two commissioners was striking. 'Went to the Admiralty yesterday', he recorded, 'and saw Sir George Cockburn and Captain Gordon; that latter appeared not at all inclined to make any alterations. But Sir George was very condescending and after putting a few questions to me ask'd me what I would propose to be done. I told him what I thought would be best and he order'd it to be done immediately'.[33]

It would be wrong to attribute all the administrative difficulties encountered at the Admiralty to the system of individual responsibility and the political incompatibility of the commissioners. Cockburn himself was not an easy colleague. He could assume, as Briggs recalled from their first meeting, 'a very imperious and very overbearing' tone.[34] Sir George Seymour, his principal opponent for two and a half years, was thus answered soon after he joined the Admiralty—having objected to changes in captain's pay structure: 'Sir George will learn 'ere he has been much longer at the Board that however specious in theory that suggestion may be . . .'.[35] Experienced, knowledgeable, precise and determined, Cockburn's expertise and authority were difficult to counter, especially from a junior situation. Capping Cockburn's competence was a lucidity on administrative matters that defied contradiction. His rough minutes were model memoranda, full, expository, logical and easy to read.[36] They bespoke a command of Admiralty administration that, while helpful to Haddington, was no doubt stifling to Seymour. For him, there was probably little alternative but to challenge the opinion of the senior lord in a manner likely to verge on, and provoke, hostility. Perhaps inevitably, he was replaced at the Board in May 1844.

Political Logistics

Between 1841 and 1846 the defensive capabilities of the British fleet became again a critical political issue. Over the previous quarter-century the fleet had been run down, but had maintained its reputation for strength mainly on account of the weakness of its rivals, its presence in most oceans, and the readiness of the British government to use its influence wherever necessary and possible. During this time, the navy's capability of defending the British Isles from invasion had not been seriously questioned. However, after 1841 the threat from France, the danger of her being joined by the United States, the weakness of the British fleet in the Channel, and its deficiencies in steamers, all called into question the adequacy of fleet management. While Peel and Haddington assisted in allaying fears, the task of ensuring the fleet was up to strength and of keeping his political masters informed, fell principally to Cockburn. His confidence provided reassurance indispensable to the steadiness of ministers.[37]

For in the Cabinet, despite the calm front maintained in public, confidence in the British navy was at a low ebb. Relations with France were uncertain. The Near East crisis of 1840, involving a confrontation between French and British Mediterranean forces, brought Britain closer to Russia whose extra ships assumed diplomatic importance.[38] Both France and Britain were strained to the limits of their peacetime finance to oppose one another, and there was no guarantee the situation would remain stable. Indeed another crisis in Anglo-French relations recurred four years later. In Britain it was fuelled by the publication in France in May 1844 of a pamphlet written by the Prince de Joinville to enhance French naval ambitions; and by the Tahiti incident of 1844, when the French imprisoned the British consul, a missionary, whose subsequent return home gave rise to a great demonstration in London. Coinciding as it did with the bombardment of Tangier by the French fleet, in London war was 'generally regarded as inevitable'.[39]

The possibility of a real rupture with France was complicated by an equal threat from across the Atlantic. Economic growth and nationalism in the United States enhanced her readiness to dispute her Canadian borders with Britain. Hostilities were averted in 1841 by the promise of definition of the Maine frontier in August 1842. But in 1845 a dispute over the Oregon boundary gave rise to a naval race on the Great Lakes until this line too was settled in June 1846. On both occasions the Cabinet responded by requiring increases in the naval forces in, or ready for, North American waters.[40] Even then, early in 1846 the Admiralty was conscious that the United States were stronger in the Gulf of Mexico and, should American differences with Mexico be settled, could easily turn upon Britain's Caribbean possessions.[41]

As these animosities grew and subsided, it was Cockburn's responsibility to ensure sufficient vessels of the necessary type were stationed in appropriate waters. The business of distribution was less simple than it appeared. Numbers of vessels were limited; increases on some stations could only be made at a cost to others. Between 1835 and 1845 it was possible to increase the number of ships on the East Indies and China station, on patrol against slave traders off the coasts of Africa and South America, and at home to face France, only by reducing the number in the Mediterranean and Pacific, at the Cape of Good Hope, and on the North American and West Indies stations.[42] On these stations the functions performed by some vessels were not all essential. The number surveying for example—26 in 1845—was subject to the availability of vessels. But the costs associated with the Treaty of Nanking terminating the first China War of 1842 were unavoidable. The treaty provided for the stationing of one British warship at each of the five treaty ports, and necessitated the establishment of Hong Kong as a naval base for the China Seas.[43] This further stimulated exploration: equipping the Franklin expedition to the Arctic in 1845, for instance, although this was a minor cost that might have been repaid many times over by trade to the Pacific through a shorter route than that by the Capes.[44]

The number of ships commissioned was still funded in terms of numbers of seamen and marines to be maintained throughout the financial year. By 1841, apart from reductions under the Whigs, total numbers voted in the House of Commons had been rising steadily since 1816. In 1832 they amounted to 27,000; by 1841 they were 43,000. Numbers of men actually borne—rising from 27,328 to 41,389— indicate a growth in the size of the navy in commission of almost fifty per cent.

Between 1841 and 1844 the strain of an increased volume of work was enhanced by pressure to perform the same range of tasks on reduced resources. For, in keeping with Peel's aim to reduce expenditure, the number of seamen voted was reduced by 21 per cent between 1842 and 1844, with a resulting fall in commissioned ships from 257 to 225. This decline was limited by the relative increase in the number of smaller vessels employed in place of ships of the line. By 1844 there were only eleven vessels of this large size in commission.

That year, as the crisis with France developed, politicians were horrified to learn there were only four ships of the line immediately available for defence in home waters.[45] Public fears of an invasion increased when Palmerston claimed in Parliament that steam power permitted a 'steam bridge' to be constructed across the Channel capable of landing 30,000 troops overnight. Concern concentrated on the readiness of a steam force able to intercept such an invasion. Partly in consequence, between 1844 and 1846 most marked growth occurred in the number of steamships in commission, the number rising from 59 to 71; moreover, contracts were made to increase that force further to 86 active steamers by 1847.[46]

Each decision to commission or build a ship of the line, a steamship or a smaller vessel was taken individually. Defence had to be weighed against surveying, the needs of home stations against foreign. In the final analysis, decisions were matters of opinion and contentious. Sir George Seymour submitted his contrary opinions in writing to Haddington.[47] But in this critical area Cockburn had the dominant influence and his opinion prevailed most of the time. In consequence, he also had a vital influence on the development of the navy. For in the changing emphasis from sail to steam, those vessels the navy lacked it had to build or purchase. Planning and decision-making in this area were determined by the composition of foreign navies, the patterns of obsolescence in the British navy, the demands of new duties and stations, the availability of labour and facilities in dockyards, and the expertise of its contractors. The opinion of the Surveyor was considered, but the orders were authorized by Cockburn.

Improving the Sailing Ship

Cockburn was depicted by J.H. Briggs as the archetypal reactionary.[48] Inevitably such comment deeply influenced historians of the early Victorian navy. Until recently the whole Admiralty establishment was considered conservative in almost all matters connected with technological innovation.[49] That this was not so is evident from the attempts to improve sailing-ship design, and to introduce the latest technology into the navy's steamships. Progress was inevitably hesitant and halting for, although the pace of technological innovation was increasing, many so-called 'improvements' were not proved reliable. Meanwhile, it was natural and necessary to adhere to what was known to be effective.

Before 1846 the largest sailing battleships were still the main fighting units of the British fleet. Cockburn always believed 'a certain strength of line of battle ships fit for service of paramount importance'. He considered them 'far more powerful in fact as well as in the effect on the minds of foreigners, than razées [cut down ships of the line] or other frigates'.[50] Befitting this continuing importance, interest in Parliament as well as at the Admiralty continued to focus on the ability of naval architects to produce efficient sailing vessels.

In spite of the advances scientific theory had achieved in other areas, naval architects were still struggling to design ships according to principles that would predetermine their sailing qualities. Although designs were subjected to a series of carefully staged trials, observation, calculation and theory had still not reached the stage at which hull shape, displacement and stability could be calculated in advance of actual construction, and the nascent science of hydrodynamics taken into account. It was understood to be a remarkably complex field. Combinations of sea and wind provided an infinite variety of conditions, baffling attempts to separate and correlate differences in design and performance. There was, in any case, 'a want of sytematic arrangement in the elements of construction, as well as of a proper register of the results'.[51]

Ship trials were tantamount to 'sailing matches' from which superior vessels were selected as models for their class.[52] During the 1820s the deductions that could be drawn from these trials remained confused from the lack of systematic planning of observations, from unplanned alterations in rig and trim, and from the spirit of rivalry that divided the designers, Seppings, Hayes and Symonds.[53] The speed of the latter's vessels under favourable conditions and his appointment as Surveyor by the Whigs in 1832 earned his vessels regular praise from their commanders. Yet in trials during the 1830s ships designed both by Hayes and by Seppings outsailed those of Symonds, but without conclusively proving that his were inferior under all conditions.[54] By 1841 no designer or design had been shown to be superior to any other. Admiralty shipbuilding policy was still based upon individual ships judged by 'sailing races'. Sir William Symonds remained in office as Surveyor but—as suggested by Cockburn's criticisms of *Vernon* in 1833—did not have the confidence of the first naval lord.[55]

Cockburn's response to these problems of design emerged in the House of Commons in 1844 when the Admiralty came under attack for its apparent failure to find a practical solution.[56] To his mind, the objective was to 'get an exact principle, and have nothing further to do than determine size'. Yet there seemed so many ideas and no impartial means of judging them. Captain Hayes 'had a plan, but no system; his plan was to take certain distances from the midship section'. Lord Dundonald 'had stated that a perfect parabolic curve was the curve of least resistance, and consequently would prove the best for passing through the water'. Meanwhile, 'the Admiralty were every day—almost every hour—listening to proposals for improvements, and examining as to how these improvements could be carried out'. It was not always practicable to refer these to the Surveyor, Symonds, to whom the Admiralty acknowledged a debt for improvements that he had made in the past. At the same time, Cockburn 'was free to say that he did not think his ships were perfect and he knew that when persons took up a system, they sometimes became too exclusively attached to it; so it was felt right that some check should be kept on that valuable officer'.[57]

That 'check', instituted in 1841, soon after Haddington's Board came into office, was a committee of dockyard Master Shipwrights sitting at Woolwich. In March 1842 Cockburn

> hoped the result of their deliberations would be to obtain the best possible mode of building ships, and also how to place as many guns as could be fought consistently with strength, not forgetting the more important points of sailing against head seas and off lee shores.

Significantly, Symonds' vessels were known neither for their capabilities against headwinds, nor for their stability as gun platforms.[58] The recommendations of the Woolwich committee were nevertheless referred to Symonds and most were adopted, though 'modified to a certain extent by the Surveyor's observations'.

The Board of Admiralty next selected three of the most able graduates of the former School of Naval Architecture (abolished by the Whigs in 1832) 'to meet as a committee to examine scientifically the errors of construction of our former system of building'. The committee was also commissioned to 'submit to the Admiralty the lines they would propose for a ship of each class as the most perfect according to the principles their science should dictate'.[59] This committee's immediate product was the *Espiegle* brig, which in the autumn of 1844 was put on trial with seven other experimental brigs. These included the *Flying Fish*, designed by Symonds, and the *Daring*, built by Mr White of Cowes, a private shipbuilder. Unfortunately White's *Daring* 'had decided advantage of the whole on a wind', while *Flying Fish* beat the *Espiegle*.[60] For theoreticians the result was a disappointment. Cockburn showed no surprise, but did authorize further trials. He noted to Croker in February 1845: 'The Surveyor and the Schoolmen not being pleased at having been beat by the Mr White, a mere practical shipbuilder without science, requested certain alterations to be made' to see if their vessels could be brought 'more on a par with *Daring*'.[61] The reruns occurred in March 1845 but, the brigs, to the students' dismay, failed to produce the expected performances, even over a series of eleven trials. So dubious were the results that no inferences could be confidently drawn from them.[62] Indeed they seemed simply to confirm Croker's opinion of the value of such races.

> I am quite aware of the results (as they are called) of the late trial of the brigs, having read what the papers have given of the reports;—but if I had not read a word, I should have been nearly as well informed, for the reports are just of the same vague and unsatisfactory kind that every report that I ever remember now near 40 years has been. One is better on a wind, another better, pie:—one stows better but slow; another fast but cannot stow, one beats everything, but she also beats herself by carrying away her own masts and spars and so ad infinitum, and the result is a kind of algebraic equation of various qualities really incommensurable and coming to no absolute and intelligible standard of merit.[63]

There were other trials of brigs and battleships in 1844 and, 'more important', a 'grand trial of the line of battle ships of each class' in 1845.[64] However, the details of these last experiments produced 'scarcely any occasion to draw an inference' even under the scrutiny of systematic 'theoretical' shipbuilders. In March 1845, under pressure in the House of Commons, Cockburn had to admit the difficulty of finding 'any exact principle which could be said to be really best'.[65] It was an admission he took seriously. By November 1845 he had become convinced that scientific principles would not emerge of their own accord.

> The Board [of Admiralty] has done much towards improving both the sailing and the steam ships by encouraging competition amongst the practical constructors of the day instead of confining the whole to one individual, but this does not afford much promise of bringing us to any fixed unerring principle of construction, and I consider the extraordinary

results of the late experimental cruises strongly call upon us to take measures for placing the matter on a more satisfactory footing, . . . I take the view of it expressed by Lord John Russell in the House of Commons when Sir Charles Napier, Captains Rous and Harris and others wanted to have the matter transferred to a committee of the House. His Lordship on that occasion said he would not consent to take the power and responsibility out of the hands of the Admiralty, but he threw out for our consideration the propriety of establishing some scientific Board of Construction under the Admiralty to aid and advise the Admiralty on a topic of so much importance and cost to this country—this certainly does appear to me to be the wisest, most moderate and best course to pursue.

It is in my opinion quite clear that, with the rapid advance science is making in every other branch of profession, the naval service ought to have the full benefit of this spirit, and that naval construction ought to be formed on more fixed and certain principles. I therefore submit for consideration the propriety of establishing a supervising Board of Construction to which the Admiralty may refer for detailed explanations in favour of or against the lines or draughts of all ships or steam vessels hereafter built. . . .[66]

Haddington supported the idea: its advantage was 'too obvious to admit of hesitation'. So did Peel, who had 'made a proposal very nearly consonant' in the Cabinet a year before. So too did Ellenborough, Haddington's successor as First Lord. The 'Committee of Reference' was formed in 1846, under the chairmanship of Captain Lord John Hay, to examine all designs including those of the Surveyor.[67] The committee included two shipwright officers and Dr Inman, the late Professor of Mathematics at the Royal Naval College. Symonds was to resign in 1847.

Far from being obstructive to the improvement of naval architecture, Cockburn was thus clearly instrumental in forwarding its progress. There were also other less visible products of his tenure as First Sea Lord. After many years' criticism, steps were taken to replace 10-gun 'coffin' brigs.[68] In 1844 schools for the instruction of shipwright apprentices were established in the dockyards, succeeding (though not replacing) the Portsmouth School of Naval Architecture which had been closed in 1832; from these schools the most able were to be selected for further training as yard officers.[69] Under Cockburn the most able of the existing officer corps were already being appointed to principal yard posts. John Fincham became Master Shipwright at Portsmouth dockyard in 1844; and as he indicated in his *History of Naval Architecture*, the sailing trials of 1844 and 1845 were not devoid of instruction. Observations of the sailing qualities of the brigs of 1844 were recorded in accordance with a range of detailed questions first proposed by Fincham in 1832. These carried the analysis of sailing qualities to the highest level yet attained. Partly from these trials he was to realize the value of testing vessels in pairs, one of them always to remain the 'control' while the other was altered as necessary to improve her performance.[70]

At this time the financing of the navy did not allow the retention of vessels purely for experimental purposes. Even the three brigs at the centre of attention in 1844 were sent off to Sir Thomas Cochrane in the Pacific after their second series of cruises together: the costs entailed to the number of men voted in the annual estimates would not permit the Admiralty to keep them 'at home for such trials longer than necessary'. In such circumstances, Cockburn could and did claim with justice, in June 1846, that the Admiralty had done everything possible 'to obtain every scientific information on the subject of the design of vessels.[71]

Steam and Defence

By 1840 there were about 800 steamers in the United Kingdom, over 70 being built each year. While nearly 500 were only river steamers or coasters, 282 were sea-going vessels. In 1838 the *Great Western* crossed the Atlantic in 15 days, the *Sirius* in 19. After a passage of 3,500 miles with over 300 passengers and crew, the *Great Western* still had fuel enough for another 1,500 miles. This event, and subsequent voyages, proved that large steamships could traverse oceans and, when necessary, were capable of carrying large numbers of troops.[72]

In the navy, as in merchant shipping, the years following these ocean voyages saw a great growth in the number of steamers. Hitherto there had been relatively few: in 1830 only three; by 1835 twenty; and in 1838 still only 21, their numbers growing markedly to 28 in 1839, 40 in 1840 and 48 in 1841. Partly to maintain parity with the French, under Cockburn the growth continued to 54 in 1843, to 62 in 1845 and 71 in 1846.[73] Cockburn thus presided over a remarkable expansion in the use of steamships: a growth in numbers of 48 per cent, with a corresponding expansion in steam factories—at Woolwich, Portsmouth and Plymouth—to service the new fleet.[74]

The period was one of education. Cockburn had become involved in the development of steamships before 1830 when he had been thrilled at the power they possessed over adverse seas. The ships built and purchased for the navy between 1841 and 1846 drew upon lessons learned from their construction and performance over the previous two decades. As Cockburn pointed out in 1845: 'it was not to be supposed that former Boards of Admiralty should at once have learned by inspiration to make perfect steamers: but, unless they had built the boats they had built, the present Board would not have known how to improve the building as they would not have had the opportunity of finding out the defects of previous constructions'.[75] Chief among those at the Board who approved changes after 1841, Cockburn, in his turn, took decisions that were to determine conclusions later in the decade and to shape the building of vessels in the 1850s.

Needless to say, contemporary understanding of the technological variables was, to the modern mind, simplistic; in this respect Cockburn conformed to the thinking of his age. The aspect of construction with which he first experimented was that of size. Before 1841 the average tonnage (builders' measure) of steamers in the navy was 458, their mean engine horsepower only 92, giving a power to weight ratio of almost 1:5. Even the largest steamers built were on the whole less than 1,000 tons. Among them the steam sloop *Gorgon* of 1837 and steam frigate *Cyclops* of 1839 stood out as exceptions at 1,111 and 1,195 tons respectively, each with 320 horsepower, and consequent power to weight ratios of 1:3.5 and 1:3.7.[76] 'One of the first things that struck me on my return to office', Cockburn wrote to Peel in September 1842, 'was the want of power and efficiency of the steam ships of the navy, to remedy which evil the Surveyor of the Navy has been ordered to build a steam ship of war of much larger dimensions than any hitherto constructed in our dockyards, and engines have already been ordered to be prepared for her of double the power of any we have hitherto used'. Launched in 1843, this vessel was to become the *Retribution* of 1,641 tons and 800 horsepower. She was designed by Symonds' chief clerk and assistant, John Edye, with whom Cockburn had a good working relationship.[77]

As with *Retribution*, so with other vessels. In 1843 the *Penelope*, a 46-gun frigate, was lengthened by 65 feet amidships and given engines of 650 horsepower. The experiment was a disappointment, increasing her weight too far in relation to her displacement, and lowering her too much in the water. However, in 1845 the 1,850-ton steam frigate *Terrible* was completed, having even more powerful engines of 800 horsepower. With this tendency to build bigger, and with more orders for steamships being placed, the average tonnage in the navy between 1841 and 1845 rose over 100 tons to 620, while the mean horsepower more than doubled to 207. Particularly on account of this increase in engine size, across the complement of steamships the power to weight ratio of the navy declined dramatically from almost 1:5 to 1:3, where it was to remain for the remainder of the decade.[78]

Because paddle-steamers like *Gorgon* could be armed only with a small broadside (*Gorgon* carried two 32-pounders a side) while their bow and stern guns were of long range and could be equally well carried by smaller vessels, some, like the shipwright officer John Fincham, later questioned the value of building larger steamships. With similar power to weight ratios, moreover, smaller vessels may well have been able to move as quickly as larger ones. But other factors affecting speed— engine weight, location and efficiency, as well as hull form—were also under trial, and at the time the only sure way of realizing the actual effect of varying any aspect of design was to try it in actual construction.[79]

An initial check on experimentation in design was the prerogative of Symonds, the Surveyor, to approve the drafts of ships to be built. Cockburn consciously worked to circumvent that influence. In August 1842, for example, he wrote encouragingly to his political opponent in the House of Commons, Sir Charles Napier:

> If you and Blake [Master Shipwright at Portsmouth, 1826–30] will lay your heads together to make a draft for a steam vessel of war of the description mentioned in your letter to me of the other day I shall be much inclined to give my vote for your being allowed to construct her, if when we take the plan into consideration there does not appear to be any reason to the contrary. You will of course state the nature of the armament you propose to carry when you send in the draft.[80]

Others too were encouraged to submit drafts, and in 1844 the Earl of Dundonald had one accepted for a steamer of 763 tons and 200 horsepower. From 1845 the number of vessels built to Symonds' plans was radically reduced. That year only two iron gun-vessels to his design were launched from a private yard at Blackwall, while the number being built from the designs of others markedly increased. These too were of iron, a material being increasingly used instead of timber. Three iron steamers of over 300 tons were built by contractors. At the same time Sir Charles Napier launched the paddle-steamer *Sidon*; built to Admiralty specifications she had to carry a broadside armament, to roll less than usual, so as to be capable of using her guns, and all at a reduced draught of water. The opportunities obtained by these designers encouraged others to put forward drafts. From 1846 all such proposals were submitted to the newly formed 'Committee of Reference'. These included the drafts prepared by the Surveyor.[81]

These measures provided both a variety of designs and the organization by which they could be assessed.[82] In the light of these developments, Cockburn's claim in the House of Commons in March 1844 that 'Government were trying everything they possibly could' to improve steamships rings true. So also does his declaration that 'they saw of what great importance they must soon become and they were endeavouring to find out the best description for sea service'.[83]

Yet, at least until 1846, their design and equipment was very hit and miss. Many criticisms of the vessels built could not be denied. Their draught seems to have been specially unpredictable, preventing them carrying the armament or the number of troops expected. Sir Charles Napier was particularly virulent in his attacks on Admiralty construction, denying for example in May 1845 'that any material improvements had been made . . . since the *Gorgon* and *Cyclops* were built ten years ago'. His claims that the steam navy was 'unfit for war purposes' was deeply challenging, especially with the deterioration in relations with the French and a tendency for most politicians to believe that steam could create a bridge across the Channel. It could only be acknowledged that the steam navy was still in its infancy, that naval commanders had been learning how best to employ their steamers under war conditions for little more than a decade, and that they had as yet no real experience of the value of the new larger vessels.[84]

To Cockburn's mind in 1845, steam was still subsidiary to sail as the main defensive force of the country. However, he believed that Britain could, and would if necessary, turn out a larger steam force than France or any other power. Public confidence in Britain's overwhelming number of merchant steamers assisted him, for it was assumed that a proportion of the largest vessels would be armed and employed with the navy.[85] Proposals for combined manoeuvres of steam fleets from both the navy and the merchant marine were considered seriously. In the United States and France, in the spring of 1845, manoeuvring squadrons of steam-frigates were formed for the first time.[86] They had their problems, not least the physical concentration of the force and the temporary abandonment of regular commitments.[87] Yet, even without manoeuvres, Cockburn was confident that a French invasion force stood little chance of success. As he explained to Haddington in June 1845, on Sir Charles Napier expressing alarm:

> From the period when the first large seagoing steam vessel was successfully completed, it became evident to everybody that a facility, never before existing, must be afforded thereby for sudden invasion of this country from the opposite shores of France, and, although of course fortified and secure harbours on our coast must prove useful to a certain extent in the event of attempts of such description, yet as it is quite clear that the whole line of coast from Dover to the Lizard cannot be so secured, and it is equally clear that an enemy intending a hostile landing would and could by means of steam select a spot for landing where no important fortifications existed, it will be wise of us to take for granted that it will be in his power to effect such a landing by watching favourable opportunities, if he make up his mind to risk the issue. Such issue, however, will be great if we manage to keep a reasonable force of regular troops and militia in the neighbourhood of the exposed coasts, and also maintain, as I trust we shall, the naval command in the Channel.

Cockburn relied for this naval command of the Channel upon a greater force of ships of the line, of which sufficient were 'in an advanced state for commissioning' and could be at sea as quickly as they received men.

He reasoned that the French at that time had only three vessels over 450 horsepower built or building, while Britain could anticipate possession of 17 between 500 and 800 horsepower by the end of the following year. Also, French steamers of 450 horsepower, resulting from the 1840 ocean-going packet programme, were underpowered.[88]

> Considering their large size and draft of water . . ., it will afford to our ships so much greater power in proportion to their size, a most important superiority, by placing it in the power of ours to choose their position for attack, to close or to retreat as may be most desirable under the circumstances in which they discover the enemy's vessels.

Superior steamers in greater numbers, supported by a larger fleet of ships of the line, would destroy a French invasion force should they not immediately withdraw, leaving any French soldiers that had been landed unsupported and in a disadvantageous position. Having himself discussed Napoleon's invasion plans with the French Emperor, Cockburn was able to argue that his plan had been to avoid all serious fighting until he reached London, and was very far from what a contemporary invasion force might achieve.

I have no idea of their attempting anything by the change of means of warfare attaching to steam beyond perhaps occasionally some sudden predatory attacks on the undefended parts of our coast, and which we must guard against by numerous steamers in-shore and larger ships outside, and I have no doubt that in spite of Sir Ch^s [Napier's] croaking we shall be equally able, as we have heretofore been, to disappoint the Prince de Joinville or any other French officer who Sir Charles may point out to be desirous of gaining laurels on *our coasts*.

The one point upon which Cockburn felt the British steam fleet lay at disadvantage 'in the event of *early* sudden war' with France was in its distribution. 'Our colonies and distant foreign relations oblige us to have quite out of reach no fewer than 28 of our most efficient steam ships of large size.' This was a quarter of the whole steam fleet, whereas the French had only six beyond reach, with all the rest situated in home waters. However, Britain had enough close at hand to be collected at short notice in the narrow part of the Channel which, with those then in advanced state for commissioning, would soon form 'a tolerably efficient steam squadron for guarding the coast until others can be collected'.[89]

In that summer of 1845, the degree to which the British steam fleet was dispersed became the cause of some alarm to Peel. He feared the accounts Cockburn employed to deduce fleet strengths were 'erroneous'.[90] For comparisons of strength in steam applicable to 'any sudden and unlooked for rupture' he wished Cockburn to use the dispersed strength of the British fleet, and to set for the standard on the home station a force equal to that of any two other countries.[91] However, Cockburn argued that the degree of British weakness in the Channel simply reflected government priorities 'for, as fast as we get steam vessels of war fit for service, they are called for some pressing duty abroad and we are obliged to detach them'. He simply urged they 'keep determinedly' a certain number of steam vessels for home service, 'the Admiralty to be authorised not to furnish them for any distant duty without special directions from the Cabinet'.[92]

The Introduction of the Screw Propeller

The importance steam had assumed in strategic thought, even by 1840, demanded that its potentialities be fully developed to the benefit of the British navy, especially to prevent rivals—France or the United States— gaining advantage through more rapid development. The technological innovation in the British navy almost wholly dependent on the

Plate 9. HM Steam sloops *Rattler* and *Alecto* towing stern to stern for the purpose of testing the relative powers of the screw propeller and the paddle wheel. The trial took place in a dead calm in the North Sea on 3 April 1845.
(National Maritime Museeum)

Haddington Board, and in particular on the attitude of Cockburn, was the introduction of the screw propeller.

During its own lifetime, the Board was accused of dragging its feet over the introduction of the 'Archimedean screw'.[93] Technological historians, reflecting Isambard Kingdom Brunel's view of Admiralty bureaucracy, were initially happy to perpetuate the allegation. As late as 1958 'the tedious and repetitive lag between invention and general adoption' was said to be 'particularly evident in the slow transition from the paddle-wheel to the screw-propeller'.[94] The view was clearly based on a limited knowledge, both of the problem that confronted those in office and of the attitudes those officials possessed. Recent scholarship, based on Admiralty correspondence, has done much to clarify the managerial difficulties and the interests of the different parties involved.[95] Reputations, once impaired by allegations of prejudice, have been cleared. Far from resisting the introduction of the screw, Admiralty officials are now known to have possessed clear aims and to have assisted encouragingly in the process by which experimentation and innovation was managed. Caution is now regarded as having been proper and necessary, while the time lapse between a decision to experiment and the launch of ships equipped with the screw has been shown to have been remarkably short.[96] Private shipping companies were quick to try the new propeller; but in the process of refinement, demanding investment beyond the means of private industry, the navy played a greater part.[97]

The process of experimentation had already begun before Cockburn returned to the Admiralty in September 1841. Naval officials had not been impressed at being towed in the Admiralty barge by John Ericsson's screw-propelled launch in April 1837. But they had taken interest in Francis Pettit Smith's launch which later that year weathered heavy seas on a trip down the Thames to Hythe. She had received an official trial in March 1838. Smith's subsequent 237-ton *Archimedes* proved herself in May 1840 in races with cross-Channel packets operated by the navy, and received favourable reports from the naval officer appointed by the Admiralty to observe the trials. A decision to build a screw-steamer had been taken at the Admiralty by the end of that year, the early months of 1841 being devoted to details of design. Disagreement arose between the Surveyor's Department and the new Steam Department, created in April 1837, over the size of the opening to be built into the stern of the vessel, so that Brunel, who was building the screw-steamship *Great Britain*, was invited to direct 'the mechanical arrangements' of the new vessel.[98] She was to be a sister ship to the paddle-sloop *Polyphemus*, and was to be named the *Rattler*. However, before work could proceed much beyond consultations over design, the Board of Admiralty altered.

In this transition, the project got off to a poor start. Cockburn's first impressions of Brunel's intentions were probably formed by his old adversary, Sir Edward Codrington, then commander-in-chief at Portsmouth, who took up and urged Brunel's plans with the new Board.[99] Symonds did not help: for the first meeting between Cockburn and Brunel he sent to the Admiralty a cut-away model of the stern of a three-decker showing, according to the label, 'Mr Brunel's mode of applying the screw to Her Majesty's ships'. In consequence Cockburn's first words to Brunel were 'Do you mean to suppose that we shall cut up Her Majesty's ships after this fashion, sir?' Brunel's denial virtually ended the interview, while the source of the model was investigated.[100]

Subsequent misunderstandings arising from conflicting objectives did not help either. The Admiralty was interested in the screw as an aid to sail. Brunel on the other hand was intent on using the screw as the principal means of propulsion.[101] Peel also had influence in requiring economy. At the Admiralty there was consequently a preference for cheap experiments, and in February 1842 it was decided to place the engines ordered for *Polyphemus*'s sister ship, now temporarily suspended, into an existing sloop, *Acheron*. She was similar to the paddle-sloop *Alecto* and a comparison would have been fair. However, on a protest from Brunel, which was supported by Symonds, on the necessity that the vessel be suitable for the screw and comparable in sailing qualities to the *Polyphemus*, the order was replaced by one to continue building the *Rattler*.[102]

This hiatus in proceedings seems to have convinced Brunel that the Admiralty was half-hearted about introducing the screw. But only five weeks were wasted, and thereafter plans were prepared rapidly. The sheer draught was approved on 6 April 1842, the profile on 1 July, other drawings being sent to Sheerness dockyard as they were prepared. The screw-sloop *Rattler* of 888 tons was launched on 13 April 1843. She received her engines in the East India Docks and had her first trial run on 30 October.[103] This was little more than two years after the Haddington ministry had taken office, and only twenty months after the decision to resume work on *Rattler*.

Throughout this period, Cockburn figured as a co-ordinator between the Surveyor, the Steam Department and Brunel, endorsing recommendations, authorizing action, even concerning himself with trials of pressure acting upon a safety-valve. He was fully informed of what was being done and commanded a position that gave control over the whole procedure. Undoubtedly aware of French progress in building a screwship—the *Pomone*, completed in 1845—he was also conscious of his own limited knowledge of the technological problems involved. In consequence, the steam enthusiast, Lieutenant John Hoseason, became his travelling agent and consultant. Hoseason's help and advice ensured that after February 1842 hold ups to construction and experimentation were minimal.[104]

In line with contemporary naval thought, Cockburn aimed to produce an auxiliary screw-warship that stowed its propulsive machinery largely below water level and left the sides of the vessel clear to mount a full broadside.[105] In October 1843 the *Rattler* was still not the warship he had in mind. Her gearwheel, an afterthought, was still exposed, like the machinery of her paddle-wheel contemporaries. But her construction, combined with contemporary developments, contributed to the creation of more satisfactory vessels. Fortunately, at that time, lighter, less bulky tubular boilers were tried in the paddle-frigate *Penelope*; their use in screw-steamships reduced the weight and space of this equipment. In mid-1844 the Ship Propeller Company, formed to build the *Archimedes* and exploit Pettit Smith's patent, proposed a geared crankshaft that would also save space and confine the machinery. The *Niger*, ordered early in 1845, consequently had all her machinery low down. Compared to paddle-steamers, screw-vessels required greater speed of drive, for which direct-acting engines were, by 1845, considered possible.[106] There was concern about hull shape, to provide the greatest thrust and least slip, and problems in the rapid wear of the propeller shaft and bearings. Above all, however, the shape of the most effective propeller had to be determined. After various alterations, this was the main task of the *Rattler* between February 1844 and January 1845. During that time as many as 32 different propellers were tried.[107] In view of their cost in casting and fitting, it was a series of trials that could only have been performed by the Admiralty.

Even before these experiments were completed, Cockburn knew enough to declare in the House of Commons on 1 March 1844 that 'his impression . . . was that they would arrive at the knowledge of a screw which would be better than the paddle-wheels'.[108] Within a year that knowledge was obtained. A second experimental screw-vessel, the *Dwarf*, had been purchased in June 1843, and after her stern was subject to numerous modifications to ascertain the most appropriate shape, she was employed in 1845 on trials of 24 types of screw propeller. Then, almost as a publicity stunt, to complete the *Rattler* trials against her paddle-sloop half-sister, *Alecto*, on 3 April 1845 the two vessels were linked stern-to-stern and set to a tug-of-war. The *Alecto*, given a sporting chance, moved off first and was towing the *Rattler* at 2 knots before her screw began to turn. Five minutes later the *Rattler* had arrested her sternway and was towing the *Alecto* at nearly 3 knots. There could remain few who doubted the screw's superiority.[109]

Nevertheless, even after this demonstration, there were some who did so, and Sir Charles Napier was among these.[110] But Cockburn was more than convinced. He informed Haddington in June 1845,

> The proofs we have lately had of the efficiency of the screw as a propeller on board the *Rattler* convince *me*, that it will be in future generally adopted and we are now adapting those building for that description of propeller. . . . The French I believe have only one or two with screw propellers. We are therefore taking the lead in this important change of getting rid of the cumbersome paddle wheels, and with the advantage that a screw vessel may if required be converted into a paddle vessel but a paddle vessel cannot be converted to a screw vessel without much alteration and expense. . . .[111]

In public Cockburn had gone further, declaring in May 1845 that he 'was in hopes before long to have all the vessels fitted with screw instead of paddles', and that 'they were now building with the view of . . . placing the machinery below the water mark . . .'.[112]

The building he referred to was probably the *Amphion* that was eventually fitted with direct-acting engines. In June 1845 he explained to Haddington that they were at that time 'fitting the *Amphion*, a large frigate, with a screw and small engine of 300 horses as an auxiliary to her sails. If we find this to answer, more of that class of ship and indeed our ships of the line may be so fitted at moderate expense without inconvenience to their interior arrangements.'[113] At that time, as a result of the 1844 commission on the state of coast defences, four 74-gun ships of the line—the *Edinburgh*, *Hogue*, *Blenheim* and *Ajax*—and some frigates were also under orders for adaptation to an auxiliary screw to act as blockships in the approaches to the dockyards. During 1845 the Board of Admiralty ordered 26 engines for installation in screw-ships, including those for bomb-vessels *Erebus* and *Terror*, to be used by Franklin in his expedition to the Arctic north-west.[114]

Much of this work went ahead in secrecy. On account of fears of the inadequacy of the British steam force in the Channel, the government regarded this enlargement of its steam fleet as necessary rearmament. Thus Peel authorized Haddington to press ahead with the fitting of the battleships and frigates 'with as little of parade as possible and, if it be practicable, without newspaper comment'.[115] Such secrecy has concealed the transformation of the steam fleet. Between 1845 and 1847 the number of screwships in the navy grew from 9 to 41.[116] At the same time officers were steadily being trained in screw navigation, partly in consequence of the continued use of the *Bee* by the Royal Naval College. The *Bee*, a 42-ton tender, had been authorized to carry screw as well as paddles in February 1841.

The *Amphion*, the Royal Navy's first screw-frigate with all her machinery and boilers below the water line, was launched in January 1846. The *Ajax* and *Blenheim*, the first line-of-battle ships equipped with the screw, went to sea in September 1846.[117] This was less than six years since *Rattler* had been proposed and less than four and a half years since the beginning of her construction. In view of the number of experiments and trials involved, this period of research and development was remarkably brief. Nothing better confutes Cockburn's reputation for resistance to technological change.

Iron Ships and Shells

In 1841 the navy had just started to mount shell-firing guns on ships of the line and frigates. Shells had been successfully tested by the French in 1824 and by the British navy in 1829. Shell-firing guns were then confined to a few paddle-steamers. However, in 1837 the French took steps to introduce them more generally, to which the British Admiralty responded by deciding in 1839 to mount them in thirty ships of the line and forty frigates.[118] By 1841 such guns were thus mounted not only in paddle-steamers—five had been used to shell enemy positions during the Syrian campaign of 1840—but also alongside conventional cannon in some sailing warships. Early shells had less range than shot due to the eccentric weight of the fuse and their usually smaller charge. Yet the explosive power of a single well-planted shell might do the work of numerous broadsides.[119] In 1838 this effect had been demonstrated at 1,280 yards on the three-deck *Prince George*. The problem between 1841 and 1846 was to improve the accuracy of fire sufficiently to ensure that shells would always find their mark at long range.[120]

Proposals for improvements in gunnery were repeatedly being received. Cockburn was in regular contact with the Master General of the Ordnance, General Sir George Murray, to decide which suggestions should be given trial.[121] Peel as well as Haddington was involved, as were naval officers like Sir Edward Owen and Sir Thomas Hastings, captain of the gunnery school HMS *Excellent*, and their army counterparts, Sir Howard Douglas and Colonel Pasley, who investigated the actual operation of particular proposals.

Cockburn admitted in Otober 1841 that he viewed 'with jealousy and doubt all these explosive inventions'.[122] Probably typical of his response was that to an 'exploding case' invented by Mr S.A. Warner, who claimed for his invention both power on detonation and accuracy of direction over a distance of six miles. Peel was anxious that these claims should be considered, though aware the invention might prove 'more dangerous to the employer than to his enemy'. Evidence suggested interest in the invention from a foreign power ready to pay a significant sum.[123] Yet a year later Warner complained that his claims for his invention were 'treated with suspicion', that he had been 'cruelly tainted' in the House of Commons for not being a theoretical man of science—as if he was 'a detected imposter'—and that Cockburn had expressed satisfaction he 'was not an officer in the naval service', as if he had been 'guilty of hoisting false colours'.[124] Warner wanted five thousand pounds to demonstrate his invention. Another year later, however, Cockburn was still resisting a payment of such magnitude. He admitted the probable power of Warner's 'exploding case' but as to Warner's second claim:

> If he could really send a shell with precision six miles, he would be able to effect what nobody else has hitherto attained and he would be entitled to a considerable reward from the Government. It appears, however, he has hitherto invariably insisted on proving first the former (in my opinion) minor experiment which causes me to entertain the strongest doubt of his being able to execute the latter more important object.

He thus considered 'no very great sum' should be provided to enable Warner to demonstrate his shell, an opinion with which Peel concurred.[125]

Advances in ordnance encouraged the Haddington Board to find a means of resisting as well as projecting shot and shell. In December 1841 the committee of master shipwrights was appointed 'to consider the best mode of strengthening ships of war and to recommend improvements, to give greater power of attack and defence without interfering with the powers of sailing'. One of the first suggestions taken up was from an inventor named Belmano for laminated armour. The idea of armour was not new: in 1827 two layers of wrought iron bars laid at right angles had been tried without success. Belmano's proposal was for layers of plate iron, three eighths of an inch thick, to be riveted together. In 1842 fourteen layers were tried, giving over five inches total thickness; later as many as 28 layers were used—however, neither stopped solid 32-pounder shot at 400 yards and in January 1843 the Surveyor concluded that the necessary quantity of armour would add too much weight to a vessel's topsides.[126] Thereafter interest focused on the use of iron purely for constructional purposes.

Iron had long been used for merchant vessels. But even they could not safely go out of sight of land until the problem of the magnetic compass was solved. This was achieved by the Admiralty in 1838, and in that year an iron sailing vessel of 260 tons crossed the Atlantic. Metal was most commonly used for steamers, and some builders had become particularly experienced in iron: William Laird of Birkenhead had 44 iron vessels built or building by September 1842. He proposed an iron frigate to the East India Company in 1836, built two iron paddle-steamers for the Company in 1839, and built an iron paddle-frigate for the Mexican government in 1842. The Admiralty also used Laird, having an iron paddle-packet built in 1839–40 and six small iron steamers for the American Lakes in 1840–41.[127]

Under Cockburn, building resumed in January 1844. He was impressed by the performance of the East India Company's iron steamship *Niger* in the First China War, from which it returned in November 1843. He began moderately, with orders for six small iron steamers for use as tenders to flagships. But by mid-1845 five large frigates and 25 gun-vessels, packets, tenders and schooners were ordered or building. Moreover, of these, four of the frigates were ordered as screwships.[128] Had this course been pursued, significant advantage may have accrued from the greater tensile strength of iron and its ability to resist vibration and wear. However, Cockburn attended tests at Woolwich which suggested the damage sustained by iron from gunfire made it questionable for the construction of warships.[129] Shot-holes on the nearside of a hull were clear and stoppable but those on the other, where jagged edges pressed outward, could not be stopped. In 1846 the succeeding Whig Board of Admiralty ordered the iron frigates of 1845 to be converted to transports.[130] Subsequently, for fifteen years, iron was used only for the construction of packet-steamers, gun- and mortar-vessels; and the building programme instigated by Cockburn was condemned.

Nevertheless, in 1845 Admiralty orders gave grounds for optimism. The Royal Navy was at the forefront of technological developments among European powers. 'With all these efforts and improvements in continual progress, in which we are decidedly taking the lead and are therefore in advance', Cockburn reassured Haddington in June, 'I feel very confident there is no just ground for . . . alarm'.[131]

Outside the Admiralty opinion was less complaisant. Parliamentary commissions of inquiry of 1840 and 1844 recommended the construction of a series of 'harbours of refuge' both for merchant vessels in distress and as stations for armed steam vessels during wartime.[132] Three for the south-east coast of England were proposed in June 1845— for Portland, Dover and Harwich—with the addition of three more in the Channel Islands, as recommended by a committee of army and naval officers in 1842.[133] Cockburn contributed to these proceedings by nominating members, commenting on reports, and obtaining engineers' proposals. He approved of the recommendations for the south coast but could 'scarcely feel so satisfied' with those for the safety of the Channel Islands.[134] Efforts were also being made to improve the landward defences of the dockyards. But Cockburn did little more than collect estimates. His main interest lay in the equipment of ships with screws to act as blockships.[135] His primary concern continued to be the strengthening of the fleet, for which the invasion threat simply enhanced his opportunity.

Flogging and Desertion

The conditions under which seamen served in the Royal Navy had been a subject for agitation on the part of reformers since the 1820s. It seemed that their terms of employment, in particular the brutality of punishments to which they were subject, encouraged seamen to desert, deterred them from enlisting, and obliged the Admiralty to maintain its right to impress seamen when circumstances made it necessary. The argument had a superficial logic which, in an age of conscious humanitarianism, the Admiralty found difficult to resist, especially in the 1840s when the reforming movement received reinforcement from technological change. For steam, and the speed with which the Channel could be crossed, seemed to demand an improvement in the means by which ships in reserve could be quickly manned.[136]

By the early 1840s there can be little doubt that conditions of service were already better in many respects than they had been half a century earlier. Some like Sir Charles Napier denied this improvement. But in 1844 Rear Admiral Dundas asserted that, after knowing the navy forty years, he had 'never known it in better condition. The men were better educated, better fed, with much less punishment than formerly, and better exercised at the guns.' Parliamentary influence could be seen at work in questions about payment and leave, and even regarding the welfare of individual ships. The trouble was that improvements in material conditions did not seem to have the desired effect in altering the behaviour of seamen. In consequence punishments and desertion continued.

In the 1830s this had been a cause of disappointment to those of Whig reforming mind. Yet Cockburn, even then, had been sceptical of their hopes. While still commander-in-chief on the North American station in August 1835, his opinion had differed from that of Rear Admiral Adam at the Board who believed that the increased comforts of the men ought to have produced a more favourable result.

> I can only say that I do not believe they have, or that any thing which could be done for them would have the slightest effect towards checking the generality of our sailors from following the bent of their inclinations when seized by any whim or attracted by any present temptation, especially if holding out to them novelty and change.[137]

Of all the conditions to which seamen were subject, their apparent exposure to arbitrary punishment was regarded as the priority for reform. The forms of punishment had been restricted, but flogging remained.[138] Here, campaigners took heart, having achieved the abolition of slavery in the colonies (a condition once likened to that of seamen on board a ship of war) and successfully worked for a reduction of flogging in the army.[139] In the navy, limits were achieved through the introduction in 1830 of reports of punishments to the Admiralty, summaries of which Parliament could and did demand. By the 1840s these registered a significant decline: a return of 1846 revealed a decline from one punishment for every 17 men in the navy in 1839, to one for every 33. However, reformers now argued that the very existence of flogging still deterred men from joining the navy. As Joseph Hume observed, when diet, clothing and cleanliness could be no better 'there must be some cause to keep the men away from it'.[140]

Reformers' attention focused upon the navy's Articles of War. Deriving from original articles drafted in the mid-seventeenth century, they had last been revised in 1749. They provided trial by court martial and the death penalty for 20 of their 36 articles. But at the same time they allowed all crimes not capital to be punished either as the court saw fit, or according to the custom of the service, at the discretion of ships' captains. Because court penalties for crimes were so severe, and in order that prompt retribution be given, men were regularly punished by their captains. The reforming case maintained that the Articles should be revised, punishments moderated according to the seriousness of offences, and every offender given the right to trial by court martial.[141]

Cockburn objected to the view that the Articles of War were administered harshly. Although he agreed it was a harsh code he maintained that the provision for punishment at the discretion of the captain ensured that its worst sanctions were avoided. Captains, like Justices of the Peace on shore, could deal with the majority of offences, being minor crimes, with minor punishments.[142] These were limited to 48 lashes and governed by restrictive regulations, with particulars to be observed in returns of the causes of punishment and of the evidence upon which it had been awarded. Where crimes demanded greater punishment, they could be referred to court martial. But, were all offences referred to a court martial, Cockburn was sure there would not only be a great consumption of the time of officers who would have to form the court, but also a great increase in punishments. As things stood, captains had incentive to prevent punishments, these being now regarded at the Admiralty as discreditable to the captain; the latter therefore 'often checked the complaints of their officers when displeased with their men'. Seamen accordingly 'looked up to the captain' as their 'father and protector', and their 'best friend'.[143]

Cockburn used the language of paternalism, but did not disguise his faith in discipline as the principal aspect of management in the navy, and his reaction to the threat of parliamentary interference was based on study and tested experience. While still on the North American station, he had been asked by Lord Aukland to explain variations in the number of corporal punishments in different ships, and had been convinced then from his 'own anxious observations'

> that at least nine times in ten it will be found a ship in which there are the fewest corporal punishments will be in the best order and have on board the best and most efficient officers; for it depends in my opinion in a very main degree on the ability and vigilance with which the officers give their constant personal attention in superintending the general conduct of the men, . . . to *prevent* such crimes as call for corporal punishment; whereas when on the contrary officers (I allude particularly

to the lieutenants) give but little superintending personal attention to the men, and satisfy themselves with merely giving their orders, looking for the captain to punish all infringements of them, the petty officers and seamen, so left to themselves, are but too apt very negligently to obey the orders so given and to fall into excesses which render a resort to corporal punishment ultimately necessary.[144]

Cockburn acknowledged that two features in the nature of seamen made management of crews more difficult—both had a bearing on Admiralty policy. First, he accepted that drunkenness was the 'incurable national vice of the lower grade of Englishmen' from whom sailors and soldiers were recruited. As drunkenness was 'usually the primary and main cause of the heaviest crimes committed in our ships', the prevention of spirits being secretly smuggled into ships would reduce the need for punishments. Secondly, Cockburn recognized that there were some men of a 'hardened refractory character' with whom 'the best efforts of the very best and most attentive and temperate officers fail to produce any good effect'. It was 'quite inconceivable to those who had not witnessed it, how much one or two such discontented and refractory men will keep a ship's company in a constant state of disquiet and dissatisfaction, and the number of necessary punishments they will cause'. Cockburn considered such men should be discharged with disgrace. This was, after all, 'the course pursued with refractory servants on shore'. It was wrong and impossible to force captains 'to endeavour to flog men of perverse and evil dispositions into good behaviour'.[145]

By 1844, to mitigate this problem of management, Cockburn claimed that officers had become 'more particular than they used to be in the selection of the seamen they would receive'.[146] This and the discouragement given to corporal punishments had had the effect of steadily reducing the number of floggings. Those reported in returns to the Admiralty amounted to 2,472 in 1842 (when 43,105 men were borne), and 1,411 in 1844 (with 38,343 men); by 1846 (with 43,314 men) there were only 1,077.[147]

Even so, seamen still seemed too ready to leave the navy, deserting at a cost to themselves in back pay and pension rights to an extent that seemed to confirm the necessity for reform. The introduction of pensions in the early 1820s had been an attempt to commit men to long service, rights to pensions being earned by men serving 21 years, even if discontinuously.[148] Breaks of service were inevitable when a ship's commission was terminated by seamen being paid off, while their entry for another naval vessel was far from assured when crimping placed them in the debt of merchant masters.[149] Pensions were thus devised as much to draw seamen back into the navy as to deter them from abandoning a ship in commission. Those who went absent without leave automatically had their pension right cancelled, the onus being placed on them to disprove any intention to desert.[150]

Pensions for terms of service shorter than 21 years were considered early in Haddington's administration. Cockburn favoured the idea.[151] Yet they were, in his opinion, of secondary importance to several other factors affecting desertion. In 1835, throughout the whole navy, one in nine men had deserted, but on the North American station the ratio had been only one in 27. At the Admiralty, it was assumed that ships in port lost most men, yet Cockburn was able to show that the *President* and *Forte*, the two ships most in port on his station, had lost the least men— less than one in fifty—while those 'constantly employed running from place to place with very short intervals at anchor' had lost more than one in seven of their men. These active vessels tended to be the smaller ones, but their size or class did not seem to him significant.[152] His view of desertion was similar to that of punishment: that the ship with the worst discipline lost the most men. The problem was 'much checked and kept under by quiet and steady discipline . . . and granting the men constant leave to go on shore whenever a fair opportunity for it offer, which last point, though it affords the facility, tends in my opinion more than anything else to check the *desire*'.

Nevertheless Cockburn knew that there was nothing 'in our power to do' that would entirely solve the problem. He believed

> it to be the nature of sailors to incline to change with headstrong inconsideration [of] their existing position, whether in the Navy or merchant service, especially if (as is generally the case when they have opportunity to desert) they have been able to get at liquor or have had present temptation held out to them.

For the majority of seamen, restraints, pecuniary or otherwise, were no check against the attraction of indulgences they had been kept from for any length of time, especially when the desire to indulge was combined with that for 'change for changing sake'. Desertion was part of a way of life which he saw no means of stopping. Moreoever, annoying and distressing though it was to officers, he attached no great importance to the loss of men in the long term.

> For the same restless disposition that causes a seaman to run from a ship of war one year induces him to leave a merchant ship the next year if not

sooner, to join some other ship of war, only entering the latter by some other name, so that they almost invariably return again to the service, and we are therefore generally enabled to keep up our complements abroad wherever we have any trade.

The only real loser in this circulation was the deserter himself who forfeited his pay and claims to a pension. The greater the back pay, in Cockburn's opinion, the greater the incentive not to desert. He therefore opposed the enlargement of monthly allowances, associating that of November 1833 with an increase of desertion, at least on the North American station.[153]

By 1846 the desertion rate was still as high as one in thirteen.[154] Yet in debates Cockburn's arguments for men running 'the tour' between the navy and merchant services were difficult to counter. For him, merchant vessels acted as a temporary repository for men trained in gunnery who could be called upon in time of war; as they spent little time at their moorings, they maintained seamanship; while 'some hard rough work', without being so well fed or cared for, made seamen willing to return to the navy. 'Besides which, this circulation of men kept up a good feeling . . . and was rather therefore a benefit than otherwise'.[155]

Impressment and Registration

The idea of men running 'the tour' was still acceptable in the 1840s because all seamen were paid off at the end of their ships' commissions, which made recruitment a constant problem. From September 1846, to keep men from being crimped into merchant vessels, the succeeding Board of Admiralty permitted seamen four to five weeks' leave *with pay* at the termination of their ships' commissions. Whether they took advantage of this facility and whether they chose a naval or a merchant ship afterwards were both optional.[156] In consequence, until there was provision for the housing of seamen at the termination of commissions, there was always difficulty in gathering sufficient trained men for crews, even when small numbers of ships were being prepared for sea.[157] Those who were recruited were generally landsmen who took some time to train.

One proposed solution was to increase rates of pay in the navy. But Cockburn rejected the idea, claiming that, whatever the naval rate, the merchant service would always pay more, resulting in a leap-frogging of pay rates. A second suggeston was to train more boys, thereby enlarging the general pool of men from which the navy drew. Again, however, Cockburn rejected the idea. He claimed that there were always more boys training or waiting for an opportunity to join, and that it was 'useless to bring forward more seamen than could find employment'.[158] Demand dictated the supply

> The country will always have as many seamen as you will give bread to, but, with the exception of a few over for relief, you will have no more, for seamen must eat like all working men.[159]

Between 1841 and 1846 this view hardened. With the reduction in the number of seamen maintained in 1844 to 38,000, the subsequent enlargement of the navy to 46,000 men in 1846 was only achieved with difficulty. The cause of this difficulty, as Cockburn saw it, was the original failure of the public to provide support for the seamen it needed.

> If the navy was reduced to the extent of 3,000 or 4,000 men in a few years, those men could not be had, ... They might educate 40,000 boys if they chose, but then if they found employment and bread for only 20,000 seamen the first number would ultimately dwindle down to the latter. The number that maintenance was provided for would always be had, and would always be retained.[160]

Difficulties of recruitment left some ships with shortages that could not be filled without delays to their date of sailing, or without men being drafted from other ships. To counter criticisms on both points, Cockburn defended two practices. First, he permitted the commissioning of ships for home waters with a complement of men even less than their official peacetime establishment—he maintained that in 1846 the available men were stretched almost ten per cent further by this means. He justified the practice by pointing out that in wartime ships were often short-handed with men sick, dead, or wounded, and his own experience of this was acknowledged. Privately he also pointed out that the establishment of the gunnery school, *Excellent*, now permitted the Admiralty to know precisely how many men were required to serve each piece of ordnance.[161] Secondly, Cockburn maintained the right of the Admiralty to turn men over from one ship to another regardless of their own preference. Some advocates of seaman's rights opposed the practice. Gentlemen officers were still expected to raise men from around their estates. It was natural for seamen to form bonds of familiarity and affection for a particular ship or officer, and removal from such surroundings was unsettling and a significant source of the desire to desert. But in war 'turning-over' had been regarded as essential; in the

1840s circumstances again made it necessary. Cockburn reminded the Commons that seamen 'entered for general service . . . [and] were subject to be sent where they were wanted, . . . not to any particular ship'.[162]

After 1844, the cause of most concern was the problem of large-scale recruitment for the mobilization of fleet reserves in case of hostilities. Steam power permitted the Channel to be crossed so quickly that old methods of obtaining men for an emergency were acknowledged— in government as well as by critics—to be too slow. At the time of the crisis with France in 1844 there were only about 3,000 seamen in ships of the line in home waters; later Cockburn was to consider 20,000 men in ships of the line and steamers necessary in case of attack. Yet, to assemble the additional men, the government had only its traditional instruments: the bounty on entry to volunteers (ten pounds in 1845) and the power, if authorized by the Crown, to impress seamen.[163] Impressment had long been opposed and in the 1840s there was uncertainty whether public opinion would still support it.

Cockburn urged its retention as expedient. At the same time he acknowledged objections to it and, in his official capacity, sought to find a practical alternative. He believed that all seamen employed on shore in government posts, whether in the dockyards, signal stations, or for the protection of revenue, as well as those in receipt of pensions for periods of royal service, should be liable to be called upon in an emergency. An Admiralty order of August 1844 thus provided that ex-seamen in the dockyards should be liable for sea service at all times. He also recalled the value of the Coast Blockade established in 1825. An anti-smuggling coastguard composed of former naval seamen, it had been called up in 1826 to man the dockyard guard-ships that had been sent as part of a squadron to the Tagus. However, the Customs and Treasury had disapproved of Admiralty 'interference' with their employees and this reserve had been abandoned.[164] Haddington revived the idea in June 1845, receiving an enthusiastic response from Peel, though he queried whether the Admiralty had the power to place the coastguards on the books of the navy and subject them to the Naval Mutiny Act without legislation. Late in 1845 all new entrants to the coastguard were made liable to sea service in the event of war.[165]

Succeeding Admiralty administrations continued the policy and over the next five years 2,000 government employees were recruited into a wartime reserve. Such was its success that in 1856 the management of the coastguard was transferred from the Customs to the Admiralty which enlarged this whole resource to 5,600 men by 1859.[166]

However, this reserve of government employees was too small to form a real alternative to impressment. The scale of manning necessary to mobilize the whole fleet necessitated a system by which men could be drawn from the whole merchant service, preferably with their own consent, or at least with public approval. Service by rota had become a possibility after 1835 with the registration of seamen. Then Cockburn had been sceptical of the scheme's value, fearing that 'it will be found very difficult to get our English sailors to adhere to any regular system of registry'.[167] Nevertheless, by 1838 it had enrolled the names of 167,000 seamen and 21,500 apprentices.[168] Plans to use the resource were drawn up by the Registrar, Lieutenant J.H. Brown, and schemes were put forward in 1838, 1841 and 1844; by the end of that last year, Brown was aware that public opinion had turned decisively in his favour. There were fears that reservists in receipt of pensions would take their stipend but not respond when called upon to serve in an emergency; yet his records provided 'an effectual check to any evasion'.[169]

Brown's confidence in his records coincided with increased attention at the Admiralty to the need to improve the competence of masters and mates in the merchant service. The initial impetus to do so arose from a recommendation of the parliamentary committee on shipwrecks of 1843 for masters and mates to be examined for their competency. Cockburn took up the recommendation on behalf of the Admiralty, writing to W.E. Gladstone at the Board of Trade in February 1844 supporting the suggestion 'inasmuch as it certainly would raise the character of our mercantile marine and probably diminish the number of shipwrecks'. Brown, the Registrar, may have taken note of Cockburn and Gladstone's arrangements for examinations, for he claimed in December 1844 that, in his opinion, the attempt at a registry in 1696 had failed due to the registration of incompetent men. The records now likely to come under his eye would provide the navy with the names of arguably the most competent seamen in the country.

To introduce examinations of competence, Cockburn sounded out and proposed a scheme which avoided both legislation and the opposition of shipowners, yet achieved the voluntary participation of masters and mates. In February 1844 he suggested to Gladstone

> whether it will not be a preferable course to endeavour to arrange with the committee of Lloyds for inserting in the Lists of the Commercial Shipping in addition to the letter and number indicative of seaworthiness

of each ship, the name of the master and whether he has passed examination, causing it also to be made known that the Government will not take up or employ any merchant vessel not commanded by a passed master.

This, two elder brethren of Trinity House had assured him, would result in ships having a passed master against their name being insured at a lower rate than equally good ships with unpassed masters. This in turn 'would naturally lead to a general voluntary adoption of the passing system', and the same course could be adopted for chief mates, as proof of their fitness to take charge should an accident occur to the master. Cockburn went on to suggest the composition and recompense of the boards of examiners.[170]

The remainder of 1844 was taken in sounding out opinion. There was some support for an Act of Parliament to make examination compulsory and to provide means at law to punish misconduct on the part of examining officers. However, Lloyds seemed likely to object to parliamentary interference with their lists, while all the principal shipping ports, except Bristol, preferred the voluntary plan. Cockburn therefore maintained that the voluntary system should be tried, which would at a minimum provide the information necessary should an Act then be considered essential.[171] Gladstone concurred with Cockburn's view.

By an order of 1845 the Board of Trade authorized voluntary examinations of competency for all men intending to become masters and mates of foreign-going British merchant ships. Five years later an Act made examination compulsory for men seeking promotion, and a consolidating Act of 1854 extended the system to masters and mates of vessels trading in home waters. As Brown might have foreseen, to maintain these records of qualifications under the Board of Trade, the Register Office at the Admiralty was transferred in 1850 to that department. From that time, therefore, as well as a register of seamen, the Registrar had in his charge registers of masters and of certificates of competency.[172] These activities paved the way for the Royal Naval Reserve Act of 1859. Through them a balanced reserve of masters and mates as well as seamen became a practical alternative to impressment.[173]

Renewing the Officer Corps

The importance Cockburn attached to the 'talent and temper' of officers in the management of seamen enhanced his desire for an active and experienced officer corps. However, by 1841 a principal feature of the corps was the proportion of its members who were inactive. In January 1814, when war was being waged against the United States as well as France, the total corps was 5,018 men. By April 1838 this total was reduced to 4,893, but by then the proportion who were inactive, yet in receipt of half-pay, was considerably greater. Whereas 2,281 were on half or retired pay at a cost of more than £326,000 in 1814, by 1838 there were 3,849 inactive men receiving over £586,000.[174]

During the early 1840s these figures remained virtually unchanged. Most officers had served in the Napoleonic War and, on account of their age, seemed unlikely to be physically capable of returning to sea; and, of those promoted by seniority, many could justifiably be regarded as inexperienced. The expense in pensions was generally accepted as a long-term cost of victory in 1815; but the efficiency of the corps was questioned. A parliamentary commission on naval and military promotion in 1840 had analysed the situation and revealed that only 20 per cent of vice-admirals were under 65 years of age, 28 per cent of captains were under 49, and only 29 per cent of lieutenants under 35.[175] Critics in the Commons, like Sir Charles Napier, claimed 'that it would be impossible to carry on a war with vigour' with superior officers of such advanced age. Probably stung—in 1842 he was himself 70— Cockburn rejected such allegations, claiming they were prompted by the arrogance of youth. Nevertheless, in debates over more than two years, he was eventually forced to admit that for 'three-fourths' of all officers on half-pay, practical skills would be lacking.[176]

The 1840 report also revealed that only one captain in eleven, one commander in ten, and one lieutenant in six, was actually needed at sea, and that almost half of all captains and commanders, and one fifth of all lieutenants, had never served afloat in the ranks they held. Lack of practice was inevitably perpetuated by a selection system which tended to favour those with most experience. In 1838, of 4,369 captains, commanders and lieutenants, about one half had never served afloat for more than 15 years, while nearly 2,000 had not served afloat for 20 years.[177]

By 1844 most of these men would have been absent from sea that much longer, and the changing technology of warfare was increasing pressure for the removal from the officer lists of men who were so out of practice. A retired list of so-called yellow admirals had existed since 1747 but this had been reunified with the active list on the recommendation of the report of 1840. Sir Charles Napier was vociferous in calling for removals to a new retired list. He raised the subject of retirement in debates six times between 1842 and 1844.[178] Peel eventually answered him in May 1844 and simply echoed the report of 1840. He pointed out that regulations for retiring elderly officers had given rise to invidious distinctions and ill-feeling; that the extra expense in pensions necessary to induce them to volunteer for a retired list would place a further financial burden on the public; and that those likely to volunteer were principally captains near the bottom of the list who despaired of a flag, while those at the top would hang on in hopes of a flag at the next promotion. The wrong men would thus volunteer. 'The advantage to be gained by the public in clearing the list would not be commensurate to the expense.'[179]

Later that year the evident need for rapid action should an invasion threat materialize obliged reconsideration of this position. Confidence in the defensive capabilities of the government would increase with a weeding of the active list. A plan for retirements was thus produced in 1845. But funding was inadequate, too much reliance being placed on the status of rear-admiral to attract captains to apply for retirement in the higher rank.[180] Another scheme containing 'higher bidding'—the offer of higher rates of pension—was approved by the Board of Admiralty and recommended to Peel in January 1846. It began a succession of periodic removals to a 'reserve half-pay' which significantly reduced the active list in 1847, 1851 and 1864.[181]

Cockburn took little part in creating this pension scheme. He concentrated on ensuring that the younger able men needed at sea received the experience that was essential to their proficiency. In 1840 the system of promotion was described as one of selection up to the rank of captain, and advancement after that by seniority, the qualification for receipt of a higher rank being service at sea in command of a rated ship.[182] Since 1830 the Admiralty had restricted promotions of lieutenants, commanders and captains to one in every three vacancies arising from death or removal from the rank above. Three officers were promoted annually for service in the coastguard, while sometimes an action or duty deserved immediate reward.[183] A commander-in-chief on a foreign station could fill death vacancies, while a home port commander-in-chief and an admiral striking his flag could nominate a lieutenant or midshipman. Otherwise officers were selected for promotion by the Board of Admiralty.[184]

Such a tight restriction on promotion limited the number of rising officers in 1838 to 35 commanders, 50 lieutenants, and 60 passed midshipmen with experience as mates.[185] Naturally enough, names and numbers were studied jealously. In 1845, a principal criticism was that 'the Admiralty was placed too high to hear the real merits of naval officers'. It was an ignorance Cockburn denied. 'He had always found that officers gave their opinions of those who had served with them with sincerity and fairness.' With such information, 'the utmost attention was paid . . . to the claims of persons, whether for length of service, or for service afloat'. In 1842 he even declared his belief that he could give a satisfactory reason for every promotion that took place.[186]

Nevertheless, it was still maintained that officers were selected more for their political connections than for their professional qualities.[187] It was undeniable that connection, aristocratic or naval, was still of value to those seeking appointments.[188] Indeed it was considered necessary to have 'men of high rank and influence' in senior positions in the navy.[189] In 1842 a scheme was seriously proposed for the purchase of promotion by mates, lieutenants and commanders in order 'to tax the sons of those men of high rank and influence who must and will be promoted over the heads of hundreds'.[190] Cockburn supported the idea. He claimed he had raised it before both the Lord High Admiral in 1828 and the commission on naval and military promotion in 1838. However, the idea was not well received.[191] On the contrary, parliamentarians pressed the Admiralty to ensure merit took primary place in its considerations.

In consequence, there were regular preparations behind the scenes for defending appointments that had been made. In July 1844, for example, Cockburn prepared to defend the promotion of the son of Sir George Seymour, his principal antagonist at the Admiralty. Haddington notified Peel that Hume (who intended to make an issue of the case) was 'supposed to blame that promotion because Seymour is a young officer'.

> Cockburn and Herbert [First Secretary at the Admiralty] will be there to explain and defend the conduct of the Board. . . . What I want to show is that it is absolutely impossible for him to lay a parliamentary ground for the papers he means to move for. No regulation has been violated. The young man has served double the time required for a commander and nearly double of the time for a lieutenant. He cannot say that an unserviceable or bad appointment has been made for a most promising and active man has been promoted, as will be shown. There is and can be no allegation of corrupt influence. For these reasons I say that he cannot make a parliamentary case for a vote of implied censure, which granting his papers would amount to. . . . For the rest and for the practice of the Board on many such occasions I refer you to Cockburn.[192]

Another defence had to be mounted in May 1845 when Sir Charles Napier was not selected for command of an experimental squadron because he had 'taken so decided a part against the ships of Sir William Symonds'. He had 'proved himself to be a decided partisan', but 'there was no allusion as to any "party" except that as to shipbuilding'.[193]

Cockburn never appeared comfortable discussing promotions in the House of Commons. He knew that political influence was inevitable in some appointments and promotions. The navy was, after all, a royal service in which reasons of state had their place.[194] But, as first naval lord, Cockburn had to continue to ensure that sea officers and dockyard posts were filled with men of the appropriate qualifications. So far as surviving records show, he was never himself expected to subordinate professional priorities to political purposes.[195] As before 1830, the First Lord made appointments and ordered dismissals, while Cockburn provided advice on the ranks, seniority, and persons appropriate to the posts available.[196] Professional considerations accordingly dominated his thoughts; so much so indeed that, when asked for nominations to posts, he did not hesitate to consider officers of doubtful political connections,[197] or, in the case of officers of professional distinction, to ignore their politics altogether.[198]

This diffidence on the politics of professional officers reflected a view that politics should not ideally affect the selection of officers for appointments. He held to the simple principle that advancement to a higher rank should be dependent upon a period of sea service in the preceding rank. Consequently one of the first changes Cockburn tried to achieve on entering office was to have the three annual promotions of lieutenants for service in the coastguard—introduced by the Whigs in 1833—made dependent upon their serving afloat for the equivalent of two years in the navy. He objected to officers 'being employed as inferior custom house officers, somewhat on a par with Tidewaiters of the Customs' (posts often given to gentlemen's servants), and condemned the Whig innovation as 'most mischievous'. For 'all the various details of conducting and managing ships and fleets . . . were wholly lost to individuals passing their time in walking up and down along the shore watching for smugglers'. Moreover, it had entailed 'the transfer of awarding the highest rewards of the profession (namely promotion) from the miliary government of the Admiralty and the highest naval officers, to an assemblage of civilians such as the Board of Customs', thereby opening 'a door to innovations which have been taken advantage of for mere political objects to the manifest injury of the service'. Accordingly, in 1841, he agreed only 'with a bad grace' to continue promotions for coastguard service after Haddington altered his intentions for them.[199]

What informal influence Cockburn wielded was through existing relationships with family or friends. The most important of these natural connections was with Peel. Peel's son William embarked on a naval career in 1841, and for the first five years Cockburn kept an avuncular eye on him. He had William appointed as a midshipman for a trial voyage to Canada and back; advised on his spending money; cast an eye over his letters to Peel; advised the appropriate next step in his career; commended his achievements at gunnery school; urged him promoted to lieutenant; and saw him placed in his first command in a steamer. So interested did Cockburn become that in 1849, on William Peel's promotion to captain, he was still providing advice on the choice between the captaincy of a flagship or that of a small frigate.[200] This relationship with Peel was highly personal. Peel rarely asked Cockburn to do anything for other people, and then not necessarily for political advantage. However, in return, equally occasionally, Cockburn was able to pass to Peel requests received for appointments in the gift of the First Lord of the Treasury, and to use his influence on behalf of members of the Cockburn clan.[201]

This relationship with Peel was replicated with other principal members of government departments, although with them appeals on behalf of clansmen were less common. Significantly, there were few appeals for assistance to friends with commands in the navy. Moreover, of these, requests with an unambivalent political purpose were exceptional, and all were for assistance towards a career in which an Admiralty appointment had already been made.[202]

In concentrating on the training of the relatively small proportion of officers who were promoted, Cockburn continued to favour not only those qualities that made them compatible within the wardroom and attentive to their men, but those that permitted them to represent and defend the interests of their country. Hence, for example, he condemned the performance of Commander Gordon of the *Cormorant* in dealing with the French at the time of the Tahiti incident: 'nothing could have been more weak and unsatisfactory than his whole correspondence and conduct'. He failed in evincing 'the spirit required for maintaining his independence and the respect due to our national colours'.[203]

Because he concentrated on the training of this small proportion of officers, Cockburn was necessarily elitist. Briggs suggested he was also prejudiced against the sooty appearance of the steamship captain. This was probably so. He believed officers should be proud of their appearance. Moreover, the officer profession was becoming specialized, and it was impractical to have officers responsible for sailing warships whose previous experience had been confined to steamships. In his time, the steamship captain could not have the career path, nor yet the ultimate fleet responsibility, of the sailing warship captain. Neither did steamship engineers yet have the status of quarterdeck officers. The most senior engineers were not appointed by Admiralty commission until 1847; but the master, surgeon, purser and chaplain were all admitted to the officers' wardroom and appointed by Admiralty commission from 1843.[204] Admittance to this privilege in their case was not so much on account of a lack of prejudice as a wish to enlarge Board of Admiralty control over those appointments. For control was above all what the first naval lord wanted.

Ideas for Improving the Admiralty

Cockburn's experience at the Admiralty led him to abhor the subjection of the officers corps to civilian politicians. In his view their emancipation from this control could only be achieved through further reorganization at the Admiralty. He set out his recommendations for this reorganization after his departure from office. Following his death, these proposals were found under his will in a secret drawer and published in *The Times* in February 1855.[205] At that time, the Crimean War was raising questions about the efficiency of administration in the army as well as the navy, and the proposals were prefaced by a note from James Scott who claimed, from recollections of conversations with Cockburn, that his ideas embraced both services. Later in 1855, Cockburn's opinions were published in a pamphlet,[206] and in 1861 were considered by witnesses called before a House of Commons Select Committee on the constitution of the Board of Admiralty.[207]

The principal aim of his proposals was to remove 'the pernicious effects of political influence' on appointments within the navy. He believed the navy as well as the army[208] should be led by a professional officer as commander-in-chief who, as a professional man, would be 'alone competent to form an independent and impartial opinion of professional merit'. The heads of neither service would be in the Cabinet, as hitherto, but be equally subject to a Minister of War, to whom they would act as counsellors. Instead of a Board of Admiralty, the commander-in-chief of the navy would have two admirals to assist him, with whom he would sit in council. The executive of the operational navy would thus be entirely composed of professional men; moreover it would be an executive independent, so far as this was possible, of parliamentary politics.

> The naval Commander-in-Chief and his two councillors may or may not be in Parliament, as deemed best by the Government; but I am of opinion they (especially the former) should not be in Parliament, to render it unnecessary to change the governing system of our navy with every change of Ministers, which keeps the naval service in a constant state of unsteadiness and uncertainty, very detrimental to its complete and unvarying efficiency—an evil which would be remedied by the commander-in-chief and his colleagues being relieved from all political character.

He provided for the management of finance and accountancy, at the same time separating it from the management of operational business, by recommending the appointment of a civilian Controller of Naval Expenditure subject to the parliamentary process. He would 'be in constant and cordial co-operation' with the commander-in-chief, arrange with him the proposed expenditure for each year, to be approved by the Treasury, and submit the yearly estimates to the House of Commons, where he would answer all questions relating to naval finance. While responsible for proper procedure, the Controller would not possess authority for expenditure. This would remain with the commander-in-chief 'whose directions relative to the number of ships to be built or repaired or fitted for service' would be deemed sufficient to provide for payment.

Having separated the accountant and parliamentary business of the navy as far as possible from that of the commander-in-chief and his counsellors, Cockburn believed these last three officers would 'be more at liberty to give full attention to the more professional objects of maintaining and improving the efficiency' of the fleet and dockyards. Conscious of the work involved in supervising the latter, he recommended 'the appointment of a flag officer under the Admiralty to be continually visiting the yards in succession to insure uniformity of practice and working in all'. Yet this officer would not be responsible for the design of ships. Recalling the controversies that had arisen from the appointment of a Surveyor of the Navy ('whether himself a shipbuilder or not') and over the qualities of the ships that that officer produced, Cockburn proposed the continuation of the 'scientific board of construction, as lately established, to advise and offer suggestions on all points relating to shipbuilding'.

Assistance and guidance would thus be available to the commander-in-chief and his counsellors, but the former would retain control of decision-making in all areas affecting the operational performance of the navy. He could delegate as necessary to his two counsellors, they to sign 'conjointly, such documents as he may not deem necessary to be signed by himself'; yet such delegation would be only on his authority, and it was 'to be clearly understood' that he alone would be responsible for whatever was done under his authority.

Even as he drafted his proposals, Cockburn was aware of the objections that would be raised against having a naval officer at the head of the naval service. He would be suspected of showing partiality to those officers who had served with him and whose abilities he knew. But he believed a naval officer 'would evince as much real impartiality as any other individual of any other class or rank'. He pointed out that such partiality had never been found 'a sufficient objection' to the existence of a commander-in-chief of the army; and, even should 'such favourable feelings towards any particular officers . . . be entertained by a commander-in-chief', they would mainly tend to the benefit of the navy, for junior officers would be encouraged to secure the good opinion of their superiors. Secondly, he knew that a naval officer would be regarded as unsuited from 'his earlier habits and education' for the non-naval matters that came before the Cabinet. But, emphasizing that a commander-in-chief need not be in the Cabinet, he claimed that 'very many superior naval officers would prove as efficient Cabinet Minsters as many of those gentlemen' he had known in the Cabinet.

In 1855 these opinions inevitably fuelled public debate.[209] That year an internal Admiralty committee investigated the problems of the office of Admiralty Secretary, but did not alter its organization. Likewise, the Board commissioners remained overloaded, and in 1861 a Select Committee of the House of Commons investigated their operations.[210] But by then Cockburn's ideas were considered irrelevant, for after the Crimean War the office of commander-in-chief of the army itself was abolished, and thus 'condemned as not the best model'. The Duke of Somerset, at that time First Lord, was also able to claim that the foundation for Cockburn's reasoning, 'the political character of the Board', had by then passed away as not one of its four naval members sat in the House of Commons. Sir George Seymour, his old antagonist, effectively buried Cockburn's proposals, refusing to see anything in them besides his former superior's ego: they 'meant that a man like himself was to be supreme' with two others who were to have a 'sort of nominal responsibility. . . . The plan means Sir George Cockburn and means nothing else'.[211]

An 'Irksome and Difficult Station'

Seymour's intolerance of Cockburn's ideas was based on less than three years Admiralty experience twenty years earlier—a time for Cockburn of perhaps the greatest difficulty and stress in his whole career. In 1842 he turned 70 years of age and his health began to fail; in that same year his wife, never strong, became seriously ill.[212] A holiday in September seemed to put both to rights, but subsequently in January 1843 Cockburn himself suffered what was described as the 'rupture of a blood vessel in the lungs'. Prince Albert was advised for the information of the Queen.[213] Attended by Dr Alexander Nisbet, a naval surgeon at the Royal Hospital, Greenwich, he was apparently restored to health by March 1843. Cockburn himself acknowledged the illness had been dangerous, and for some months even his private correspondence was suspended. That summer a Continental holiday was deemed necessary and in the winter of 1843–44 he was advised to avoid attendance at the House of Commons whenever possible, advice he followed until after Easter. Early in 1844 he felt uncommonly well, but by mid-1845 he was keenly looking forward to the end of the parliamentary session, 'my work in the office all day and in the House of Commons all night being almost too much for anybody'.[214]

Within London's naval circle, the difficulties Cockburn laboured under were soon common knowledge. In the House of Commons in May 1845, during a debate on naval supplies, the opposition raised the subject in an attack on the constitution of the Board of Admiralty. No natural political friend, Sir Charles Napier took up Cockburn's situation. Criticizing the lack of real responsibility of Admiralty lords for operations within their respective branches, Napier condemned the system of having a civilian at the head of the Board, and the amount of work with which the first sea lord was burdened. 'It was impossible for the right honourable and gallant Admiral at the head of the Board of Admiralty to perform all the duties that were imposed upon him. He had more duties to attend to than mortal man could get through, and the consequence was that the work was badly done'.[215]

The situation in which Cockburn found himself not only damaged his health and his reputation as a man of business, but also his confidence and capacity for managing public affairs. Peel still had faith in him, and in 1844 requested permission to have Cockburn's portrait painted to place in his new gallery at Drayton where he was forming 'a collection of portraits of the most distinguished public men with whom' it had been his 'good fortune to be connected'.[216] Yet by mid-1845 both Haddington and Peel recognized that the strain sustained by Cockburn had produced in him a morbid sensitivity on some professional matters; for example, on the subject of the retirement of naval officers generally. Peel feared his own expressions, written in haste, 'might give pain to Cockburn or others'; 'professional men are so touchy on professional points' that he and Haddington needed 'to exercise a due degree of caution'.[217] Thereafter, both co-operated closely in handling certain issues, an effort sustained by their affection for their elderly colleague. Thus, in December 1845, Haddington warned Peel: 'If you write to Cockburn again do not begin your letter "My dear Sir George *Cockburn*"; omit the family name or the "Sir George"!! He is a little hurt at the apparent formality. I laughed at him and treated it as pure accident. I think it as well to tell you tho', trifle tho' it is.'[218]

Surprisingly easy for Peel and Haddington to handle was the Cabinet reshuffle early in 1846. To strengthen his government in the House of Lords, Peel recruited Lord Ellenborough but was obliged to offer him office at the head of the Admiralty, from where Haddington was happy to remove to become Lord Privy Seal.[219] To facilitate the transfer Peel requested Cockburn stay on as first naval lord to serve Ellenborough as he had done Haddington. Yet Cockburn was hurt at not being offered the post of First Lord himself:

> after having filled my present irksome and difficult station at the Admiralty seventeen years and being now nearly at the head of the list of officers of the navy, it is painful to me to add that I do not consider that attention has been shewn to me which I think I had reason to look for on this occasion.

The option of appointing Cockburn had not escaped Peel, but, as he later told Ellenborough, he preferred 'a civilian to a professional man for the office of First Lord'. At the same time he believed the labour would have been too severe for Cockburn considering his 'advanced age and infirm health'.[220] Piqued, Cockburn was unwilling to be included at all in the next Admiralty patent, although he declared a readiness to stay on for a while should difficulty arise in filling his place. Peel readily seized the offer. He was, he claimed, forced into the arrangement by the necessities of the public service 'and a sense of my duty to the Queen, under the circumstances H.M. required me to resume office'. Cockburn was grateful for the 'obliging tenor' of Peel's letter which 'tended greatly to tranquillize' his feelings.[221]

Underlying Cockburn's willingness to have his feelings smoothed lay the knowledge that his own resignation would have left Peel in difficulties. He and Haddington had 'gone over the whole flag list' and found only two men—Sir Byam Martin and Sir Bladen Capel—to whom 'the post of first naval lord could be offered, if health and political considerations combined to recommend them'.[222] Such a shortage of suitable candidates—a product of that accumulation of non-retirable admirals blocking the promotion of more youthful men from the captains' list—made the offer to stay on almost obligatory to a man with a strong sense of service. But it could not be for long. For, as Haddington observed to Peel, Cockburn was 'drawing many nails into his coffin'. It would be well 'if he stays to force the dockyard[s] from him and have the usual business of his position only—but it would be like taking a bone from a hungry mastiff. Besides to whom could they be given?'[223]

Initially unaware of such concerns, Ellenborough eased his way into Cockburn's affections.[224] An able parliamentary speaker, and an enthusiast for efficiency, there was much in the new First Lord that Cockburn could respect. They shared an interest in gaining more youthful men on the flag list, in effective dockyard appointments, and in the improvement of health on board ships in the tropics. Moreover, Ellenborough ran foul of Corry and Herbert, adversaries of Cockburn at the Board, a circumstance certain to have brought the first naval lord to his assistance. But Peel and the Cabinet rejected the First Lord's impatient demands for higher naval expenditure and he left office in July 1846 a disappointed man.[225]

With the complete change of government, Cockburn too resigned in July 1846. He feared the mischief a minority Whig government supported by 'repealers and radicals' would do 'to the true interests of the nation'. But for himself he could only celebrate. As he explained to Sir Thomas Cochrane, the labour of office, 'the constant drudgery of it, and the very little relaxation it is possible to take from it, made it a great sacrifice of all other social enjoyments'. He thus returned to his house at High Beech, Essex, 'like a boy leaving school for the holidays'.[226]

Conclusion

After his departure from the Board of Admiralty, Cockburn soon became noticeably frail. He suffered a mild stroke affecting his left arm about Christmas 1848, and was affected severely by rheumatism. He died in August 1853 at Leamington Spa. Characteristically, only a few days before, he declined to attend the 'grand naval review' at Spithead on account of the health of his wife.

In these seven years of retirement, Cockburn retained his previous confidence in the capabilities of the British navy. In September 1850 he observed to Sir Thomas Cochrane, who had been to view the improvements to the French naval arsenal at Cherbourg, how much more efficient the French navy then appeared in contrast to their recollections of it forty years earlier. But he was not surprised to hear that Cochrane had seen nothing to cause either of them

> in any degree to doubt our sea girt and commercial country continuing to maintain our natural *naval* superiority over our continental neighbours, whose habits and feelings are drawn more particularly to land operations and views, and which tend to make me very confidently believe they never can be able to wrest from us the empire of the seas, whatever efforts they may make at improvements in aggressive means.[1]

Cockburn became Admiral of the Fleet in 1851 and was still consulted on various matters: for example, in 1852 by the parliamentary committee on manning the navy. But out of office he was not one to foist his views on government; and the absence of an Admiralty lord such as Cockburn, with his supreme confidence in the British navy and his influence with politicians, was soon felt. His immediate successors at the Admiralty were inexperienced Whig desk admirals, political lightweights who were no match for Palmerston at the Foreign Office nor for Wellington as commander-in-chief of the army.[2] Their fears of invasion on the back of a French steam fleet consequently held the centre ground, resulting in vast investment in shore defences against invasion.

These great shore defences were, however, more than just a product of the power of personalities. The fortifications around dockyards and the harbours of refuge symbolized a new era in military defence planning. The government under Russell, who succeeded Peel, was dominated by the question of land defence in all its forms. Partly because the process by which defence was planned was dominated by men partial to the army, and partly because the navy was inadequately represented—and with the reputation of being in decline—it was regarded as unable to meet the demands placed upon it.[3] This, combined with the passing of the Conservative government, made the year 1846 more than just the end of a period of economic thought and of a particular political grouping: it represented the end of a military era in which the navy had held its own in planning against the land forces. The resignation of Cockburn from the Admiralty consequently coincided with what was probably the nadir in the reputation of the navy in the nineteenth century.

One contribution which Cockburn was able to make to this new era was in the appointment, late in 1847, of Captain Alexander Milne as a naval lord at the Board of Admiralty. He became one of the most able naval administrators of the nineteenth century and was to remain at the Board until 1858. Cockburn recognized his ability, provided him with advice, and favoured his continuity at the Board through succeeding Whig and Tory administrations 'to afford information of passing events to newcomers'.[4] He eventually outstayed four changes of ministry and returned to the Board again in 1866–8 and 1872–6; his continuity, like that provided by Cockburn under Tory ministries, provided the means by which administrative practice was perpetuated.

Needless to say, however, naval officers were no more trusted as political administrators after 1846 than they were before. Consequently they continued to be excluded from the highest level of naval management, the office of First Lord. The prejudice against them inevitably affected anyone who supported Cockburn's ideas for improving the Admiralty by excluding political influence. When the Admiralty was eventually reorganized in 1869 by the ruthless politician Hugh Childers, less than a month after his appointment, the scheme adopted bore some resemblance to that drafted by Cockburn. The Board was abolished and the First Lord became a central directing authority over commissioners who acted as executive heads of separate departments. However, with a politician at its head, this new arrangement did even less than the old one to relieve the naval lords of their workloads or to co-ordinate the subordinate departments. Yet with the increasing pace of technological change, good communication and co-ordination were even more necessary. After stark evidence of a calamitous failure in the decision-making process—the capsize of the newly launched *Captain*—the previous system of Board management was reintroduced with little change.[5]

That civilian politicians continued to fear appointing a naval officer to the highest position of management in the navy was also partly a legacy of the influence wielded by Cockburn. He contributed to a long-held belief, traced back to the administrations of Lord St Vincent and Howe, that naval officers did not make good politicians and were not therefore desirable as First Lords of the Admiralty. Paradoxically, this fear was a product of the refusal of naval First Lords to compromise the standards of the navy by appointments and practice of political expediency, a stand which was indispensable to the preservation of the navy as an efficient fighting force, as well as to its confidence and morale.

That Cockburn maintained this morale, at the price of his reputation as a politician, was a tribute to his professional dedication. His contribution to confidence in the navy did not die with him, living on through the officers who imbibed his views. Sir Thomas Cochrane, the son of Cockburn's commander-in-chief in 1814–15, was to survive until 1872. His contemporaries Sir James Scott and Sir Watkin Pell, subordinates and supporters of Cockburn, also lived into the mid-Victorian era. There were many others. Through such men, the sentiments expressed by Cockburn survived to influence naval historians like Mahan at the end of the century.

Cockburn's influence was also felt through the administrative and technological changes to which he contributed—changes which remained in the navy's evolutionary fabric. His record in the area of ship technology was remarkable in view of his later reputation as a conservative reactionary. His period of control of the navy's physical development between 1841 and 1846 was noteworthy for the great growth in the number and size of steam warships. Most of these were propelled by paddle. But Cockburn's great achievement was to oversee experimentation with screw propulsion to the point at which it was sufficiently developed to be adopted in the navy. In this respect Cockburn made a direct contribution to the shape of the future warship.

His achievement was the greater as he was not assisted by confrontations he suffered at the Board of Admiralty or by the necessity he felt to circumvent the strong influence of Sir William Symonds, Surveyor of the Navy, in ship design. That in this respect he achieved his end was not just a personal triumph, although clearly his relationship with Symonds was never a happy one. He seems to have been aware that development in steam and sail could no longer rely on the opinions of a limited number of men in privileged positions: the navy had to be opened to the thinking of the whole seafaring community. That he was open to these ideas was evinced by the retention of Brunel as an adviser to the introduction of the screw propeller, and by his introduction of committees to consider proposals and make recommendations on technological subjects relating to ship design. These were in part a political device to reduce Symonds' influence, but they culminated in the 1846 Committee of Reference which attempted to blend judgements drawn from traditional practice with those based on science. His own trial of iron ships ran into disrepute, but that was the sort of risk he was prepared to take. He was aware of his own deficiencies, especially in the new fields of naval science, and accordingly employed advisers like John Hoseason. That the latter became a confidant is suggested by Hoseason's entry into the Cockburn household and marriage to his daughter in 1856.

The breadth of Cockburn's thinking, encompassing the merchant as well as the naval community, was demonstrated by his tolerance of the nature of seafarers' lives. Even in 1852 he was averse to any limited plan of recruitment that precluded the opportunity (to be taken if necessary) of resorting of impressment.[6] But at the same time he was aware of inclinations that encouraged seamen to desert and rejoin the navy, and of the need to care for their interests while within the service. The characteristic feature of his attitude was the deep vein of tolerance, care and service to seamen that ran like a thread through his career: during his experience while commander-in-chief on the North American station in 1833–6, and back to the management of his crews in the 1790s. Thus, though an advocate of the maintenance of corporal punishment, he recognized its limitations and discouraged its use, preferring to indulge, rather than repress, natural desires in seamen for pleasures such as shore leave.

Such thinking can be traced back to his experience on board his own ship *La Minerve* during the Revolutionary War against France. At that time, shore leave, patronage and paternalizm seem to have minimised impulses to mutiny and the necessity for punishment: indeed floggings ceased to be recorded in periods of frequent shore leave at foreign ports.

Cockburn was then able to rely on his crew as his greatest human resource, a view of seamen in the Revolutionary War that goes against the received opinion of them as the navy's Achilles' heel, given to mutiny and desertion. It hints at the strong necessity for a study of their behaviour that avoids focusing on the political dissenters and mutineers among them.

During the Revolutionary War Cockburn's ability was recognized by Hood, Nelson and St Vincent. Their appreciation of him is not only a tribute to their discernment, but a tribute to patronage as a system for selecting officers for advancement. Of course the system worked as much to the advantage of superiors as subordinates, as acknowledged in the debts of honour repaid by Nelson. In a society that valued conduct guided by honour, the reciprocity of human relations provided an underlying social harmony, not to be confused with the obligatory services performed according to a hierarchy of command. Debts of honour were thus incurred with subordinates as well as superiors; that Cockburn was able to maintain good relations with both was as much a measure of his quality as a man, as of his ability as an officer.

This knowledge of the social basis of the navy was carried with him into the mid-nineteenth century, when society was rapidly changing. The opportunities for the most able to be raised as Cockburn was (almost by serendipity) no longer provided sufficient men of outstanding abilities. Population growth and the increasing reinforcement of class divisions also increased the number of aspirants demanding to be noticed, even though they lacked connections. At the same time, centralization of patronage enabled the introduction of publicly accountable procedures for the selection of men for appointments which, with technological change, were in any case becoming increasingly specialized. Under these changing conditions, Cockburn represented an awareness both of the human qualities that had to be observed, and of the managerial mechanics by which the navy was administered.

The social balance and logical coherence of his views gave him strength as an administrator. His understanding of the mechanics of self-interest lay at the foundation of his contribution to the beginnings of examination and registration of the mates and masters of merchant ships. Equally, that understanding informed his defence of the interests of the navy in the House of Commons, and of the Admiralty against the Foreign Office. His grasp of legal technicalities placed him in the front line of constitutional debates—a position that was not always a comfortable one, as in his confrontation with the Lord High Admiral.

But his pride and temper reinforced his intellectual knowledge. His refusal to surrender his integrity gave him the reputation of an ungovernable man. Yet he was precisely what the Admiralty needed during difficult and demanding episodes in its history.

During his 17 years at the Admiralty, Cockburn was in a sense a martyr to the politics of the period. Although he entered wholeheartedly into parliamentary affairs, his first allegiance was always to the navy. Under pressure, subject to abuse or allegation of party prejudice, he always maintained that the Admiralty should pursue its 'straight course', especially with regard to court martial proceedings. By pursuing this course, he meant of course that the procedures of the navy should be maintained, whatever the pressures that were brought to bear on administrators. In resisting these pressures, like many officer-administrators before him, he preserved the internal discipline of the navy. His role in this capacity was not a visible one. But in drafting the General Printed Instructions and acting in many respects as the navy's legal adviser, he ensured not only that the Admiralty emerged from periods of Tory administration with a relatively clean reputation, but that officers were given clear guidance as to the spirit and conduct demanded of them.

Cockburn's contribution to the development of the officer corps was the least tangible, but perhaps the most important of his contributions to the post-war navy, for his clear duty was to maintain the practical skills of an élite group in the officer corps while neglecting that of the majority. Unemployment, however, generated resentment and allegations of political patronage. Politics could not be excluded entirely; but Cockburn believed they should be and, by his own example, did much to foster an ethic of non-political service to the Crown.

The politics of the post-war period have had a tendency to obscure Cockburn's role in the wars against France and against the United States. The controversy surrounding his regime in the Chesapeake and his role in the attack on Washington naturally reflected the attitudes of writers and officers of different party or service allegiance. However, there can be no doubting his successful persuasion of people in the middle-eastern seaboard of the United States of the ill wisdom of pursuing war against Britain. His achievement in interning Napoleon on St Helena demands equal recognition. His control of the former emperor goes virtually unacknowledged in accounts of Napoleon's career; but Cockburn, like Wellington, was one opponent who was not intimidated by that personality. Moreover, unlike Hudson Lowe, he managed to maintain uneasy relations with Napoleon to the very end of his term as Governor of St Helena. His confidence at that time came, of course, from earlier experience. There were few other naval officers who were so consistently employed on diplomatic duties throughout the Napoleonic War. His appreciation of the political problems underlying Spain's relations with her colonies, his employment both at Flushing and in Martinique to negotiate the surrenders of French garrisons, and his appointment to carry to India the payments of compensation made by the United States to War of Independence loyalists, all underline the respect others had for his intellectual and military qualities.

The confidence so accrued, and his willingness to argue his views, did not endear him to administrative opponents, while unquestionably his arrogant manner offended them. But those who maligned him on personal grounds seem to have had their own motives for doing so. Briggs' later depiction of Cockburn as a conservative reactionary is misleading in the extreme. Cockburn undoubtedly tended to overstate his case, almost as a provocation and challenge to antagonists, yet he remained abreast of the changes which society and the navy were undergoing—often more so than others who had seen less service, who were less well acquainted with the resources of the navy, and who were less experienced in how those resources might be employed. Few were as perceptive as Cockburn. His great strength lay in his combination of this experience and perception. In addition he possessed a sense of duty which never failed the Crown. His importance lies in his willingness to serve under changing conditions, his ability to defend what was of value from the past, and his capacity for considering and integrating what was useful from the new.

Cockburn's contribution to the administration of the British navy probably did more to help it through the difficulties of the peacetime years between the Napoleonic and Crimean Wars than that of any other single officer. His contemporaries—Peel, Wellington, Melville, Croker, even the Whig Graham—appreciated this contribution and Cockburn's outstanding competence. In 1828 George IV described him to his brother, the future William IV, as 'the most useful and perhaps the most important naval officer in my service'. It was a tribute that was applicable over a great length of Cockburn's service, and should be better known.

Notes

Abbreviations used in the Notes

BL	British Library
EHR	*English Historical Review*
GC	George Cockburn
HMC	Historical Manuscripts Commission
IOLR	India Office Library and Records
LC	Library of Congress, Washington, District of Columbia
LG	*The London Gazette*
MM	*The Mariner's Mirror*
NLS	National Library of Scotland
NMM	National Maritime Museum
NRS	Navy Records Society
PP	British Parliamentary Papers
PRO	Public Record Office
RA	Royal Archives
SRO	Scottish Record Office
SUL	Southampton University Library
WLC	William L. Clements Library, University of Michigan
WRP	William R. Perkins Library, Duke University, North Carolina

Introduction

1. Bartlett, 7.
2. J. Pack, *The Man who Burned the White House* (Havant, 1987).
3. 'Memoir of Services', NMM, COC/11.
4. [Evans, De Lacy], 5–6.
5. Van der Voort, 68–70; G.C. to James Scott, 23 Dec 1837, NMM, MRF/D/8.
6. Van der Voort, 87–9.
7. G.C. to A. Milne, 19 Feb 1852, NMM, MLN/165/2.
8. Briggs, 6–15.
9. Penn, 22.
10. Brown, *Before the Ironclad* (1990); Lambert, *Battleships in Transition* (1984); Lambert, *Last Sailing Battlefleet* (1991).
11. See for example, Hamilton, *Anglo-French Naval Rivalry*, 47.
12. Buckingham and Chandos, *Memoirs*, II, 43.
13. G.C. to M. Shawe, 2 Mar 1810, BL Add MSS, 37, 291, f 230.

14. Both Shawe and Croker earned affection by sending Cockburn newspapers, a luxury on a foreign station. In Croker's case they were in French, and were passed on to the St Helena captives by Cockburn. Croker to G.C., 25 Jan 1816, WLC Croker papers.
15. Only semi-official personal papers survive in the Library of Congress and National Maritime Museum.
16. *Naval Chronicle* (1812), XXVII, 264; C. Shorter, 116.
17. A. Cockburn to J.W.C. Croker, 10 Oct 1853, NMM CKE/7.
18. Briggs, 11, 13.
19. Attributed to Lord Chesterfield (1694–1773).
20. Cockburn-Hood, 62–3.
21. 'A narrative of Sir James Cockburn, Bart., Services in Germany', memorial of 1782, Wentworth Woodhouse Muniments, Sheffield City Library, R108-137-1.
22. Namier and Brooke, II, 229.
23. ibid, 103–6.
24. J.G. Parker, 59; Sutherland, 228, 245.
25. Namier and Brooke, II, 230; Almon, *Parliamentary Register*, 1777, VII, 212–13.
26. Fortescue, V, 469.
27. Aspinall, *Later Correspondence of George III*, V, 232–3.
28. Thorne, III, 468.
29. Warren, 85–7, 146–7, 151. Thanks are due to Mrs Gillian Hughes for this information.
30. PRO, ADM 36/9536; /10212; /10988.
31. Log of the *Termagant*, PRO, ADM, 51/976, parts 4 and 5.
32. Log of the *Ariel* kept by G.C., LC Cockburn papers, container 1.
33. Lewis *Social History*, 160; Rodger, *Wooden World*, 298. For the sort of questions asked in these oral examinations before a committee of the Navy Board, see NMM, MID/9/3, 7 Jan 1789.
34. For his journals for the *Hebe* and *Romney*, see LC Cockburn papers, cont 1.
35. Lewis, *Navy in Transition*, 22.
36. Fremantle, II, 121, 144, 164–5.
37. See his bank account records: Coutts Customer Ledger No 6 in particular.
38. Archdeacon William Paley, *Principles of Moral and Political Philosophy*, quoted in Clark, 147.
39. Lewis, *Navy in Transition*, 47.

Chapter 1: The Georgian Navy in the French Revolutionary War, 1793–1801

1. Morriss, *Royal Dockyards*, 14.
2. Log of HMS *Britannia*, kept by G.C., 28 Apr–8 May 1793, LC Cockburn papers, cont 1.

The Mediterranean theatre
3. Log of HMS *Britannia*, LC Cockburn papers, cont 1.
4. Rose, *Lord Hood and the defence of Toulon*, 11.
5. Log of HMS *Britannia*, 8 July 1793.
6. Rose, 19–23.
7. Log of HMS *Victory*, PRO, ADM. 51/1028, parts 5, 6.

8. Rose, 24.
9. Napoleon was directing part of this bombardment. Cronin, 85.
10. Log of HMS *Meleager*, NMM, ADM/L/M/145, 6–13 June 1794; James, *Naval History of Great Britain* (1847), I, 215.
11. NMM, ADM/L/M/145, 9–14 Mar 1795, 6–14 July 1795.
12. Mackesy, *War in the Mediterranean*, 13.
13. Morriss, in *Français at Anglais*, 171–180.
14. NMM, ADM/L/M/145, 31 July–5 Nov 1794.
15. ibid., June 1794.
16. Oman, 153–54.
17. Nicolas, *Dispatches and Letters of . . . Nelson*, II, 155, 176; VII, p.lxxvii; *London Gazette*, 1796, 614; NMM, ADM/L/M/145, May 1796.
18. Nicolas, II, 182.
19. ibid., II, 270, 283, 285; Nelson to G.C., 4 Oct 1796; Jervis to G.C., 21 Oct 1796 (2 letters); G.C. to Jervis, 24 Oct 1796, LC Cockburn papers, cont. 9, 13.

Trade suppression
20. Nelson to his wife, July 1795, in Nicolas, II, 59.
21. Lieutenant's log of the *Inconstant*, NMM, ADM/L/J/57; and *Meleager*, NMM, ADM/L/M/145.
22. Sir Francis Drake to G.C., 25 September 1795, and G.C. to Captain Sawyer, 13 July 1796, LC Cockburn papers, cont. 13, 9.
23. Copy of Bomieter's letter to Sir Hyde Parker, 11 Feb 1794, in LC Cockburn papers, cont. 13.
24. NMM, ADM/L/M/145.
25. The following account of procedure is from two sets of instructions, 'Hints for examining ships at sea, West Indies 1797', NMM, Kittoe papers, MS87/005, and another set, *c*.1809, NMM, MS89/038.
26. G.C. to Messrs McArthur, Pollard and Udney at Leghorn, 8 Sep 1795, 14, 18 Jan 1796, LC Cockburn papers, cont. 9.
27. ibid., 11 Feb 1796; LC Cockburn papers, cont. 9.
28. Deposition of John Corado in G.C. to Nelson, 7 Aug 1795, LC Cockburn papers, cont. 9.; see also Nicolas, II, 58.
29. G.C. to Nelson, 7 Aug 1795, LC Cockburn papers, cont. 9.

Serving a superior: Nelson
30. Nelson to G.C., 15 May, 20 Oct 1796, LC Cockburn papers, cont. 13.
31. G.C. to E.P. Brenton, 6 Dec 1822. Brenton, Box 1, Beinecke Lib., Yale Univ.; see also Brenton, *Naval History of Great Britain*, II, 223; and Nelson to Jervis, 31 May, 2 June 1796, Nicholas II, 176; VII, p. lxxvii.
32. The name of this ship is hereafter given as *La Minerve* because contemporaries referred to her as such even after she was captured and brought into British service.
33. Nelson to Jervis, 30, 31 May, 3 June 1796, Nicolas, II, 175, 176–7, 180.
34. Nelson's account is in Nicolas, II, 312–3. For comparison of wording, see G.C.'s log of *La Minerve*, 20 Dec 1796, LC Cockburn papers, cont. 2.
35. Nicolas, II, 416.

36. Drinkwater-Bethune, 13–15.
37. Log of *La Minerve*, 12 Feb 1797.
38. Drinkwater-Bethune, 16–17.
39. Nelson to Jervis, 13 June 1797; Nicolas, VII, p. cxlii.
40. Nelson to Jervis, 10 July 1797; Nicolas, VII, p. cxlvi.
41. NMM, COC/11, f.56.
42. Nelson to G.C., 2 Oct 1796, LC Cockburn papers, cont. 13.
43. G.C. to Nelson, 1 June 1798, BL 34,907, f.3; Nicolas, V, 11, 13–15.
44. G.C. to Nelson, 19 Apr, 24 July 1797, BL 34,906, ff. 28,205.
45. G.C. to J. Croker, 11 Apr 1845, NMM. CKE/6.

Morality and discipline
46. Nicolas, II, 281, note 4; VII, p. cxiii. Sawyer was found guilty of 'sundry indecent familiarities with persons belonging to the said ship, and of not taking public notice of mutinous expressions uttered against him'. PRO, ADM.12/27E, 18 Oct 1796.
47. The whole correspondence is included as evidence with the minutes of the courts martial of Sawyer and those he accused. PRO, ADM, 1/5337. I am grateful to Dr John Dann of the William L. Clements Library for a copy of these minutes.
48. See also Rodger, *Wooden World*, 278.

The management of seamen
49. *Hansard*, 2nd series, XIII, 1825, cmn 1098.
50. In the *Ariel* in 1788, Cockburn had witnessed Thomas Smith being obliged to run the gauntlet for theft, a form of punishment abolished in 1806. The practice of 'starting' was also forbidden by Admiralty order in 1809. See G.C.'s log of the *Ariel*, 30 June 1788, LC Cockburn papers, cont. 1; also Kemp, 185–6.
51. Byrn, *Crime and Punishment in the Royal Navy*, 121–2, 184–5.
52. Muster books of *Meleager*, 1793–5, and *La Minerve*, 1797, PRO ADM. 36/13083, 13135.
53. Muster books of *La Minerve*, 1797 and 1801, PRO, ADM. 36/13135, 13816. For 13 months before April 1798 *La Minerve* carried at least one female, the wife of a marine. See Rowbotham, 44.
54. There were 102 entries and re-entries in *La Minerve*'s muster book over the summer of 1798, while the ship was at Portsmouth, and 118 between then and 1801. It was of course in the interests of seamen to volunteer if it became clear they would not escape impressment.
55. Numbers of punishments for different offences are derived from Cockburn's logs for *La Minerve*, LC Cockburn papers, cont. 2–3. In many cases punishments were awarded for two offences; for numerical purposes, the first-mentioned offence has been taken as the principal one and counted; the second one has not been counted.
56. These figures presume that drunkenness was punished as an offence against the whole shipboard community.
57. This balance was even more marked in *Meleager*. Of 90 punishments for which offences were recorded in lieutenants' logs for *Meleager*, 29 (32 per cent) were for

drunkenness; 19 (21 per cent) for fighting, quarrelling and theft; 33 (37 per cent) for neglect of duty and/or disobedience; 1 (1 per cent) for mutiny. NMM, ADM/L/M/145.

58. Byrn, 108, 114.

59. Byrn, 147.

60. It may be noted that the scale of punishment by flogging was not an issue with the Spithead mutineers, though petitions from the later Nore mutineers complained of the cruelty of some officers. Punishments of course also took other informal forms, such as running the gauntlet and 'starting', respectively forbidden in 1806 and 1809, which are not often mentioned in logs and therefore cannot be used as an index of the tenor of relationships.

61. Jervis to G.C., 22 May 1797, LC Cockburn papers, cont.13.

62. G.C. to Nelson, 24 July 1797, BL34,906, f.205.

63. The offences were punished with 36, 32 and 24 lashes respectively. G.C. log for *La Minerve*, LC Cockburn papers, cont.2.

64. G.C. to Sir P. Parker, 20 Sep 1798. LC Cockburn papers, cont.9.

65. G.C. followed events in Ireland closely while on leave in 1798, writing to Nelson on 1 June 'The news from Ireland today is something better but in general I think there reigns a complete chaos of confusion'. BL 34,907, f.3–5.

66. Gradish, *Manning of the British Navy*, 144; Rodger, *Wooden World*, 82–5.

67. G.C. to Victualling Board, 3 June 1796, 6 Apr 1801; *La Minerve*'s surgeon to G.C., 14 Dec 1796, 27 June 1797, LC Cockburn papers, conts. 9, 13.

68. Nelson to Jervis, 30 May 1796; Nicolas, VII, p. lxxv; G.C. Log of *La Minerve*, Oct 1799. LC Cockburn papers, cont. 3.

69. See Admiralty order to G.C., 30 May 1798, reiterating an order in council of 28 May concerning the equipment of destitute pressed men. LC Cockburn papers, cont. 13.

70. G.C. to Navy Board, 18 May 1799; G.C. to Lieutenant-General O'Hara, 28 Oct 1797, LC Cockburn papers, cont.9.

71. For example, requests on behalf of men who had served in the *Tarleton* prior to *La Minerve*. G.C. letters to Navy Board, 5 Oct 1798, 17 Dec 1801, LC Cockburn papers, cont.9.

72. G.C. to Navy Board, 15 July 1798; to the master of the *Weymouth*, 28 Apr 1798; to Messrs Noble, Penson and Sons, 28 Apr 1798; and to John Bedingfield, Navy Pay Office, 22 Oct 1798, LC Cockburn papers, cont. 9.

73. A further example of Cockburn's representation of seamen was his letter to the Secretary of the Post Office in London in 1806 on behalf of a seaman in his ship at that time, the *Captain*. The man had sent his mother eight pounds through the post office at Plymouth in May 1805 but the woman had been unable to obtain the money. 'I have therefore thought it right to forward her letter to you, fully convinced you will take such steps as will be most likely to procure these poor people redress and enable them to recover their money'. G.C. to Francis Freeling, 7 Nov 1806, LC Cockburn papers, cont.9.

74. G.C. to Navy Board, 5 Oct 1798, LC Cockburn papers, cont.9.

75. Robert Galway, aged 29 in 1796, had transferred to *La Minerve* as an able seaman and served as a master's mate before becoming master sailmaker. PRO, ADM. 36/13135.

76. G.C. to Navy Board, 9 July, 20 Sep, 1798; G.C. to Lord Keith, 21 Aug 1800, LC Cockburn papers, cont.9.
77. G.C. to Navy Board , 11 July 1798, 20 Aug 1800, LC Cockburn papers, cont. 9. The son in *La Minerve* was William Gregory, aged about 19; another son may have been Jonathan Gregory who served as a midshipman in the *Meleager* May 1793–May 1794.
78. G.C. to Vice-Admiral Sir W. Hotham, 31 Sep 1795; J. Gymm, 9 Nov 1797; Sir P. Parker, 6 Aug 1798, LC Cockburn papers, cont.9.
79. For the recommendation of T.M. Hardy to Jervis, see G.C. to Nelson, 24 July 1797, BL 34,906, f.205.
80. Significantly, the only time Cockburn referred to the crew of *La Minerve* as her 'people' was on the last day of her commission on 20 Feb 1802. LC Cockburn papers, cont.3. Indicative of the interest he showed in them is his recollection 40 years later of the humour of the crew of *La Minerve* early in 1797. See letter of Walter Devereux to his mother, 20 Jan 1836, NMM, Devereux papers, MS 83/062.

Trade protection

81. G.C. to St Vincent, 7 Nov 1797, LC Cockburn papers, cont.9.
82. For the common nature of this experience see Crowhurst, *Defence of British Trade*, 73.
83. Not only were these printed and additional instructions essential to convoy discipline, no owner of a vessel could claim for a loss under a policy 'to sail with convoy and arrive', unless the master had received a copy of the printed instructions. Crowhurst, 73, 96–7.
84. G.C. to Evan Nepean, Admiralty secretary, 7 Apr 1798, LC Cockburn papers, cont.9.
85. For this record of relations with masters of vessels in the convoy see log of *La Minerve* kept by G.C., 11 Mar–7 Apr 1798.
86. Crowhurst, 71.

Reasserting command at sea

87. Log of *La Minerve*, 4 Jan 1800; G.C. to Sir J.T. Duckworth, 21 Jan 1800, LC Cockburn papers, cont. 3, 9.
88. G.C. to Sir J.B. Warren, 14 Jan 1801, ibid., cont.9.
89. G.C. to Duckworth, 15 Dec 1799, LC Cockburn papers, cont. 9
90. NMM, COC/11, ff. 57–62, G.C. to Lord Keith, 20 Mar 1801, LC Cockburn papers, cont.9.
91. 'Captain Cockburn's journal between 19 March and 9 April 1801', NMM Keith papers, KE1/20/1.
92. NMM, COC/11, f. 63–6.
93. ibid., ff. 66–71; log of *La Minerve*, 1–3 Sep 1801.

Chapter 2: *The Napoleonic War, 1803–1812*

1. NMM, ADM. A/2962, 10 Mar 1803.
2. LC Cockburn papers, cont 9.

The United States payments

3. G.C. to Admiralty Sec., 10 Nov 1803; Vice-Admiral Sir A. Mitchell to G.C., 19 Jan 1804; G.C. to Mitchell, 14 Dec 1803. LC Cockburn papers, cont.9, 14.
4. G.C. to T. Barclay, 11 Nov 1803, ibid., cont.9.
5. G.C. to De Witt Clinton, 14 Nov 1803, ibid., cont.9.
6. G.C. to Clinton, T. Barclay, A. Merry, 28, 29, 30 Dec 1803, ibid., cont.9.
7. NMM, COC/11, f.17.
8. A. Merry to G.C., 20, 30 Dec 1803, 2 Jan 1804; G.C. to Merry, 26 Dec 1803, 16 Jan 1804; G.C. to T. Barclay, 29, 31 Dec 1803. LC Cockburn papers, cont.9, 14.
9. J. Hamilton to G.C., 15 Jan 1804; G.C. to Hamilton, 16 Jan 1804, ibid., cont.9, 14.

The Governor-General of India

10. Graham, *Tides of Empire*, 59–61; G.C. to Captain J. Osborn, 17 Sep 1804, LC Cockburn papers, cont.9; NMM, COC/11, f.78.
11. Pellew to G.C., 26 Apr 1805, G.C. to Pellew, 1 May 1805, LC Cockburn papers, cont.9, 14. In these waters, he spent some time assessing military defences. See G.C. to commanding officer, Visagapatnam, 18 May 1805, ibid., cont.9; and 'Extracts of military letters from Fort St George', 5 June 1805 to 12 Feb 1806, IOLR, F/4/200, Board's collections 4525.
12. PRO, ADM. 1/1648, f.346.
13. Butler, *The Eldest Brother*, 366; NMM COC/11, f.79.
14. IOLR, H.481, ff.1313–41.
15. PRO, ADM. 1/1648, f.346, dated 28 July 1807.

The taking of Martinique

16. Garcia, *A History of the West Indies*, 196; Jenkins, 'Martinique', 35.
17. The following account of the operations in Martinique is based on the reports printed in *The London Gazette*, 1809, 398–403, 481–90.
18. General Maitland to Rear-Admiral Sir A. Cochrane, 3 Feb 1809, NLS, 2316, f.85.
19. NMM, COC/11, f.82.
20. Log of the *Pompee*, LC Cockburn papers, cont.5; *LG* 1809, 488–9.
21. NLS, 2316, ff.112, 114B; also *LG* 1809, 487–8.
22. G.C. to Lieutenant-General Sir G. Beckwith, 28 Feb 1809, BL Add MSS, 40166.
23. PRO, ADM.1/1653, 16, 20 May 1809.
24. G.C. to Cochrane, 12 Mar 1809, NLS 2316, f.172.
25. G.C. to Sir W. Pole, Admiralty Commissioner, via gun brig, *Encounter*, 23 Apr 1809, PRO, ADM.1/1652.
26. Report of G.C., PRO ADM.1/1653, 15 May 1809.

The Walcheren expedition

27. Bond, *The Grand Expedition*, 6–12
28. NMM, COC/11, f.86.
29. Bond, 14, 17, 172.
30. George III to Lord Chatham, 16 July 1809; Vane, VI, 285, quoted in Bond, 23.
31. Log of the *Belleisle*, LC Cockburn papers, cont.5.

32. Bond, 45–65.
33. NMM, COC/11, ff.88–9.
34. ibid., f.89; *LG*, 1809, 1322; 'Narrative of the second period during the investment of Flushing', NMM, COO/2/B/2.
35. Bond, 80, 110–19.
36. ibid., 123–7; Vice-Admiral Sir R. Strachan to G.C., 31 Aug 1809, NMM COC/11, ff.89–90.
37. ibid., f.90; PRO, ADM 1/1654, 9 Sep 1809.
38. *A Collection of papers relating to the expedition to the Scheldt, presented to Parliament in 1810* (1811), 490–4.
39. Bond, 139, 157–9.

The attempt to rescue Ferdinand VII
40. See Severn, *A Wellesley Affair*, 1–21.
41. Severn, 22–39.
42. Severn, 43–7, 194–5.
43. BL Add. MSS. 37, 291, ff.214–17.
44. G.C. to Colonel M. Shawe, BL 37, 291, f.230.
45. G.C. to Wellesley, ibid., f.253.
46. G.C. to Admiralty Secretary, 10 May 1810, PRO, ADM. 1/1657.
47. Severn, 113; G.C. to Wellesley, 21 May 1810, BL 37, 292, f.11; G.C. to Croker, 21 May 1810, WLC Croker papers.
48. G.C. to Captain Garth, Lieut Dickinson, Lieut Crawford, BL 37, 292, ff. 13–15.
49. The Admiralty too benefitted from captured codes of signals brought back by Cockburn. PRO, ADM. 1/1657, 21 May 1810.
50. G.C. to Shawe, 7 June 1810, BL 37, 292, f.31.
51. See [Cockburn] *Extract from a diary*, 17–18; Severn, 113–15.
52. George III nevertheless signified his approval of Cockburn's efforts. Wellesley to G.C., 13 July 1810, BL 37, 292, f.45.

Mediation and Spanish America
53. Severn, 115–117; NMM, COC/11, ff. 92–3.
54. *London Gazette*, 1810, 1,445.
55. G.C. to Keats, 29 Aug 1810, NMM, KEA/14.
56. Eusebio de Bardaxi Yatzara to H. Wellesley, 26 Aug 1810; NMM, COC/11, f.93.
57. G.C. to J.W. Croker, 13 Sep 1810, WLC Croker papers.
58. Severn, 78. See the proposal, 14 Sep 1809, from the Spanish Secretary of State, and Spencer Perceval's letter to Lord Wellesley, 19 Apr 1810, WRP/30.
59. Severn, 140–1.
60. See Gough, 'Specie conveyance', *MM*, 69 (1983), 419.
61. Copies of letters relating to shares claimed by Sir Charles Cotton and others, 20 Aug–11 Sep 1811, are in NMM, MKH/116.
62. G.C. to J.W. Croker, 6 May 1811, WLC Croker papers.
63. Severn, 141–3, 180–5.
64. NMM, COC/11, f.97.
65. Butler, 453–4.

66. See register of Foreign Office correspondence re Spain, from 2 Sep 1811, PRO, FO. 802/534, f.251; Severn 194–5.
67. NMM, COC/11, f.98; PRO, ADM 1/1661, 28 Nov 1811.
68. G.C. to Luis Lopez Mendez, 22 Dec 1811, PRO, FO. 72/156.
69. LC Cockburn papers, cont.18; PRO, FO. 72/156, 10 Dec 1812, 6 Jan 1813.
70. Severn, 201.
71. G.C. to Castlereagh, 22 Mar 1812, PRO, FO. 72/156.
72. G.C. to Castlereagh, 27 Mar 1812, ibid.
73. Observations of the American Deputies on the offer of mediation 'Communicated by Commodore Cockburn in Aug. 1812', PRO, FO. 72/156, 10 July 1812.
74. G.C. to Croker, 4 Aug 1812, PRO, ADM. 1/1663.
75. G.C. to Castlereagh, 11 Aug 1812, PRO FO. 72/156. Draft and retained neat copy in LC Cockburn papers, cont. 18.
76. Foreign Office draft letter to Spanish ambassador in London, 2 Sep 1812, PRO, FO. 72/136.

Chapter 3: The War with the United States, 1813–1815

The offensive under Warren
1. D.G. Shomette, *Flotilla*, 150, quoting Lord, 36
2. Watson, 553.
3. G.C. to respective captains, 29 Oct, 20 Nov 1812, LC Cockburn papers, cont. 9.
4. Folder 4, NMM Troubridge papers.
5. G.C. to Vice-Adm. Martin, 6 Nov 1812, and to Capt. R. Barrie, 7 Nov 1812, LC Cockburn papers, cont. 9; G.C. to Adm Sec., 6 Nov 1812, and Lord Clancarty to Lord Liverpool, 24 Nov 1812, BL 38, 250.
6. Dent, 245.
7. Vice-Adm. J.B. Warren to Lord Melville, 18 Nov 1812, NMM, LBK/2.
8. Warren to Melville, 19 Feb 1812, NMM, LBK/2.
9. Dent, 241–4.
10. R. Peel to Earl of Dessart, 7 Oct 1814, BL 40, 287, f.158. I am grateful to Mr R. Thorne for this reference.
11. G.C. to Barrie, 16 July 1814, WLC Barrie papers.
12. Dent, 246, 248, 249.

The Chesapeake in 1813
13. Warren to Melville, 19 Feb 1813, NMM, LBK/2.
14. Lieut Gleig, Royal Marines, quoted in Shomette, 154, 157.
15. G.C. to Warren, 13 Mar 1813, LC Cockburn papers, cont. 9.
16. G.C. to Warren, 23 Mar 1813, ibid., cont. 9.
17. G.C. to Warren, 23 Mar 1813, ibid., cont. 9.
18. Warren to Melville, 29 Mar 1813, NMM, LBK/2.
19. Allen, ii. 420–2.
20. G.C. to Warren, 19 Apr 1813, LC Cockburn papers, cont. 9.
21. G.C. to Warren, 29 Apr 1813, ibid., cont. 9; Auchinleck, G, 265; *London Gazette*, 1813, 1331.
22. G.C. to Warren, 2 May 1913, LC Cockburn papers, cont. 9; Auchinleck, 267; Cockburn's own 'Memoir of Services', NMM, COC/11, f. 107.

23. ibid., f. 104.
24. Auchinleck, 267; G.C. to Warren, 2 May 1813, LC Cockburn papers, cont. 9.
25. G.C. to Warren, 2 May 1813, ibid., cont. 9. Warren also referred Cockburn to the same 'large iron foundry of great consequence to Baltimore situated near Perry Point at the mouth of the Susquehanna by a small creek. It is stated as a principal work and certainly deserves notice.' Warren to G.C., 1 May 1813, WLC, War of 1812 papers. Cockburn annotated letter 'I destroyed foundry. Received after foundry was destroyed.'
26. NMM, COC/11, f. 111.
27. NMM, Troubridge papers, folder 5.
28. Warren to Melville, 1 June 1813, LBK/2.
29. Auchinleck, 268.
30. G.C. to Warren, 16 June 1813, LC Cockburn papers, cont.9.
31. G.C. to Warren, 17 June 1813, ibid., cont. 9.
32. Shomette, 11.
33. G.C. to Warren, 16 June 1813, LC Cockburn papers, cont. 9.
34. NMM, COC/11, f.111. James, *Naval History of Great Britain*, (1902), VI, 90.
35. Warren included a diagram of the geography for Melville, 23 June, NMM, LBK/2.
36. *London Gazette*, 1813, 1576.
37. ibid., 1576–7; NMM COC/11, f. 114.
38. Warren to Melville, 6 July 1813, NMM, LBK/2.
39. *London Gazette*, 1813, 1746–7.
40. G.C. to Warren, 12, 19 July 1813, LC Cockburn papers, cont. 9.
41. Shomette, 14.
42. Cockburn was the subject of more than just newspaper articles. On 22 Dec 1813 he wrote to Captain Barrie 'The book against me which you sent has afforded some amusement to those who have had time to read it and Sir John Warren is now going through it. I really have not had leisure to throw away upon it, but shall keep it for sea amusement . . . '. WLC, Barrie papers.
43. G.C. to various local inhabitants, 28 Jan, 13, 19 Mar, 17 June, 8 July, 1813, LC Cockburn papers, cont. 9.
44. Shomette, 10–11. Some companies of French troops were particularly condemned by Warren after the attack on Norfolk. Warren to Melville, 6 July 1813, NMM, LBK/2.
45. G.C. to squadron commanders, 12 July 1813, LC Cockburn papers, cont. 15.
46. NMM, COC/11, f. 110.

The offensive under Cochrane
47. While Cockburn went to Bermuda, Barrie was left in the Chesapeake for the purpose of 'keeping my Yankee friends on the fret'; G.C. to Barrie, 23 Dec 1813, WLC, Barrie papers.
48. Warren to Melville, 6 Sep 1813, NMM, LBK/2.
49. Dent, 249–50.
50. Vice-Admiral Sir Alexander Cochrane to Melville, 17 July 1814, NLS 2345, f. 13.
51. Draft by Cochrane, *c.* 27–28 Apr 1812, NLS 2574, f. 3.

52. Cochrane to Melville, 17 July 1814, NLS 2345, f. 13.
53. G.C. to Cochrane, 2 Apr 1814, NLS 2574, f. 91.
54. Shomette, 34; Bullard, 1.
55. G.C. to Cochrane, 10 May 1814, NLS 2574, f. 103.
56. G.C. to Cochrane, 10 May 1814, NLS 2574, f. 103.
57. Shomette, xi, 20, 30.
58. Shomette, 36–55.
59. G.C. to Captain Robert Barrie, 25 June, 11, 16 July 1814, WLC Barrie papers.
60. G.C. to Cochrane, 25 June 1814, NLS 2574, f. 135; NMM COC/11, f. 127.
61. G.C. to Barrie, 11, 16 July 1814, WLC Barrrie papers.
62. G.C. to Barrie, 16 July 1814, WLC Barrie papers.
63. G.C. to Cochrane, 10 May 1814, NLS 2574, f. 103.
64. For this anxiety, see G.C. to Barrie, 3 July 1814, WLC Barrie papers.
65. G.C. to Cochrane, 25 June 1814, NLS 2574, f. 135. Cockburn reiterated to Barrie his main recommendations to Cochrane; see G.C. to Barrie, 26 June 1814, WLC Barrie papers.

The burning of Washington

66. However, about 15 July Cockburn heard from Sir Thomas Cochrane at Halifax that 'there were great commotions on the continent and that things were by no means settled in Europe'. G.C. to Barrie, 16 July, WLC Barrie papers.
67. G.C. to Barrie, 16 July, WLC Barrie papers.
68. Cochrane to Cockburn, 1 July 1814, NLS 2346.
69. Cochrane's letter probably arrived with ships on 15 July. Cockburn reported to Captain Robert Barrie on 16 July its main contents.
70. G.C. to Cochrane, 17 July 1814, original NLS 2333, ff. 173–7; transcript NMM, COC/12.
71. G.C. to Cochrane, 17 July 1814, NLS 2574, f. 142.
72. On 16 July Cockburn had already outlined his intentions to Barrie; see his letter in WLC Barrie papers.
73. Shomette, 116, 134.
74. NMM, COC/11, ff. 129–130.
75. Cochrane to rear-admirals, 18 July 1814, NLS 2346, f. 8.
76. Lieut Barker to Messrs Cox and Son, navy agents, 29 July 1814, NMM, MS85/050.
77. NMM COC/11, f. 132.
78. *London Gazette*, 1814, 1965.
79. [Evans, de L.], *Facts relating to the capture of Washington*, 5–6.
80. Cochrane's official report to the Admiralty confirms that Commodore Barney's flotilla in the Patuxent 'afforded a pretext for ascending that river'. Printed in *Naval Chronicle*, XXXII, 342, and quoted in Mahan, *Sea Power and its Relations to the War of 1812*, II, 341.
81. Shomette, 155–7; Auchinleck, 359.
82. Shomette, 158–161, 162–3, 171–3.
83. Shomette, 177.
84. James, *The chief naval occurrences*, appendix 81, cxxxv; *London Gazette*, 1814, 1941–3; NMM, COC/11, f.133; Shomette, 183–4.

85. James, *The chief naval occurrences*, cxxxv.
86. Lord, 52; Shomette, 189.
87. [Evans, de L.], 10.
88. [Evans, de L.], 11.
89. Evans took issue in particular with the essay on Cockburn printed in J Ralfe's *Naval Biography of Great Britain*, III, 257–307; see also criticisms of this account 'by an old Sub', Sir Charles Napier, in 'Recollections of the expedition to the Chesapeake . . . ' in *United Services Journal*, 1840, part 1, 35.
90. NMM, COC/11, f. 134–5.
91. G.C. to Cochrane, 23 Aug 1814, NLS 2329.
92. Auchinleck, 360.
93. Lord, 95–6.
94. Briggs, 14.
95. Lord, 99.
96. Shomette, 190.
97. Estimates in NLS 2329, f. 79; Auchinleck, 365; James, *The chief naval occurrences*, appendix 83, cxliv.
98. Reminiscences of members of the expedition record his collection of mementoes and settlement of personal scores. See Lord, 115–132. However these should be used with caution. He would have been the first to observe the orders against looting and wanton destruction.
99. Reilly, 159; James, *Naval History of Great Britain*, (1902), VI, 180.
100. NMM, COC/11, f. 137.
101. Shomette, 191.
102. NMM, COC/11, f. 137.
103. Melville to Cochrane, 28 Sep 1814; Bathurst to Cochrane, 29 Sep 1814, NLS 2574, f. 174.
104. J.W. Croker (Admiralty Secretary) to G.C., 30 Sep 1814, WLC Croker papers.

The attack on Baltimore
105. NMM, COC/11, ff. 137–9.
106. ibid., f. 141.
107. James, *Naval History of Great Britain*, (1902), VI, 189. Of interest for its bearing on Cockburn's relationship with Ross is Marina Ross's reply to Cockburn's letter of condolence, 29 Oct 1814, WLC 'War of 1812' papers.
108. Brook to Bathurst, 17 Sep 1814, *London Gazette*, 1814, 2074–5; Cockburn to Cochrane, 15 Sep 1814; *London Gazette*, 1814, 2077–8; original NLS 2234, f. 20; Auchinleck, 378.
109. The phrase 'the rockets' red glare' in the United States National Anthem is generally believed to have arisen in connection with the attack on Fort McHenry.
110. Cochrane to Cockburn, 13 Sep 1814, quoted in NMM COC/11, ff. 145–6.
111. ibid., f. 146.
112. James, *Naval History of Great Britain*, (1902), VI, 191–2; *London Gazette*, 1814, 2074.
113. Melville to Cochrane, 25 Oct 1814, NLS 2574, f. 203.
114. Lord Liverpool to Cochrane, 28 Sep 1814, NLS 2574, f. 175.

Cumberland Island

115. Melville to Cochrane, 29 July 1814, NLS 2574, f. 146.
116. James, *Naval History of Great Britain* (1902), VI, 193; NMM COC/11, f. 146; G.C. to Cochrane, 30 Oct 1814, NLS 2574, f. 187.
117. G.C. to Cochrane, 3, 10 Oct, 3, 13 Nov, 1814, NLS 2574, ff. 187, 189, 207, 221.
118. Melville to Cochrane, 10 Aug 1814, NLS 2574, f. 171.
119. Cockburn reported to Barrie on 27 October: 'It was likewise stated that Lord Hill had actually sailed in a frigate from Portsmouth for Cork, thence to take command of a large division of troops destined for this country . . . . I hope it may be correct . . . '. WLC Barrie papers.
120. Cochrane to Bathurst, 2 Sep 1814, PRO WO/1/141, p. 66; quoted in Bullard, 3. I am indebted to Mary R. Bullard for bringing her *Black Liberation on Cumberland Island in 1815* to my notice.
121. NMM, COC/11, f. 149.
122. Bullard, 47–52.
123. Bullard, 26–7.
124. Cockburn paid ten dollars to each of three black men 'for conducting us to where a new gunboat . . . had been concealed at the head of a very woody covered creek'. The gunboat was sent to Bermuda. G.C. to Admiralty Sec., 5 May 1816, LC Cockburn papers, cont. 12.
125. NMM, COC/11, f. 150; Bullard, 52.
126. Bullard, 26, 50. A former British officer named Fitzgerald was here of much use. He had married and lived in Georgia for many years. With the war he had been obliged to leave the area and had offered his services to Cochrane, who sent him to Cockburn. The latter appointed Fitzgerald to raise a company of 'coloured natives' and charged him 'with keeping the neighbouring woods and roads' around St Mary's vigilantly watched and providing Cockburn with 'quick and certain intelligence from the enemy's camp by confidential people'. Cockburn was fully satisfied with Fitzgerald's performance, the British never being surprised by the enemy and seldom more than four hours without information from the American camp. 'One woman in particular used to go to the American officers' tents and converse with them to endeavour to hear among them the general ideas respecting their intended plans'. Cockburn spent 218 dollars in total on these services, but Fitzgerald's people refused to sign receipts to avoid exposure. G.C. to Admiralty Sec., 5 May 1816, LC Cockburn papers, cont. 12.
127. G.C. to Cochrane, 26 Jan 1815, NLS 2575, f. 5; NMM, COC/11, f. 150.
128. G.C. to Croker (Admiralty Sec), 28 Jan 1815, quoted in Bullard, 54–5.
129. His whole military force on the island amounted to 1,100 men. G.C. to Admiralty Sec., 5 May 1816, LC Cockburn papers, cont. 12.
130. Bullard, 54, 57, 60; NMM, COC/11, ff. 151–2.
131. Bullard, 57, 101–4, 106.
132. Bullard, 12, 68–74, 103.
133. For earlier experience see G.C. to Commodore Andrew Evans, 2 Oct 1813, LC Cockburn papers, cont.15.
134. Don Sebastian Kindelan, Governor of E. Florida, to G.C. 31 Jan 1815, and G.C. to Kindelan 13 Feb 1815, PRO, ADM 1/509, ff. 12–36. I am grateful to Mrs G. Hughes for the reference.

135. Kindelan to G.C., 18 Feb 1815, ibid., ff. 37–44.
136. G.C. to Kindelan, 22 Feb 1815, ibid., f. 45. Other copies of the correspondence are in PRO, WO/1/144 pt. 1, ff. 56–66, which were used in Bullard, 76–8.
137. G.C. to Cochrane, 28 Feb 1815, quoted in full in appendix A, Bullard, 122–5.
138. G.C. to Admiralty Sec., 9 Mar 1816, LC Cockburn papers, cont 12.
139. NMM, COC/11, f. 152; Bullard, 83–4.
140. Bullard, 126.
141. G.C. to Thomas Spalding and Capt Thomas Newall, 7 Mar 1815, quoted in Bullard 88–9. Mrs Louisa C. Shaw, who inhabited Dungeness House on the island, wrote to Cockburn on his departure to thank him for his 'many acts of goodness to us' and agreeing that her loss in slaves was small; 'all of any value have returned to us'. See WLC 'War of 1812' papers. In 1825 Cockburn was still willing to assist Mrs Shaw in her claim for other losses. See his reply to her, 7 Aug 1825, WLC 'War of 1812' papers.
142. Cochrane to G.C., 5 Apr 1815, quoted in full in NMM COC/11, ff. 153–4.
143. Although 38 schooners and sloops were captured in the Chesapeake in two relatively routine months in 1814, 17 May to 10 July, a fifth of them were burned. *London Gazette*, 1814, 1964.
144. Sir James Cockburn to Broughton, 30 Jan 1815, LC Miscellaneous MS Collection, COA–COE, 50.
145. G.C. to Cochrane, 31 May 1821, NLS 2576, f. 46.
146. Barrett, 'Naval recollections . . . ' in *United Services Journal*, 1841, part 2, 17.

Chapter 4: Napoleon and St Helena, 1815–1816

1. Lord Bathurst to Lord Melville, 30 July 1815, NMM, COC/2.
2. Admiralty Sec to G.C., 31 July 1815, NMM, COC/3.
3. 'Memoranda', War Department, 30 July 1815, NMM, COC/1.

Mastering the 'General'

4. Ross had been Cockburn's flag captain in four successive vessels since 1813.
5. G.C. to Melville, 2 Aug 1815, SRO, GD51/2/1081/10.
6. The senior officers 'absolutely refused to attend the examination of the baggage or the counting of money', G.C. to Admiralty Sec., 7 Aug 1815, LC Cockburn papers, cont. 12.
7. Shorter, 40, 60.
8. Cockburn's diary was published in Boston, USA, in 1833 and in London in 1888; see *Extract from a diary of Rear-Admiral Sir George Cockburn* . . . . Glover's was published in 1893, 1895 and 1906, on the last occasion under the title *Napoleon's Last Voyages*.
9. For the MS of Cockburn's diary see BL, Wellesley papers, Add. MSS. 37, 294, ff. 72–134; for a photocopy of Glover's see NMM, XJOD/2. For the minutes corrected by Cockburn see G.C. to Melville, 22 Oct, 11 Nov 1815, NLS, 886, ff. 165–174.
10. W. Hastings to General G. Hastings, 24 Sep 1815, HMC Hastings MSS, iii, 379.
11. G.C. to Mr Dedasckoff, Russian ambassador to USA, 1 June 1813, LC Cockburn papers, cont. 9.

298   NOTES TO PAGES 127–135

12. Shorter, 44.
13. ibid., 73; Roseberry, 109–11.
14. G.C. to Croker, 9 Aug 1815, WLC Croker papers.
15. *Extract*, 6; NMM, XJOD/2, f.7; for the embarrassment felt by the three, see Shorter, 84–92.
16. The following account of the course of relations is derived from *Extract*, 10–76; and NMM, XJOD/2, ff.16–39, 152.
17. G.C. to Melville, 24 Aug 1815, SRO, GD51/2/1081/19.
18. NMM, XJOD/2, ff. 140, 165. Cockburn also noted their change of mood. G.C. to Croker, 22 Oct 1815, LC Cockburn papers, cont. 12.

Governor of St Helena
19. 'Memoranda', War Department, 30 July 1815, NMM, COC/1, ff.5–12.
20. 79 foreigners, soldiers and their wives were transferred to the Cape. These included three gunners of the Royal Artillery who behaved badly on the voyage out. Cockburn was sorry that the whole of the Royal Artillery embarked at Portsmouth (except officers and non-commissioned officers) were 'Irishmen to a man and by no means the description of people I could have wished to have had with me on this service'. Three foreigners were sent back to Europe as well as a French servant smuggled on board the *Northumberland*. G.C. to Admiralty Sec., 22 Oct 1815, LC Cockburn papers, cont. 12.
21. His proposals for guardboats were included in the letter of 22 Oct 1815, ibid.
22. Shorter, 62.
23. G.C. to Colonel G. Bingham, 10 Nov 1815, BL Add MSS. 20,114, ff.266, 269.
24. G.C. to Captain Poppleton, 11 Dec 1815, BL 20,114, f.283.
25. By the time the French party moved to Longwood, Cockburn was 'confident not only of it being quite impracticable for the General or any of his followers to escape . . . , but even for them to have communication with any person whatever without my sanction.' LC Cockburn papers, cont. 12.
26. Count Bertrand to G.C., 5 Nov 1815, BL 20,114, f.260.
27. G.C. to Bertrand, 6 Nov 1815, ibid., f.265.
28. G.C. to Bathurst and to Admiralty Sec., both 11 Nov 1815, ibid., ff. 273, 277.
29. Two of four transports with prefabricated housing arrived in mid-December, LC Cockburn papers, cont. 12.
30. G.C. to Admiralty Sec., 11 Nov 1815, BL 20,114, f.273; G.C. to Admiralty Sec., 9 Feb 1816, LC Cockburn papers, cont.12; H. Chamberlain to G.C., 17 Apr 1816, BL 20,115, f.55. Mules were necessary owing to the local farmers' oxen being overworked and ill fed.
31. See BL 20,114, ff. 271, 307. When supply ships did arrive, Cockburn then faced a storage problem. Provisions for 6–7 months were placed in the *Northumberland* and some in the timber houses not in use by troops. LC Cockburn papers, cont. 12.
32. Lieut General Lord Charles Somerset to G.C., 29 Dec 1815, BL 20,114, f. 307.
33. See BL 20,114, f.299; 20, 115, f.43.
34. Shorter 63; NMM, XJOD/2, f.147; G.C. to Admiralty Sec., 13 Dec 1815, LC Cockburn papers, cont. 12.
35. NMM, XJOD/2, ff. 149–150.

36. G.C. to Capt. Poppleton, 18 Dec 1815, BL 20,114, f.288.
37. General Count de Montholon to G.C., 21 Dec 1815, BL 20,114, f.293.
38. G.C. to Montholon, 22 Dec 1815, ibid., f.300.
39. J.R. Glover to Poppleton, n.d., BL 15,729, f.17.
40. NMM, XJOD/2, f.151.
41. BL 20,114, ff.304, 309–10; 20,115, ff.30, 70. On 4 June 1816 Cockburn advised the Admiralty that £1,757, or nearly half of the 4000 napoleons had been spent. LC Cockburn papers, cont. 12.
42. G.C. to Bathurst, 12 Jan, 17 Mar 1816, BL 20,115, ff.2, 36.
43. G.C. to Bertrand, 14 Mar 1816, ibid., f.30.
44. Dr O'Meara to J. Finlaison, 16 Mar 1816, ibid., f.31.
45. G.C. to respective officers, 17 Feb 1816, ibid., f.25; G.C. to Hudson Lowe, 13 May 1816, BL 15,729, f.25. See also G.C. to Bertrand, 22 Mar 1816, BL 20,115.
46. H. Chamberlain to G.C., 17 Apr 1816, ibid., f.57.
47. A copy of the letter is located among papers *c.* April 1816, ibid., f.185.
48. 'Extract from Colonel Wilks remarks', *c.* Apr 1816, BL 20,115, f.43.
49. Admiralty Sec. to G.C., 27 Dec 1815, NMM, COC/5. Ascension was 'only three days run from St Helena'. Although not previously thought necessary, Cockburn had proposed occupation of the island on his arrival at St Helena, 'not only to give us a stronger right to examine any vessels arriving there and take from them any persons who may have escaped from hence, but more particularly to prevent America or any other nation from planting themselves there as upon a hitherto unoccupied and unowned island . . . for the purpose of favouring sooner or later the escape from hence of General Bonaparte or any of the persons unwillingly detained here.' G.C. to Admiralty Sec., 22 Oct 1815, 12 Jan 1816, LC Cockburn papers, cont. 12.
50. Sir H. Lowe to Sir H. Bunbury, 22 Apr 1816, BL 20,115, f.79.
51. NMM, XJOD/2, f.168; Hobhouse, i, 343.
52. Bathurst to G.C., 5 Aug 1816, NMM, COC/11, f.157.
53. Major I. Barnes to G.C., 24 July 1816, NMM, COC/7; NMM, XJOD/2, f.163. For Lowe's instructions from the Secretary of State, 12 Sep 1815, see BL 20,114.
54. H. Lowe to Bathurst, 21 Apr 1816, BL 20,115, f.74.
55. Sir P. Malcolm to G.C., 5 Sep 1817, NMM, COC/8.

Chapter 5: Parliament and the Admiralty, 1818–1830

1. J.W. Croker to Robert Peel, 8 Aug 1816, in Pool, 37; Croker to G.C., 29 Aug 1816, WLC Croker papers.
2. G.C. to Croker, 6 Mar 1818, WLC Croker papers.
3. Sainty, *Admiralty Officials*, 103–4.
4. Lewis, *Navy in Transition*, 66.
5. Lambert, *Last Sailing Battlefleet*, 16.
6. On account of the internal politics of the navy, as well as the feuding between government departments, management of the navy at the highest level still demanded statesmanship. The assessment of N.A.M. Rodger, *The Admiralty*, 95, of the talents of the second Viscount Melville as 'only moderate' requires revision. Recent work—by, for example, M. Fry, *The Dundas Despotism* (Edinburgh,

1992)—does not do justice to Melville as a naval administrator either. His achievement requires full and detailed re-examination.

Champion of liberty
7. G.C. to Sir J. Gore, 1 Nov 1818, NMM, MS 76/101.
8. For Byron's rhyme on this subject see Bartlett, 15.
9. For these traditional appeals see G. Jordan and N. Rogers in *Journal of British Studies*, 28 (1989), 201–224; thanks are due to Peter le Fevre for this reference.
10. Thorne, II, 187–9.
11. *Hampshire Telegraph and Sussex Chronicle*, 1 June 1818. For the election of the other Admiralty officials, see J. Barrow to J.W. Croker, 18 June 1818, WLC Croker papers.
12. ibid., 9 Mar 1820; *Hereford Journal*, 8 Mar 1820; Pack, 247–8. In 1826 Cockburn was to be returned again for Weobley, which was under the control of the Thynne family, Marquesses of Bath.
13. G.C. to Croker, 25, 29 May, 8, 11 Sep, 3, 7 Oct 1820, 15 May 1821, WLC Croker papers.

The House of Commons
14. G.C. to Sir T. Cochrane, 31 May 1821 NLS 2576, f.46; *Hansard*, 2nd series, V, 524, quoted in Pack 264; G.C. to Rear-Admiral Adam, 10 Aug 1835, WLC private papers.
15. Gash, *Mr. Secretary Peel*, xii.
16. G.C. to J.W. Croker, 4 Mar 1822, WLC Croker papers.
17. *Hansard*, 2nd series, V, 525; XXIV, 751.
18. ibid., XXIV, 751–2.
19. ibid., XIX, 715.
20. ibid., X, 168.
21. ibid., X, 175.
22. ibid., XXIII, 958.
23. G.C. to J.W. Croker, 8 May, 8 Aug 1827, 16 Jan, 13 June 1828, 14 Aug 1829, WLC Croker papers.

The defence of naval interests
24. G.C. to Croker, 1 Dec 1822, 29 July, 5 Aug 1827, 15, 29 Aug 1829, WLC Croker papers; G.C. to Sir Robert Barrie, 3 July, 24 Aug 1826, WLC Barrie papers. See also Bartlett, 55–84; Hamilton, *Anglo-French Naval Rivalry*, 1–5; and Lambert, 'Preparing for the long peace', *MM* 82 (1996), 41.
25. Bartlett, 21.
26. G.C. to Barrie, 15 Mar 1820, WLC Barrie papers.
27. Admiralty Board to Liverpool, 3 Nov 1818, 28 Dec 1820, BL Add. MS 38,274, f.58; 38,288, f.380.
28. Liverpool to Bathurst, 6 Sep 1821, HMC Bathurst MSS (1923), 516. See Cockburn's 'General Consideratons by which I was activated in advising that Her Late Majesty's remains should be embarked at Harwich and should be conveyed hither by land', given to Liverpool, in Aspinall, *Letters of King George IV*, II, 454–464.

29. G.C. to Croker, 23 Oct 1822, WLC Croker papers.

30. Sainty, *Admiralty Officials*, 27–8.

31. G.C. to Croker, 19 June 1833, NMM CKE/5. Accountant business included even allowances of table money. The public responsibility for striking officers from the list was nonetheless jointly taken by members of the Board. See Cockburn's denial of personal responsibility for the removal of J.M. Hanchett in his letter to the latter, 18 Oct 1835, LC Cockburn papers, cont.13.

32. Speech, 18 Mar 1819, *Hansard*, XXXIX, 1055–8.

33. Barrow, 337–8.

34. Admiralty letters to the Navy Board for Jan 1822, BL Add. MS 41,401, ff.52–284.

35. PRO, ADM. 3/190, Admiralty rough minutes, Jan–June 1818.

36. Briggs, 14–15.

37. See for example G.C. to Croker, 1 Dec 1822, 25 Oct 1823, WLC Croker papers.

38. Barrow, 338; Briggs, 10.

39. G.C. to Croker, 17 Oct 1822, WLC Croker papers.

40. PRO, ADM. 3/262, 263.

41. G.C. to Croker, Good Friday 1833, NMM, CKE/3.

42. G.C. to Croker, 12, 26 Nov 1823, NMM, CKE/1; 25 Oct, 28 Nov 1823, WLC Croker papers.

43. W.H. Fremantle to the Duke of Buckingham, 4 Feb 1824, in Buckingham and Chandos, *Memoirs*, II, 43.

44. G.C. to Croker, 23 Aug 1824, WLC Croker papers.

45. G.C. to Croker, 18, 19 Sep 1819, ibid.

46. Bartlett, 17.

47. G.C. to Sir J. Gore, 1 Nov 1818, NMM, Melville papers, MS 76/101.

48. G.C. to Melville, 22 Aug 1818, NMM AGC/2/19.

49. ibid.; also G.C. to Croker, 1 Dec 1822, 25 Oct 1823, 20, 21 July 1827, WLC Croker papers.

50. G.C. to Croker, 13 Nov 1818, 24 Oct 1821, 30 Sep 1822, WLC Croker papers.

Defying the Lord High Admiral

51. Pool, 75; Ziegler, 134–5.

52. Bagot, II, 391; Ziegler, 131; C Arbuthnot to Lord Bathurst, 15 July 1827, HMC Bathurst MSS (1923), 641.

53. Dillon, II, 482.

54. Wellington, V, 10.

55. ibid., V, 10; IV, 514–6.

56. See for example PRO, ADM 3/215, 22 June, 8, 13 Nov 1827.

57. Briggs, 2–5.

58. Hints of Cockburn's irritation at the extent to which Clarence could command the time of his more experienced subordinates, even on the dockyard visitations, are found in his two letters to Croker, 23 Sep 1827: 'I look to much advantage from your visit to Chatham, that is if the Duke allowed you time to scrutinize the manner of conducting the business of the dockyards . . . '; and 11 Oct 1827: 'we had a wretched day yesterday at Woolwich and you must have rejoiced at having escaped being one of the party'. WLC Croker papers.

59. NMM, ADM. BP/47, 6 May, 19 Sep 1827.
60. Codrington to G.C., 31 Aug 1827, NMM, COD/8/6, f.108.
61. NMM, ADM. BP/47C, 31 Oct 1827.
62. The fear of interruption to regular succession was expressed by the Navy Office messengers who had held their places 33, 28 and 24 years respectively: NMM, ADM. BP/48A, 24 Mar 1828. Instead of succeeding to an established post (the number of which had been reduced in 1822) one extra clerk at Plymouth was discharged without recompense after nearly 12 years service in the dockyard (and 11 more years as apprentice and shipwright) in spite of being promised the next vacancy. The Navy Board observed in 1830 'the expectations which were held out to this unfortunate individual . . . would have been realized without doubt if His Royal Highness . . . had not been pleased to fill the vacancies alluded to . . . by the entry of clerks new to the service, without attending to the hopes . . . which had been held out by this Board . . . in consequence of reduction'. NMM, ADM. BP/50B, 1 Apr 1830.
63. Dillon, II, 485.
64. Croker to Wellington, 2 Sep 1828, Wellington, V, 7.
65. G.C. to Huskisson, 12 Oct 1827, BL Add. MS. 38,751, f.200.
66. Pool, 115.
67. Briggs, 6.
68. The correspondence of 8–18 July 1828 between Cockburn, Clarence, Wellington and George IV is printed in Wellington, IV, 514–539.
69. MS copy also in RA 45,195.
70. RA 24,522.
71. The King's letter of 11 Aug 1828 is quoted fully in Ziegler, 140.
72. The correspondence of 13–22 Aug 1828 between Wellington, Peel, Clarence, Croker and George IV is printed in Wellington, IV, 599–602.
73. Wellington to Duke of Cumberland, 24 Sep 1828, Wellington, V, 77.
74. Croker to Wellington, 22 Aug 1828, ibid., IV, 651–2; Wellington to Peel, 26 Aug 1828, in Parker, *Sir Robert Peel*, II, 42; see also Aspinall, *Letters of King George IV*, III, 422, 425, 426.
75. Ziegler, 141; see also G.C. to Croker, 6, 11 Sep 1828, WLC Croker papers.

Managing the officer corps
76. G.C. to Sir J. Gore, 1 Nov 1818, NMM, MS76/101.
77. G.C. to Sir C. Morice Pole, 30 July 1819, NMM, WYN/105.
78. G.C. to Sir R. Barrie, 15 Mar 1820, WLC Barrie papers.
79. *Hansard*, XIV, 21 Feb 1826, 683.
80. G.C. to Pole, 19 Dec 1823, NMM, WYN/105.
81. Briggs, 13.
82. *Hansard*, XIV, 21 Feb 1826, 683.
83. S. Araban to G.C., 9 July 1829, in G.C. to J.W. Croker, 12 July 1829, WLC Croker papers; also Lieutenant K.B. James in 'The Fortunes of War', 1822, BL Add. MS 38,886.
84. G.C. to J.W. Croker, 6 Nov 1814, WLC Croker papers.
85. Lewis, *Navy in Transition*, 73–87.
86. R.C. Maunsell to G.C., 9 Oct 1830, WLC Melville papers.

87. R. Fitzroy to F. Fitzroy, 12 Sep 1822, in Ellis, *MM* 72(1986), 123.
88. G.C. to J.W. Croker, 8 Sep 1820, 17 Oct 1822, 13 Dec 1825, 3, 5 Aug 1827, WLC Croker papers.
89. T. Hoskins to G.C., 31 May 1830, WLC Melville papers.
90. Peel to G.C., 10 Feb 1826, BL Add. MS 40,385, f.199.
91. G.C. to Wellesley, 6 Dec 1823, BL Add. MS 37,310, f.235.
92. D. of Sussex to G.C., 12 Jan 1830, WLC Melville papers; G.C.'s answer described in Catalogue 1049, published by Francis Edwards Ltd, item 78. See also complaints about treatment in Dillon, II, 483–4.
93. G.C. to Barrie, 15 Dec 1818, WLC Barrie papers.
94. Letters sent 24 Jan 1829 to 24 Nov 1830, LC Cockburn papers, cont.11.
95. G.C. to Melville, 1829–30, WLC Melville papers.
96. G.C. to Melville, 10 Aug 1830, ibid.
97. W. Padwich and H. Hughes to G.C., 2 Jan, 30 Aug 1830, ibid.
98. NLS, 2266, f.60; 2267, f.23; 2576, f.46.
99. G.C. to Melville, 1 June 1829, 10 Aug 1830, ibid.
100. G.C. to Melville, 15 Dec 1827, ibid.
101. G.C. to J.W. Croker, 11 Dec 1822, 15 Oct 1825, WLC Croker papers.
102. 'Conversation that passed between myself and Sir G. Cockburn, 17 February 1825', NMM, BAY/104.
103. G.C. to Captain J. Talbot, 26 Feb 1813, LC Cockburn papers, cont.9
104. G.C. to J.W. Croker, 24 Oct 1821, 22 Feb, 7 Nov 1822, *c.* Sep 1826, 15 July 1827, WLC Croker papers.
105. G.C. to Croker, 26 July 1820, ibid.; 19 June 1833, NMM, CKE/5; G.C. to J.M. Hunchett, 18 Oct 1835, LC Cockburn papers, cont.12.
106. G.C. to Croker, 19 Oct 1821, 18 Oct 1823, 22 Apr 1824, 10 Sep 1826, WLC Croker papers.
107. For his instructions and events in the Mediterranean in 1827, see Bourchier II, 585–598.
108. To supply Codrington with these skilled men, Cockburn authorized him to retain volunteer carpenters or caulkers from ships returning to England. The measure was suggested by the Comptroller of the Navy Board, Sir Thomas Byam Martin. NMM, ADM BP/47C, 19 Sep 1827.
109. Codrington to G.C., 31 Aug 1827, NMM, COC/8/6, f.108.
110. Codrington to G.C., 12 Sep 1827, NMM, COD/8/6, f.133.
111. Woodhouse, 161–176.
112. Codrington to the D. of Clarence, 26 Feb 1828, NMM, COD/8/7. f.75.
113. Codrington to the D. of Clarence, 22 July 1828, NMM, COD/8/7, f.253 [Codrington], *Documents relating to the recall of*, 21–26.
114. G.C. to Croker, 24 May 1828, WLC Croker papers.
115. Codrington to Hon. Captain Spencer, *c.* 20 July 1828, NMM, COD/8/7. f.239.
116. G.C. to Melville, 11 Oct 1828, NMM, AGC/2/21.
117. Codrington to Sir B. Hallowell, 13, 7 Dec 1828, NMM, MS73/126.
118. [Codrington], *Documents*, 82–91.
119. *Memoir of the Life of . . . Codrington*, II, 440–1.
120. G.C. to Croker, 20, 24 Aug, 2 Sep 1829, WLC Croker papers.
121. Woodhouse, 134–5, 174–5.

122. *Hansard*, second series, XXII, 1319, 5 Mar 1830.

The beginnings of reform
123. *The Royal Devonport Telegraph and Plymouth Chronicle*, 7 June 1828.
124. G.C. to Sir Watkin Pell, 6 Mar 1842, NMM, PLL/6.M.
125. Parnell, *On Financial Reform*, 161–7.
126. *Hansard*, second series, IV, 343 (1821); VI, 1196 (1822); XII, 350 (1825); XVIII, 307–10 (1828); third series, II, 983 (1831).
127. ibid., XVIII, 310–11, 355; XIX, 736, 766, 814 (1828).
128. *Report of the Select Committee on Finance*, 1828, 154–5, 224–7.
129. Parnell had been associated with the Whig party in 1806–7 and had particular interests in finance and Ireland. See Thorne, IV, 723–6.
130. *Hansard*, second series, XX, 627, 630; XXI, 632, 1054 (1829).
131. Memorandum of a conversation with Lord Melville, kept by Sir T. Byam Martin, BL Add. MS, 41,368, f.219; *Navy List*, 1829.
132. NMM, ADM. BP/49A, 11 Mar 1829.
133. *Hansard*, second series, XIX, 754 (1828); XXIII, 942 (1830). Cockburn kept closely in touch with reform of payment procedures in the dockyards. See PRO, ADM 106/3571, 20 Nov 1829.
134. *Hansard*, second series, XXI, 613, 1053 (1829).
135. H. Parnell, 152.
136. J. Hume, on 2 Mar 1830, *Hansard*, second series XXIII, 285.
137. ibid., VI, 873–4.
138. *Report of the Select Committee on Finance*, 1828, 69; Parnell, 151.
139. *Hansard*, second series, XXIII, 280–87.
140. ibid., XXIII, 945–60.
141. Gash, *Mr. Secretary Peel*, 631.
142. NMM, ADM. BP/50B, 8 May 1830. In 1833 Cockburn regretted the proposed abolition of the sinecure Colonel and General of Marines posts because he believed they were a reward to deserving men, for whom the navy had few such allowances compared to the army. G.C. to D.P. Bouverie, 23 Dec 1833, NMM, MRF/D/8.
143. *Hansard*, second series, XXIV, 751–2.

Chapter 6:   *Opposition and North America, 1830–1840*

1. G.C. to J.W. Croker, 25 July 1830, WLC Croker Papers.
2. PRO, ADM.3/263, 6 Nov 1830.
3. G.C. to Sir R. Barrie, 9 Jan 1831, WLC Barrie Papers.

Resisting revolution
4. Hamilton, Sir R. Vesey, ed, *Journals and Letters of Sir T. Byam Martin*, III, 239–265, contains Byam Martin's account of this election. The relations with the new Whig government are fully outlined in Lambert, *Last Sailing Battlefleet*, 28–9.
5. The following account of the election is taken from the 7 May 1831 issue of the *Plymouth Devonport and Stonehouse Herald*.
6. G.C. to Croker, 15, 19, 26 May 1831, NMM, CKE/2/2.

7. G.C. to Croker, 19, 26 May 1831, NMM, CKE/2/2. For Croker's attitude, see his memorandum, 21 Sep 1831, in Pool, 143–4.
8. *Hansard*, 3rd series, X, 55–6.
9. G.C. to Croker, 12 May 1832, NMM, CKE/2/5.

Administrative reform
10. *Hansard*, 3rd series, II, 981.
11. Lambert, *Last Sailing Battlefleet*, 27–30.
12. *Report of the Select Committee on the Board of Admiralty*, PP 1861 (438), V, 145.
13. J. Graham to Earl Grey, 7, 13 Dec 1831, Univ. of Durham, Grey papers.
14. Lambert, *Last Sailing Battlefleet*, 30–1.
15. *Hansard*, 3rd series, X, 349–355.
16. G.C. to Croker, *c.* 20 Feb 1832, NMM, CKE/2/4.
17. *Hansard*, 3rd series, X, 355–360.
18. G.C. to Croker, *c.* 2 Feb 1820, WLC Croker papers.
19. G.C. to Admiralty Sec., 5 May 1816, LC Cockburn papers, cont.12.
20. *Hansard*, 3rd series, X, 364; XI, 1333–6.
21. G.C. to Croker, 12 May 1832, WLC Croker papers.
22. Melville to Graham, 30 Mar 1832, and Graham to Melville, 11 Apr 1832, SRO, GD 51/2/726/6 and 7.

Divided loyalties
23. See the observations of J.D. Thompson, Navy Board commissioner, 1805–32, NMM, Middleton papers, MID/13/5. f.10.
24. *Hansard*, 3rd series, XI, 338–9, 924, 926.
25. G.C. to Croker, 4 Nov 1832, NMM, CKE/2/6.
26. G.C. to Croker, 3 Dec 1832, NMM, CKE/3/1.
27. G.C. to Peel, 4 Dec 1832, BL 40,403, f.138.
28. LC Cockburn papers, cont. 13, 30 Apr, 18 July 1834.
29. G.C. to Sir J. Graham; 20 Apr 1833, ibid., cont. 13.
30. See G.C. to Croker, 19 June 1833, NMM CKE/3/5.
31. G.C. to C Mackenzie, 26 Dec 1833, LC Cockburn papers, cont. 13.
32. G.C. to Capt. Hamilton, 23 Dec 1833, ibid., cont. 13.
33. G.C. to Sir C. Ogle, 22 July 1834, ibid., cont. 13.
34. G.C. to Croker, 26 Jan 1835, NMM, CKE/3/6.
35. G.C. to Peel, 7 Feb 1835, BL 40,413, f.312.
36. G.C. to Sir J. Rowley, 14 June 1835, LC Cockburn papers, cont. 13.
37. G.C. to Sir R. King, 8 May 1834, ibid., cont.13.

The Vernon *affair*
38. Brown, *Before the Ironclad*, 32–3; Lambert, *Last Sailing Battlefleet*, 68. See also D.K. Brown's paper 'The Speed of Sailing Warships' given at the Anglo-French maritime history conference in Portsmouth, 1988, and published in *Les Empires en Guerre et Paix* (Vincennes, 1990).
39. For Symonds' system of building, see Lambert, *Last Sailing Battlefleet*, 68–72.
40. G.C. to Graham, 27 Mar 1833, NMM, MRF/D/8.
41. G.C. to Sir Thomas Hardy, 1 Mar 1833, NMM, MRF/D/8.

42. G.C. to Graham, 5 Nov 1833, NMM, MRF/D/8.
43. G.C. to Graham, 21 Dec 1833, NMM, MRF/D/8. D.K. Brown doubts 'the trivial differences in hull form affected *Vernon*'s pitching'. In his view, it was 'most likely that the period of encounter with the waves happened to be in resonance with her own natural period of pitch'. That the same thing happened eight months later in the same area suggests to him that wave frequency was the cause.
44. G.C. to Sir Robert Seppings, 21 Dec 1833, NMM, MRF/D/8.
45. Walter Devereux to his parents, n.d. (Torbay, Monday), and 12 Jan 1833, NMM, Devereux papers.
46. G.C. to Captain Hays, 18 July 1834, NMM, MRF/D/8.
47. G.C. to Sir George Westphal, 13 Aug 1834, NMM, MRF/D/8.
48. Lambert, *Last Sailing Battlefleet*, 67.

Management without patronage
49. G.C. to Sir Thomas Hardy, 14 Apr 1833, NMM, MRF/D/8.
50. ibid., NMM, MRF/D/8.
51. G.C. to Hardy, 5 Nov 1833, NMM, MRF/D/8.
52. *Navy List*, 1834.
53. Gough, 'Specie Conveyance', *MM* 69(1983), 419.
54. G.C. to Sir Arthur Farquhar, 30 June 1834, NMM, MRF/D/8.
55. G.C. to Sir Richard King, 8 May 1834, NMM, MRF/D/8.
56. G.C. to Captain Strono, 27 May 1834, NMM, MRF/D/7.
57. G.C. to Commodore Pell, 5 July 1834, NMM, MRF/D/8; 5 July 1834, NMM, PLL/6b.
58. G.C. to Captain Wise, 30 June 1834, NMM, MRF/D/8.
59. G.C. to Sir James Graham, 27 Mar 1833, NMM, MRF/D/8.
60. G.C. to Commodore Pell, 26 June 1834, NMM MRF/D/8.
61. G.C. to Captain Ross, 2 Jan 1834, NMM, MRF/D/8. Captain Charles Bayne Hodgson Ross had been Cockburn's flag captain in the *Marlborough*, *Sceptre*, *Albion* and *Northumberland* in 1814–15. He had married a sister-in-law of Cockburn's in 1803 so that his son was in fact Cockburn's nephew.
62. G.C. to Sir Thomas Hardy, 7 May 1834, NMM, MRF/D/8.
63. G.C. to Sir Colin Campbell, 28 Dec 1833; and to Lord Rodney, 17 July 1834, NMM, MRF/D/8.
64. G.C. to Captain Ross, 2 Jan 1834, NMM, MRF/D/8. For fuller discussion of points raised here, see N.A.M. Rodger, 'Officers, Gentlemen and their Education' in *Les Empires en Guerre et Paix* (Vincennes, 1990).
65. G.C. to Sir James Graham, 20 Apr 1833, NMM, MRF/D/8.
66. G.C. to Commander Hamilton, 5 Sep 1833, NMM, MRF/D/8.
67. Walter Devereux to Viscount Hereford, 12 June 1833, 1 June 1834, NMM, Devereux papers, MS83/062.
68. G.C. to Captain of *Vernon*, 12 July 1834, NMM, MRF/D/7.
69. G.C. to Captain of *Scylla*, 9 Jan 1836, NMM, MRF/D/8.
70. Kemp, 191.
71. G.C. to Commander Carpenter, 9 Jan 1836; to Sir William Parker, 4 Feb 1836; and to the Admiralty Secretary, 3 Mar 1836, NMM, MRF/D/8. Carpenter remained on half-pay, 1836–41, but was then given command of the steam sloop

Geyser in the Mediterranean, after which he was advanced to post rank. Thereafter he remained on half-pay to at least 1849.

72. G.C. to Sir Thomas Hardy, 7 May 1834, NMM, MRF/D/8. Pears was employed again in the *Hastings* in 1838–40. In 1845, after five years on half-pay, he obtained command of a coastguard station where he remained until 1849.
73. G.C. to Admiral Horton, 21 Dec 1833; and to Viscount Melville, 6 Jan 1834, NMM MRF/D/8.
74. Farquhar was not employed again, although he was promoted rear-admiral in 1837. He died in 1843.
75. For the situation of a commander-in-chief in the mid-eighteenth century, see Rodger, *The Wooden World*, 282–7, 303–8.
76. G.C. to Mrs Brane, 10 May 1834; see also G.C. to Mrs Cumberland, 8 May 1834; NMM, MRF/D/8.
77. G.C. to J. Backhouse, 13 May 1833; and to J. Posite, 12 Aug 1834; NMM, MRF/D/8.
78. G.C. to Captain Hamilton, 23 Dec 1833, NMM, MRF/D/8. Hamilton was not employed again after the *Cornus* was paid off in 1836, although he was advanced to post rank in that same year.
79. G.C. to Sir Josias Rowley, 28 Dec 1833, NMM, MRF/D/8.
80. G.C. to Lieut Demman, 22 Nov 1834; and to J.H. Pelly, 26 Dec 1833; NMM, MRF/D/8.
81. G.C. to Sir James Graham, 29 Apr 1833, NMM, MRF/D/8.
82. Walter Devereux to his parents, 11 Aug 1833. NMM, Devereux papers.
83. ibid., 19 Feb 1834. NMM, Devereux papers.
84. G.C. to Sir Watkin Pell, 2, 26 Sep 1834, 12 Oct, 17 Dec 1835. NMM, PLL/6d. The two deaths in 1834 were those of the surgeon in the *Forte* and Commander Bertram of the *Tweed*.
85. Thomas Woodman to Lieut Willis, 25 Sep 1834, NMM, MRF/D/8.
86. G.C. to Colonel Hawker, a Plymouth constituent, and the Marquess of Sligo, Governor of Jamaica, both 5 July 1834, NMM, MRF/D/8.
87. G.C. to Major-General Sir Lionel Smith, 7 May 1834, NMM MRF/D/8.
88. G.C. to Lord Lyttleton, 9 July 1834, NMM MRF/D/8.
89. G.C. to Admiralty Secretary, 29 Apr 1833, and to Captain Ross, 2 Jan 1834, NMM, MRF/D/8.
90. Walter Devereux to his mother, 20 Jan 1836, NMM, Devereux papers.
91. G.C. to Commodore Pell, 26 Sep, 21 Oct 1834, NMM, Pell papers.
92. G.C. to Captain Quae, 9 July 1834, NMM, MRF/D/7.
93. Walter Devereux to his parents, 25 June, 11 Aug 1833, NMM, Devereux papers.
94. G.C. to Samuel Triscott, 7 Sep 1833, NMM, MRF/D/8.

North American affairs
95. G.C. to Captain King, 27 July 1833, NMM, MRF/D/7.
96. G.C. to Hardy, 10 May 1833, MRF/D/8.
97. G.C. to Captain Strong, 25 Jan 1836, MRF/D/8.
98. G.C. to Captain Walpole, 15 Dec 1833, MRF/D/8; and to the pro-consul, Cartagena, 16 Dec 1833, 31 Jan 1834, MRF/D/7 and 8.
99. G.C. to Sir Robert Porter, 23 Jan 1836, MRF/D/8.

100. G.C. to Sir Richard King, 8 May 1834; and to B.H. Wilson, 11 July 1834, MRF/D/8.
101. G.C. to the Governor of Cuba, 17 Oct 1835, MRF/D/8.
102. G.C. to Sir Richard King, 8 May 1834; to Sir Charles Ogle, 22 July 1834; to Lord Aukland, 6, 8 Dec 1834; and Commodore Pell, 31 Mar 1836, MRF/D/8.
103. G.C. to Lord Aukland, 8, 15 July, 10 Aug 1835; and to B Balfour, 13 July 1834, MRF/D/8.
104. G.C. to Sir J. Graham, 5 Nov 1833; to all commanding officers, 2 Nov 1835; and to Commodore Pell, 25 Mar 1836, MRF/D/8.
105. G.C. to Sir T. Usher, 21 Jan 1834; and to Sir J. Graham, 10 Feb, 30 Apr 1834, MRF/D/8. It was later reported in the House of Commons that 82 slavers were taken, 1831–5, of which 7 were empty; and 247 in 1836–41, of which 143 were empty. *Hansard*, third series, LXXX, 5 May 1845, 217.
106. G.C. to Sir J. Graham, 20 Apr, 13 May, 27 July, 5 Nov 1833, 30 Apr 1834, MRF/D/8.
107. G.C. to Commander Hamilton, 7 Apr 1834; to the Marquis of Sligo, 5 July 1834, 12 Aug 1835; to Earl de Grey, 15 Feb 1835; and Lord Aukland, 15 July 1835, MRF/D/8.
108. G.C. to the Bishop of Nova Scotia, 29 Nov 1835, MRF/D/8.
109. G.C. to Captain Beaufort, Oct and 26 Dec 1833, MRF/D/8.
110. G.C. to Captain Kitson, 9 Sep 1834, MRF/D/7; and to Sir L. Smith, 3 Jan 1835, MRF/D/8.

Leadership without office
111. G.C. to Captain Arthur, 26 Jan 1835, LC Cockburn papers, cont. 13; G.C. to Sir T. Cochrane, 14 Apr 1837, NLS 2278, f.42.
112. G.C. to Croker, 3 Oct 1837, NMM, CKE/4/1; *Hampshire Telegraph and Sussex Chronicle*, 31 July 1837.
113. G.C. to Minto, 27 Dec 1839, BL 12,058, ff.296–301.
114. G.C. to Croker, 29 Feb 1840, 9 Mar 1841, 8 Aug 1842, NMM, CKE/5/4; G.C. to Wellington, 20, 21 May 1839, 26 June 1844, SUL 2/5/28-29; 2/121/61. G.C. to Peel, 24 June 1844, BL 40,547, f.196.
115. G.C. to Sir T. Cochrane, 4, 9 June, 2, 4 July 1840, NLS 2,280, ff.48, 54, 71, 67.
116. G.C. to Wellington, 31 Aug, 11, 14 Sep 1840, SUL 2/70/147–153, 2/71/32-3; G.C. to Sir T. Cochrane, 9 June 1840, NLS 2,280, f.54.
117. G.C. to Peel, 5, 7 Sep 1837, 15 Dec 1839, BL 40,424, ff.124, 133; 40,428, f.471.
118. *West Kent Guardian*, 3 July 1841.
119. *The York Courant*, 30 Sep 1841.

Chapter 7:   The Early Victorian Navy in Transition, 1841–1846
1. *Hansard*, third series, LXI, 4 Mar 1842, 201; LXXIII, 1 Mar 1844, 486.
2. Bartlett, 165–174.
3. G.C. to Sir T. Cochrane, 5 Aug 1843, 6 Feb 1844, 7 July 1845, and 26 July 1846; NLS, 2284, f.94; 2285, f.27; 2286, f.213; 2287, f.205.

The Admiralty reformed

4. Bartlett, 183.
5. G.C. 22 July 1844; *Hansard*, third series, LXXVI, 1230–1.
6. [Cockburn] *Opinions*, 4–5.
7. 'Observations copied from Admiral Sir T. Byam Martin's private naval memoranda', 1837, BL 41,369, f.201.
8. Note by Haddington, n.d., with Peel to Haddington, 19 June 1841, ibid., ff.240, 244.
9. G.C. to Martin, 9 Sep 1841; BL 41,369, f.136.
10. Haddington to Melville, 26 Mar 1842, SRO, GD51/2/739.
11. Bartlett, 10–11.
12. Hamilton, 'Selections from the Phinn Committee of Inquiry', 431–2.
13. Briggs, 74.
14. [Cockburn], *Opinions*, 5–6.
15. Haddington to Melville, 26 Mar 1842; SRO, GD51/22/739.
16. See O'Ferrall, Napier, 22 July 1844, 16 May 1845; *Hansard* LXXVI, 1234, LXXX, 493. With the heads of five major departments, including the Admiralty, in the Lords, Peel could not all the time be expected to answer for them in the Commons, in addition to being Leader of the House. It was thus natural to leave much to departmental spokesmen. See Gash, *Sir Robert Peel*, 527.
17. The responsibilities of each set of Commissioners varied from Board to Board. See Hamilton, 'Selections from the Phinn Committee of Inquiry', 385. For a memorandum by Cockburn on factors affecting the selection of ships for particular stations, see PRO, ADM. 3/265, n.d.
18. Behind the parliamentary scene, Peel minutely supervised the work of every department. See Gash, *Sir Robert Peel*, 528.
19. Peel to G.C., 5 Apr 1845, BL 40,564, f.94.
20. Martin to W. McPherson Rice, 16 Nov 1841, NMM REC/3.
21. For example, 7, 25 July 1842, *Hansard* LXIV, 1465; LXV, 619; also letter written 23 Oct 1841, BL 43,238, f.105.
22. See ADM. 3/247, June–Aug 1839; G.C. to Peel 9 Oct 1842, BL 40,516, f.279.
23. Hamilton, 'Selections from the Phinn Committee of Inquiry', 391; *Report of the Select Committee on the Board of Admiralty*, PP 1861 (438), V, 280, 284.
24. Earlier critics included Sir Charles Middleton, Comptroller of the Navy Board, 1778–1890.
25. [Cockburn] *Opinions*, 6.
26. Rodger, *The Admiralty*, 101.
27. 'Naval Officers in Coast Guard Services', n.d., *c.* Apr 1842, PRO, ADM. 3/265.
28. Briggs, 67.
29. [Cockburn] *Opinions*, 7.
30. Seymour was replaced by Sir W. Bowles in May 1844.
31. Briggs, 67, 74.
32. [Cockburn], *Opinions*, 7.
33. NMM, JOD/83, 20–21 Nov 1845.
34. Briggs, 73.
35. PRO, ADM. 3/265, n.d., *c.* Apr 1843.
36. For examples of his memoranda, see PRO, ADM 3/265.

Political logistics

37. Cockburn's confidence was displayed to most advantage in speeches in the House of Commons. See, for example, *Hansard*, LXXVI, 1232.
38. Bartlett, 130–1, 140–5.
39. Bartlett, 161, 181.
40. ibid., 149, 174–5; G.C. to Peel, 7 Apr 1845, BL 40,564, f.96.
41. Bartlett, 176, 182.
42. ibid., 1533; Hamilton, 'Selections from the Phinn Committee of Inquiry', 431.
43. Bartlett, 151–2; G.C. to Sir T. Cochrane, 6 Dec 1843, 6 Feb, 6 Dec 1844, NLS 2284, f.130–2; 2285, ff. 27, 269.
44. Peel also considered other visionary schemes like that for the occupation of a chain of Pacific islands. Peel to G.C., 7 Dec 1841, BL 40,497, f.14.
45. Bartlett, 148, 152–4, 339–40.
46. Bartlett, 158, 170, 342.
47. For the battles Cockburn waged, see his argument for commissioning battleships instead of 'razees' or frigates, headed 'with reference to Sir George Seymour's Minute delivered to Lord Haddington', PRO, ADM 3/265, n.d.

Improving the sailing ship

48. Briggs, 11, 75.
49. See, for example, Baxter, 13, 34.
50. G.C.'s answer to 'Lord Seymour's minute delivered to Lord Haddington', PRO, ADM 3/265, n.d., *c.* 1843.
51. For the many factors influencing design in the period—tactics, gunnery, timber supply and naval policy—see A. Lambert, *The Last Sailing Battlefleet*, 91–118; also D.K. Brown, *Before the Ironclad*, (1990), 15–43, and his paper 'The Speed of Sailing Warships' in *Les Empires en Guerre et Paix* (Vincennes, 1990). Fincham's *History of Naval Architecture* provides a survey by a contemporary attempting to grasp the theoretical implications of the previous three decades of trials. John Scott Russell's *Mechanism of Waves* (1834) is discussed by G.S. Graham in *MM* 44 (1958), 35. The only systematic experimentation in resistance hydraulics in Britain before 1860 is discussed by T. Wright in 'Mark Beaufoy's Experiments', *MM* 75 (1989), 313–327.
52. Fincham, 221. In 1832 there was even an Anglo-French trial from which the French identified national characteristics of designs. See Fincham 255–64.
53. For an examination of Symonds' term of office as Surveyor, 1832–47, see Lambert, 'Captain Sir William Symonds', *MM* 73 (1987), 167–179; also his *Last Sailing Battlefleet*, 68–87.
54. Fincham, 221–8. See also NMM, SPB/21, 'Diagrams of the experimental trials of HM Frigates *Inconstant*, *Pique* and *Castor* with other ships during the years 1836 and 7'.
55. For contemporary comment on the 'races' see speech of Captain Pechell, 13 Feb 1845 in *Hansard*, LXXVII. Cockburn corresponded with both Hayes and Seppings about their designs; for the former, 3 July 1834, 4 Feb 1836, see NMM, MRF/D/8; for the latter, see Lambert, *Last Sailing Battlefleet*, 67, which also considers his relationship with Symonds, 81–3.

56. From Cockburn's speeches in the House of Commons, 1 Mar 1844, 31 Mar 1845; *Hansard*, LXXIII, 482; LXXVIII, 1263–6.

57. Speeches, 1 Mar 1844, 31 Mar 1845, *Hansard* LXXVIII, 481; LXVIII, 1261, 1265.

58. D.K. Brown more precisely observes that 'the problem with Symonds' ships was not lack of stability but an excess, which led to rapid rolling.'

59. Speeches, 4 Mar 1842, 13 Feb 1845, Hansard, LXI, 99; LXXVII, 411–412.

60. Fincham, 228–30; see also NMM, SPB/22 'Diagrams of the experimental squadron of brigs under the command of Captain AY Corry', 29 Oct–2 Dec 1844.

61. G.C. to JW Croker, 2 Feb 1845, NMM, CKE/6.

62. Fincham, 233.

63. J.W. Croker to G.C., 26 Feb 1845, NMM, CKE/6.

64. G.C. to J.W. Croker, 25 Feb 1845, NMM, CKE/6. For a product of the 1844 battleship trials see 'Journal kept on board HMS *Queen* during the experimental cruise on the coast of Portugal from 23 October to 27 November 1844 by P Cracroft', in NMM.

65. Fincham, 239; Speech 31 Mar 1845, *Hansard* LXXVIII, 1265.

66. It appears this proposal was submitted to the rest of the Board, PRO, ADM 3/265, n.d.; see also minute 15 Nov 1845, BL 40,458, f.241.

67. Haddington to Peel, 26 Dec 1845, Peel to Haddington, 27 Dec 1845, and Ellenborough's comments, n.d., BL 40,458, ff.246, 259, 266–7; Fincham, 334. See also G.C. to Ellenborough, 5 Apr 1846, PRO, ADM 3/265.

68. Bartlett, 36; *Hansard*, LXXIII, 474.

69. Morriss, 47; *Hansard*, LXXVIII, 1265.

70. Fincham, 228, 230.

71. G.C. to J.W. Croker, 25 Feb 1845; NMM, CKE/6; G.C. to Sir T. Cochrane, 6 Dec 1844, NLS 2285, f.269; Hansard, LXXXVII, 627.

Steam and defense

72. *The Penny Magazine of the Society for the Diffusion of Knowledge*, No.536, 8 Aug 1840.

73. Bartlett, 342. Between 1841 and 1843 the French built 18 large ocean-going steamers; see Roberts, *MM* 73 (1987), 273–86.

74. Bowles, *Short Remarks . . .* (1846).

75. G.C. to J.W. Croker, 6, 12 Sep 1830, NMM, MRF/D/8. *Hansard*, LXXX, 816.

76. Fincham, 332–3, 401, 403. The two vessels were designed as sister ships but differences in rig placed them in separate classes. *Gorgon* took part in the Syrian campaign of 1840. See D.K. Brown, *Before the Ironclad*, 62.

77. G.C. to Peel, 23 Sep 1842, BL 40,515, f.325; Fincham, 328; D.K. Brown, *Before the Ironclad*, 69.

78. Fincham, 333–4, 401, 403; Lambert, *Last Sailing Battlefleet*, 72.

79. Fincham, 333–4. It is now known, as D.K. Brown has pointed out, that smaller ships in fact require more power per ton than larger ones.

80. D.K. Brown, 67–69; Lambert, *Last Sailing Battlefleet*, 72–3; G.C. to Sir C. Napier, 20 Aug 1842, NMM, NAP/3; thanks are due to Dr Lambert for this reference.

81. Fincham, 334–5.

82. Assessment focused in particular on the efficiencies of the hull shape and engine design and arrangement. See Fincham, 337–9.
83. *Hansard*, LXXIII, 472.
84. *Hansard*, LXXVIII, 1261, 1283–4; LXXX, 819–820; LXXXVII, 1460.
85. *Hansard*, LXXIII, 321, 472; LXXVI, 1232; LXXVII, 413–4.
86. Suggestion of Mr Ellice, 22 May 1845, enclosed in G.C. to Peel, 9 June 1845, BL 40,458, f.64. Peel was anxious to ensure plans for mobilizing the merchant marine were properly considered and prepared. See Peel to Haddington, 2 July 1845, BL 40,458, ff. 100–103. Bartlett, 156.
87. Peel to G.C., 17 Aug 1845, and G.C. to Peel, 17 Aug 1845, BL 40,550, ff. 117, 119. Manoeuvring squadrons were formed annually 1846–48 and 1849–53.
88. See Roberts, *MM* 73 (1987), 273–286. An additional French weakness was their shortage of good steam coal; they were trying to stockpile Welsh coal for time of war. Thanks are due to D.K. Brown for this point.
89. 'Memo for Lord Haddington in consequence of the note of Sir Charles Napier to Sir Robert Peel', 9 June 1845, BL 40,458, f.57. See also N. Gash, *Sir Robert Peel*, 520–1.
90. C.S. Parker, III, 217–8; Haddington advised Peel on 18 June 1845 that Cockburn had not used the latest French navy list, BL 40,458, f.76.
91. Peel to G.C. 15 Aug 1845, BL 40,571, f.383.
92. G.C. to Peel, 16 Aug 1845, BL 40,572, f.250.

The introduction of the screw propeller
93. *Hansard*, LXXIII, 489.
94. Brunel, 286; Rolt, 219; Graham, 'The transition from paddle-wheel', *MM* 44 (1958), 35–48. D.K. Brown, who has done much recent research in both the Admiralty and the Brunel papers, confirms that the Brunel family account of the introduction of the screw propeller was 'seriously misleading'.
95. Lambert, 'The Royal Navy' in *Innovation in Shipping and Trade*, 61–88.
96. Brown, 'The introduction of the screw propeller' in *Warship* 1 (1977), 59–63.
97. For comment on this relationship between the public and private sectors see Fincham, 303.
98. For precise details and chronology of these stages, see Lambert, 'The Royal Navy', and D.K. Brown, *Before the Ironclad*, 99–111.
99. ibid., 70.
100. Brunel, 285.
101. Lambert, 'The Royal Navy', 63–67.
102. Brunel, 286.
103. Lambert, 'The Royal Navy', 72; Brunel, 287.
104. See Lambert, 'The Royal Navy', 75; also PRO, ADM. 7/614, G.C. minute of 21 Jan 1842; Hoseason, 19.
105. Bartlett, 223.
106. Lambert, 'The Royal Navy', 80–81; *Hansard*, LXXX, 816.
107. Brown, 'The introduction of the screw propeller', 60.
108. *Hansard*, LXXIII, 472.
109. Bartlett, 220, 223.
110. *Hansard*, LXXXVII, 628.

111. 'Memo for Lord Haddington . . . ', 9 June 1845, BL 40,458, f.57.
112. *Hansard*, LXXX, 816.
113. Lambert, 80; 'Memo for Lord Haddington . . . ', 9 June 1845, BL 40,458, f.57.
114. Brown, 'The introduction of the screw propeller', 60; Fincham, 358–9; Bourne, *Screw Propeller*, Appendix xxxiii.
115. Peel to Haddington, 25 June 1845, BL 40,458, f.92.
116. Bartlett, 223.
117. Graham, 44; Brown, 'The introduction of the screw propeller', 62.

Iron ships and shells
118. Bartlett, 216–7.
119. 'Directions for the use of shell guns' were included in the instructions given to gunners in HMS *Excellent*, the gunnery school, by 1842. See NMM, GUN/4, 6.
120. Hamilton, *Anglo-French Naval Rivalry*, 23–4.
121. See their correspondence in BL Add MSS 46.9/12–16.
122. G.C. to Sir G. Murray, 23 Oct 1841, BL 43,238, f.105.
123. Peel to G.C., 3 Oct 1841, BL 40,490, f.189.
124. S.A. Warner to Sir G Murray, 9 Sep 1842, BL 40,516, f.243.
125. G.C. to Haddington, 3 Sep 1843, BL 40,532, f.328.
126. Baxter, 28, 55–6.
127. D.K. Brown, *Before the Ironclad*, 74–5; Baxter, 33–5.
128. D.K. Brown, *Before the Ironclad*, 75–9; Baxter, 36; Bartlett, 218; Fincham, 391. The latter lists 28 iron steamers ordered between 1841 and 1846, 13 propelled by paddles, 15 by screw.
129. Graham, 'The Transition from paddle-wheel', *MM*, LXIV, 35–48. The main structural problem about building in iron was the ability to make rigid joints which would resist shearing forces. Thanks are due to D.K. Brown for this point.
130. Baxter, 37–9.
131. 'Memo for Lord Haddington . . . ', 9 June 1845, BL 40,458, f.57.
132. Gash, *Sir Robert* Peel, 517–523.
133. M.S. Partridge, 'A supplement', *MM* 72 (1986), 17; Fincham, 358.
134. 'Memo for Lord Haddington . . . ', 9 June 1845, BL 40,458, f.57.
135. Peel to G.C., 17 Aug 1845, BL 40,572, f.254; Bartlett, 182, 240–4; Hansard, LXXXVII, 1456. Lambert, *Last Sailing Battlefleet*, 44–6.

Flogging and desertion
136. *Hansard*, third series, LXIV, 196; LXXIII, 183, LXXX, 221.
137. G.C. to Rear-Admiral Adam, 10 Aug 1835; LC Cockburn papers, letters sent, private, cont. 13.
138. Lewis, 174, 188; Kemp, 185–6, 191; Lloyd, 220, 248.
139. Speech of Sir Francis Burdett, 13 July 1830 in *Hansard*, XXV, 1207. Dinwiddy, 'The early nineteenth-century campaign against flogging in the army', *EHR*, 97 (1982), 308–31.
140. *Hansard*, LXXXVII, 1343–4, 1346.
141. The 1749 Articles of War remained in force until the Naval Discipline Act of 1860, when flogging was prohibited without Court Martial. See Rodger *Articles of War*, 11; Bartlett, 308.

142. For the similarity between the jurisdiction of Justices of the Peace and naval captains see Byrn, *Crime and Punishment in the Royal Navy*, 26–7.
143. *Hansard*, LXXXIV, 1260–70; LXXXVII, 1345–5.
144. G.C. to Lord Aukland, 10 Aug 1835, LC Cockburn papers. Letters sent, private, cont.13.
145. G.C. to Sir W. Parker, 10 Aug 1835, LC Cockburn papers, Letters sent, private, cont.13.
146. *Hansard*, LXXVI, 1233; LXXX, 219.
147. Bartletter, 313, fn.2.
148. Lewis, 178, 184–6.
149. For Cockburn's opposition to crimping, see *Hansard*, LXXX, 450.
150. G.C. to Capt. Barrie, 3 July 1826, WLC, Barrie Papers.
151. *Hansard*, LXI, 106; see also Cockburn's evidence, 30 Aug 1852, before the Committee on Manning, in 'Naval Papers', PP 1859 (45) and in NMM, PHL/5/1.
152. The figures sent by Cockburn to Aukland were 'extracted from the weekly accounts between 1 August 1834 and 31 August 1835'; G.C. to Aukland, 10 Aug 1835, LC Cockburn papers, cont.13. For comment on an earlier period see Rodger, *The Wooden World*, 188–204, 354–8.
153. G.C. to Aukland, 10 Aug 1835; LC Cockburn papers, cont.13.
154. Bartlett, 308.
155. *Hansard*, LXXIII, 473.

Impressment and registration
156. Lewis, 183. See also Taylor, *MM* 44 (1958), 302.
157. *Hansard*, third series, LXXX, 219.
158. *Hansard*, LXI, 92.
159. ibid.
160. *Hansard*, LXXX, 447.
161. ibid., 449, 453; LXXXVII, 1456; G.C. to Peel, n.d. (Aug 1844?), BL 40,457, f.243.
162. *Hansard*, LXXX, 220, 454. For comment on the effects of 'turning over' in the previous century see Rodger, *The Wooden World*, 195–7.
163. Bartlett, 162; *Hansard*, LXXX, 222; evidence of Cockburn, 30 Aug 1852, before the Committee on Manning, PP 1859 (45) and NMM, PHL/5/1.
164. ibid.; *Hansard*, XIX, 751, 764; Bartlett 76.
165. Haddington to Peel, 18 June 1845, and Peel to Haddington, 2 July 1845; BL 40,458, ff.77, 92, 110; Bartlett, 307.
166. Bartlett, 306; evidence of Cockburn, 30 Aug 1852 before the Committee on Manning, PP 1859 (45) and NMM, PHL/5/1; Lewis, 182–3, 188–9.
167. G.C. to Rear-Admiral Adam, 10 Aug 1835, LC Cockburn papers, cont 13.
168. Lewis, 181, 184.
169. 'Proposal for establishing a naval reserve', 23 Dec 1844, PRO, ADM. 7/714; *Hansard*, LXXX, 222, 495.
170. G.C. to WS Gladstone, 9 Feb 1844, LC Cockburn papers, Letters sent, Miscellany, cont 12.
171. G.C. to W.S. Gladstone, 21 Dec 1844, with copy of J. Lefevre to W.S. Gladstone of 18 Dec 1844, LC Cockburn papers, cont 12.

172. Cox, *Maritime History* 2 (1972), 168–188.
173. Lewis, 189–90.

Renewing the officer corps
174. *Report of the Commission for inquiring into Naval and Military Promotion and Retirement*, 1840, xlv.
175. The above commission in 1840 revealed only 8 Admirals (of 41) less than the age of 70; 11 vice-admirals (of 54) less than the age 65; 13 rear-admirals (of 64) less than 59; only 185 captains (of 670) less than the age of 49; 174 commanders (of 887) less than age 41; and 835 lieutenants (of 2,879) less than 35. Ibid., xlv– xlviii.
176. *Hansard*, third series, LXI, 91–2, 94; LXXIII, 482–3; LXXIV, 1217.
177. *Report . . . Promotion and Retirement*, xlvii–xlviii.
178. *Hansard*, LXXIV, 1203–5.
179. *Hansard*, LXXIV, 1212–14.
180. G.C. to Captain Slade, 10 Aug 1845, LC Cockburn papers, Letters sent, Miscellany, cont 12.
181. Haddington to Peel, 12–18 Jan 1846, BL 40,458, ff. 283–304; Lewis, 116–121. See also Beeler, *MM*, 81 (1995), 300–12.
182. *Report . . . Promotion and Retirement*, xliv–xlv.
183. Promotion was given as a reward for valour in diverting disaster, and for survival in spite of extraordinary adverse conditions. See *Hansard*, LXXXII, 1064–5.
184. *Report . . . Promotion and Retirement*, l–li.
185. ibid., li.
186. *Hansard*, LXXX, 823; LXV, 857.
187. *Hansard*, X, 287; LXV, 151; LXXIV, 1221–2.
188. Using W. O'Byrne, *A Biographical Dictionary* (London, 1849), M. Lewis compared the parentage of 834 entrants to the navy after 1815 to the parentage of 1800 pre-peace entrants. While business and working-class parentage declined from 10.6% of pre-peace entrants to 0.4% of post-1815 entrants, the proportion with peers and baronets as parents increased from 12% to 17.8%. Naval parentage was also an asset. Parents in the professions increased from 50% for pre-1815 entrants to 54% of post-1815 entrants, of which the proportion who were of the naval profession rose from 48.2% in the pre-1815 category to 61.5% in the post-1815 group. See Lewis *Navy in Transition*, 20–26.
189. See the opinion of Lord Ellenborough in 1846, when First Lord of the Admiralty, in Bartlett, 316.
190. *Hansard*, LXI, 88–9; LXV, 151, 856–8.
191. ibid., LXI, 94–5; LXXIV, 1217.
192. Haddington to Peel, 9 July 1844, BL 40,457, f.159.
193. *Hansard*, LXXX, 824–6.
194. For Cockburn's personal concern with the Queen's travel arrangements see PRO, ADM. 3/265, 7 Sep, 7 Oct 1844.
195. For a refusal to promote before an adequate term had been served in a dockyard post, see G.C. to Lady Nicholson, 3 Mar 1846, NMM, MRF/D/8.
196. Thus he wrote for Haddington to Sir C. Napier, 12 Nov 1841, BL 40,021, f.34.
197. In 1841 Cockburn recommended an officer 'of a whig family' to command the Mediterranean fleet. Haddington to Peel, 11 Sep 1841, BL 40,456, f.1.

198. See, for example, his recommendation of Sir John Ross 'of polar celebrity' for the Commissionership of Greenwich Hospital. Haddington to Peel, 10 Feb 1844, BL 40,457, f.94.
199. PRO, ADM. 3/265, n.d. (ca. Nov. 1841).
200. These letters of advice are scattered through Peel's correspondence in the British Library.
201. For example, Peel's request to Cockburn on behalf of the son of Mr Haydon, 8 Oct 1841, BL 40,491, f.208; and Cockburn's to Peel for the place of Gentleman Usher of the Order of the Bath for the son of Sir William Woods, 5 Nov 1841, BL 40,494, ff.49–51. For Cockburn's requests on behalf of his brother and a nephew, see Alexander Cockburn to Peel, 27 Sep 1843, BL 40,516, f.75; and G.C. to Peel, 24 June 1846, BL 40,594, f.191.
202. G.C. to Sir T. Cochrane, 4 May 1842, NLS 2283, f.102.
203. G.C. to Peel, 17 Aug 1844, BL 40,550, ff.117, 119.
204. Lewis, 139–149.

Ideas for improving the Admiralty
205. See *The Times*, 1 Feb 1855, p.8; 2 Feb 1855, p.7.
206. *Opinions of the late Right Honourable Sir George Cockburn Bt., GCB, Admiral of the Fleet, on the necessity of remodelling the Admiralty Board* (London, 1855).
207. *Report of the Select Committee on the Board of Admiralty*, 72.
208. Others too compared the administration of the navy to that of the army. See [Bowles] *Remarks on the Conduct of the Naval Administration of Great Britain since 1815.*
209. See *The Times*, 30 Jan 1855; *Report of the Select Committee on the Board of Admiralty*, 33.
210. See the comment of Sir James Graham in *c.* 1853, in Rodger, *The Admiralty*, 103–4; also Hamilton, 'Selections from the Phinn Committee of Inquiry', 371.
211. *Report of the Select Committee on the Board of Admiralty*, 279–80.

'An irksome and difficult station'
212. G.C. to Peel, 29 Sep 1842, BL 40,516, f.102.
213. Haddington to Prince Albert, 20 Jan 1843, RA, M51/100.
214. G.C. to Sir T. Cochrane, 5 Aug, 6 Dec 1843, 6 Feb 1844, 7 July 1845; NLS 2284, ff.99, 130; 2285, f.27; 2286, f.213; G.C. to Sir W. Pell, 1 Nov 1844; NMM, PLL/6a.
215. *Hansard*, third series, LXXX, 493.
216. Peel to G.C., 1 June 1844, BL 40,546, f.30.
217. Peel to Haddington, 11 June 1845, BL 40,458, ff.53, 55.
218. Haddington to Peel, 29 Dec 1845, BL 40,458, f.271.
219. Bartlett, 176.
220. Peel to G.C., 27 Dec 1845, BL 40,583, f.353; Peel to Ellenborough, 1 Jan 1846, BL 40,473, f.35.
221. G.C. to Peel, Peel to G.C., 29 Dec 1845, BL 40,583, ff. 355–7; Haddington to Peel, 29 Dec 1845, BL 40,458, f.271; G.C. to Peel, 1 Jan 1846, BL 40,581, f.359.
222. Haddington to Peel, 29 Dec 1845, BL 40,458, f.271.

223. ibid., BL 40,458, f.271.
224. Peel to Ellenborough, 27 Dec 1845, Ellenborough to Peel, 28 Dec 1845, BL 40,473, ff.25, 29. I am grateful to Dr A. Lambert for this reference.
225. Bartlett, 179–182.
226. G.C. to Sir T. Cochrane, 26 July 1846, NLS 2287, f.205.

Chapter 8: Conclusion

1. G.C. to Sir T. Cochrane, 15 Sep 1850, NLS 2291, f.176.
2. Hamilton, *Anglo-French Naval Rivalry*, 19–21.
3. Partridge, *Military Planning*, 21–64; and 'The Russell Cabinet and National Defence', 240.
4. See G.C.'s letters to Milne, NMM, MLN/165/2; Bartlett, 8.
5. Sainty, 17; Rodger, *The Admiralty*, 110–112; Hamilton, 'Selections from the Phinn Committee of Inquiry', 378; Hattendorf, *British Naval Documents*, 661–8.
6. G.C. to Sir G.E. Hammond, 5 Mar 1852, W.R. Perkins Lib, Duke Univ, N. Carolina.

Bibliography

MANUSCRIPT SOURCES

The principal manuscript sources used to write this book are listed by the retrieval reference as cited in the notes for this book.

LIBRARY OF CONGRESS, WASHINGTON, D.C.

Cockburn's official and semi-official papers were purchased by the Library of Congress in 1909 from Catalogue 361 of Karl W. Hiersemann, Konigstrasse 3, Leipzig. The papers are now catalogued according to the container in which they are grouped.

Container 1.	Logbooks for HMS *Ariel*, 1788–1790; *Hebe*, 1791–2; *Romney*, 1792; *Pearl*, 1792; *Britannia*, 1793.
Containers 2–3.	Logbooks for HMS *La Minerve*, 1796–1802.
Container 4.	Logbooks for HMS *Phaeton*, 1803–5; *Howe*, 1805–6; *Captain*, 1806–7.
Container 5.	Logbooks for HMS *Pompee*, 1808–9; *Belleisle*,1809; *Implacable*, 1810–11; *Alfred*, 1811.
Container 6.	Logbooks for HMS *Grampus*, 1812; *Marlborough*, 1813; *Sceptre*, 1813–14; *Albion*, 1814.
Container 7.	Logbooks for HMS *Albion*, 1814–15; *Northumberland*, 1815; journal, 1833.
Container 8.	Journals, 1833–5.
Container 9.	Journals, 1835–6; and copies of miscellaneous letters sent, 1794–1802; 1803–7; 1812–14.
Container 10–11.	Miscellaneous letters sent, 1814–16, 1829–30; 1832–5.
Container 12.	Miscellaneous letters sent, 1835–6; 1844–6; and letters to the Admiralty, 1815–16.
Container 13.	Letters to the Admiralty, 1832–6; private letters sent, 1833–6; and letters received, 1794–1801.
Container 14.	Letters received, 1801–7; 1812–15; 1815–16.
Container 15–17.	Orders received and issued, 1794–1808; 1810–1811; 1812–37.
Container 18.	Orders received and issued, 1833–6, including secret orders, 1834; secret dispatches relating to the attempted rescue of Ferdinand VII; expence account book relating to the mediation attempt with Spain's American colonies; an appraisal of the advisability of

British intervention in Spain's colonies; and draft proposal for reorganization in the Board of Admiralty, 1847.

The Library's miscellaneous manuscript collection also contains letters by Sir James Cockburn, brother of George.

NATIONAL MARITIME MUSEUM, LONDON

Admiralty Papers

ADM/A/2962	In-letters, bound, from the Navy Board, 1803.
ADM/BP/47–50	In-letters, unbound, from the Navy Board, 1827–30.
ADM/L/J/57	Lieutenant's logs for HMS *Inconstant*, 1794–1802.
ADM/L/M/145	Lieutenant's logs for HMS *Meleager*, 1793–1800.

Personal Papers

BAY/104	Nias Papers, 1815–67.
COC/1–13	Cockburn Papers, 1814–18.
COD/8/6 and 7	Codrington Papers, 1827–8.
COO/2/B2	Owen Papers, 1809.
CKE/1–8	Croker Papers, 1822–46.
HLW/6	Hallowell Papers, 1827–9.
KEA/14	Keats Papers, 1790–1813.
KEI/20/1	Keith Papers, 1801.
MID/9/3 & 13/5	Middleton Papers, 1787–1832.
MKH/116	Hood Papers, 1810–11.
MLN/165/2	Milne Papers, 1850–2.
NAP/3	Napier Papers, 1842.
PHL/5/1	Phillimore Papers, 1852–9.
PLL/6A & 6M	Pell Papers, 1834–51.
WYN/105	Pole Papers, 1819–23.

Single Items

AGC/2/19 & 21	Cockburn Letters, 1829.
GUN/4&6	Gunnery Instructions, HMS *Excellent*, 1842–3.
JOD/83	Journal of Edward Pearn, Master of the transport *Athol*, 1845–6.
LBK/2	Warren Letters to Melville, 181–14.
SPB/21	Diagrams of experimental trials, 1836–7.
SPB/22	Diagrams of the experimental squadron, 1844.

Reproductions

MRF/D/1–11	Microfilm of Cockburn papers in the Library of Congress.
XJOD/2	Photocopy of the diary of J.R. Glover, 1815.

Uncatalogued Papers

MS76/101	Melville Papers, 1818.
MS83/062	Devereaux Papers, 1833–6.
MS85/050	Papers of Cox and Sons, Navy agents, 1802–38.
MS87/005	Kittoe Papers, 1795–1820.
MS84/070	Troubridge Papers, 1813–15.

BRITISH LIBRARY, LONDON

Add MSS 15,729, 20,114–20,115	Lowe Papers
Add MSS 34,904–34,913	Nelson Papers
Add MSS 37,291–37,310	Wellesley Papers
Add MSS 38,250–38,294	Liverpool Papers
Add MSS 38,751	Huskisson Papers
Add MSS 40,021	Napier Papers
Add MSS 40,166	Miscellaneous Papers
Add MSS 40,287–40,608	Peel Papers
Add MSS 41,368–41,369	Byam Martin Papers
Add MSS 41,401	Admiralty Papers
Add MSS 43,232–43,24	Aberdeen Papers
Add MSS 46,883	Drake Papers

PUBLIC RECORD OFFICE, LONDON

Admiralty Records

ADM 1/509	Admiralty In-letters, Admirals, North America, 1815.
ADM 1/1629–63	Admiralty In-letters, Captains, 1800.
ADM 1/4238–40	Admiralty–Secretary of State correspondence, 1819–26.
ADM 1/5337	Court Martial Records, 1796.
ADM 3/190–247	Admiralty Board Rough Minutes, 1818–39.
ADM 3/262–5	Admiralty Board Special Minutes, 1816–57.
ADM 7/614	Captain Carpenter's screw propeller, 1838–55.
ADM 7/714	Proposal for a reserve of seamen, 1841.
ADM 12/124–151	Admiralty Indexes, 1807–12.
ADM 36/10,212, 10,681, 10,988, 11,109, 13,083, 13,135	Muster Books of ships, 1781–1802.
ADM 50/191, 51/652, 51/976, 51/1028	Log books of ships, 1787–1793.
ADM 106/3571	Suggestions for reforms in procedure, 1817–29

Foreign Office Records

FO 72/127–156   Correspondence relating to Spain, 1810–12.
FO 802/534   Register of correspondence relating to Spain, 1810–15.

War Office Records

WO 1/144   Expedition to the Southern coasts of the United States, 1815.

Chatham Papers

PRO 30/8/369   Letters from Strachen, 1809.

SCOTTISH RECORD OFFICE, EDINBURGH

GD 18/3542, 3572   Clerk of Pencuik Papers
GD 51/2/712, 720, 726,
739, 1081   Melville Papers
GD 157/2023   Scott Papers

NATIONAL LIBRARY OF SCOTLAND, EDINBURGH

MS 2316–2576   Alexander Cochrane Papers
MS 2266–2293   Thomas Cochrane Papers
MS 886   Melville Papers
Adv MS 46.8, 9 Murray Papers

ROYAL ARCHIVES, WINDSOR

RA 24,522–3   William IV Papers
RA 45,194–5   George IV Papers
RA M51/100   Prince Albert Papers

WILLIAM L. CLEMENTS LIBRARY, MICHIGAN

Croker Papers
Melville Paprs
Barrie Papers
Goulburn Papers
War of 1812 Papers

OTHER LIBRARIES

Beineke Library, University of Yale, New Haven, Conn: Brenton Papers
Durham University Archive, Durham, England: Grey Papers
India Office Library and Records, London: Board's Collections, 4525; F/4/200; H/481.
Southampton University Library: Wellington Papers.
W.R. Perkins Library, Duke University, Durham, North Carolina: Wellesley Papers and
Hammond Papers.

PARLIAMENTARY PROCEEDINGS AND REPORTS

Almon, J, *The Parliamentary Register...1774 to...1780*, VII, 1777.
Hansard, T.C., *The Parliamentary Debates...from 1803*, IXL–XLI, 1819–20; second series,
    I–XXV, 1820–30; third series, I–IIXC, 1830–1846.
*3rd and 4th Reports from the Select Committee of Inquiry into the state of Public Income and
    Expenditure*, PP 1828 (480, 519) V, 479, 543.
Report of the Commissioners for inquiring into Naval and Military Promotions and Retirement,
    PP 1840 (235) XXII, 1.
Report of the Select Committee of Inquiry into the Constitution of the Board of Admiralty, PP
    1861 (438) V, 1.
Report of the Commissioners appointed to inquire into the best means of Manning the Navy, PP
    1859 (45) VI, 1.

CONTEMPORARY PERIODICAL PUBLICATIONS

Hampshire Telegraph and Sussex Chronicle, 1818.
Hereford Journal, 1820.
London Gazette, 1796–1814.
Naval Chronicle, 1812.
Navy List, 1829.
Plymouth Devonport and Stonehouse Herald, 1831.
The Penny Magazine of the Society for the Diffusion of Knowledge, 536, 1840.
The Royal Devonport Telegraph, and Plymouth Chronicle, 1828.
The Times, 1855.
West Kent Guardian and Gravesend and Milton Express, 1841.
The York Courant and Original Advertiser, 1841.

BOOKS AND ARTICLES

Allen, J., *Battles of the British Navy* (2 vols, London, 1852).
Allen, H.C., *Great Britain and the United States. A History of Anglo-American
    Relations:1783–1952* (London, 1954).
Aspinall, A., ed., *The Letters of King George IV, 1812–1830* (3 vols, Cambridge, 1938).
Aspinall, A., ed., *The Later Correspondence of George III* (5 vols, Cambridge, 1962–70).

Auchinleck, G., *A History of the War between Great Britain and the United States during the years 1812, 1813 and 1814* (Toronto 1855, reprint 1972).

Bagot, J., *George Canning and his Friends* (2 vols, London, 1909).

Barrett, R.J., 'Naval recollections of the late American war', *United Services Journal* 1841, part 1, 455–67; part 2, 13–23.

Barrow, Sir J., *An Autobiographical Memoir* (London, 1847).

Bartlett, C.J., *Great Britain and Sea Power, 1815–53* (Oxford, 1963).

Baxter, J.P., *The introduction of the Ironclad Warship* (Cambridge, Mass, 1933).

Beeler, J., ' "Fit for Service Abroad": Promotion, Retirement and Royal Navy Officers, 1830–1890', *MM* 81 (1995), 300–12.

Bond, G.C., *The Grand Expedition. The British Invasion of Holland in 1809* (Athens, Georgia, 1979).

Bourchier, Lady, *Memoir of the Life of Admiral Sir Edward Codrington* (2 vols, London, 1873).

Bourne, J., *Screw Propeller* (London, 1867).

Bourne, J.M., *Patronage and Society in Nineteenth Century England* (London, 1986).

Bourne, K., *Great Britain and the Balance of Power in North America, 1815–1908* (London, 1967).

[Bowles], *Remarks on the conduct of the naval administration of Great Britain since 1815 by a flag officer, with a preface by Rear Admiral Bowles* (London, 1847).

Bowles, Sir William, *Short remarks on the present state of the navy* (London, 1846).

Brenton, E.P., *The Naval History of Great Britain, 1783–1822* (London, 1823).

Briggs, J.H., *Naval Administrations 1827–1892. The experience of 65 years* (London, 1897).

Bromley, J.S., *The Manning of the Royal Navy. Selected Public Pamphlets, 1693–1873* (Navy Records Society, 1976).

Brown, D.K., *Before the Ironclad. Development in Ship Design, Propulsion and Armament in the Royal Navy, 1815–60* (1990).

Brown, D.K., 'The introduction of the screw propeller into the Royal Navy', *Warship* 1 (1977), 59–63.

Brown, D.K., 'The Speed of Sailing Warships', *Les Empires en Guerre et Paix* (Vincennes, 1990).

Brunel, I.K., *The Life of Isambard Kingdom Brunel, Civil Engineer* (London, 1870).

Buckingham & Chandos, *Memoirs of the Court of George IV, 1820–1830* (2 vols, London, 1859).

Bullard, M.R., *Black Liberation on Cumberland Island in 1815* (Delean Springs, Florida, 1983).

Butler, I., *The Eldest Brother: the Marquess Wellesley, the Duke of Wellington's eldest brother* (1973).

Byrn, J.D., *Crime and punishment in the Royal Navy. Discipline on the Leeward Islands Station, 1784–1812* (Aldershot, 1989).

Christie, I.R., *Wars and Revolutions. Britain 1760–1815* (London, 1982).

Clark, J.C.D., *English Society, 1688–1832* (Cambridge, 1985)

[Cockburn, Sir G.], *Buonaparte's voyage to St Helena, comprising the diary of Rear Admiral Sir G Cockburn, during his passage from England to St Helena in 1815* (Boston, 1815).

[Cockburn, Sir G.], *Extract from a diary of Rear Admiral Sir George Cockburn with particular reference to general Napoleon Bonaparte on passage from England to St Helena in 1815 on board HMS Northumberland* (London, 1888).

[Cockburn, Sir G.], *Opinions of the late Right Honourable Sir George Cockburn Bt, GCB, Admiral of the Fleet, on the necessity of remodelling the Admiralty Board. Reprinted from the Times* (London, 1855).

Cockburn, Sir Robert, & Cockburn, Henry A., *The Records of the Cockburn family* (Edinburgh, 1913).

Cockburn-Hood, T.H., *The House of Cockburn of that ilk, and the cadets thereof with historical anecdotes of the times in which many of the name played a conspicuous part* (Edinburgh, 1888).

[Codrington, Sir E.], *Documents relating to the recall of Vice Admiral Sir Edward Codrington from the Mediterranean command in June 1828* (printed for private distribution, 1830).

Cox, N., 'The records of the Registrar General of Shipping and Seamen' *Maritime History* 2 (1972), 168–188.

Cronin, V., *Napoleon* (Bungay, Suffolk).

Crowhurst, P., *The Defence of British Trade 1689–1815* (Folkestone, 1977).

Dent, K.S., 'The British Navy and the Anglo-American war of 1812–15' (Unpublished University of Leeds MA thesis).

Dillon, Sir W., *A narrative of my professional adventures, 1790–1837* (2 vols, Navy Records Society, 1953, 1956).

Dinwiddy, J.R., 'The early nineteenth-century campaign against flogging in the army', *English Historical Review*, 97 (1982), 303–31.

Drinkwater-Bethune, Colonel, *A Narrative of the Battle of St Vincent* (London, 1797, reprint 1979).

Dudley, W.S., ed., *The Naval War of 1812. A Documentary History* (2 vols, Washington, 1985, 1992).

Ellis, F.E., 'Robert Fitzroy: Midshipman Aboard HMS Hind, 1822–26' *MM* 72 (1986), 123.

Evans, De Lacey, *Facts relating to the capture of Washington in reply to some statements contained in the memoirs of Admiral Sir George Cockburn, GCB* (London, 1829).

Fincham, J., *A History of Naval Architecture* (London, 1851).

Fortescue, Sir J., ed., *The Correspondence of King George III from 1760 to December 1783* (6 vols, London, 1927–28).

Fredriksen, J.C., comp, Free Trade and Sailors' Rights: A bibliography of the War of 1812 (Westport, Conn, 1985).

Fremantle, A., ed., *The Wynne Diaries* (3 vols, Oxford, 1935–1940).

Fry, M., *The Dundas Despotism* (Edinburgh, 1992).

Garcia, A., *A History of the West Indies* (London, 1965).

Gash, N., *Aristocracy and People. Britain 1815–1865* (London, 1981).

Gash, N., *Mr Secretary Peel. The Life of Sir Robert Peel to 1830* (Harlow, Essex, 1985).

Gash, N., *Politics in the Age of Peel. A Study in the Technique of Parliamentary Representation 1830–1850* (London, 1953).

Gash, N., *Sir Robert Peel. The Life of Sir Robert Peel after 1830* (Harlow, Essex, 1986).

Glover, J.R., *Napoleon's Last Voyages* (London, 1893, reprints 1895, 1906).

Gough, B.M., 'Specie conveyance from the west coast of Mexico in British warships', *MM* 69 (1983), 419.

Gleig, G.R., *The campaigns of the British army at Washington and New Orleans in the years 1814–1815* (London, 1836).

Gradish, S.F., *The Manning of the British Navy during the Seven Years War* (London, 1980).

Graham, G.S., *Tides of Empire: discursions on the expansion of Britain overseas* (Montreal, 1972).

Graham, G.S., 'The transition from paddle-wheel to screw propeller' *MM* 44 (1958), 35.

Hamilton, C.I., *Anglo-French Naval Rivalry 1840–1870* (Oxford, 1993).

Hamilton, C.I., ed., 'Selections from the Phinn Committee of Inquiry of October–November 1855 into the state of the office of Secretary to the Admiralty' in *The Naval Miscellany, v* (Navy Records Society, 1984), 431–2.

Hamilton, Sir R. Vesey, ed., *Journals and letters of Sir Thomas Byam Martin* (3 vols, Navy Records Society, 1900–1902).

Hattendorf, J.B., et al., eds, *British Naval Documents, 1204–1960* (Navy Records Society, 1993).

Head, Sir F.B., *The Defenceless State of Great Britain* (London, 1850).

Hobhouse, J.C., ed., *Recollections of a Long Life. By Lord Broughton* (6 vols, London, 1909).

Holland, F., *Remarks on the Manning of the Fleet* (London, 1845).

Hoseason, J.C., *The steam navy and the application of screw propellers to sea-going line of battle ships* (London, 1853).

James, W., *The Naval History of Great Britain* (6 vols, London, 1847; reprinted 1902).

James, W., A full and correct account of the chief naval occurrences of the late war between Great Britain and the United States of America (London, 1817).

Jenkins, H.J.K., 'Martinique: The British occupation,1794–1802', *History Today* 31 (1981), 35.

Jennings, L.J., *The Croker Papers. The Correspondence and Diaries of the Right Honourable J. W. Croker* (London, 1884).

Jordan, G. & Rogers, N., 'Admirals as Heroes: Patriotism and Liberty in Hanoverian England', *Journal of British Studies* 28 (1989), 201–224.

Kemp, P., *The British Sailor* (London, 1970).

Lambert, A., *Battleships in Transition. The creation of the Steam Battlefleet, 1815–60* (London, 1984).

Lambert, A., 'Captain Sir William Symonds and the ship of the line, 1832–1847' *MM* 73 (1987), 167–179.

Lambert, A., 'Preparing for the long peace: the reconstruction of the Royal Navy, 1815–1830' *MM* 82 (1996), 41–54.

Lambert, A., *The Last Sailing Battlefleet. Maintaining Naval Mastery, 1815–1850* (London, 1991).

Lambert, A., 'The Royal Navy and the introduction of the screw propeller, 1837–47' in *Innovation in Shipping and Trade*, ed. S. Fisher (Exeter, 1989).

Lewis, M., *The Navy in Transition 1814–1864* (London, 1965).

Lewis, M., *A Social History of the Navy, 1793–1815* (London, 1960).

Lloyd, C., *The British Seaman, 1200–1860. A Social Survey* (London, 1968).

Lord, W., *The Dawn's Early Light* (London, 1972).

Mackesy, P., *The War in the Mediterranean, 1803–10* (London, 1957).

Mahan, A.T., *Sea Power and its relations to the War of 1812* (2 vols, Boston, Mass., 1905).

Morriss, R.A., 'Problems affecting the maintenance of the British fleet in the Mediterranean, 1793–1815' in *Français et Anglais en Méditerranée de la Revolution francais a l'independance de la Grèce 1793–1830* (Paris, 1992), 171–180.

Morriss, R.A., *The Royal Dockyards during the Revolutionary and Napoleonic Wars* (Leicester, 1983).

Murray, O.A.R., 'The Admiralty' parts 6 and 7, *The Mariner's Mirror* XXIV (1938), 329, 458.

Namier, L. & Brooke, J., *The History of Parliament: The House of Commons 1754–1790* (London, 1964).

[Napier, Sir Charles], 'Recollections of the expedition to the Cheaspeake and against New Orleans in the years 1814–15. By an old Sub', *United Services Journal* 1840, part 1, 443–67; part 2, 25–36, 182–95, 337–52.

Nicolas, Sir Harris, ed., The *dispatches and letters of Vice-Admiral Lord Viscount Nelson* (7 vols, London, 1844–6).

O'Byrne, W., *A Naval Biographical Dictionary* (London, 1849).

Oman, C., *Nelson* (London, 1950).

Pack, J., *The Man who Burned the White House* (Havant, 1987).

Parker, C.S., *Sir Robert Peel from his Private Papers* (3 vols, London, 1891–9).

Parker, J.G., 'The Directors of the East India Company 1754–90' (Unpublished University of Edinburgh PhD thesis, 1977).

Parnell, H., *On Financial Reform* (London, 1830).

Partridge, M.S., 'A Supplement to the naval defence of Great Britain; harbours of refuge, 1814–1870' *MM* 72 (1986), 17.

Partridge, M.S., *Military Planning for the Defense of the United Kingdom, 1814–1870* (Westport, Connecticut).

Partridge, M.S., 'The Russell Cabinet and National Defence, 1846–1852', *History* 72 (1987), 231–50.

Penn, G., *Up Funnel, Down Screw. The story of the Engineer* (London, 1955).

Pool, B., ed., *The Croker Papers* (London, 1967).

Ralfe, J., *The Naval Biography of Great Britain* (4 vols, London, 1828).

Reilly, K., *The British at the Gates* (London, 1974).

Roberts, S.S., 'The French transatlantic steam packet programme of 1840' *MM* 73 (1987), 273–286.

Rodger, N.A.M., *The Admiralty* (Lavenham, Suffolk, 1979).

Rodger, N.A.M., *Articles of War. The statutes which governed our fighting navies 1661, 1749 and 1886* (Havant, 1982).

Rodger, N.A.M., *The Wooden World. An Anatomy of the Georgian Navy* (London, 1986).

Rodger, N.A.M., 'Officers, Gentlemen and their Education', *Les Empires en Guerre et Paix* (Vincennes, 1990).

Rolt, L.T.C., *Isambard Kingdom Brunel* (Harmondsworth, Middlesex, 1970).

Rose, J. Holland, *Lord Hood and the defence of Toulon* (Cambridge, 1922).

Roseberry, Lord, *Napoleon. The Last Phase* (London, 1937).

Rowbottom, W.B., 'Soldiers and seamens' wives and children in H M ships', *MM* 46 (1961), 42.

Sainty, J.C., *Admiralty Officials 1660–1870* (London, 1975).

Scott, James, *Recollections of a naval life* (3 vols, London, 1834).

Severn, J.K., *A Wellesley Affair. Richard, Marquess Wellesley and the conduct of Anglo-Spanish Diplomacy, 1809–1812* (Tallahassee, Florida, 1981).

Schenk, H.G., *The Aftermath of the Napoleonic Wars* (London, 1847).

Shomette, D.G., *Flotilla. Battle for the* Patuxent (Solomons, Maryland, 1981).

Shorter, C., *Napoleon and his Fellow Travellers* (London, 1908).

Sutherland, L.S., *The East India Company in Eighteenth Century Politics* (Oxford, 1952).

Taylor, R., 'Manning the Royal Navy: the Reform of the Recruiting System, 1852–1862', *MM* 44 (1958), 302.

Thorne, R.G., ed., *The History of Parliament. The House of Commons 1790–1820* (5 vols, London, 1986).

Van der Vort, P.J., *The Pen and the Quarter-deck. A study of the life and works of Captain Frederick Chamier*, RN (Leiden, 1972).

Vane, C.W., ed., *Correspondence, despatches, and other papers of Viscount Castlereagh* (6 vols, London, 1851).

Warren, C.D., *The History of St Peter's Church, Petersham, Surrey* (London, 1938).

Watson, J.S., *The Reign of George III, 1760–1815* (Oxford, 1960).

Wellington, Duke of, *Despatches, Correspondence and Memoranda of Arthur Duke of Wellington (New Series) 1819–1832* (8 vols, London, 1867–80).

Woodhouse, C.M., *The Battle of Navarino* (London, 1965).

Wright, T., 'Mark Beaufoy's nautical and hydraulic experiments', *MM* 75 (1989), 313–327.

Ziegler, P., *King William IV* (Bungay, Suffolk, 1973).

Index